T0292872

Profits, Politics and Panics

Profits, Politics and Panics

Hong Kong's Banks and the Making of a Miracle Economy, 1935–1985

Leo F. Goodstadt

香港大學出版社
HONG KONG UNIVERSITY PRESS

Hong Kong University Press
14/F Hing Wai Centre
7 Tin Wan Praya Road
Aberdeen
Hong Kong

© Leo F. Goodstadt 2007

ISBN 978-962-209-896-1

British Library Cataloguing-in-Publication Data
A catalogue record for this book is available from the British Library.

Secure On-line Ordering
http://www.hkupress.org

Printed and bound by Liang Yu Printing Factory Limited in Hong Kong, China

Contents

Preface

This is the second of three books reviewing the connections between government and business in Hong Kong. The first, *Uneasy Partners: The Conflict between Public Interest and Private Profit in Hong Kong*, investigated the political coalition between officials and the business élite. This new book examines the government's relations with banking and finance, a sector which played a crucial role in the creation of Hong Kong's economic 'miracle' between 1935 and 1985. In the process, bankers had to survive the Japanese invasion and the Cold War and to overcome a protracted US embargo against the Mainland and the constraints of UK trade and exchange controls. It was also the one sector in which the Hong Kong government abandoned laisser faire and intervened — usually reluctantly — more regularly and directly than anywhere else in the economy.

The consequences were paradoxical. Banking was enormously successful, ensuring that investors and entrepreneurs were always able to raise the funds they needed to build their businesses. Yet, arguably, Hong Kong had a more unstable banking system than any other British colony before 1986, when sweeping reforms were introduced at last. These put an end to the recurrent bank runs and financial scandals as abruptly as the establishment of the Independent Commission Against Corruption (ICAC) in 1974 had halted misconduct and malpractice in the public sector. Also puzzling was the way that both the government and the banking industry found it easier to overcome the stresses of wars, revolutions and radical political change than to adjust to breakneck economic growth. Individuals in both government and business were generally shrewd and far-sighted in their responses to political challenges. They were far less willing to adapt their policies and business models to match the different stages of Hong Kong's economic transformation. As a result, during 50 years of 'miraculous' performance by the economy as a whole, the banking industry's record was tarnished by resistance to reform and adaptation.

The book seeks to explain this strange state of affairs. A major factor was the role of the government. Banking and finance were deeply influenced by official decisions about how much supervision was required to prevent bank runs and public panics but also about how laws and regulations should be policed. Because banking enters into every part of a modern economy, government policies — particularly towards real estate and stock markets — had serious but often unanticipated consequences for banking performance. In the background, there was also the problem of integrity because throughout much of the period covered by this book, the public sector and the business world were heavily affected by corruption and malpractices.

The colonial political structure was a further complication. Officials were not accountable to the public for their errors, and the government was under no compulsion to take either business or the wider community into its confidence about economic, monetary or any other policy. Although the political system was dominated by representatives of the business and professional élite, they were incapable of holding the colonial administration to account. Decisions were made by a handful of officials, who were mostly remote from the experiences of the community, the realities faced by ordinary businesses and the technicalities of modern banking and monetary affairs. In addition, the colonial administration was not nearly as efficient as is widely supposed, while business itself frequently lacked the resilience and adaptability with which it is usually credited.

My concern with the government-business nexus began as a Commonwealth Scholar in 1962 and was subsequently fostered by appointments to eight statutory bodies and official advisory bodies between 1966 and 1989, whose agendas ranged from public utilities to housing and from statistics to employment. Banking and monetary policy were also an occasional issue while I was head of the Hong Kong government's Central Policy Unit (1989–97).

Hong Kong's financial affairs became a professional priority when I worked for the *Far Eastern Economic Review* (1966–76). Readers were fascinated by HSBC as a quasi-central bank, the vulnerability of local Chinese-owned banks, Hong Kong's special value to the Mainland and the complex colonial relationship with the UK government. Later on, the editors of *Euromoney* and *Asiabanking* were equally keen on coverage of Hong Kong's emergence as an international financial centre and the turmoil caused by its unstable monetary conditions. These publications gave me access to the owners and senior executives of a wide range of banking institutions, including many that fell victim to their own mismanagement. I also became familiar with the officials who were responsible for banking affairs and monetary matters. Although they had little respect for journalists, the colonial administration had learnt during the 1965 banking crisis that it could not afford to allow misconceptions and misinformation to circulate, particularly overseas. Officials had an additional incentive for briefing the *Review* to counterbalance the views of HSBC which provided the magazine's Chairman. After I left the *Review*, I worked as a private sector economist until 1989, and among my clients was a number of financial institutions, including Hang Seng Bank, Standard Chartered Bank, N. M. Rothschild & Sons Ltd and County NatWest Securities.

While the book thus reflects personal and professional experience of both government and banking, it is not based on personal reminiscences or recollections from previous employment. Its backbone is an examination of the unpublished government documents that preserve the colonial administration's policies and practices in the Hong Kong Public Records Office. These files also contain a wealth of information about the business models and lending policies of a large number of individual banks. The picture which this hitherto confidential material presents is far from flattering to many of the parties concerned.

The banking failures and corporate collapses are not so shocking because these scandals — but not always their real causes — were widely reported at the time. Nevertheless, government files are sometimes astonishing in their revelations of how obviously a firm was being mismanaged and how self-inflicted was its downfall. Much more unexpected is the poor performance of the officials involved. Very few — not even such respected personalities as Sir John Cowperthwaite, Sir Philip Haddon-Cave, Sir Jack Cater or Lord MacLehose — emerge with much distinction from their own minutes and memoranda.

Many of the officials who figure in this book were unfailingly kind and considerate to me, socially as well as professionally; so that I have a sense of regret that I have had to challenge the myths about them. In looking at the records of the past, a question of fairness arises. It is easy to judge individuals in terms of today's standards, which, in the financial field, reflect professional skills and modern technical resources that were unavailable to previous generations. However, I have not assumed that in earlier decades, the colonial administration would operate at the same level of efficiency as I experienced while at the Central Policy Unit. Instead, I have endeavoured to assess individuals in terms of expectations in their own period, with which I had some familiarity through serving on public bodies set up to advise the colonial administration. As a further safeguard against unfairness towards institutions as well as individuals, I have tried to cite the documentary evidence for each assertion and every criticism, even at the cost of providing far more detailed references than would normally be necessary in a work of this kind.

Since 1997, my interest in banking and monetary affairs has been entirely academic, and I have focused on researching the financial foundations of modern Hong Kong first under the auspices of Trinity College Dublin and subsequently at the University of Hong Kong's Centre of Asian Studies and the Hong Kong Institute for Monetary Research. No previous client or employer has been consulted or otherwise involved in the preparation of this book, and none of its contents has been discussed with, reviewed, or approved by officials of any government.

My research trips to Hong Kong have been made all the more pleasant by the kindness and hospitality which my friends and former colleagues at the Central Policy Unit so generously offer me. Among those I can acknowledge here with gratitude are Barry Cheung, Helen Cheng, T. L. Tsim, Dr Rikkie Yeung, Professor Cecilia Chan and their families, who have gone to endless trouble to look after me. It is a pleasure to record my thanks to Dr Colin Day of Hong Kong University Press who, once again, proved himself to be the best of editors and a most efficient publisher.

Acknowledgments

I am happy to acknowledge the considerable assistance from the Hong Kong Institute for Monetary Research (HKIMR) towards the research on which this book is based. This included the award of research fellowships in 2005 and 2007 and publication of four Working Papers which are cited extensively in the chapters that follow. Dr Hans Genberg, who as Executive Director (Research Department, Hong Kong Monetary Authority) is responsible for the HKIMR, has given me unflagging personal support and encouragement during the last three years, which I deeply appreciate. I am also most grateful to Dr Matthew S. Yiu, the HKIMR's Senior Manager, and his team who have been untiringly helpful during my visits.

The Centre of Asian Studies at the University of Hong Kong provided me with generous use of its facilities in the course of drafting this book during 2006. I am especially indebted to Professor Wong Siu-lun, SBS, JP, for all his help over many years and for the warm support which I received from so many of his Centre's staff during this research project.

It is a pleasure to record my thanks to the Government Records Service and, in particular, Mr Bernard Hui Sung-tak and his colleagues in the Public Records Office, who made every effort to facilitate my access to the unpublished government documents on which the success of my research depended so heavily.

I am indebted to the School of Business Studies, Trinity College, University of Dublin, and in particular to Professor John Murray, for their interest and kindness, as well as for their facilities, throughout my stay in Ireland.

None of the institutions or individuals referred to in these Acknowledgments has any responsibility for any part of the contents of this book or the views which it expresses.

Introduction

Hong Kong is among the most remarkable of the twentieth century's economic 'miracles'. It overcame the constraints on economic progress that beset the rest of China and the Third World after World War II, despite the loss of its traditional Mainland markets and in the face of rampant protectionism in Western countries. An 'industrial revolution' transformed the war-ravaged British colony from a coastal trading port into a leading exporter to Western Europe and North America by the 1960s. In the following decade, it made the transition from manufacturing for export to become a substantial international financial and business centre. When China started to dismantle the Maoist era's barriers to foreign trade and investment at the end of the 1970s, Hong Kong embarked on a second 'industrial revolution', this time creating a major manufacturing base in southern China.

A Proud Record

This exceptional economic record required the support of a substantial and sophisticated financial infrastructure. Hong Kong had a vigorous indigenous banking community which had played an active part in China's development until 1949 when the Chinese Communist Party defeated the ruling Guomindang in the civil war. In addition, major international banks as well as China's principal financial institutions had long recognised the colony's special advantages in financing Mainland China's foreign trade and investment, and they dominated the local banking scene. Thus, throughout the twentieth century, Hong Kong possessed an open and multi-national banking system which could offer a range of services and a level of expertise to match the standards set by the principal Western banking centres. Chapter 11, 'The Exceptional Colony', will argue that no other colony could boast a comparable range and quality of banking services.

Hong Kong's banks were able to meet in full the business community's demands for finance from 1935 to 1985. They underwrote each new transformation of the economy, no matter how daunting the political or commercial risks. During these 50 years, they adapted to the threats created by Japanese hostilities, civil war and revolution. They shifted their focus from China trade to global markets. They overcame the barriers created by UK exchange controls and the US ban on all China-related transactions which lasted until 1971. Hong Kong was Asia's premier banking centre up to World War II (although its status was not widely acknowledged before the 1970s).[1] It retained this ranking after 1945, thanks to its free exchange market and its sophisticated international banking institutions. Not until 1960 did it slip to second place behind Tokyo after Japan had completed its recovery from the war.[2]

The quality of Hong Kong's financial institutions was put to the test by the 1997 Asian financial crisis, when it was credited with having the most effective banking regulation in the region.[3] The crisis threatened to topple banks and currencies across the region. Hong Kong's banks, however, were never in danger, although by the end of that year, property prices had fallen by 30 per cent and share prices by more than 40 per cent as Hong Kong plunged into its first recession since the 1950s.[4] As the recession bit harder in the following year, the banks absorbed the strain through lower profit levels before resuming business growth in 1999.[5] By the end of the century, Hong Kong could claim to have the freest and most stable financial system in the region.

A Scandalous Background

Despite its impressive performance in financing rapid economic development between 1935 and 1985, the colony was no exception to the rule that 'the history of banking is the history of bank failures'.[6] A conspicuous feature of the banking industry throughout this half-century was its lack of stability and integrity, and Hong Kong endured recurrent bank crises and financial scandals that grew worse by the decade.

- Bank runs in 1935 threatened to topple the economy and caused such extensive panic that London officials and local business leaders demanded sweeping reforms, including professional regulators.
- The early 1950s saw the widespread collapse of locally owned Chinese banks, and 52 of them had closed by 1955.[7]
- Between 1961 and 1965, three licensed banks failed, and another six had to be rescued from imminent collapse, including Hang Seng Bank, then the colony's second largest bank.
- In the 1970s, the government grossly mismanaged the currency. The money supply spiralled out of control, while the banking system was

allowed to fuel excessive speculation in shares and property, creating conditions for a collapse of the exchange rate in 1983.

- Between 1982 and 1986, the financial markets were beset by corporate collapses, corruption and scandal, leading to the failure of seven licensed banks and the closure of 94 deposit-taking companies (DTCs).[8]

The colonial administration's response to the ample evidence of mismanagement and misconduct among bank owners and executives was a scandal in itself.

- During the 1950s and 1960s, according to the unpublished official archives, such distinguished colonial officials as Sir John Cowperthwaite and Sir Jack Cater proved ignorant and incompetent when personally involved in monitoring standards of banking behaviour.
- During the 1970s, the public speeches of Sir Philip Haddon-Cave revealed him to be persistently ill-informed and complacent when confronted with unmistakeable signs that imprudent and illegal practices had reached perilous levels.
- In the 1980s, the Independent Commission Against Corruption (ICAC) launched investigations into the regulators of the banking industry and the stock exchange. The Deputy Public Prosecutor in charge of criminal cases relating to three major bank failures in this decade was gaoled on corruption charges relating to their affairs.

The failures of banking regulation and monetary policy hardly seemed to matter, however, since the rest of the economy did so well. Success appeared to be a natural state of affairs for Hong Kong. It escaped from poverty ahead of anywhere else in Asia, it has been claimed, and it attained prosperity faster than any other society in modern history.[9] It financed its own success, starting with rapid recovery from the Japanese occupation after World War II and then the creation of an industrial base which made Hong Kong a leading exporter to Western markets. Unlike other Third World economies, the colony received only token foreign aid and remarkably little direct investment from abroad to finance its economic take-off.[10] The local stock exchange raised virtually no funds for industrialisation.[11] Yet, unlike almost every other Third World economy, Hong Kong's development was never constrained by a shortage of the capital needed to finance high-speed growth.[12]

If Hong Kong's industrial take-off defied the usual obstacles to Third World growth, its subsequent expansion was no less impressive. Its GDP growth rates have been described as 'one of the world's most remarkable achievements'.[13] From at least 1961 when national income statistics were first compiled, GDP increased in real terms every year without exception until 1998.[14] Such unbroken growth was astonishing by any historical criterion. By the 1990s, the colony had transformed itself into a world-class, post-industrial society and, in the process, set a new benchmark for deindustrialisation with minimum social strain.[15] In the mid-1990s, this Chinese city could claim to be:[16]

> ... the world's eighth largest trading entity, with the world's eighth largest stock market, seventh largest financial reserves, fifth largest foreign exchange market, third busiest airport ... the world's busiest port.

Hong Kong's 'economic miracle' had another dimension which was no less impressive than the sustained growth of its domestic economy during the second half of the last century: its contribution to the Mainland's emergence as a major economic power after Deng Xiaoping's reforms created a new growth momentum from 1978. 'Without Hong Kong's involvement', it has been argued, 'China would face a much more difficult, if not impossible, task of successfully growing and modernizing its economy'.[17]

A Neglected Model

These achievements would have been impossible without a banking system of considerable scale and sophistication which was able to ensure that, between 1935 and 1985, growth was never hindered by a shortage of finance. Nevertheless, any attempt to identify the banking industry's true place in the history of Hong Kong's economic development faces serious obstacles. Confusion has surrounded the process from the very start. The colony's early industrial growth was so phenomenal that it left contemporary observers bewildered.[18]

> On the face of it, Hong Kong is not at all well suited to be a manufacturing centre ... Yet there has taken place this remarkable development of manufacturing during recent years, under a régime of almost complete free trade, and without any subsidies, tax concessions, or other forms of financial encouragement by the Government. How can it be explained? ... Why should little Hong Kong, rather than some other Asian country, have succeeded in alleviating the post-war shortage of manufactured goods? Why should capital and entrepreneurs and skilled workers have come to Hong Kong rather than elsewhere?

Contemporary economists, for the most part, had no satisfactory answers to these questions because Hong Kong broke the rules which were supposed to govern the economic destinies of Asia and the rest of the Third World after World War II. Most governments, both in Asia and the West, believed that the state was far more capable of ensuring national prosperity and social progress than free-market capitalism. Governments took charge of the economy, and the private sector was subject to extensive controls in capitalist as well as socialist countries.[19] Foreign trade was attacked as a form of colonial and capitalist exploitation, and the newly independent Asian and African nations were advised to replace imports from the industrialised nations with domestic products manufactured in local factories and protected by tariffs and import controls.[20] These theories remained fashionable until the 1980s, partly because of the ideological commitments of political leaders but also because of the reluctance of economists to examine the poor results achieved by these policies.[21]

Against this background, Hong Kong and its growth experiences seemed an anomaly which was irrelevant to the development issues facing the rest of the world.[22] This colony had stuck to political arrangements and economic policies that were little changed from the heyday of the British Empire. It retained an unreformed colonial political structure managed by an expatriate élite. Its government espoused free trade, minimal interference with market forces and no direct involvement in economic management. This sort of economic liberalism was to remain out of favour until late in the twentieth century. In addition, Hong Kong seemed a transitory society without a political future and whose survival as a flourishing economy was unlikely.[23] By 1966, Hong Kong had emerged as 'the leading developing country in supplying the developed world with labor-intensive manufactures'.[24] Yet, its sustained business boom was seen as an incidental by-product of the Cold War and vulnerable to changes in Asia's political balance.[25] After Hong Kong's transformation into a services-based economy in the 1970s, many observers forecast that Hong Kong could expect only a limited future as an international services centre. There was little confidence in Hong Kong's ability to survive competition from the Mainland in the 1990s, and the prediction was that Hong Kong would soon be overtaken by Shanghai.[26]

Painful Adjustments

With an economy which generated positive real growth every year from the mid-1950s until the end of the century, Hong Kong's banks should have faced few threats to either their stability or their profitability. Rapid economic development was neither a smooth nor a comfortable process, however. It involved the radical transformation both of Hong Kong's basic industries and of their business practices, a process which the banks managed to finance almost single-handed. But the banking system's own adjustment to a changing economic environment was often painful and sometimes self-destructive.

Hong Kong's banks were unique among British colonies, it was noted earlier, because they offered services comparable to those of international financial centres. Throughout the last century, the banking system was divided into four distinct groups, each with its own business model, its separate markets and its specialised functions.

China state-owned banks. These had been active in Hong Kong before 1949. After the Chinese Communist Party came to power and established total control over external trade and finance, these banks formed a tightly disciplined group under the Bank of China implementing state policies and little involved in Hong Kong's domestic economy.[27]

Local Chinese-owned banks. Until the 1960s, a distinction was often made between the modern commercial banks in this group and 'Chinese native banks' which were believed to adhere to traditional business practices. In practice, apart from corporate status, the group shared much the same business model after World War II. These banks preferred to specialise in property, currency and gold dealing.

Foreign-owned banks. The group included branches of the world's leading commercial banks and formed the backbone of Hong Kong's activities as an international financial centre. These banks were largely free from constraints on their ability to make loans well in excess of their local deposit base.

HSBC. This was the colony's largest bank group. Unique among British colonies, Hong Kong's dominant financial institution was not controlled from London (as Chapter 11 will explain). Its management was totally British, although, reportedly, Chinese shareholders were in the majority.[28] HSBC enjoyed considerable monopolistic advantages, thanks to its size and its role as the colonial administration's principal banker until the government started to strip it of its central banking functions from the mid-1980s.[29]

How each of the four banking groups adapted their business strategies in response to the challenges of economic transformation had a profound effect on the stability of the banking system. Yet, the importance of their different business models is generally overlooked when analysing the periodic bank runs and corporate collapses that were so regular a feature of Hong Kong's growth process. It is easy to regard 'bank fragility [as] a symptom of a deeper malaise in an economy', sometimes caused by business trends and sometimes by political events.[30] Hong Kong banks were, indeed, hit by internal events — notably, by downturns in the property market in the mid-1930s, the mid-1960s and the early 1980s. They also suffered because of external developments: United Nations and US embargoes in 1949–50 and political panics during the Korean War in the 1950s, the Maoist Cultural Revolution in 1966–68 and the deadlock in the 1982–84 Sino-British negotiations over the colony's future. But these dramatic incidents were only the immediate triggers for bank runs and currency crises. The fragility within the financial system which they uncovered was caused by unsound business practices over a considerable period.

Conservative Communists

Until almost the end of the period covered by this book, the China state-owned banks stayed largely aloof from Hong Kong's domestic economy. Once the Chinese Communist Party had come to power in 1949, their role in Hong Kong was confined almost exclusively to Mainland-related transaction. The political risks of trading with the Mainland during the extremism of the Maoist era thus fell mainly on this group. In the Cold War, these banks were the conduit by which the Chinese government obtained the convertible foreign exchange that the centrally controlled economy needed, a process which created a new role for Hong Kong as an international financial centre (as Chapter 4, 'Financial Centre under Siege', will explain).

The business priorities for these banks were set by the Mainland where the government's policies were extremely conservative.[31] The Bank of China and its 'sister banks' in Hong Kong thus steered clear of real estate and the property and share markets, and maintained high levels of liquidity.[32] Their involvement in 'capitalist' business in Hong Kong started only after 1978 and the introduction of Deng Xiaoping's reforms.

Local Traditions

Historically, the local Chinese-owned banks had played a conspicuous role in Hong Kong banking. They financed and organised trade with the Mainland regardless of wars, revolution and invasion. After the Chinese Communist Party took control of China's banking and external trade after 1949, this group did not realise how radically the economic environment was changing. Because the colonial administration was determined to preserve 'traditional' banking, this group was given 'informal' exemption from the 1948 Banking Ordinance and other legislation, which minimised the incentives for these banks to modernise their business practices. (These issues are explored in detail in Chapter 6, 'The Rise and Fall of Chinese Banking'.)

Traditionally, local Chinese bankers preferred to make their money from currency dealing, gold and property. The first two activities remained largely illegal from the end of World War II until the late 1960s. The colonial administration tolerated gold and currency smuggling without realising how easily they could contaminate a bank's culture. In addition, the government's property policies encouraged high levels of real estate speculation in which this group of banks was heavily involved. Local Chinese-owned banks stayed aloof from the manufacturing boom, and their traditional business model seemed to flourish in the 1950s. Hang Seng Bank, for example, went from unincorporated money changer to the second largest bank in the colony within three decades. But, by the 1960s, the group had lost its market power and its credibility with the public. Not even Hang Seng Bank was able to survive under Chinese ownership. Chapter 7, 'A Dangerous Business Model', and Chapter 8, 'An Avoidable Crisis', will demonstrate how the relationship between economic change, government policies and the business strategies of this group determined the rise and fall of the local Chinese banks.

The Dominant Players

When the manufacturing take-off began after World War II, HSBC and the foreign-owned banks were no more enthusiastic than the local Chinese-owned group about adjusting their business models to the loss of traditional Mainland markets. Cultural factors deterred them from lending to Chinese entrepreneurs who did not belong to the small Westernised elite. When the 'industrial revolution' began, it was barely noticed by contemporaries, and its potential for sustained growth was grossly under-estimated by bankers and bureaucrats alike. Chapter 5, 'Industrial Take-off: Cut-price and Self-financed', will explain how HSBC and the foreign-owned banks gradually overcame their prejudices and, through their willingness to finance the new manufacturing class, transformed Hong Kong into a major export centre. This chapter also identifies how foreign banks benefited throughout the last century from a 'liquidity loophole' because the colonial administration did not apply the same restrictions to their lending activities as were imposed on HSBC and local Chinese-owned banks.

In the 1970s, foreign-owned banks were to face problems with their business models which were very similar to the dangers that had overtaken the local Chinese-owned banks in earlier decades. Chapter 9, 'From Banking Crisis to Financial Catastrophe', reviews how during the transition from manufacturing to a services economy in the 1970s, foreign banks moved outside the highly conservative trade and industrial finance which had been so profitable and so secure in the previous 20 years. Corporate relationships became increasingly important, and foreign banks started to rival local Chinese-owned banks in their appetite for deals that involved significant legal as well as commercial risks.

Government policy proved dysfunctional. Officials were determined not to extend regulation beyond the licensed banks, and a banking moratorium prevented newcomers to Hong Kong from obtaining licences. Thus, unregulated DTCs proliferated, and inferior professional standards soon contaminated the banking system as a whole. Reluctant regulation had much the same damaging consequences for the behaviour of foreign bankers in the 1970s as the refusal to oversee Chinese banks had in an earlier era. The quality of regulation, not racial or cultural differences, was the decisive factor. Chapter 11 will show how the colonial administration lost control of the money supply in this decade, so that there was an ample supply of cheap funds for almost any speculative venture. The crisis that followed in the 1980s finally made drastic reforms unavoidable.

The Case for Regulation

Modern economists have become increasingly sceptical about the merits of government efforts to oversee financial markets. The self-inflicted losses incurred by Barings, Daiwa and Credit Lyonnais, and the involvement of prominent banks in such corporate disasters as Enron Corporation have been taken as evidence that regulators can do little to prevent fraud and misconduct. Furthermore, special measures to police the banking industry become harder to sustain as the boundaries blur between different types of financial institution and as banks themselves no longer concentrate on loan and deposit business but rely increasingly on marketing a range of financial products. The growing integration of financial services, institutions and markets through modern technology is an additional obstacle to effective regulation. Nevertheless, the overall conclusion of this book will be that effective regulation would have made a difference.

The case for regulation in Hong Kong starts, as it does everywhere, with the special nature of banking business. Historically, banks have needed relatively little capital. They are financial intermediaries, recycling money deposited with them so that the bulk of their 'working capital' comes from the funds entrusted to them by their depositors. The barriers to imprudent behaviour are probably lower than in other businesses because a bank's owners stand to lose far less than the depositors if the bank fails. In the absence of banking regulations, they can actually lend out more to their customers than they have received from their depositors. Again, if there are no official restrictions, banks can try to compensate for low profits and outright losses by making loans which involve greater risks but for which higher interest can be charged.[33] In addition, the opportunities for corruption among bank owners and executives are considerable. These individuals can demand commissions over and above the interest payable to the bank from applicants for loans who are unable to obtain funds from more conservative banks. In these cases, borrowers are approved because they bring personal benefits which are not shared either by the bank's shareholders or its depositors.

Early in colonial history, the colonial administration showed little understanding of the importance of a legal structure to ensure the stability of the financial system. In 1895, for example, the Attorney General had to confess to the legislature that the entire currency in circulation lacked legal sanction.[34] By the mid-1930s, senior officials no longer seriously questioned the need to ensure the stability and integrity of the banking system. The colonial administration was aware that the most effective way to improve the quality of banking management was professional regulation. The leading banks were advocates of reform. Yet, the government's reluctance to regulate persisted, as this book will relate, for 50 years. What is striking about the government's refusal to oversee the banks was its defiance of London's pressures before World War II and its specific directive to colonial governments after the war to protect the public's bank deposits.[35] To a large degree, this attitude was inspired by the colonial administration's general repudiation of direct responsibility for the well-being of the community.

The case for regulation was reinforced in Hong Kong by the special role of the banks by comparison with other Third World economies. Whether as an entrepôt, a manufacturing or a services-based economy, Hong Kong's dependence on external trade meant that a very high proportion of all business transactions had to be conducted through the banking system. Any threat to the good standing of this essential financial infrastructure could damage Hong Kong's credit ratings with its import sources and its export markets. Furthermore, Hong Kong lacked protection against a sudden collapse in depositor confidence and an abrupt flight of capital because the colony did not enforce the exchange controls and investment restrictions which, from World War II until late in the last century, defended the solvency of most countries.

Political factors were also important. Hong Kong needed to keep China's leaders convinced of the colony's value to the Mainland. Unstable banks could easily be seen in Beijing as evidence of deep economic malaise. At the same time, the government had to persuade London that the colony would not become a financial liability to the UK through turmoil in local financial markets. As a colony, the government was very vulnerable to public unrest. This threat was aggravated by the high population densities which meant that in a bank run, large queues of depositors could form, legitimately seeking to recover their money, and these crowds might prove difficult to disperse peacefully if the bank ran out of cash. That scenario was an argument in favour of regulation that officials could never entirely ignore.

Paradoxically, as the business of banking became more complex in the late twentieth century, the stability of Hong Kong's financial institutions improved dramatically. The last banking crisis took place in the mid-1980s, and the last bank failure occurred in 1991 when the local branch of the Bank of Credit and Commerce International (BCCI) could not survive the downfall of its overseas parent, although its Hong Kong business was solvent.[36] Hong Kong's banking system withstood the Asian Financial Crisis in 1997, as was pointed out earlier. This substantial improvement in performance, compared with earlier decades, must be attributed largely to the government's implementation of effective regulations following the banking and currency disasters of the early 1980s. Hong Kong's banking record in the second half of the twentieth offers a very powerful refutation of claims that the stability and integrity of the banks are best left to free market forces and the informed judgment of investors and depositors.[37]

The 'Data Deficit'

A daunting obstacle to a full evaluation of Hong Kong's growth performance and the development of the banking industry is a large and insoluble 'data deficit'. Hong Kong appears to have the worst record in Asia for compiling and publishing official economic and social statistics.[38] For example, almost every other Asian government was releasing estimates of national income and balance of payments by 1950.[39] The earliest official estimate of Hong Kong's GDP is for 1961, and the data for the 1960s were not released until 1973.[40] Publication of official balance of payments statistics had to wait until 1999, by which time the colonial administration had ended.[41] The absence of reliable figures has long frustrated research into Hong Kong's economic performance. As one economist lamented in the 1970s:[42]

> In order to evaluate the speed and magnitude of post-war industrialization, one would normally turn to industrial production statistics, but in the case of Hong Kong this is impossible, for none exist. There is, in fact, a scarcity of published economic statistics of every kind, and a total absence of national income accounts. This situation is the direct result of the Government's anachronistic economic policy, which attaches little value to comprehensive economic and social statistics.

The government published almost no data that can be used to trace Hong Kong's transformation into a major manufacturer and exporter of textiles and other consumer goods. Reliable benchmarks are available only for the period after Hong Kong had already become a mature industrial economy and a leading banking centre for the region.

- The GDP series started only in 1961.
- The bulk of the output from local factories was sold overseas so that the official trade statistics ought to be a good measure of the expansion of total industrial production and of output by manufacturing sectors. Publication of the domestic exports series started only in 1959.
- Data on the number of factories and on employment and wages should be good indicators of industrial trends as well as incomes. In 1952, however, the colony's labour statistics were condemned in a confidential government report as 'based on hearsay' and 'almost useless'. They did not match the standards of other Asian economies and did not comply with international standards until after 1970.[43]
- The socio-economic characteristics of the population were obscure, and even its total size was uncertain until 1961 because the colonial

administration steadfastly refused to organise a census before that date on the grounds that such an exercise would not help tackle the government's problems and would focus public attention on its unsolved social issues.[44]

The statistics available on banking and financial trends are also unsatisfactory.

- Banking statistics were collected from the industry in the 1950s but in the face of considerable misgivings among bankers. The figures were not comprehensive, and the consistency and reliability of the data are suspect.[45]
- The banks' published balance sheets were not an adequate substitute. Banks with headquarters outside the colony did not publish separate accounts for their Hong Kong operations. Local banks were permitted to obscure their true financial positions until the mid-1990s through window dressing to conceal their inner reserves.[46]
- The colonial administration sought to avoid the release of banking data that might reveal China's financial activities in the colony during the Cold War.[47]
- Reliable and comprehensive statistics on licensed bank are available only from December 1964.[48]
- The colonial administration refused to collect data from non-bank DTCs until 1978 on the grounds that this statistical exercise might imply an obligation to ensure the prudent management of the DTCs.[49]

The best-known authority on the history of Hong Kong banking has made an heroic effort to compile key banking data for the period 1954–63 before the government started to collect comprehensive statistics. Professor Catherine R. Schenk's study has also demonstrated how invaluable analyses of banking developments and official policies are in the unpublished data gathered by the Banking Commission for later years.[50] In addition to these statistical sources, this book will make use of confidential banking and currency data supplied to the author in the course of contemporaneous background briefings by the Economic Branch of the Hong Kong government.[51] These statistics are limited and incomplete, however.

It is almost certainly too late to statistically reconstruct the past . The sources of information needed to overcome the data deficit never existed in the first place. Well-resourced government agencies with extensive access to confidential data failed miserably in the 1950s to produce satisfactory estimates of key financial data for Hong Kong. 'Pretty worthless' was the unflattering verdict of the Colonial Office's Statistics Department on the Bank of England's attempt at statistical analysis of Hong Kong, for example.[52] In the case of national income statistics, the government finally bowed to pressures from

London and started work under university auspices in 1962. Officials were unhappy about the outcome of this exercise, and its results were not published until 1969.[53] Not surprisingly, there is a gap between the national income estimates subsequently reconstructed by the government for the 1960s and the work of other academics who were not so well-resourced. It is significant, too, that the colonial administration's first efforts to build a retrospective GDP series for the 1960s later required considerable revision.[54] The statistical void is yet another example of how different Hong Kong and its economic management were from the rest of Asia after World War II.[55]

The data deficit was of more than academic interest. It meant that the colonial administration deliberately made policy without the statistics needed to analyse policy proposals or to assess their outcome. Officials had to rely on instinct and anecdote to oversee banks and manage monetary affairs throughout most of the period. These were unreliable guides for action in managing an increasingly complex economy, as this book will demonstrate repeatedly. The deficit also deprived the colonial administration's constituents of the information needed for constructive political dialogue. In a 1950 discussion of statistical standards within the British Empire, one distinguished colonial official claimed that where a territory had good statistics, 'these owed their origin to the need of supplying information to active Legislatures and an interested and inquiring public, both of which were lacking in most of the British Colonies' before World War II'.[56] Hong Kong officials were not to face elected members of the legislature until 1985, and the colonial administration took full advantage of the opportunity to manipulate the flow of statistical information before that date.

Unravelling History

In addition to a dearth of financial data, the contribution made by the banking industry to Hong Kong's development has been obscured by political and academic controversies. Industrialists lobbying for government subsidies and other incentives have repeatedly accused the banks of ignoring manufacturers' requirements.[57] The industrialists' attacks on the bankers have been widely accepted among academics.[58] Critics allege that bank-lending policies had three damaging consequences.

- Hong Kong's industrial growth was impeded by a lack of capital caused principally by the failure of the banks to comprehend the needs of the new manufacturing businesses.[59]
- Industrialists could obtain only short-term bank finance on onerous terms, which 'necessarily limited the scale and expansion of manufacturing firms'.[60]
- The economy became over-dependent on textiles and was dangerously

deprived of large-scale projects and advanced technology that required ample development capital.[61]

The allegations that Hong Kong's development in the second half of the last century was hindered by a lack of bank support are refuted by the way Hong Kong's industrial expansion outperformed everywhere else in Asia and the rest of the Third World. The only significant obstacles to even faster growth in the 1950s were the mounting restrictions imposed by Western countries on textile imports and Hong Kong's increasingly severe labour shortage at the end of that decade. Chapter 5, 'Industrial Take-off: Cut-price and Self-financed', will present evidence that the banks were the chief source of finance for the creation of Hong Kong's manufacturing sector.

As a British colony, the UK's role has inspired both controversy and conspiracy theories. There is a very natural presumption that the colonial administration was duty-bound to promote British financial and commercial interests at the expense of Hong Kong and to collaborate with London in using the colony's resources to protect the UK economy in general and its currency in particular — regardless of Hong Kong's own well-being.[62] The government had to deny persistent allegations that 'as a Colony [Hong Kong was] compelled to hand over our surpluses and reserves to Britain, as if it were some form of tribute'.[63] The evidence shows that the colonial administration almost never displayed such 'patriotism' and that it made its own decisions with minimal interference from London, leaving colonial officials with no one to blame for their mistakes except themselves. The relationship between Hong Kong and the UK is examined in depth in Chapter 11 and, in the context of the Cold War, in Chapter 6.

But the conspiracy theories did not always lack justification. The most striking example is the link between the gold smuggling and drug trafficking. After sensational media reports in the 1960s, officials in both London and Hong Kong tried hard to smother public interest in this topic. However, the public records offices in both places reveal how high-level decisions were made to facilitate illegal shipments of gold to the colony by restricting police and customs service surveillance of smuggling activities. Officials knew that narcotics dealers would be able to take advantage of the tolerance shown towards the illegal movement of gold.[64]

The most misleading assumption about Hong Kong's economic history is that what happened before World War II or before the start of the Cold War at the end of the 1940s had little relevance to Hong Kong's subsequent success. In reality, banking policies and performance were heavily influenced by pre-war decisions and the rapid economic reconstruction after the Japanese occupation. The historical background is described in Chapter 2, 'Chinese Revolutionaries, Colonial Reformers' and 'Chapter 3, 'Post-war Emergencies: from Boom to Bust'.

A Colonial Case Study

The focus of this book is deliberately parochial. The role of the state in the economic achievements of the 50 years from 1935 and in the history of the banking industry are examined from a strictly Hong Kong standpoint. The wider context of Hong Kong's development has already been well explored by distinguished historians. The imperial background and the role of the UK have been described in a masterly volume by Dr. Steve Tsang.[65] The relationship between the Colonial Office and Hong Kong has been illuminated in a variety of essays by Professor David Faure. British and other overseas archives have been mined assiduously by Professor Schenk for a series of authoritative investigations of Hong Kong's financial institutions and the international dimensions of the colony's financial markets. Their scholarship sets the frame for much of the analysis in the chapters that follow.

The starting point for this book is the colonial administration's own record, especially as recorded in its own unpublished files. The picture that emerges from these sources is not flattering to Hong Kong's former rulers. The contemporaneous record of how they went about the daily task of running an increasingly prosperous and complex economy offers few instances of effective administration. There was little vision and not much internal pressure to inspire good performance. The files give a sense of isolation from the concerns of society in general, and there was little to link the personal interests of the expatriate mandarins to the well-being of the Chinese community. Very occasionally, the colonial mood changed, most notably for a few years before and after World War II when new governors felt the urgency of new policies and brave reforms. On the whole, however, senior officials were not inspiring figures.

Banking regulation and monetary affairs are important in their own right because they shaped the financial infrastructure on which Hong Kong's economic success depended. But they were also a test of the quality of colonial government and its leading personalities. Unlike social policies, the management of Hong Kong's money left little room for debate about conflicts between economic progress and public welfare. In the period covered by this book, banking regulation — almost always — wasstraightforward and involved no more than the normal standards of business integrity and sensible commercial practice. Special financial expertise was rarely required because, until the 1970s, banking business was not complicated by the technical sophistication that globalisation and the digital revolution were to bring. Monetary affairs should have been a matter of economic common sense: the adoption of policies that would ensure a monetary system free from improper or imprudent activities and stable financial markets.

The British Record

There are contradictory views on the British record as economic managers. Economic and monetary affairs were under the almost exclusive control of whoever occupied the post of financial secretary. These economic overlords were supported by the tiniest of teams until the late 1970, and they delegated little to their subordinates.[66] Yet, three of them, Sir Sidney Caine, Sir John Cowperthwaite and Sir Philip Haddon-Cave, earned the respect of the business community and came to be regarded overseas as distinguished authorities on economic affairs. Thus, the history of the colonial administration's management of monetary affairs is very much an account of the individual performance of the seven men who were financial secretaries between 1935 and 1985. It is also important to emphasise that they personally dictated the management of monetary affairs. They retained personal control even after a Monetary Affairs Branch had been established with its own policy secretary.

Despite the powerful personalities of the colony's Financial Secretaries and their public stature, there is a general assumption that, in Hong Kong, the state had no direct role of any significance in economic growth because of the government's commitment to laisser faire and its minimal intervention in either economic or social affairs. The colonial administration took a much less 'ideological' view of its agenda, however. Officials never saw themselves as locked into non-interventionism by colonial tradition. For them, laisser faire was not a matter of principle but motivated by political convenience and economic expediency.[67] The continued governability of Hong Kong was their overwhelming concern. Thus, under threat of Mainland sanctions in 1947 and of civil unrest because of bank runs in later decades, the colonial administration became more directly involved in the management of the banking industry than in the affairs of any other sector of the economy. This was a political decision, and it will become apparent in later chapters that officials felt no concern for the well-being of depositors or even the protection of the public from fraud.

This book devotes considerable attention to the impact of government intervention on banking. Chapter 1, 'Mismanaged by Mandarins', explores the priorities and preconceptions of the expatriate members of the élite Administrative Service who personally supervised the banking industry until the establishment of a professional Banking Commission in 1964. As regulators, they were handicapped by an almost invincible ignorance of even the simplest business arithmetic. They were indecisive in dealing with recalcitrant bankers and indulgent towards those whose activities were as much unlawful as unprofessional. The colonial mandarins were also responsible for overall economic and financial policy, and Chapter 10, 'Colonial Money and its Management', examines the quality of their policy-making. With no reliable national income estimates before the 1970s, the coordination of monetary policies with overall economic trends depended more on guesswork than credible analysis. Decisions were based very often on misconceptions about how the financial system worked. In the 1970s, the statistical situation improved. Now the problem was that the government totally misunderstood the consequences of the break with sterling and the way its management of a floating exchange rate would fuel inflation, encourage speculation and lead to financial failures and collapse of the currency in the following decade. These developments illustrate the well-known phenomenon that the regulators' own policies often lead a banking industry into dangerous business practices.[68]

Far more damaging, however, was the propensity of Hong Kong officials to discredit the regulatory system by disregarding their statutory obligations. The colonial administration appeared totally unaware of the close connection between the quality of the legal environment and banking developments.[69] The result was to create conditions that actually encouraged imprudent and illegal banking practices. Legislation and official policies are, of course, a powerful influence on business behaviour generally. They shape 'the rules of the game' which the entrepreneur follows because of their potential impact on profits. Where laws or official practices are misguided, it has been argued, the 'rules' may encourage business behaviour that is both self-destructive for the entrepreneur and damaging to the economy as a whole.[70] This assertion is a fair summary of the interaction of officials and bankers in the colony from the introduction of statutory regulation in 1948 until the radical reforms introduced after 1985.

Throughout this book, history appears to repeat itself. The past was easily forgotten, and its lessons ignored. Crises were recurrent, with little change in their causes or in the reluctance of the colonial administration to adopt the obvious remedies. Immigrants from the Mainland were often accused of being mere sojourners with no real commitment to Hong Kong and its well-being. The real birds of passage were the colonial mandarins who could escape the consequences of their erroneous policies because they lived in splendid isolation from the community and thought of somewhere else as home.[71] These were problems which the colony's political system could not solve. Indeed, between 1935 and 1985, its unreformed political arrangements did not foster the sound management of monetary affairs. The classical advocates of laisser faire in the UK had always realised that a government can ignore threats to the stability and integrity of the financial system only at considerable cost to the rest of the economy.[72] That was to be Hong Kong's experience during this period. Fortunately, its remarkable community generated such sustained growth in these years that the colony could afford to write off the costs of the government's policy and regulatory blunders without crippling the economy.

1

Mismanaged by Mandarins

Throughout the twentieth century, anti-imperialism and a deep resentment of foreign interference were among the most powerful political emotions of the Chinese people. Before World War II, the nation was bent on reforms to modernise social institutions, industrialise the economy and establish democratic government. Western nations began to lose the privileges they had seized in the previous century, and the expulsion of foreign interests got underway. Opposition to the UK's role in China was particularly severe, and London began the retreat from its 'informal' empire on the Mainland. By 1945, Hong Kong was the last remaining British possession in China, and the tide of anti-imperialist sentiment now forced the colonial administration to bow to the ruling Guomindang and its demands for Hong Kong to cooperate with the Mainland in the regulation of both banking and foreign trade. (Chapters 2 and 4 will review these political developments and their impact on Hong Kong.) In 1949, the Chinese Communist Party came to power, determined to remake every feature of the nation's life. At the same time, radical political changes were transforming the rest of the British Empire as colonial rule gave way to democratic legislatures and self-government.

There was no obvious reason why Hong Kong should survive as a separate political entity under British rule . Nor did Hong Kong officials seem likely to organise their own survival. They had made some effort between the two world wars to make their administration more responsive to the community's needs. But this reforming spirit soon evaporated after World War II, and the government showed no interest in improving its political credibility by introducing democratic reforms, despite London's instructions that all colonial territories should do so. The colonial administration refused to bid for popular support through adopting the programmes for social and economic development that post-war British governments recommended and which became a standard feature of most Third World countries. But British rule was not overthrown; Hong Kong did not become ungovernable; and the community never demanded to be reincorporated into the Mainland. The colony remained largely free from the political violence and social clashes endemic in most Asian societies of the period, although Hong Kong retained the colonial attitudes, political institutions and economic policies inherited from the nineteenth century.[1]

Political scientists have argued that an important factor in the survival of British rule was the superior quality of colonial administrators and their policies which brought them 'performance legitimacy'.[2] The colonial administration created 'a very efficient organization with excellent managerial skills, [and] an impressive record of policy implementation'.[3] As long as the government achieved 'technical efficiency and administrative effectiveness', it is claimed, it had no need of 'an elaborate mechanism of political mobilization, control and repression' and could ignore 'political values and principles'.[4] It was acknowledged that Hong Kong officials had their failings, among them 'a fetish for formal rules and codes'.[5] But even this fault could be passed off as bureaucratic zeal.

This chapter will demonstrate that if performance legitimacy had depended on the government's record in dealing with banking issues during the 50 years from 1935, British rule would have collapsed. There was a pattern of imprudent lending and incompetent management in banking that had made the financial system vulnerable to downturns in the business cycle before World War II and which forced officials to recognise that a special case existed for the supervision of bankers and their behaviour. The same defects were to persist throughout the post-war period, causing chronic crises until the mid-1980s.

Leading bankers and businessmen repeatedly urged the colonial administration to become involved in regulating the banking system to ensure its stability and integrity. The weaknesses of the banking system were plain enough, and so were the counter-measures the colonial administration ought to adopt. Yet, throughout the period from 1935 until 1985, its performance was deeply flawed. Inferior management and technical incompetence went unchecked and unrebuked among officials responsible for managing monetary affairs. Policy was confused and mainly influenced by political expediency and cultural misconceptions. Duties imposed by law, both on officials and on bankers, were frequently diluted or deliberately ignored until 1964, and stubborn resistance to formal regulation prevailed among senior officials until the late 1970s.

The repeated attempts to disclaim responsibility for the state of the banks had little to do with Hong Kong's long-standing commitment to laisser faire. Senior officials felt no great attachment to this traditional colonial ideology and regularly considered interventionist measures when confronted with serious economic challenges.

- In the years before World War II, there was considerable support for tariff protection for local industry, an industrial promotion programme and the allocation of factory sites on concessionary terms, and as Governor, Sir Geoffry Northcote, was an ardent supporter of initiatives to develop the economy (as the next chapter will explain).

- Another Governor, Sir Robert Black, was prepared to introduce import controls to protect local manufacturers in 1958[6] and to make a general retreat from traditional laisser faire in 1964 if significant benefits seemed likely to result.[7]

- In 1960, the Financial Secretary, A. G. Clarke, called for public discussion of the case for abandoning laisser faire to counter mounting protectionism in Hong Kong's export markets.[8]

- The official regarded as the colonial administration's most uncompromising opponent of government involvement in the economy, Sir John Cowperthwaite, advocated several departures from laisser faire. He proposed, for example, cheap land and subsidised finance to promote manufacturing in 1947[9] and anti-monopoly controls on public utilities in 1957.[10] During the 1960s, he was ready to consider help for 'infant industries' and the introduction of building licences to control the over-heated property sector.[11]

- The next Financial Secretary, Sir Philip Haddon-Cave, tried to recycle laisser faire as 'positive non-interventionism', which he defined as 'taking the view that, in the great majority of circumstances it is futile and damaging … to plan the allocation of resources available to the private sector and to frustrate the operation of market forces'.[12] Yet, he introduced cheap industrial loans in 1972[13] and later actively sought to facilitate the shift from manufacturing to services.[14] He presided over a 1979 report urging government support for initiatives to take advantage of the expected oil boom in the South China Sea (which did not materialise).[15]

Almost never were proposals to interfere with market forces rejected because of laisser-faire principles.[16] They were discarded, nearly always, because they were considered economically hazardous or politically inconvenient.

The discussion that follows will explore why the colonial administration's management of banking affairs was bedevilled by misguided policies and chaotic administration. It begins with the handicaps of the bureaucratic élite and reviews the colonial government's flawed approach to policy-making generally. It will explain how administrative officers prevented experienced professionals from contributing to the supervision of banking until 1964. Unpublished government records reveal an ignorance among senior officials of even the most routine features both of simple accounting and of business practices. This evidence also shows that these expatriates were unable to negotiate with local bankers or maintain the government's authority. Finally, the chapter will look at the part played by individual financial secretaries in allowing poor-quality banking regulation to persist for half a century.

The Policy Vacuum

Much of the blame for the colonial administration's poor performance can be attributed to the overweening confidence in the superiority of the Administrative Service and the extensive disregard for professional and technical expertise, which were the hallmarks of British rule. As a result, policy was made in a vacuum, remote from the economic and social realities of Hong Kong. 'Administrative officers' were specially selected and trained to be able to function effectively in the Chinese world. They were a small group of generalists who were supposed to make the British rulers seem less alien and remote by building direct and comfortable links between the colonial administration and its Chinese constituents.[17] This élite was dominated by expatriates, who numbered a mere 42 in 1950, 67 in 1964 and only 86 a decade later.[18] Between the first banking legislation in 1948 and its revision in 1964, financial secretaries relied on a handful of administrative officers — less than a dozen all told — to take charge of banking policy and the enforcement of the minimal statutory provisions governing the banks.

There were some who displayed outstanding qualities, but most senior administrative officers assigned to banking duties showed little knowledge of Chinese business and less concern for the well-being of the Chinese depositor. Yet, many went on from incompetent supervision of the banking system to reach the highest posts in the government. They included a future chief secretary, two future financial secretaries, a well-regarded director of commerce and industry, a commissioner of labour and, after a minor banking role, a future governor. The 1964 Banking Ordinance seemed to bring their reign to an end by creating a professional Banking Commission. Nevertheless, a tiny band of administrative officers continued to decide not only policy but its implementation, despite the regulators' pleas for more autonomy.[19]

The colonial culture did not encourage a rational approach to policy-making. The administrative officer's priority was to find a quick, convenient and, above all, a cheap solution for each problem confronting the colonial administration. In contrast to colonial officers in most other territories, officials in Hong Kong did not believe in coordinated policy-making. Constitutionally, a formal structure existed which passed policy proposals upwards towards the governor and the Executive Council via the colonial (later chief) secretary or financial secretary. In practice, Hong Kong adopted a casual, *ad hoc* approach to issues, particularly in deciding how policies should be interpreted, implemented or amended. Policy was assumed to evolve almost spontaneously in this piecemeal process.[20] On the whole, policies were not recorded systematically as a coherent guide to decision-making but left to be discovered, almost haphazard, from a variety of seemingly unconnected files.[21]

The most dangerous deficiency in the policy-making process was a deep mistrust of statistics within the Administrative Service that defied severe criticism from London and discounted the risks of making policy in ignorance of the facts. As early as 1938, the Governor had denounced a chronic shortage of the data essential for good government.[22]

> The statistical information at the disposal of this Government is deficient … there is a serious lack of machinery for the co-ordination of such statistics as exist, and in nearly every case these are crude. In such circumstances it might with some truth be alleged that figures are given to us to conceal the facts.

Such obvious good sense became unfashionable in Hong Kong after World War II. In the 1950s, officials candidly declared that data should not be collected because they were afraid of being compelled to introduce new and better programmes if the public had fuller information on economic and social conditions.[23] Even a population census was regarded as dangerous politically and useless for policy purposes.[24] The first post-war Government Statistician was treated almost as a subversive for trying to introduce a modern statistical system. His opinions were distorted; his professional performance denigrated; and his position made impossible.[25]

From the start of the post-war era, London complained fruitlessly about the absence of Hong Kong data, but the colonial administration was particularly opposed to collecting banking data even if the figures were strictly for confidential circulation among officials.[26] The banks shared the colonial administration's mistrust of releasing statistical information. HSBC, for example, was afraid that its true financial position might be deduced from published statistics even if the data were consolidated for the industry as a whole.[27] Not until 1959, after considerable pressure from London, did Hong Kong fall in line with the rest of the British Commonwealth and start to publish some banking data, although in a highly abbreviated form and on an incomplete basis.[28] As a result, when a Bank of England official was preparing the 1962 policy document to set up a modern system of banking regulation enforced by statute, his report was remarkably lacking in statistical and economic analysis. It consisted mainly of generalisations based on anecdotal evidence.[29]

The colonial administration did not rectify the data deficit and start to collect accurate and comprehensive statistical information about banking until December 1964. The published statistics remained minimalist, however, until the mid-1980s. The reluctance to release information extended to the government's own appointees to the legislature, even when its discussions were taking place behind closed doors. There was almost a constitutional crisis in 1965, for example, when the government requested additional funds for banking supervision after serious bank runs that year. The colonial administration outraged legislators by refusing to show them the Bank of England report which officials invoked to justify the increased spending.[30]

The statistical situation appeared to improve in the 1970s, when a new Financial Secretary, Haddon-Cave, ended Cowperthwaite's ban on the compilation of such macro-economic data as national income and balance of payments estimates. However, this liberalism did not extend to comprehensive coverage of financial institutions. As the unlicensed deposit-taking sector ran amok in the 1970s, he declined to use statutory powers to obtain the statistics from DTCs urgently required to assess the extent of their problems and the measures needed to resolve them. He later excused his decision on the grounds that it would have been improper to collect information showing depositors to be at risk when there was no legislation to protect them.[31]

> … the implication of the Government receiving those monthly returns is that the Government accepts a degree of responsibility for the prudential supervision of those companies. How far is it right for the Government to accept that responsibility, if it does not have the power to ensure that all is well in the companies?

He could, of course, have used the information to justify new statutory powers to intervene in the DTC sector on the public's behalf. At the end of the 1970s, when effective regulation had become imperative, Haddon-Cave confessed publicly that the government lacked the statistics needed to make policy decisions.[32] That administrative handicap was counter-balanced by a political advantage: the public did not have the information to challenge government policies. Only when the system came close to collapse in the early 1980s was the colonial administration no longer able to conceal how it had allowed 'imprudence, mismanagement, and malpractice' to flourish. Some 40 per cent of the DTCs had closed their doors between 1978 and 1987, amidst considerable scandal.[33]

The Amateurs Take Charge

It would be hard to imagine a worse recipe for the regulation of a banking system than to have policy made by a group of officials deeply indoctrinated in a colonial culture that resented outside opinions, whether from its own hand-picked representatives in Hong Kong's ruling councils or from the Colonial Office, and who did not believe that accurate data was good for policy-making. The absurdity of this situation was compounded by the lack of qualifications among these officials. When it came to banking, they were amateurs who, no matter how gifted, would have benefited from professional expertise and commercial experience. These resources were available within the colonial administration, but administrative officers were determined to limit the influence of their professional colleagues.

The rejection of a role for professionals had begun before World War II. After a banking crisis in 1935, legislation was drafted to make banks a special class of company that would come under the professional supervision of the Registrar of Companies. This official's department was already complaining of gross overwork, however, and the proposal did not survive.[34] In any case, the question of entrusting bank supervision to professionals seemed of secondary importance. Any official should have the intelligence, it was argued, to ask the auditors for all the explanation needed to understand a bank's balance sheet.[35] By 1939, the Financial Secretary was determined to prevent the appointment of a professional 'banking examiner' whom he portrayed, unconvincingly, as expensive and too difficult to recruit. His real reason was the conviction that the government ought not to employ professional regulators to safeguard depositors:[36]

> The primary object of all this [discussion of banking regulation] is the protection of the public. I do feel, however, that the public is not entitled, and should not be encouraged, to expect Government to replace private prudence.

A similar attitude persisted after the war. Clarke, a future Financial Secretary, declared that the 'small measure of control over banks' introduced by the 1948 Banking Ordinance 'cannot be made effective unless we have a competent staff of accountants', but no attempt was made to recruit them.[37] This decision cannot be explained by a lack of money. Although Hong Kong was a struggling economy in the first decade after World War II, the banking industry was well able to pay for investigations of suspect banks through the annual licence fees collected from the industry.[38] Financial secretaries, however, were determined to retain the revenue derived from licensing for general government expenditure, while rejecting any responsibility to pay for effective banking regulation.[39]

The government's own professionals could not always be excluded from banking matters. For example, there was the crucial question of who would be qualified to hold banking licences. Senior legal and commercial officials warned that licences were being issued improperly to smaller local Chinese-owned banks which were owned by 'associations' or partnerships. The administrative officers persisted with this unlawful procedure even after being informed that, under the new law, licences could only be granted to individuals or limited companies. The Financial Secretary recognised the potential dangers of this practice. If a bank which had been improperly licensed got into trouble, there would be no party whom the government or the depositors could pursue. The Financial Secretary did not believe that the danger was serious, and he decided to tolerate the situation but to threaten to withdraw a bank's licence if it failed to disclose information about the proprietors if requested.[40] As a result, licences were issued to applicants even when disqualified under the 1948 Banking Ordinance or the 1932 Companies

Ordinance.[41] Subsequently, when the government wanted to bring pressure to bear on a mismanaged bank, it was often too late to identify who was legally liable.[42] In addition, bank licences were being transferred between unidentified partners, which made it all the more difficult to monitor suspect bankers.[43]

A related problem was that the indiscriminate licensing of virtually all applicants meant that banks were being endorsed whose operations were fraudulent from the very start. A test case came with the China Industrial Bank, which an internal government report found had been operating fraudulently since it first applied for a licence. The Registrar General was unwilling to overlook the serious danger to depositors created by this bank's obvious disregard for the ordinary criminal and commercial laws. He argued that the government had a duty under the 1948 Banking Ordinance to safeguard depositors from malpractice or misconduct by any licensed bank. The Registrar General pointed out the obvious parallels with his own department which regulated insurance and trust companies. These had to lodge a security deposit with the Hong Kong authorities if they did not match UK standards for minimum paid-up capital and margins of solvency. The 1948 Banking Ordinance did not impose such stringent requirements, but the Registrar General could not see why banks were not compelled to comply with its far-from-onerous provisions as well as with the laws that applied to business in general. The administrative officers involved were willing to admit among themselves the validity of his complaints. Nevertheless, the Financial Secretary insisted that the government had no duty to police the banks because, he declared, 'the grant of a licence in no way implies any Government assurance of the standing of the bank'. The climax to this dispute over regulatory standards came when the Registrar General asked that China Industrial Bank's licence fee be used to institute bankruptcy proceedings to recover some of the depositors' money. The Financial Secretary rejected this request, together with the plea for stricter enforcement of the 1948 Banking Ordinance.[44] The Registrar General found himself unable to make any further representations on how the law should be applied to banks. But he used his department's powers in bankruptcy cases to protect depositors' interests when banks, which had been incorporated, went into liquidation during the 1950s.[45] The administrative officers, nevertheless, had won what was to prove a lasting victory in 1952. They were left free thereafter to decide for themselves how to oversee the banks, regardless of the letter of the law.

Would it have made a significant difference if greater use had been made of the legal and commercial expertise within the colonial administration? A scandal nine years later shows how the Registrar General's department might have contributed to better banking. It also indicates that the administrative officers had learnt nothing from the bank failures of the 1950s. In 1961, the Registrar General drew attention to the latest accounts of the Chiu Tai Bank, which suggested that it was already insolvent. From his past experience of winding-up banks which had failed, he suspected that the bank's accounts were probably too optimistic about its chances of survival. His recommendation was that the licence should be withdrawn without delay.[46] His first memorandum on Chiu Tai Bank was a model of commercial insight and sound judgment unmatched by any analysis of an ailing bank from an administrative officer in the available government archives. This contrast was not surprising. A professional department could learn from experience because its staff had the technical background and professional training to analyse corporate behaviour and to evaluate managerial practices. Administrative officers lacked these advantages, were unable to accumulate knowledge in this way, and could not apply experience creatively. Even with the best will in their world, they were grievously handicapped by their inability to understand the simplest accounts and their unfamiliarity with routine banking. The response of the administrative officers to the plight of the Chiu Tai Bank will be discussed in some detail later. But their readiness to accept the assurances of its management and their failure to exert any appreciable influence over the bank's conduct allowed it to continue in business for another two years.

The Missing Accounts

The 1948 ordinance required banks to prepare annual accounts. These balance sheets were the only means by which the government could establish whether banks were solvent — apart from newspaper reports of writs and bank runs.[47] They provided the starting point for a relationship between an official and a banker, and they were the best basis for any serious discussions between the two sides. Initially, it was found that that the original ordinance compelled licensed banks to display their annual reports on their premises but imposed no obligation to submit them to the government.[48] Even after this omission was rectified, banks often failed to send in their accounts within the legal time limits. To Clarke, there seemed no point in trying to compel the smaller banks to comply with the law, and he directed that they should not be pursued for their accounts.[49] He and his colleagues failed, apparently, to understand that the obvious reason why a bank would hold up its accounts was the dismal picture of its performance they would reveal. The significance of the missing accounts was illustrated dramatically by one of the worst bank collapses of the 1950s. The government was alerted to the plight of the Fu Shing Bank in 1952 by press reports of a creditor's meeting. No annual accounts had been supplied to the government, of course. Clarke displayed a relatively indulgent attitude towards the bank. It had closed its doors after investing heavily in the manager's factory and fishing projects. The manager 'seems unable at the moment to distinguish between his own personal debts and the bank's debts', Clarke noted, while believing — erroneously — that the manager might still rescue the business.[50] He did not. Other banks continued to miss their statutory deadlines, and when their managers were belatedly compelled to comply with the law, their businesses were found, all too often, to be in poor shape.[51]

Once a bank's accounts had been received, it was the administrative officers' job to review them and then to advise the Financial Secretary when a bank was badly run; how much fresh capital should be injected; and whether its licence should be withdrawn. Administrative officers frequently found these tasks beyond them even though the accounts of the banks quoted in this chapter involved the simplest kind of book-keeping and were far less complicated than the financial records maintained by a typical government department. The Yue Man Bank, for example, had lost all its capital within two years of being licensed. Its owners undertook to raise additional finance. 'Although this sum still leaves the paid-up capital below a desirable minimum', the official responsible advised, 'the Bank have done as much as can reasonably be expected to improve the capital resources of the Bank', and so it was permitted to remain in business. It continued to run at a loss, and another official commented complacently on the annual accounts: 'As the loss for 1951 was comparatively small I assume no action need be taken on this matter'. Fortunately, the Financial Secretary was more alert and noticed that the auditors had qualified the accounts, pointing out that its loans were in such a bad state that its solvency was in doubt. There was no rebuke for his subordinate who had failed to read the accounts properly, and the blunder did not check his eventual promotion to the post of commissioner of labour.[52] Possibly this indulgence reflected the Financial Secretary's own casual attitude towards statutory returns from local Chinese-owned banks. On one occasion, he noted that a bank had sent in 'somewhat unorthodox accounts'. He decided to overlook this deficiency, even though he was aware that the beneficial ownership of the bank was in doubt and that it was being run at a loss.[53] It did not survive.

Baffled by Business

Administrative officers could not be relied on to comprehend even the most ordinary features of banking business. A future financial secretary, Cowperthwaite, was mystified as to how a bank's financial statement could show current accounts under 'liabilities' (being owed to its depositors) and also under 'assets' (being owned by the bank). He seemed, as yet, unaware that banks maintained deposit accounts with other banks (typically, for clearing purposes).[54] This same official seems to have felt no special urgency about recommending the withdrawal of a licence when a bank's lending practices were plainly perilous although he knew that a bank ought to keep reasonable cash balances.[55] The larger issues of management of bank liquidity and how banks created credit also seem to have baffled Cowperthwaite. When he was informed by a Belgian executive that his bank's 'loans and advances to commerce and industry far exceed our deposits', Cowperthwaite's response was one of incredulity. He believed that such a high ratio of loans to deposits was impossible and must reflect unorthodox treatment of items in the bank's accounts. The Belgian took the trouble to show him that accounting errors were not the explanation, but Cowperthwaite steadfastly refused to believe that banks could create loans on this scale.[56]

His misunderstanding of the lending policies of foreign banks did no harm in this period because their high ratios of loans to deposits created a liquidity loophole which was invaluable in financing Hong Kong's industrial take-off after World War II, as Chapter 5, 'Industrial Take-off: Cut-price and Self-financed', will discuss. But the ratio of loans to deposits went to the heart of the prudential supervision of bank lending and was vital to the stability of the overall banking system. Cowperthwaite seemed unaware that even the limited statistical information available to him showed that, during the 1950s, banks in general were becoming significantly less conservative. The overall loan/deposit ratio was estimated at 48 per cent in 1954; 67 per cent in 1959; and 70 per cent in 1964 — the eve of a major banking crisis.[57] This crude but useful indicator of a bank's risks went unrecognised by most officials. They were taken by surprise when, between 1961 and 1965, nine local Chinese-owned banks were brought to the point of collapse through over-exposure to property in particular. It is fair to say that if Cowperthwaite had been less convinced that bankers did not know their own business, he could have acted earlier to impose adequate liquidity ratios on the banking system, thus reducing the risk of banks runs in the 1960s.[58]

The personal encounters of administrative officers with Chinese bankers highlighted the cultural disabilities of the expatriate. For example, a run started on Shun Foo Bank and forced it to close its doors in November 1952, after it was involved in the insolvency of another bank. The Managing Director expressed optimism about reopening later in the month when interviewed by Cowperthwaite who seemed to have taken a very trusting view of the bank's affairs. He recorded on file: 'There is no indication that the bank's policy has been unsound'. In fact, its loan portfolio was in a dreadful state. According to the auditors' view of the 1952 accounts, 'the large majority' of loans and advances were overdue, collateral was inadequate and 'a very substantial amount should be provided against possible losses'.[59] Cowperthwaite had shown himself incapable of assessing a Chinese bank executive and his business standing.

Later in the decade, a Shanghainese operator of a cinema chain applied to open a bank of which he would be Managing Director. In 1961, not long after it was licensed, he called on Cowperthwaite in search of advice. Should the bank's liquid funds be invested in local equities? Cowperthwaite suggested that a sound bank would place surplus funds in the inter-bank market (with which he was now more familiar than he had been when dealing with bank accounts in 1955, as mentioned above). What about a flour mill? Cowperthwaite 'suggested that flour milling was not a proper business for a bank'. Real estate was the Managing Director's main interest. He had registered some of the bank's properties in his own name, he explained, because 'he had frequently forgotten to take his bank's seal with him when he went to execute the deed'. He promised to rectify the situation, but Cowperthwaite advised the Financial Secretary: 'I think we will have to continue to watch this bank very carefully'. Cowperthwaite reported that he had 'read him a lecture about keeping banking business and other business strictly separate'. But, for all Cowperthwaite's powerful personality in English and his very real authority in banking matters, he failed to convince this Shanghainese to take either him or the government seriously. The banker displayed no great enthusiasm, according to government files, about complying with Cowperthwaite's advice.[60] Despite continuing difficulties in persuading the Managing Director to distinguish between his own property and the bank's investments, official interest in this bank does not appear to have lasted for very long.[61] Not surprisingly, this bank was to require government assistance during the widespread bank runs in 1965.[62]

To be fair, the ability of the businessman to get the better of expatriate officials and ignore their laws and regulations was not confined to the banking world. Manufacturers, for example, sometimes submitted fraudulent applications for export licences to sell textiles overseas. Even after a decade of administering this quota scheme, there was no file containing clear working instructions on how to deal with suspect applications. In addition, expatriates were nervous that industrialists might withdraw their cooperation from the colonial administration if penalised or they might simply prove too smart to be convicted if prosecuted. As with banking, the officials involved included some destined for outstanding careers. Behind this failure to enforce legislation lay misleading expatriate preconceptions about Chinese social values and political attitudes.[63]

Beyond Salvation

The fallout from a bank failure in 1961 discredited the cursory approach to bank regulation preferred by administrative officers. The Liu Chong Hing Bank got into trouble because of imprudence and misconduct, and its Managing Director misappropriated HKD8 million. It was rescued because it was too large to be allowed to fail.[64] In the aftermath of this scandal, officials took the line that the 1948 Banking Ordinance was not conducive to taking prompt and effective action against offending banks.[65] New legislation was unavoidable, and a Bank of England official was brought in to update the 1948 Banking Ordinance. His 1962 report proposed a thoroughly modern system of regulation with professional staff qualified to investigate a bank's affairs, and accurate and comprehensive statistics.[66] But the proposals did not become law until 1964.

In the meantime, the inability to establish effective dialogue with local bankers was threatening the stability of the entire system. After the Chiu Tai Bank's fragile position had been identified by the Registrar General, as mentioned earlier, the case was taken over by an expatriate administrative officer, who later became well thought of as director of commerce and industry. He interviewed the Managing Director, and the official record of the discussion shows the official taking a very mild, almost hesitant, line in urging more prudent behaviour. His approach was so unimpressive that a subordinate suggested in vain: 'Can you not tell this "bank" that they must not accept any more deposits from the public?'. The bank did not improve, and by 1963, a future Chief Secretary (Sir Jack Cater) was dealing with its Managing Director. The interview notes show that Cater, too, was apologetic about troubling this executive with questions about his bank's dishonoured cheques, its outstanding debts and its dubious business practices. By this date, the bank was beyond salvation.[67]

The same two officials who had figured in the Chiu Tai Bank fiasco were to respond in a very similar way to even grosser mismanagement and misconduct in the case of the Canton Trust and Commercial Bank. Its collapse in 1965 was to trigger the banking crisis that year. When its senior staff were charged with criminal offences, the two officials gave evidence. They admitted that in 1962, the government had known the bank was dangerously over-exposed to property. They swore that officials had attempted to warn its management that they were acting imprudently. Cater admitted that this advice had not been heeded by the time he took over the file in 1963. He claimed, however, that he had become satisfied with the improvements which he witnessed. These apparent changes for the better had come from false accounting, it later became clear.[68]

The official files show that administrative officers who took over banking supervision in the early 1960s felt more helpless than their predecessors. They do not appear to have been given much leadership by Cowperthwaite who had become Financial Secretary in 1961. He adopted the traditional stance of his predecessors and proved a reluctant regulator who made little effort to enforce the existing legislation. Not until after the banking and political emergencies of the mid-1960s did he acknowledge that depositors could not be treated as if they were investors in a limited company. The depositor's interests, he now suggested, should rank higher than those of the bank's shareholders.[69] Banking stability had become a political necessity for the colonial administration, but was not yet perceived as vital to Hong Kong's economic performance.

History Repeated

Cowperthwaite's successor was Haddon-Cave. He too shared a marked reluctance to expand supervision of the banks. He came into office with a professional regulatory system well able to cope with threats to the integrity of commercial banks. In the 1970s, however, DTCs of all sorts mushroomed in Hong Kong. Illegal and imprudent management of financial institutions grew on a scale unmatched in Hong Kong's history, as Chapter 9, 'From Banking Crisis to Financial Catastrophe', will describe. The new Financial Secretary reacted much as his predecessors had done before the 1964 reforms. He repudiated responsibility for safeguarding any depositors except the customers of licensed banks.[70] He also disclaimed any duty to secure even 'the prudent conduct of business' by any deposit-taking firms not licensed as banks. Mounting alarm within business circles compelled him to bring these unlicensed firms under a degree of official supervision in 1975, but the measures taken were as nominal as those which the 1948 Banking Ordinance had espoused. They were strengthened later in the decade but were still minimalist, and they proved ineffectual in preventing a series of bank runs and corporate collapses, which will be analysed in Chapter 9. The causes of these failures had much in common with the mismanagement and misconduct of the 1950s that had led to the scandals and bank crashes from 1961 to 1965. Although Hong Kong had professional regulators from 1964, their scope was limited to commercial banking. They were isolated from the administrative officers who, in their turn, were making decisions on economic and financial issues without adequate experience or the expertise to assess the implications for the integrity and stability of the banks and other financial institutions.[71]

This hands-off approach to regulating the new DTCs had a disastrous effect on the standards of banking regulation in general. By the 1980s, such highly reputable banks as HSBC and Citibank seemed happy to take at face value transactions with secondary banking institutions later found to have engaged in extensive frauds. Bank auditors expressed no alarm about lax bank attitudes towards credit controls and the quality of their loan portfolios. The Banking Commission focused on the technical requirements of its legislation, assuming that bankers would solve any other problems through their commercial good sense. Banks found it easy to exploit this regulatory strategy which took no account of the underlying patterns of banking behaviour. The Financial Secretary was too busy resisting pressures to clean up the DTCs to tackle the failings of the regulators.[72]

The Men at the Top

In the final analysis, the chronic banking failures that persisted after World War II until the mid-1980s can be traced back to the attitudes of the men who, as financial secretaries, were responsible for overseeing the colony's financial institutions. Before the war, there had been a worldwide depression and the chaotic conditions on the Mainland to excuse Hong Kong's banking crises. After the defeat of Japan, there could have been no such defence. Chapter 2, 'Post-war Emergencies: From Boom to Bust', will recount Hong Kong's astonishingly rapid recovery from the Japanese occupation and its subsequent remarkable success as a manufacturing centre, in spite of the constraints of the Korean War and the two decades of Cold War that were to follow.

There was a striking similarity about the outlook that the financial secretaries brought to the job, which can be summarised here and will form the background to the analysis in later chapters of the banking sector's development up to 1985. Their ultimate concern was political — the avoidance of public unrest. They were all unenthusiastic about introducing effective regulation and generally enforcing the colony's commercial laws unless the financial system was in direct danger from bank runs and related scandals. They seemed to have little interest in the economic gains from promoting stable financial institutions whose integrity was assured. The interests of the mass of depositors meant even less to them. Financial secretaries also suffered from the same distaste for structured policy-making that was typical of the Administrative Service as a whole, combined with an astonishing ignorance of the basic technicalities of banking and business, as this chapter has discussed in some detail.

Trusted Talent

Clarke was Financial Secretary from 1952 until 1961. However, he had shaped policy even before his appointment. His predecessor, Sir Charles Follows, had considerable trust in his talent and allowed him to dominate the banking scene. Under Clarke, Hong Kong made full use of its freedom from the exchange controls and other constraints that applied to other colonial territories, and Hong Kong developed a modern, international banking sector which comfortably financed the colony's 'industrial revolution' in the 1950s. (See Chapter 5.) Hong Kong also laid the foundation for its emergence as a major regional financial centre by meeting China's needs for a convertible international currency throughout the 20 years of intense economic blockade by the US.

During Clarke's term of office, banking seemed free of serious scandals. There was, nevertheless, a severe and often painful contraction of the industry.

Between 1948 and 1955, 52 local Chinese-owned banks disappeared.[73] Many of these closures were painless, but several involved crashes that were among the largest corporate failures of the decade.[74] They attracted little political attention, partly because mass banking had not yet developed. In any case, against a background of Mao Zedong's revolutionary changes on the Mainland and an international environment of war, economic embargoes and growing protectionism, individual bank failures did not capture the public imagination as they would in later decades. Clarke's political life was made easier by the lack of popular representation in the legislature and an absence of statistical information about banking and the economy in general. In short, there was no forum in which to debate the government's banking performance, and little information with which to assess it.

Recipe for Disaster

Clarke's successor, Cowperthwaite, occupied the post from 1961 to 1971. Before his appointment as Financial Secretary, he commanded even more respect from senior members of the colonial administration for his policy-making abilities than Clarke had done at a similar stage of his career. But, unlike Clarke, Cowperthwaite showed no great personal interest in banking matters. Until he became Financial Secretary, he functioned at about the same level of ignorance and incompetence as his colleagues, as this chapter has noted already.

Cowperthwaite seemed blind to the way in which mismanagement and misconduct would prove a recipe for banking disasters. He knowingly accepted compromises to the 1964 Banking Ordinance that allowed grossly imprudent lending practices to continue.[75] Although he presented himself as bowing to irresistible lobbying by influential bankers, he can be criticised for neglecting to rally business support for the new legislation at an early stage. He was also at fault for failing to disclose publicly how the near-collapse of the Liu Chong Hing Bank in 1961 justified a tough regulatory régime for the industry as a whole.[76] His technical limitations were to prove costly. Chapter 8, 'An Avoidable Crisis: The 1965 Bank Runs', will show that he completely misread the dangerous trends in the property sector in the early 1960s, thereby creating the conditions that precipitated the bank runs in 1965. It will also discuss his mismanagement of the economic consequences of the 1965 banking crisis and the damage done by his adoption of measures designed to suppress competition in the local banking industry. Unlike the 1950s, there could be no discreet disasters, for mass banking had arrived. The public was outraged when large numbers of depositors lost their savings through the illegal and imprudent activities of bank owners and executives, of which officials should have been aware. Under Cowperthwaite, three local banks collapsed, while another six had to be rescued, either directly with public funds or indirectly with the aid of government guarantees.

Colonial Throwback

Haddon-Cave, who was Financial Secretary from 1971 to 1981, lacked his two immediate predecessors' experience of Hong Kong and its business affairs. He was franker in his public discussion of his banking policies and problems than any previous financial secretary. He had little choice, given the changing political scene of which aggressive pressure groups and collective protests became regular features.[77] He also recognised the limitations of the colonial administration's expertise in managing financial affairs. He dropped Cowperthwaite's aversion to 'experts' and borrowed younger staff from the Bank of England and elsewhere in the British government. They lacked the seniority, the Hong Kong background and the administrative support to make a significant difference to the government's performance. But they did inject a degree of professionalism into Hong Kong's management of monetary affairs that was to prove crucial to the reforms of the 1980s.

Haddon-Cave's handicap was his fidelity to colonial traditions from an earlier generation. He revived the attitudes of officials before World War II and of Clarke in the 1950s, although he had no personal contact with them or even their files. There was no question of reversing the 1964 Banking Ordinance or abolishing professional regulation. But he mounted a stubborn campaign to prevent regulation from being extended beyond the licensed banks. This approach would have been less dangerous for financial integrity and less damaging to the economy if Haddon-Cave had not been woefully ignorant of the mechanics of Hong Kong's financial system and the creation of liquidity. In the first half of the decade, he fumbled badly because he was baffled by the new floating exchange rate and its impact on the government's reserves.[78] He spent the rest of the decade tinkering fruitlessly with formulas to bring liquidity under official control.[79] The result was a credit explosion that financed a bubble economy and encouraged the worst banking excesses, as Chapter 9 will discuss. He did not have to take personal responsibility for these failures. As with Clarke, the poisoned fruits of Haddon-Cave's erroneous policies were left as a legacy for his successor. The government was forced to spend HKD3.8 billion on rescuing and restructuring collapsed banks during the 1980s in order to avert public panic and a collapse of business confidence.[80] (This sum was equivalent to total government spending on public housing in 1983–84.[81])

It was unfortunate that the Governor during this period was Sir Murray MacLehose. He had made a brief appearance on the banking scene as Political Adviser, the diplomat appointed by London to handle relations with Beijing and other foreign governments and to deal with intelligence and related matters. In this capacity, he had tried to block a 1959 transaction with Thailand by one of Hong Kong's China state-owned banks, alleging 'somewhere there is a racket'. He was displaying the same ill-informed attitude towards banking business as the typical administrative officer. He had not bothered to check the relevant files, and the British Embassy in Bangkok had to point out to him that the transaction was authorised by an international agreement relating to the partition of Vietnam.[82] As Governor, MacLehose tried to strike a populist attitude. He blamed the stock market collapse of 1973 on the way '*laissez-faire* produced excessive risks'.[83] He went on, nevertheless, to preside over the non-interventionism of Haddon-Cave for the rest of the decade, which was followed by even worse market collapses.

Conclusions

This chapter has shown the extent to which the banking crises of the period were avoidable disasters. In the last resort, the explanation for these lapses in a government that has been hailed for its efficiency was to be found in the nature of colonial rule. Expatriate officials were remote from the consequences of their own decisions. Crooked bank owners were seen as a threat to the Chinese depositor, and the corrupt bank executive as a burden on the Chinese borrower. Bank crashes were viewed as happening only in the Chinese world. The expatriate's family and friends were unaffected. Nor were there any disciplinary penalties for officials responsible for misguided policies or erroneous decisions. Careers continued to flourish for the 'high-flyers' regardless of the incompetence and even indifference they displayed towards their statutory duties. In addition, as long as there were no public disturbances, the colonial system insulated officials from most of the political liability for bad policies. There was little scope before the 1970s for informed public discussion of banking issues, and there was no means of holding the government to account for its banking blunders until the first, indirect, elections to the legislature in 1985.

2

Chinese Revolutionaries, Colonial Reformers

In the years between the two world wars, a new China emerged — and a very different Hong Kong. This was a time of political turmoil and economic crisis on the Mainland. Yet, inspired by a surging sense of Chinese nationalism, a reform process gathered momentum, propelled by a nationwide desire for unified government and the radical reconstruction of China's social and economic institutions, ranging from marriage to the tax system. The growth of large-scale industries and the creation of modern financial institutions offered the prospect of rapid economic development.[1] This national revival was even more powerful politically. It was dramatically evident in the failure of foreign powers to maintain their grasp on the country. The UK could not withstand the mounting resentment of its presence in China, and it was forced to start the retreat from its 'informal' empire on the Mainland. More striking still was the failure of Japan to bring China to its knees, either through undeclared war up to 1937 or the launch of full-scale hostilities thereafter. Japanese forces seized territory, bombed cities and caused economic havoc. But Japan did not capture the Mainland, destroy the economy or bring to a halt the appetite for reform and development. China, for all its political conflicts and economic backwardness, was no longer in the parlous state that had made it unable to defy foreign powers in the final period of Manchu rule.

As China changed, so did Hong Kong. Still a British colony, the community was, at this time, more closely integrated socially and economically into the Mainland, than it would be again until the resumption of Chinese sovereignty in 1997, and it could not be isolated from the nationwide drive for reform and development. The nature of colonial rule was also changing. Within the UK itself and throughout the British Empire, there was a growing tide of reform that questioned the foundations on which colonial rule was based. Unlike the Indian Empire, democratic reforms were never on the agenda for Hong Kong. Yet, its senior officials briefly became less wedded to colonial traditions than they would be again until the 1980s. A readiness to retreat from laisser faire and to promote industry went hand in hand with a willingness to raise taxes and expand welfare. Colonialism, it seemed, no longer involved an unconditional commitment to what later decades labelled 'non-interventionism', either in economic or in social affairs. The period demonstrates what reforms the colonial administration could have achieved if the Japanese war against China and the occupation of Hong Kong had not halted the momentum of economic and social innovation.

These years mark a crucial period in the history of Hong Kong's economic development, laying the foundations for the manufacturing take-off in the second half of the century. At the same time, however, the relationship with the Mainland became so close between the wars, and economic integration was so visible, that a sense of dependence on the Mainland and on the China trade dominated Hong Kong's economic outlook. As a result, officials and business leaders in the early post-war decades found it almost impossible to see that the foundations for industrial growth laid before the war were more than adequate to make up for the Mainland business that Hong King lost after 1949.

The inter-war period was also important in Hong Kong's financial history. Between the wars, banking became the first major industry for which the colonial administration recognised, though without enthusiasm, that government direction was necessary. Banking policy after World War II was to follow very closely the attitudes towards bank regulation that had grown up in the inter-war period, despite the very different economic environment.

This chapter will explore how political and economic trends on the Mainland affected Hong Kong and why the colonial administration developed a new sense of responsibility for social and economic progress. It will show that the colonial administration sought to maximise its freedom from London's control in order to protect a financial system unique among colonial territories for its autonomy and sophistication (whose remarkable characteristics are analysed in Chapter 11, 'The Exceptional Colony'). The present chapter will also focus on how the official attitudes towards banking and financial affairs that evolved during the inter-war years created a cultural legacy that resisted the regulation of banking and financial markets and which later adopted an indulgent, almost protective, stance towards local Chinese bankers and their traditional business model.

Strengths and Weaknesses

Hong Kong took a suitably modest view of its place in the world between the two world wars. An official report in 1935 described it simply as part of China, despite its political status as a British Crown Colony.[2]

> Hong Kong consequently is not an economic entity even in the most restricted sense of the word ... As a community and as a trade centre it is a portion of China from which it is separated by political barriers. It shares in the strength of weakness of its neighbour's conditions and institutions.

Because Hong Kong was so closely integrated into the Chinese economy before World War II, the fortunes of its own economy and of its banking industry mirrored very closely the Mainland's business environment. During this period, the Mainland made considerable economic progress. The country was hardly affected by the slump that overtook the world economy in the 1920s. The currencies of both Hong Kong and the Mainland were linked to silver, rather than to gold, sterling or the US dollar. As a result, neither the Mainland nor the Hong Kong economies suffered the severe deflation that affected the rest of the world in this decade. On the contrary, because the price of silver declined until 1931, the Mainland saw a prolonged period of rising prices which boosted profits and encouraged investment.[3] In addition, the Mainland benefited from efforts to modernise the country, create Western-style industries, unify the currency and overhaul public finances.[4] Although these reforms were implemented very patchily, the economy was able to expand impressively until the price of silver started to rise from 1931. This caused a severe economic downturn that lasted until the link with silver was abolished in 1935 and banking reforms were introduced to stabilise the currency.

Nevertheless, throughout this period, contemporary commentators tended to disregard the positive economic trends and to portray the Chinese nation as being in a state of acute crisis. This sense of catastrophe reflected the political turmoil that constantly reoccurred. The ruling Guomindang Party, with its ambitions to create a modern, unified state, was an improvement over the control of the warlords which it replaced. But its authority was widely disputed and frequently defied, and not just by the Chinese Communist Party. Warlord remnants continued to disrupt the economy in the 1920s, halting railway traffic, for example, thus bringing the important mining industry close to bankruptcy.[5] The Guomindang defended its right to rule with military campaigns which were a constant drain on public revenues. In financial desperation, its leaders suppressed independent business associations and used criminal gangs to extort funds from leading capitalists, even in Shanghai.[6]

Paradoxically, the laudable efforts to overhaul the tax system did nothing to encourage industrial development. The reforms left Chinese manufacturers at a serious disadvantage in competing not only against imported products but against the output from modern, foreign-financed factories on the Mainland.[7] Management of the nation's financial affairs was made all the more difficult by the freedom with which peripheral areas could opt out of the national economic system. Thus, Guangdong and several other southern and western provinces enjoyed considerable financial independence from the central government, symbolised by their local currencies whose circulation added to the general commercial confusion.[8]

Advantage Hong Kong

The sorry financial situation of the Guomindang was indirectly beneficial to Hong Kong. The exactions imposed on the business class revealed the vulnerability of Chinese capitalists, even in Shanghai despite its British and other Western 'protectors', in marked contrast to the political and legal security which they enjoyed in Hong Kong. As for taxation, when the Colonial Office had directed in 1922 that all colonial territories should introduce income taxes, most had complied. Hong Kong declined to do so, however, on the grounds of 'the peculiar circumstances of Hong Kong and the Chinese attitude towards income tax'.[9] Hong Kong imposed no direct taxes until the eve of World War II, and even then, no taxes were levied on dividends or capital gains, on offshore profits and earnings; and there was no conventional income tax.

Similarly, the economic 'separatism', which more remote local governments exercised at the expense of the Guomindang authorities, allowed Guangdong Province to introduce a successful programme of financial and economic reforms and generally to seek to insulate itself from the misrule that afflicted so much of China.[10] The result was that Hong Kong's own hinterland was in better shape than many other parts of the Mainland. Overall, Hong Kong was able to profit from the modernisation and expansion of China's economy, no matter how uneven and disrupted this process was.

On the banking scene, the balance of advantage was also in Hong Kong's favour. The Mainland's commercial banks were not a prime source of industrial finance. Bankers understood the importance of manufacturing for the country's future prosperity, and industrial loans expanded during the inter-war years. Nevertheless, the banks' most useful role appears to have been indirect: the creation of sophisticated arrangements to provide factories with working capital in a country where adequate security for loans was hard to come by.[11] On the whole, the banks' contribution to industrial growth was limited. One contemporary observer went so far as to allege: 'The general conclusion must be that the role of the modern Chinese bank in China's industrial life has been practically negative'. Even after the banks had been provided with modern legal and commercial structures, their part in the modernisation process remained restricted. In addition to the continued attraction of such traditional activities as gold and currency speculation, the handling of government loan issues became a major part of their business.[12] Although state bonds could be highly profitable, political turmoil between the two world wars made them a highly speculative investment, leading to a number of banking collapses. The better-run banks sought to avoid the role of government broker, although the increasingly tight control exerted by the Guomindang over the banking system made resistance difficult. As noted already, there were military campaigns to be fought, and the banks had to help finance them if the Guomindang was to survive.[13]

In Hong Kong, by contrast, banks were free from official restrictions of any kind, and they were not part of the system for financing government expenditure. Ironically, however, the colony's banks were to be attacked repeatedly after World War II for failing to provide the funds needed by the booming manufacturing sector, just as Mainland banks had been before the war. (The controversy over the contribution from Hong Kong banks to industrial finance will be discussed in Chapter 5, 'Industrial Take-off: Cut-price and Self-financed'.)

In one crucial area of financial policy, Hong Kong had no choice but to follow the Mainland. Both the UK and the colonial administration recognised that the Hong Kong economy was too dependent on China to link the colonial currency to sterling. Instead, the Hong Kong dollar was based on silver, as was China's national currency. The price of silver declined up to 1931, as explained earlier, causing a significant degree of inflation which helped to buoy profits and boost business. As a result, Hong Kong was spared the worst of the world depression in the 1920s.

In the next decade, the price of silver started to rise, driving up Hong Kong export prices and deflating the economy. The recession that followed was aggravated by problems in managing the local note issue and compounded by the currency crisis which had overtaken the Mainland. Recovery had to wait until after 1935 when both the Mainland and Hong Kong abandoned the link with silver, and the Hong Kong dollar established a fixed exchange rate with sterling.[14] Significantly, however, the link to London was not enshrined in law, which left Hong Kong free to follow any new currency arrangements which the Mainland might introduce. Temporarily at least, Hong Kong was now on the same sterling standard as almost every other colony and, therefore, backed its banknotes with reserves held by its Exchange Fund and deposited in London.

It was typical of the age and the Governor, Sir Geoffry Northcote, that he lobbied the Colonial Office to allow Hong Kong to use the Exchange Fund's income and capital gains to start an 'Improvement Fund' to finance the redevelopment of the slum areas. London accepted the scheme in principle but wanted further discussion postponed because of the war clouds that were gathering in 1939.[15] After the war, this sort of proposal was to be regarded with great suspicion by the colonial administration.

The British Retreat

Between the two world wars, China was still not in a position to reclaim all the elements of its sovereignty which had been lost to foreign powers in the previous century. The UK, nevertheless, had begun to pull back from its 'informal empire' on the Mainland and was becoming increasingly reluctant to use military force to protect either its citizens or their business interests. By the end of the 1920s, popular resentment throughout the Mainland was forcing the UK to relinquish treaty ports and concessions and to abandon the legal and commercial privileges which China had surrendered under the Unequal Treaties in the nineteenth century.[16] The British withdrawal had begun, and there were clear signs that it would accelerate. This retreat did not immediately undermine British political influence and commercial power in China, however.[17] The UK remained the Mainland's largest source of foreign capital before World War II, over 80 per cent of which was invested in Shanghai. The city was the largest and most economically advanced in China, and the world's third busiest port. As the centre of British commercial activity on the Mainland, it far outstripped Hong Kong in its importance to the UK.[18] But outside major commercial centres like Shanghai, the British faced increasingly difficult business conditions.

Even though direct British control over key areas of the Chinese economy (notably the customs service) was diminishing, considerable optimism prevailed among the British and other foreign business communities from the mid-1930s. The prediction was that stabilisation of the Chinese currency and revival of the world economy would usher in a period of rapid economic recovery for China. However, instead of the economic boom that was expected to emerge by 1937, that year saw Japan launch full-scale war against China. Extensive air attacks, including the bombing of Guangdong Province, started a flight of capital and refugees. The fighting disrupted normal commercial and financial activities, and British interests across the Mainland suffered badly. The Japanese took over British firms and markets and generally restricted their business opportunities.[19]

In comparison with the Mainland, Hong Kong was a haven of peace and security. Shanghai, for example, proved vulnerable to attack in Japan's undeclared war during the 1930s, and its hinterland, the heartland of the Chinese national economy, came under severe military and commercial pressure from the Japanese. For the time being, Shanghai remained economically far more valuable to the UK than Hong Kong, despite the rapid development of a boom in the colony's economy in the late 1930s.[20] But it was plain that colonial rule offered more substantial protection from war and other upheavals than such legal and political privileges as still lingered on the Mainland from the age of the Unequal Treaties, as the post-1945 era was to demonstrate even more dramatically.

Radical Imports

Although Hong Kong enjoyed considerable freedom from the political chaos and economic turmoil that regularly engulfed the rest of the country, it was not isolated from the revolutionary fervour that had dominated China since the overthrow of the Manchu Dynasty in 1911. The 1920s saw a serious effort to import revolution from the Mainland. The local community's growing sense of Chinese nationalism and its resentment of foreign imperialism were intensified by an upsurge in social discontent and industrial unrest early in the decade. A seamen's strike in 1922 threatened to paralyse the economy which was then entirely dependent on the China trade. Strikers forced the port to close once again in 1925, this time backed by a year-long boycott which brought the economy to the brink of collapse. The colonial administration survived this challenge mainly through mobilising the business and professional classes. This élite group was convinced that its members faced ruin, regardless of race, if the strikers won this anti-colonial campaign in which the Chinese Communist Party was prominent.[21] The fledgling Party's efforts to build a significant presence in the colony failed and were not revived until after Japan's defeat.[22] The threat of political upheaval collapsed and did not reappear during the rest of the inter-war years.

While the forces of Mainland political and social radicalism evaporated from the colony, Hong Kong faced other pressures for social and economic change.[23] These had emerged in the UK itself in the early twentieth century and were exerting a powerful influence throughout the British Empire. At the end of World War I, London had believed at first that peace would permit a return to the traditions of the past. The state controls that had been imposed on the UK's strategic industries and financial markets to mobilise resources for the war were removed. Laisser faire, free trade and the gold standard were reinstated as the guiding principles of government. But the economic problems of the 1920s undermined the general British conviction that peace and prosperity would be assured by the formula of economic liberalism, cheap food, low taxation and small government inherited from the nineteenth century.[24] The public was now demanding that the state should intervene more directly to promote the nation's economic and social well-being.

This new and more radical outlook within the UK encouraged a similar change in attitudes among Hong Kong's colonial rulers. They did not favour the sort of political liberalisation which was to bring democratic elections and a ministerial system to India and Ceylon (Sri Lanka), for example, during the 1930s.[25] Despite the evidence from the rest of China that its people were as moved by political passions as any other nation, the British were convinced that the Hong Kong community was different. In the official view, the Chinese residents were merely transients, so devoted to making money that they were content with a political system that was 'neither a despotism nor a democracy, but an effective blend of both'.[26] Hong Kong officials were sympathetic, nevertheless, to social and economic reforms, the importance of which had been highlighted by the two seamen's strikes. Even before the upsurge of industrial unrest, the colonial administration had started to recognise a duty to protect the labour force, particularly as employment in factories expanded. In 1921, an official report rejected manufacturers' attempts to defend their exploitation of child labour.[27] In 1923, another official commission, set up to tackle the acute shortage of housing and the vulnerability of tenants, felt compelled to comment on industrial matters. Its report called for the creation of 'a strong and independent tribunal' to deal with labour disputes.[28] As with most inter-war official inquiries, this commission's recommendations proved too far-reaching to be implemented until long after World War II. These official documents were evidence, nevertheless, of a growing concern among the ruling élite for the living and working conditions of the general public.

In the following decade, interest in reform was, if anything, strengthened by the currency crisis and by the mounting deflation between 1931 and 1935 which led to severe recession in Hong Kong. An official report described the population as suffering from 'poverty … so dire that many families cannot afford any rent at all'.[29] Northcote, who took over as Governor in 1937, was appalled by the way that 'malnutrition and slum housing conditions dominate … the lives of a very large majority of Hong Kong's population'. His response was a programme of reforms covering health, housing, education, welfare and employment.[30] To finance these improvements, the business community was persuaded to endorse the introduction of Hong Kong's first direct taxation.[31]

It would be a mistake, nevertheless, to view Hong Kong during the inter-war years as governed by liberal-minded officials who enjoyed the trust of a docile community content to accept uncritically the legal and administrative disabilities that colonial rule imposed on the Chinese population. After the 1925–26 boycott collapsed, Hong Kong had been remarkably free from political agitation of any kind, and the colonial administration faced no organised challenge to its authority.[32]. Yet, the grip of the expatriate on the colony was beginning to weaken. A sense of Chinese patriotism and widespread resentment of foreign rule were widespread, reinforced by the extensive social discrimination against even wealthy, Westernised Chinese.[33] Colonial privilege was forced to retreat, albeit slowly, and the colonial administration could not ignore rising Chinese aspirations. It was no longer taken for granted that foreigners were essential for the efficient conduct of business or government, and Chinese merchants and professionals became increasingly influential in virtually every field.[34]

This trend was accelerated by economic realism after the Hong Kong dollar collapsed in the early 1930s and the government had to cope with budget deficits. As a result, the civil service was unable to justify the costs of generous expatriate benefits, and the principle of equal opportunity for local officials was accepted in 1935, a policy that was not to be honoured with any enthusiasm for another half-century.[35]

Hong Kong's discussions of its economic situation in the 1930s involved direct attacks on traditional UK policies for its colonies. Economic recession led the colonial administration to set up a commission (the 'economic commission') dominated by bankers and businessmen to review Hong Kong's economic fundamentals. They produced what for that era was a very radical report. They realised that Hong Kong's future prosperity depended on two factors:

- integration into the Mainland economy to ensure the prosperity of the dominant China trade sector; and
- the growth of manufacturing to supply both local and export markets.

Its report accepted the argument that Hong Kong could not afford to abandon free trade if it were to remain a major re-export centre for China. However, it rejected unconditional laisser faire; it supported tariffs to protect local manufacturers where appropriate; and it urged the colonial administration to encourage industrialisation. The report also believed Hong Kong could afford higher taxes to finance social improvements.[36]

In this period, the UK was fearful of any colonial developments that might reduce demand for its manufactured exports and thus aggravate the already high levels of British unemployment. Hong Kong was identified by London officials as a significant source of 'unfair competition'.[37] Consequently, the economic commission's recommendations of government measures to promote industry and protect local manufacturers were in flagrant defiance of Colonial Office policies with which other colonies generally cooperated. The commission pointed out that neither the UK nor the British Empire would promote Hong Kong's interests because the colony was of little direct benefit to them. Hong Kong, therefore, should no longer be subject to Colonial Office restrictions on industrial development, the report argued, and should be free to manage its own external commercial relations.[38] The economic commission's recommendations for an industrial development policy and protection for local industries against foreign imports were never implemented. But the report's general endorsement of economic activism, coupled with social responsibility, was to be reflected, though without acknowledgment, in official policies for the rest of the decade.

War Profits

The urgency of the report's calls for government aid to business and industry was removed by the economic revival that followed the stabilisation of the Mainland and Hong Kong currencies in 1935 and, then, by the economic boom in Hong Kong that followed the outbreak of open war against China by Japan. At first, hostilities seemed to threaten the colony with social collapse. Refugees from Guangdong Province poured in as Japanese troops advanced. Hong Kong's 'natural' population of one million was swollen by 500,000 arrivals in 1938 and a further 150,000 the following year.[39] The colonial administration accepted a duty to provide the destitute with food and shelter, an awesome challenge in a society that had been grossly overcrowded before the influx.[40]

But the economy was a different matter, and here Hong Kong was in no danger of collapse. On the contrary, a boom got underway, propelled by a surge in orders for military supplies and facilitated by the refuge influx, not all of whom had come empty-handed. A few had arrived 'with financial backing … [and] transferred their commercial interests from Occupied China to this Colony', to quote an official report. Others were 'artisans, small merchants and others who have managed to save their tools, some of their stock in trade and a portion of theirs savings'.[41] 'The refugees have … brought a great deal of trade and a large number of factories and shops have been established', a senior official declared. The government — unlike the colonial administration in the 1950s — did not assume that the refugees were temporary sojourners who would quit Hong Kong promptly once China was at peace again.[42]

For the government, a serious problem was to find sufficient premises for the new workshops and factories. Most appear to have started in domestic premises, adding to the dirt, noise and overcrowding of tenement buildings. But as new trades were introduced, notably from Shanghai, business boomed — and with some pressure from the health authorities — 'the general prosperity in some trades' allowed manufacturers to move into 'new modern factory type buildings'.[43] The next priority was industrial sites. The Governor was opposed to what he regarded as out-dated procedures for allocating land strictly by public auction with no concessions for industrial development. He was also anxious that immigrant industrialists unfamiliar with colonial law should not be penalised if they bought land on which the construction of factories was technically unlawful, and he insisted that a solution be found for these 'illicit' factories.[44] Before the end of 1939, the government was reporting sharp rises in the volume of trade and an impressive recovery in public finances. Northcote, however, mistrusted the economic recovery generated by the Japanese war and was apologetic about Hong Kong's economic gains from the misfortunes of Guangdong and other nearby provinces.[45]

What was taken for granted in this demonstration of the colony's resilience was the availability of adequate finance to underwrite a sudden surge of high-speed growth. (This phenomenon was to prove no less important for Hong Kong's industrial take-off in the 1950s.) Ample funding from the banks was not a new phenomenon. During the 1920s, falling silver prices had helped to boost an influx of Overseas Chinese funds in search of speculative foreign exchange gains, and these had swelled deposits in the bank system to a level that the banks found difficult to cope with.[46] When silver prices started to surge in the 1930s, a banking boom started, with a sharp rise in the number of local Chinese-owned banks.[47] The complaint was that these firms, tempted by high interest rates, made funds too easily available for doubtful projects, particularly in the property sector.[48] In this period, the economic commission found little complaint about the banks' support for business.[49]

> No criticism can be levelled at the banks of the Colony on the score of unwillingness to finance trade and industry. Indeed few places in the world have suffered less from Exchange and Finance restrictions.

When industrial expansion accelerated in the late 1930s, the banks managed to finance this unexpected spurt in industrial expansion quite comfortably, despite the special difficulties created by disruption of normal commercial and financial relations with the banks' important customer base on the Mainland after the Japanese war began. The influx of refugee capital and the transfer of assets by Mainland banks to Hong Kong in order to evade controls imposed both by the Japanese and the Chinese authorities helped, of course. At the end of the 1930s, the colonial administration declared complacently but not without justification:[50]

> The credit and repute of the Colony's financial institutions are high and it is satisfactory to know that ample encouragement and support are available to finance any demand.

The Great Exception

The evidence is clear enough that by the 1930s, Hong Kong was served by a robust, free-standing and international banking system that met in full the financial requirements of commerce and industry, not just locally but for a significant sector of the Mainland economy. No similar claim could have been made at this time for any other colonial territory's banking system. The survival of Hong Kong's special status in colonial banking came under threat during the 1930s because of changes in the fundamental economic policies of the UK. London now sought to protect its access to Dominion and colonial markets through a combination of trade preferences and coordinated foreign exchange markets. The preservation of Hong Kong's unique banking centre required the colonial administration to seek the maximum possible autonomy from London, first in handling Hong Kong's trade relations with the rest of the world and second in managing its financial relations with the British Empire and the Sterling Area.

During the 1930s, global depression gave governments around the world the excuse to increase the protection of their domestic producers through tariffs and quotas, and the UK could no longer cling to the principle of free trade which had been the cornerstone of its imperial economic policies. London tried to counter the mounting threat of protectionism through a system of 'imperial preferences' under the 1932 Ottawa Agreements so that British Dominions and colonial territories would offer trade concessions to each other's exports. Hong Kong was treated as a separate trade and tariff entity under this system, with considerable freedom in practice to mange its own external commercial relations by lobbying overseas governments and negotiating on technical issues.[51]

As was explained earlier in this chapter, the Colonial Office in London tried to minimise the incentives for industrial investment in the colonies. The British government was particularly apprehensive about the threat from the growth of manufacturing in Hong Kong. In addition, the UK — and the rest of the British Empire — had grievances against Hong Kong because the colony was doing nothing to combat the threat to their trade from Japan. Instead, the colony's firms provided 'backdoor' arrangements for Japanese manufacturers to qualify for imperial preference in the Dominions and colonial territories at the expense of their local producers.[52] But Hong Kong's disregard for UK and imperial commercial interests could be justified by the well-founded expectation in the colony that its economic interests would not rank high among British priorities. Indeed, the economic commission had warned that there could be no reliance on London's support in international trade negotiations.[53]

The gold standard had been the other cornerstone of imperial economic policy, and after its collapse, the UK grew anxious to protect its financial interests in a world of competing currencies. The relatively liberal trading community created by the Ottawa Agreements was to be reinforced by a wider financial grouping made up of the Dominions and colonial territories, together with the other countries which relied on London's financial markets. This relationship was strengthened by the substantial and relatively export liberal markets which were available in the UK.[54] The 1930s saw this Sterling Area evolve into an effective currency bloc, with the pound sterling operating as a successful alternative to the US dollar. Its initial success was aided by the absence of central banks and similar financial institutions throughout the British Empire (including its self-governing members in 1931) — apart from the Bank of England — and was reinforced by overseas confidence in British monetary policy in the 1930s. The emergence of the Sterling Area, together with a structure for the coordination required between its emerging central banks and other monetary institutions, was a considerable feat, given the conflicts of national interest which had to be overcome.[55] It was managed from London, however, which meant that British policies were applied to the colonial empire as a whole and could run counter to the best interests of individual territories.[56]

Hong Kong was the great exception to the arrangements established between the Sterling Area and colonial economies. Initially, Hong Kong had not been part of this new currency bloc because the colony had to link its currency to the same standard as its dominant trading partner, China. As explained earlier, London accepted this reality. When the silver crisis described above forced both the Mainland and Hong Kong to abandon the traditional basis for their currencies, London was sympathetic to the serious political obstacles which prevented the Chinese government from linking to the Sterling Area, although Hong Kong did so in practice. Legally, nevertheless, the new relationship with sterling was deliberately left vague in order to preserve the option to follow China's future currency policy, which was still undecided in 1935.[57] All in all, Hong Kong had avoided the danger of being integrated into the Sterling Area. The colonial administration had retained the right to be treated as a special case in currency and related matters because economic survival depended so heavily on meeting the financial needs of China. A precedent had been set that allowed Hong Kong far more autonomy in managing its currency than other colonies and which was to have profound consequences for the development of Hong Kong banking over the next three decades, as subsequent chapters will explain.

A Free-standing System

Hong Kong's free-standing banking system and its largely autonomous currency arrangements could have been swept away in 1939 when the UK introduced controls of economic and financial resources as it mobilised the British Empire for war. Throughout the Sterling Area as a whole, all financial and commercial transactions with non-members were regulated through an interlocking system of controls on imports and exports and on ownership of and access to foreign currencies and other overseas assets. The introduction of these exchange controls meant that trade and investment now followed the currency because transactions outside the Sterling Area were so tightly controlled. The integration of colonial financial systems into the UK economy was thus increased. The UK introduced these wartime measures reluctantly and far from comprehensively.[58] Thus, there were no political or economic obstacles to granting concessions to Hong Kong, and London continued to recognise, as it had done throughout the 1930s, that the China trade gave the colony a special case to be freed from most of the constraints imposed by exchange controls on other members of the Sterling Area.[59] The exemptions granted to Hong Kong were generous and of special benefit to the Chinese community.

- Foreign trade was left almost untouched by controls, with only very gentle licensing to cover sensitive items, while the current transactions of business firms were exempt from exchange controls.
- The currency dealing and remittance business that was of special importance to local Chinese-owned banks was left uncontrolled for transactions with the Mainland. Furthermore, while British subjects had to surrender their foreign exchange to the government, Chinese and other non-nationals did not.[60]
- The right to practise 'free trade' and to operate outside the Sterling Area and its constraints was recognised, which allowed the survival of a free market for foreign currencies and the right to use them in preference to sterling and at Hong Kong's own convenience.

Thus, the economic controls of World War II did not alter the fundamentals of Hong Kong banking or the free operation of the financial markets. The colonial administration was determined to ensure that such constraints as were unavoidable would be administered with the lightest touch and with particular sensitivity to the needs of Chinese business. A privileged position was created for Hong Kong, enabling it to enjoy a larger measure of freedom from London's control than other colonies, together with much greater latitude in pursuing local interests even at the expense of the UK.

Domestic Deficiencies

The colonial administration proved adept at defending Hong Kong's trade and financial autonomy, but its approach to banking policy was deeply flawed. Although the banking system itself was impressive by the standards of the age, it suffered from serious weaknesses which threatened its integrity, and officials were under considerable pressure, both from leading businessmen and from London, to introduce legislation to regulate the industry. Surprisingly however, while the Governor and other senior officials usually favoured intervention to protect the public and, as this chapter has shown, they generally supported business, traditional laisser faire prevailed when the government was faced with glaring deficiencies in the banking sector. Officials fought hard to avoid responsibility for ensuring the stability of local banks and the protection of depositors. They were dismissive not only of the commercial costs of bank failures but also of the social hardships which these caused.

While there was little complaint about the banks' performance in meeting the expectations of their clients, Hong Kong banks suffered from two serious defects. The first was their excessive appetite for speculative business, a feature not only of the unincorporated 'native Chinese banks' but also of local banks with modern corporate structures. This situation reflected the commercial environment in which they had to operate. Trade was frequently uncertain or disrupted during this period, and manufacturing's opportunities were still limited. As a result, real estate seemed particularly attractive. Banks were prepared to invest in property projects on their own account, as well as to provide finance through mortgages. Hong Kong real estate was uncertain enough, but banks were also active in Mainland property ventures where risks were much higher.[61] By the 1930s, banks were also increasingly attracted to currency and bullion dealing, which proved even more perilous. As a prominent businessman and director of HSBC commented later in the decade: 'The Hong Kong currency [when] on a silver basis was being used as one of the easiest and most convenient forms of gambling for anyone interested to have a flutter in the metal'.[62]

The second shortcoming was the inability of financial markets to discipline banking behaviour. Even when a banking institution's accounts were prepared professionally, the auditors' reports had little impact. Officials were not interested. Directors and shareholders took no notice even of 'damning comment', while depositors 'dare not do anything' — for fear, presumably, of starting a run on the bank.[63] The accounting profession saw government supervision as the solution.[64]

The numerous 'native Chinese banks' tended to be small, and they made little distinction between capital and deposits, as both were raised largely from relatives and friends. Officials could take comfort from the fact that the failure of one of these family firms had little impact on the economy at large or on the general public. But the failure of a commercial bank could not be shrugged off so easily because it could trigger extensive bank runs. The crash of the Chinese Merchants Bank in 1924 highlighted the weaknesses of local banking and led to calls for official regulation of the industry, which the colonial administration ignored.[65] The colonial administration had to take the complaints of foreign banks a little more seriously because of the pivotal role they played in Hong Kong's foreign trade. After they lobbied for stricter controls on local Chinese-owned banks which purported to operate on modern commercial lines, the government undertook a review of the case for legal supervision of banks in 1927 and again in 1930. The Attorney General provided some unconvincing excuses for continuing to do nothing. New legal powers to oversee the banks could not be used promptly or effectively enough to prevent crises, he argued. The introduction of such legislation would create a false sense of security among the public, he went on, which would blame the government if a bank failed.[66]

The threat to banking stability worsened in the early 1930s. A number of banks got into difficulty in 1931 as the currency linked to silver ran into serious problems and recession set in. A full-blown crisis took longer to develop — a pattern that was to be repeated in the post-war era — although the warning signs of an unstable system became increasingly unmistakeable. The economic commission noted the fragility of the banking industry, which made 'a financial collapse inevitable when a major depression occurs'. Its recommendations proved confused, however. Its report published in 1935 urged the government to regulate savings banks but principally on welfare grounds rather than as a measure to reinforce banking stability. For the industry as a whole, the commission declared that 'any step tending to the adoption of sounder banking methods would increase the Colony's stability', but its members felt that legislation would be of little use in preventing bank failures.[67]

Reform Proposals

Just as the commission was providing a further excuse for the government to stand idly by, the stability of local banks as a whole came under threat in early 1935. Trouble began with Ka Wah Bank, which was to figure in scandals in later decades. But public panic only set in when the Bank of Canton suspended business. The failure of this respected institution, the oldest local bank, frightened depositors at other banks.[68] Its road to ruin had begun with its imprudent exposure to silver. Ironically, the government and the legislature had agreed to amend the law to allow this bank to gamble with its depositors' funds in this way.[69] In addition, however, its audited accounts had shown for seven years that over-exposure to property had reduced its liquidity to dangerous levels.[70] But the auditors' revelations had no effect. The bulk of the depositors were unable to read English, let alone comprehend the balance sheet of a modern corporation. The Registrar of Companies had taken no notice of the auditors' comments because his staff were too over-worked to read the accounts submitted to them. As was to happen in the 1960s and again in the 1980s, here was a bank whose collapse was predictable but also avoidable if it had been encouraged to establish a system of competent management overseen by official regulators.

The bank runs that followed were on a scale that made it impossible for the colonial administration to brush banking problems aside as it had done in the 1920s. In addition to renewed demands for reforms from the business community, there was an unusual source of political pressure. An official from the UK Treasury had been visiting Hong Kong during the crisis. He shared his experiences directly with the Colonial Office in London, thus forcing the colonial administration to abandon its usual hands-off approach. A confidential committee was set up to propose legislation for Hong Kong's banks.[71] Its report was never published, but if its recommendations had been implemented, Hong Kong would have had a modern regulatory system in place before World War

II, well-designed to cope with the challenges and crises that were to recur so frequently in the second half of the century. The committee's members were not inhibited by their own lack of experience of banking regulation. They took the trouble to examine not only British colonial models but also the banking reforms under way on the Mainland. They developed a sound grasp of the safeguards that should be put in place to protect the most vulnerable depositors.

Their report identified a set of controls for savings banks to ensure adequate liquidity and to prevent involvement in speculative lending. These were modelled on the statutory requirements already imposed on insurance companies (which had been borrowed from UK legislation). The case for these measures was simple. In a community made up of immigrants, largely unfamiliar with colonial legal institutions and modern banking practices, 'ignorance, illiteracy and apathy' made it impossible for ordinary depositors to monitor the banks where they kept their working capital and their savings.[72] This task ought to be performed on their behalf by the government. For the banking industry as a whole, the committee took a different approach. It was convinced that effective regulation of the unincorporated 'native Chinese banks' was unattainable. In any case, the committee regarded the relationship between these banks and their depositors as based on personal connections with the owners. In consequence, their report argued, regulation should be confined to incorporated businesses which were already subject to the Companies Ordinance. The key recommendations for this group of banks included:[73]

- a system of licensing which would allow the regular collection of financial information from individual banks;
- the creation of a specialised regulatory body through the appointment of a 'banking examiner'; and
- professional investigation of banks when problems were suspected.

As this chapter has already noted, it was typical of Hong Kong and the colonial administration in the inter-war years that implementation of sensible solutions to chronic problems recommended in official reports was to be delayed for several decades. Banking proved no exception, and in this case, Hong Kong had to wait until 1964 for the prudential controls on liquidity and bank lending, regular monitoring and professional regulators that had been recommended before World War II.

Depositors Don't Care

In dealing with the demands for measures to regulate banks before World War II, the colonial administration developed a pattern of bureaucratic behaviour that was to recur regularly over the next half-century. In their confidential files, officials took the line that the public either did not need, or did not deserve, to have its bank deposits protected. Hong Kong's most senior financial official produced the curious argument in the 1930s that a more stable banking system was not what the community wanted. Greater stability, he claimed, would lead to lower interest rates, which would prove unpopular with the public. 'The Chinese depositor would much rather get a higher rate of interest and lose his entire capital every twenty years or so' he insisted, 'than get a low rate of interest with security'.[74] An expatriate business member of the committee showed the absurdity of this view, but to no avail.[75]

Surprisingly, even officials known for their reforming and liberal attitudes in general lost their sense of responsibility for the public's well-being when it came to banking. As Financial Secretary, Sydney Caine, played a major role in the Northcote reforms described above and later won an outstanding reputation as a colonial administrator and an academic economist. Yet, he insisted that ordinary depositors in Hong Kong ought to be able to make their own judgments about the integrity of the banks to which they entrusted their savings. Earlier in the decade, professional auditors had warned that this attitude made no sense. He insisted, however, that 'the public is not entitled, and should not be encouraged, to expect Government action to replace private prudence'.[76] In 1940, Caine was recalled to London and replaced as Financial Secretary by H. R. Butters, who has been described as 'surprisingly liberal and reformist' and hailed for his readiness to make personal contact with ordinary workers and to cite their views in drafting measures to improve their welfare.[77] However, it may be that his un-colonial, populist approach was inspired not by personal convictions but by a new burst of enthusiasm in the Colonial Office for the welfare of the working class.[78] That would explain why, when it came to banking, Butters followed the example of his distinguished predecessor and did nothing to promote effective regulation, even of savings banks. In fact, he did his best to resist pressures both locally and from London for measures to protect depositors.[79]

Within Hong Kong, the economic boom which followed the start of the Japanese war against China in 1937 took the pressure off the banking system. But the Colonial Office was not so easily satisfied. Consequently, the colonial administration set up a new, ad hoc committee to review the 1935 confidential committee's recommendations and London's views. The Colonial Office strongly supported the appointment of a banking examiner. The Financial Secretary resisted this proposal on the grounds that a suitably qualified person would be hard to find and that the banks would not pay the costs involved.[80] In reality, the banks could hardly have refused to pay for adequate regulation through a significant licence fee in the wake of the crisis that had shaken the industry in 1935. Furthermore, by 1938, when officials were trying to bury the proposal for an examiner, Japanese hostilities were disrupting normal business throughout the Mainland, including Shanghai. Banks would have shown little resistance to paying a market price for a licence to operate in Hong Kong now that it had become the only secure financial centre left in China. Not surprisingly, however, as the local economy boomed, bankers grew worried about the impact of regulation on their business prospects and their profit opportunities. In particular, they expressed concern that an examiner might go too far and might introduce the tough regulatory approach which the US had adopted after its banking disasters during this decade.[81]

The colonial administration did not rely on arguing the merits of its case in dealing with London. It adopted a cruder strategy based on Hong Kong's remoteness from London and the Colonial Office's inability to dispute its assertions. Officials in Hong Kong claimed that they lacked the technical information to draft a banking law. London pointed out that Palestine, then under British rule, had enacted legislation which Hong Kong could imitate. The colonial administration claimed to be unable to finalise its review of the legislative proposals based on the 1935 committee's recommendations until copies of the Palestine ordinance had been supplied. Although a copy of the ordinance had been placed on the relevant file in 1936, Hong Kong officials said they were still awaiting its arrival by post two years later. With the help of this excuse, the colonial administration was able to ignore requests from London to give a higher priority to banking legislation until the Japanese invasion began in 1941.[82] The same delaying tactics resumed after World War II. When the question of a Hong Kong banking ordinance came up once more, the colonial administration renewed its request for a copy of the Palestine ordinance and mislaid its pre-war banking files (where it was to be found) until 1952.[83]

Official Ignorance

The reluctance to regulate cannot be explained away by a commitment to laisser faire or an aversion to innovation and reform. As this chapter has shown, the general trend throughout the inter-war years was to be more responsive to the needs of the Chinese community. The colonial administration was even prepared to impose direct taxation to meet the costs of better social services. So, why did it baulk at the expense of a banking examiner whose expenses could have been recovered through the licence fees payable by the industry? The colonial administration was also prepared to encourage manufacturers through easing their land problems and to give serious consideration to protection against imports. So, why was it unwilling to intervene to rectify the weaknesses of the banking industry?

One suggestion is that the government was deterred by nervousness about political opposition from the Chinese banking community.[84] In reality,

Northcote and senior officials were exceptional among Hong Kong's colonial rulers for their readiness to confront the business community. After all, they had introduced direct taxation to Hong Kong for the first time and expressed considerable disdain for their opponents in the Legislative Council in the process.[85] It is hard to believe that the colonial administration would have faced serious difficulty in managing political opposition from local bankers, especially as the Mainland authorities had also embarked on reforms to China's banking system.

A more convincing explanation is the widespread ignorance of banking within the bureaucracy. Apart from the redoubtable Caine, the government's financial and economic expertise was very limited.[86] Officials had only the sketchiest information about the financial system, its organisation and even the number of banks. The confidential files in which senior officials discussed the question of regulation, and which are cited throughout this chapter, are devoid of any serious review of policy issues and contain no statistical or economic analysis of any kind. This vagueness about banking was part of a general contempt for statistics, which was deeply embedded in the colonial culture.[87]

Ignorance was compounded by complacency. From 1937, Hong Kong — and its banking system — had absorbed the influx of refugees and overcome the disruption of normal trade and finance throughout the rest of China.[88] The banks had responded well to the surge in manufacturing and the creation of new industries. The result was a boom which laid the first foundations of the industrial take-off that was to transform Hong Kong in the 1950s, as Chapter 3 'Post-war Emergencies: From Boom to Bust', will recount. But the case for regulation seemed to shrink with such favourable business conditions. And complacency was reinforced by a vagueness about the Chinese banking world. As long as the foreign-owned banks were performing satisfactorily, it did not seem worthwhile even to count the number of local Chinese banks, as an official report indicated.[89]

> The Colony is well served by banking institutions, including branches of English, American, French, Netherlands, Japanese and Chinese banks. Besides the fourteen banks which are members of the Clearing House, there are several Chinese banks. Many native *Hongs* do some banking business.

The Shape of Things to Come

This chapter has shown how closely linked were Hong Kong's fortunes and the Mainland's progress during the inter-war years. As a result, a policy was established, accepted by ministers and officials in London, that Hong Kong belonged to the Chinese world. Hong Kong was allowed to give priority to meeting the Mainland's financial requirements rather than simply serving UK interests. This precedent was to prove crucial to Hong Kong's success as an international manufacturing and financial centre in the Sterling Area crises that were to dominate British economic policy during the 1950s and 1960s, as well as during the Cold War embargo imposed by the US from 1950 to 1971. The colonial administration successfully sought a wider autonomy from the Colonial Office in financial affairs. The failure to comply with London's directions on banking legislation in the 1930s was merely the first round of a protracted campaign of flagrant non-cooperation with London that continued until the 1970s, and which will be discussed in later chapters.

Throughout the inter-war years, the economy displayed a robust resilience in meeting local political challenges and adjusting to the crises that overtook the world economy. Hong Kong was particularly adept in making the most of its Mainland opportunities, particularly the bursts of modernisation and financial reform. In this period, a pattern of economic behaviour evolved that was not destroyed by either the Japanese war or the civil war. Nor was the colony to be bankrupted by the victory of the Chinese Communist Party in 1949. On the contrary, Hong Kong had developed the manufacturing and financial expertise between the two world wars that enabled it to rebuild a war-shattered economy by 1947; to overcome the abrupt loss of the China trade in the 1950s; and to manage the complex financial relations that emerged during the Cold War.

The parallels between the decades immediately before and after World War II are striking. The Japanese war led to an inflow of industrial capacity from Guangdong Province and Shanghai, which boosted Hong Kong manufacturing dramatically, expanded the range of its products and reduced the competition its manufactures faced on the Mainland. Civil war in the 1940s was to be followed by a similar inflow of Mainland capital and entrepreneurs. Both influxes included prominent Shanghai businessmen who introduced modern industrial production to Hong Kong.[90] Similarly, China's financial markets were disrupted by an unstable currency in the 1930s, and normal financial relations were impossible with areas under Japanese occupation. Despite the chaotic conditions, Hong Kong bankers still managed to serve their clients' financial needs. They were to perform a similar function for the Chinese government after 1949, this time by adjusting to the requirements of a centrally planned economy on the Mainland and by devising techniques that overcame the obstacles of exchange controls and US prohibitions.

Nevertheless, during the inter-war years, Hong Kong banking was displaying serious weaknesses that would continue until late into the century. Despite the obvious lessons from the 1935 banking crisis, together with demands for regulation from both the local business community and London, the officials responsible for the supervision of financial services showed a reluctance to take responsibility for the integrity of the banks that was to become a dominant feature of banking policy for the next four decades. Thus, during the inter-war years, the foundations were laid for the continuation of Hong Kong as a leading financial centre in later decades, but the colonial administration had little interest in the prevention of fraud and other criminal behaviour by banks. It attached no importance to the protection of depositors on the assumption that, in Chinese society, the relationship between banks and their customers was mostly a family matter. One official declared outright: 'If the Chinese want security they can get it in the Western banks'.[91] Whatever supervision of the banking industry might be introduced, the colonial view was that it should be extended as minimally as possible to Chinese-owned firms — with a special exemption for the 'native' banks.

Thus, Hong Kong lost the opportunity to put in place a modern regulatory system to ensure the integrity of its banks, to monitor their stability and to enforce the standards of prudent lending that would protect depositors. It was to be another three decades before the colonial administration implemented the 1935 confidential committee's proposals which had been endorsed both by leaders of the business community and by the UK authorities. The seeds had been sown for a cycle of mismanagement and misconduct that was to mar the banking industry until 1985.

3

Post-war Emergencies: From Boom to Bust

When Admiral Harcourt sailed into Hong Kong on August 30, 1945, to liberate the colony from the Japanese and establish a British Military Administration, he took possession of a ruined, though not a desperate, city.

> … at the end of August 1945, the economic life of Hong Kong was dead. The population was greatly reduced in numbers; utilities were barely functioning; there was no food, no shipping, no industry, no commerce … The people with their native industry and genius for improvisation set themselves at once to the task of restoring Hong Kong to its proper place in the commercial life of the Far East.[1]

But there were considerable obstacles in returning to business as normal. World markets no longer functioned freely, and international commercial and financial activities were severely disrupted. In the pursuit of victory — and even just to ensure survival — most governments had taken charge of the direction of their national economies. Indeed, there was a widespread belief that the war had demonstrated the state's power to raise productivity, eliminate waste, invent new technologies, create modern industries almost overnight and overcome the most daunting challenges. There seemed no reason why the state could not accomplish much of the same feats in building prosperity in peacetime as had been achieved in the midst of the battles, bombing and blockades of the war.[2] In any case, there was a desperate shortage of every kind of essential commodity, so the merchant seemed redundant, while the industrial entrepreneur was helpless unless the state could procure raw materials for the factories. For Hong Kong, the replacement of free enterprise with government intervention by so many of its traditional trading partners was a threat to the foundations of its economy. Foreign governments imposed state controls in order to replace the market and restrain free enterprise, aims which clashed with the colony's primary economic role: to promote the flow of international trade and investment with China. How could it resume this function if its commercial and financial activities were not driven by market forces but depended on the decrees of foreign bureaucrats?

At the same time, the colony's post-war reconstruction was made all the more daunting by a flood of returning residents and refugees. By mid-February 1946, the population had risen to 900,000. It then doubled to reach 1.8 million by the end of 1948.[3] It was obvious that Hong Kong itself would need extensive state involvement in the economy to overcome the acute shortages of food, raw materials and equipment of every sort that blocked the revival of the colony's peacetime economy and threatened the community's survival. This chapter will demonstrate that Hong Kong recovered from the Japanese occupation faster than any other Asian economy. In this process, the government became deeply involved in overseeing business activities and the banking industry in particular.

Emergency Powers

The immediate challenge in 1945 was to mobilise the resources to rebuild the economy. Military proclamations were issued regulating every aspect of economic life, from control of trade and financial transactions (both internal and external) to powers of requisitioning property and fixing prices. Many of these emergency measures remained in force after normal civilian rule was resumed in 1946.[4] They created a basic framework for orderly trading and the restoration of business confidence. Unlike the UK and most other governments in that era, the colonial administration soon became uncomfortable with its sweeping economic powers. There was no immediate escape from them, however, because world markets had not resumed normal operations and post-war shortages were so acute that state controls were unavoidable. As the newly restored civilian administration acknowledged:[5]

> Controls on trade have proved one of the most difficult problems in view of Hong Kong's peculiar position as an entrepôt. While the merchant's natural belief in laisser-faire could not be fully accepted, it was recognised that the fullest freedom compatible with the welfare of the people and international obligations must be accepted.

Free trade in agricultural products and other commodities was suspended. Instead, the distribution of essential supplies was entirely under government control throughout most of the world. Food supplies were allocated centrally through international negotiations in accordance with local nutritional requirements and in relation to population size. Within Hong Kong, the authorities allocated supplies of essential commodities through a rationing system supported by price controls.[6] The immediate post-war shortages were so severe that the official food ration did not meet the nutritional requirements of a 'normal worker'.[7] The colonial administration found the strain of procuring food supplies in a hungry, post-war world more than it could cope with. Although the government had promised in 1950 to provide the bulk of the population with rice, it decided in mid-1951 to stop registering any more immigrants for new ration cards.[8]

The shortage of raw materials was no less acute. Hong Kong's industrial base had expanded rapidly between 1937 and 1941, as the previous chapter explained. After the war, the government faced serious obstacles in procuring adequate supplies to meet industry's requirements. By the start of 1946, officials estimated that only 11 per cent of the factories known to the government were operating. Less than five per cent had been closed by direct war damage, and another 24 per cent were idle because their machinery had been removed during the war. The bulk had been unable to resume operations because they lacked the necessary raw materials.[9] Textile manufacturers were particularly hard hit. Although the Guomindang authorities were anxious to supply the Hong Kong market, their increasing inability to govern the Mainland effectively meant that this traditional source was shrinking fast. Japan was another threat. It was rebuilding its own industrial capacity, and its textile manufacturers competed hard for what international supplies were available. In addition, this was a world of exchange controls, and the Hong Kong authorities faced a constant battle to acquire the foreign currency needed to import raw materials from outside the Sterling Area.[10]

Breath-taking Recovery

Nevertheless, economic reconstruction went ahead at a breath-taking pace. Before the Japanese defeat, officials in London planning for Hong Kong's post-war recovery had assumed that the process would be protracted. It was suggested, for example, that business would be so 'moribund' that the colonial administration could not hope to levy taxes for at least five years after British rule was resumed.[11] Normal collection of government revenue started in mid-1946. There was a small budget deficit in that financial year but a significant surplus in the year that followed.[12] It was also assumed that because of deaths, injuries and disease, public utilities and listed companies would lack the directors to manage their affairs. These fears proved groundless. In January 1946, London was informed that the power companies and the docks were being run on normal peacetime lines (albeit with some government assistance), while the telephone and tramways companies were operating 'entirely on their own feet'.[13] By Christmas that year, the boast was that Hong Kong enjoyed 'a high degree of stability, security and prosperity unequalled elsewhere in the Far East'.[14]

Industrial production in 1947 was estimated to have reached 70 per cent of pre-war performance despite the shortages of raw materials and machinery. The following year, power supplies exceeded the 1941 figure in spite of the inability to repair wartime damage to generating equipment. By 1948, the damage and destruction suffered by buildings during the war had been made good.[15] By now, 'the average person's standard of living [in Hong Kong] was said to be the highest in the Far East'.[16] The economic boom created a labour shortage even though new arrivals were pouring in from the Mainland, and officials complained about the short supply of skilled factory workers from 1946 onwards.[17] The economy was expanding beyond all expectations.

Officials knew that state intervention was making a large contribution to Hong Kong's rapid economic recovery: for example, by stabilising wages and labour costs; procuring raw materials efficiently; and protecting local manufacturers from resurgent Japanese competition.[18] Furthermore, officials were ready to take direct action in support of business expansion. They made sure that small firms got access to overseas markets, sought out local sales outlets for new industries and made the case for cheap land and subsidised finance to promote manufacturing in 1947.[19] Yet, the colonial administration remained anxious that Hong Kong keep to a minimum the direct controls over trade and financial activities that were such a conspicuous feature of the post-war era on the Mainland and the world at large. Hong Kong was determined to abolish emergency economic powers as soon as world trading conditions allowed.[20]

This attitude appears to have been based on administrative convenience rather than loyalty to the traditions of laisser faire. Price controls proved difficult to administer. As was mentioned earlier, finding adequate supplies of food and raw materials was a nightmare made all the worse by international discrimination against Hong Kong. This colony was too insignificant geopolitically to compete for a fair share of available international supplies against such claimants as India, China and Ceylon (now Sri Lanka).[21] Controlling the public utilities was a painful and thankless task. Their executives defied even the Governor and shamelessly manipulated government funding for the benefit of their shareholders.[22] In the absence of an elected legislature to insist that the government should actively manage economic and social development, there was nothing to induce the colonial administration to retain its extensive powers once the immediate post-war emergency was over.

The banking industry proved an important exception. The British Military Administration had wide powers to impose conditions on firms wishing to operate as banks or to open bank branches in the colony and generally to regulate the industry. These controls were quickly abandoned, and it seemed likely that banking would be as free from official interference as the rest of the economy.[23] Completely forgotten were the pre-war experience of banking crises described in the previous chapter and the calls for a modern system of regulation from business leaders and the Colonial Office in the 1930s. The colonial administration had been able to circumvent these demands until the Japanese invasion. But after World War II, Hong Kong could not withstand another source of political pressure on this issue. The Guomindang threatened to impose economic sanctions if the colonial administration did not introduce legislation — including regulation of the banks — to end Hong Kong's role as a major centre for smuggling and black market activities on the Mainland. These difficult negotiations are reviewed in the next chapter. Their outcome was the 1948 Banking Ordinance which was to lead to more extensive government intervention in banking than in any other sector of the economy.

Financial Commitments

In the meantime, the banks made a crucial contribution to the colony's post-war recovery. They emerged from the war in remarkably good shape. The Japanese occupation had been a severe test for the community, which had to survive brutality, hunger and the forced reduction of the pre-war population of nearly two million to a mere 600,000 people by 1945. Those who survived inhabited what was labelled 'the most looted city in the world'.[24] Local Chinese-owned banks, like their mainland counterparts, had shown considerable ingenuity in adapting to the constraints of Japanese rule. The Bank of East Asia, for example, was able to maintain its dividends for 1942 at the pre-war level and to increase them significantly in the next two years of enemy occupation, despite strict controls on lending and interest rates. 'All in all, the Chairman believed, public confidence in the Bank grew during the [Japanese] occupation', the bank's historian records. After the Allied victory, the bank was in a very strong position to profit from the post-war boom because it had taken the precaution of transferring a substantial share of its assets to the US and the UK in the months leading up to the outbreak of war.[25]

The smaller banking houses displayed a similar capacity for survival. Many 'native Chinese banks' (i.e., banks run as family firms and in accordance with traditional Chinese business practices) were bullion dealers who benefited from buoyant demand for their services under Japanese rule. Employees left well-established firms to set up on their own account. Many did well for themselves on the wartime gold market, and, even after the war, most of them earned a better living than they would have as employees of the bigger firms.[26] The Japanese were less tolerant of black market currency dealings. The previous chapter noted that Chinese banks had continued to transfer funds even in Japanese occupied areas of the Mainland before 1941. Within Hong Kong, the Japanese were unable to suppress similar transactions despite 'employing unlimited powers of punishment'.[27] The banking industry as a whole emerged from the occupation ready to underwrite Hong Kong's economic recovery.

When British officials first returned to Hong Kong, they believed that the government would need to set up a low-cost loan scheme to be administered by the Chinese General Chamber of Commerce in order to meet a desperate need for cash until the banks resumed normal business.[28] In the event, the banking industry resumed normal services far faster than anticipated. Even before the Japanese had been defeated, HSBC's chairman in London had provided GBP700,000 to procure equipment for Hong Kong's power stations which, according to British intelligence reports, had been seriously damaged.[29] (This sum was equivalent to almost a quarter of Hong Kong's total imports from the UK in 1946.)

HSBC's confidence in Hong Kong's capacity to rebuild itself on commercial terms was matched by a similar optimism among the local Chinese-owned banks. However, HSBC and the foreign banks were handicapped in the early months after the British return by official restrictions on the release of expatriate banking personnel from military or government service and also by a shortage of transport to get them to Hong Kong.[30] Local Chinese-owned banks were under no such constraints, and the British Military Administration gave a high priority to the return of their staff from the Mainland and the resumption of banking business as quickly as possible.[31]

The local Chinese-owned banks may well have been the first business sector to start operating on a normal basis after the defeat of Japan. Immediately after the Japanese had surrendered and direct flights were resumed between Hong Kong and China's wartime capital, Chongqing, the local currency market resumed operations in earnest. Within weeks, the British Military Administration was searching for ways to control an influx of the Chinese National Currency, so large that officials feared it would destabilise the Hong Kong economy. They recognised, however, that any restrictions on financial transactions would reduce the incentives for Mainland merchants to sell vital food supplies to Hong Kong. In fact, the smuggling of currency from Mainland was impossible to stem. Hong Kong quickly became the main escape route from China for flight capital, encouraged by over-valuation of the Chinese National Currency.[32] Local banks were to profit increasingly from this business as the ruling Guomindang's political weaknesses worsened, its economic management disintegrated and its currency suffered accelerating inflation.

Apart from funding Hong Kong's own recovery, the colony's banks also profited from an expanding role on the Mainland. During this period, Hong Kong was still thoroughly integrated into China's economy, and the colony's political and commercial environment was shaped by Mainland events. The defeat of Japan had not been followed by a return to stable government and peaceful business conditions in China. As civil war intensified and the currency collapsed, elements of the Mainland banking system migrated to Hong Kong. Among them were 'native' banks. On setting up in Hong Kong, however, they preferred to register as limited companies and to adopt modern business practices, so that they did not compete directly with Hong Kong's own 'native' banks.[33] The colony was becoming the centre for a growing share of the Mainland's financial operations.

Shanghai Eclipsed

Hong Kong's banking industry benefited in particular from the eclipse of Shanghai where only the 'native' banks enjoyed decent profit opportunities. [34] These had seemed on the verge of extinction in the mid-1930s. However, they had won a new lease of life in the chaotic conditions created by invasion and inflation to which their traditional business model was well suited. They were also adept at evading the controls administered by a corrupt and ineffectual Mainland bureaucracy after the war. Shanghai's Chinese commercial banks found it impossible for to make profits for their shareholders from legitimate business because of the mounting inflation and increasing government restrictions. In addition, the Guomindang wanted Shanghai to be integrated into the national economy after World War II, and the city no longer offered the business environment required for an international banking centre. Foreign banks had lost the last of their commercial privileges when the Unequal Treaties were abolished during World War II. Post-war exchange controls barred both Chinese and foreign banks from direct participation in the free foreign currency market. The controls also deterred foreign banks from bringing funds into China to expand business. The result was to remove Shanghai as a financial rival to Hong Kong.[35]

> The overwhelming predominance in Shanghai banking of international transactions concerned with foreign trade, international short-term credits, bullion and exchange [was] now a thing of the past — of the semi-colonial century which followed upon the opening of imperial China to modern-style foreign business in 1841. That era died shortly before the recent war began; the abolition of extraterritoriality in China was its tombstone, and the foreign-exchange control regime of the Central Bank of China the seal on that tombstone.

The Guomindang's fruitless battle to impose draconian exchange controls on Shanghai and to stem the flight of funds to Hong Kong merely served to emphasise how liberal were the colonial administration's attitudes towards currency transactions.[36]

The 'Native' Banks

As Shanghai's banking role shrank, so Hong Kong expanded its activities in serving the Mainland's financial and commercial needs. In this process, it seemed that the principal contribution was made by Hong Kong's own 'native' banks. Immediately after World War II, this group came to dominate the banking landscape. The *Far Eastern Economic Review* praised them in lyrical terms.[37]

> The influence of the native banks on the Colony's commerce and finance is enormous. Many well-established and financially potent native banks often finance the biggest trade propositions as well as industrial and construction projects ... A big native bank usually has branches in Canton, and other leading towns in South China, Shanghai and North China cities: many banks extend their activities as far as Malaya, the Philippines, Siam and Indo-China ...

No statistics were available to test these impressive claims. But the magazine was repeating a long-standing conviction about the contribution of the 'native' banks, not only to Hong Kong but to China's economy as a whole, particularly when beset by political or economic disruption. Indeed, during the 1930s, a senior Mainland banker had claimed that the national economy could withstand the closure of the country's modern commercial banks but would collapse if the 'native' banks disappeared.[38] Hong Kong's 'native' banks were an extension of the Mainland system and shared its principal characteristics.[39] These banks were generally small, unincorporated family firms. They raised capital and deposits from relatives and friends, and they confined their lending to equally restricted social circles. They operated largely beyond the direction of official institutions and frequently outside the law. They maintained their own business associations and kept at a distance from the world of modern commercial banks. Above all, their business model enabled the Mainland's informal financial system to keep China's economy going no matter how adverse the political and commercial situation.[40]

By the end of 1946, the colony's 'native' banks were reported to be heavily dependent on their dealings in the Mainland currency. In theory, these were in flagrant breach both of Mainland legislation and of Hong Kong's exchange controls. Nevertheless, a free market in the Chinese National Currency flourished in Hong Kong, to which the colonial administration turned a blind eye. The bulk of this business was unconnected with trade: it was straightforward speculation on the Mainland's rate of inflation and the speed of its currency depreciation.[41] But without the facilities offered by Hong Kong and its 'native' banks to exchange the Chinese national currency for gold, US dollars and Hong Kong's own currency, Mainland businesses would have lost a major inducement to route shipments through Hong Kong. The colony and its 'native' banks offered them a haven from the collapse of their own currency.

As China's civil war intensified and Mainland business conditions deteriorated, Hong Kong's 'native' banks were to play an increasingly important role in financing China's economy. The colony's unregulated financial markets — especially the 'native' banks' currency dealings with the Mainland — led to a Sino-British crisis. The Guomindang authorities were not prepared to tolerate a situation in which their laws were flaunted with impunity from the safety of a British colony.[42] Despite the impending collapse of the Guomindang régime, its representatives were able to exert sufficient pressure on the British authorities to compel Hong Kong to introduce statutory controls on the colony's banks, as the next chapter will recount.

The defeat of the Guomindang at the hands of Mao Zedong and the Chinese Communist Party in 1949 transformed Hong Kong's relationship, not only with the Mainland but also with the rest of the world economy. Hong Kong's role as a conduit for the Mainland's international trade and investment came to an end. Yet, the economy did not collapse, and Chapter 5, 'Industrial Take-off, Cut-price and Self-financed' will describe how Hong Kong's manufacturing was already launched on a growth path that would continue unchecked for the next three decades and make the colony a major exporter to Western markets.

Invisible Growth

Despite a general awareness that rapid industrial expansion was under way in the 1950s, neither the government nor the business community had more than a vague notion of the scale and pace of the manufacturing take-off. Until 1959, there were virtually no published official data to demonstrate the speed with which the economy had switched to exporting the output from its own factories. This data deficit meant that growth rates were largely hidden from view, and this new lease of life took contemporary observers by surprise.

Hong Kong was far from ideal as a manufacturing centre, the Governor warned the legislature in 1948. 'Chinese labour can no longer be regarded as cheap in comparison with western [labour]', he declared, and 'there were … comparative disadvantages, such as limited water supply, scarcity of suitable sites, and more stringent labour regulations'.[43] Contemporaries had little sense of how sustained the growth momentum would be, even after the industrial transformation had become very visible. Labour productivity was low, and so was the level of capital investment, an observer noted in 1956. The colony's only obvious advantages were efficient administration and a reasonable infrastructure, he claimed, and the quality of its Chinese entrepreneurs.[44] The feeling that Hong Kong was ill-suited to manufacturing never entirely disappeared. Indeed, a Colonial Office report concluded that 'manufacturing, though of increasing importance, cannot replace trade in the Hong Kong economy'.[45] In 1964, the Governor urged industrialists to move 'into technically more complicated processes and into higher quality ranges' and to imitate Western countries — although he felt that 'we can never hope to catch up with them because our only competitive advantage is clearly lower labour costs'.[46] This pessimism about Hong Kong's industrial prospects seems so misplaced, in retrospect, that it has been interpreted — erroneously — as evidence that 'the Hong Kong government was determined not to pursue industrial upgrading'.[47]

In the absence of authoritative statistical evidence, contemporary commentators could hardly be blamed for their inability to gauge the scale and speed of the transformation that was underway. For a hundred years, the economy had been dominated by entrepôt activities. It thus required an enormous leap of the imagination to recognise that the value added from manufacturing would more than fill the shortfall created by the loss of the traditional China trade. By the end of 1954, the government started to realise that locally manufactured goods accounted for at least 30 per cent of total exports and were the largest source of national income. Even then, however, the colony clung to its entrepôt past. 'In a sense it is more of an entrepot than ever', the Financial Secretary argued, 'for our factories import all their raw materials, add to their value by some form of processing, and export them again'.[48] This reluctance to see how Hong Kong had broken with the past led a significant section of the business community to ignore the new markets for local products overseas in the misguided hope that China would return to 'normal' and that the traditional entrepôt trade would recover its former preeminence.[49] Most contemporary observers focused on the collapse of the entrepôt sector as reflected in the total export figures. These were the only economic data readily available, and they seemed calamitous. A fall of 53 per cent in total exports in 1952 alone was followed by a further 17 per cent decline before starting to recover in 1955 (Table I). The government had other trade statistics which pointed to considerable growth in the local economy, but they were not generally accessible. These unpublished data are included in Table I and reveal that domestic exports were growing by 136 per cent a year between 1950 and 1960, thanks to the breakneck expansion of local manufacturing. During the same period, re-exports fell by an annual seven per cent.

The Banks Stumble

The speed and significance of the industrial take-off went largely unrecognised by contemporary observers within the government, the banking industry and the business world at large. The banks had confidently underwritten the reconstruction of the economy and a remarkable revival of the Mainland-related entrepôt trade immediately after World War II.[51] Nevertheless, as Hong

Table I: Domestic Exports and Total Exports, 1950–1960 (HKD millions)[50]

Year	Domestic Exports	Re-exports	Total Exports
1950	197	3,518	3,715
1951	312	4,130	4,433
1952	486	2,413	2,899
1953	635	2,099	2,734
1954	682	1,735	2,417
1955	730	1,804	2,534
1956	1,115	2,095	3,210
1957	1,202	1,814	3,016
1958	1,260	1,729	2,989
1959	2,282	966	3,278
1960	2,867	1,070	3,937

Kong's rapid industrial take-off began in the late 1940s, even the largest banks found the experience uncomfortable. They stumbled badly in 1950, refusing to finance imports on the grounds that local warehouses were filled with unshippable products.[52] This crisis had begun the previous year when consignments destined for the Mainland could not be shipped after the Guomindang blockaded the ports in a final, fruitless effort to delay the triumph of the Chinese Communist Party. Shipments to the Mainland were also held up from late 1949 because of uncertainty about the restrictions which the new rulers were imposing on trade and bank transactions with Hong Kong. Nevertheless, the business community had started 1950 with considerable optimism about the colony's prospects.[53]

The banks, however, took a gloomy view of the future as the Korean War widened, leading to a total US ban on all commercial and financial transactions with the People's Republic of China, which was to last until 1971 (reinforced initially by a United Nations embargo). Bankers began to cut credit lines even to the biggest and most modern manufacturing plants established by immigrant entrepreneurs from Shanghai. The sudden financial squeeze almost shut down the cotton-spinning sector — the building block for Hong Kong's emergence as a major textile exporter. Catastrophe was averted by China Engineers Ltd, a trading firm founded in Shanghai in 1928.[54] In addition to importing industrial equipment, this company supported its Chinese customers with both investment and working capital. When two major Shanghai cotton manufacturers found that they could not obtain bank support in the early post-war period to set up in Hong Kong, China Engineers had come to the rescue with substantial mortgage facilities. With some justification, its British executives boasted closer relations with that city's leading Chinese businessmen than Hong Kong bankers.[55]

Until the Korean War, business had boomed for the newcomers from Shanghai. While cash flows were still robust and balance sheets attractive, it would have been easy enough to raise additional share capital or secure long-term bank credits. These immigrant tycoons saw no need to do so because they expected to finance future expansion out of their ample profits. But the banks no longer viewed them as acceptable risks when the Korean War embargoes came into effect and their sales suffered a sharp downturn. They now faced ruin because their bankers were reluctant to finance the purchase of raw materials unless a factory had confirmed export orders for its finished products. The mills were in danger of going out of business. China Engineers organised a rescue operation and created the 'Hong Kong Cotton Mills Pool' to buy yarn on a group basis. HSBC and the Chartered Bank were sufficiently reassured by this cooperative venture to provide enough funds to keep the spinning industry alive.[56]

Needless Panic

The government took no direct action to help either the banks or industry during the crisis which followed the outbreak of the Korean War. Initially, the colonial administration's principal economic anxieties had been the general threat to business sentiment as the Chinese Communist Party swept towards victory in the summer of 1949 and the need to retain the trust and cooperation of the public utilities in particular. By the end of 1950, officials were convinced that business confidence was on the point of collapse. In order to cut their Hong Kong risk, the Financial Secretary warned the Governor confidentially, 'many people would be glad to unload [their assets] at any reasonable price'.[57] The colonial administration then became convinced that mass unemployment was imminent, creating a 'political' rather than an economic threat. Officials were alarmed by internal government estimates of unemployment (although these were little better than guesses).[58] These claimed that from 25 to 30 per cent of the industrial labour force was already without work, although the government's own, relatively reliable social surveys in squatter areas — then the most vulnerable and deprived group in the community — recorded less than two per cent of males aged 14 and above were without jobs .[59] The US assessment was that its embargo had cut profit margins for Hong Kong firms but had little impact on demand for labour.[60] There was no employment crisis in fact, and one prominent businessman, Lawrence (later Lord) Kadoorie, advised the government that the credit squeeze was causing more harm to the economy than the embargoes themselves. He urged officials to 'intimate to the lending banks that [the government] will stand behind approved industrial and commercial loans'.[61] Manufacturers pleaded with officials to persuade the banks not to reduce credit facilities in early 1951. The colonial administration did not regard the crisis as a liquidity problem for which there was an obvious financial solution, however. So, government departments were instructed to draw up schemes to create work and provide unemployment relief, while trying to persuade large employers not to close down or lay off staff. Yet by August 1951, it should have been obvious that there was no crisis because officials knew that the textile industry was moving towards three-shift production to meet increasing orders.[62]

This rejection of reflationary measures and the reliance on Victorian make-work and relief programmes were inspired by the colonial administration's mistrust of Keynesian economics (an important feature of the colonial culture which is analysed at length in Chapter 10, 'Colonial Money and its Management'). But the immediate cause of this policy blunder was Hong Kong's refusal to comply with the Colonial Office's advice to compile comprehensive trade statistics and estimates for industrial production and gross capital formation.[63] As a result, the colonial administration had no reliable data by which to gauge economic performance. Officials were victims of their own data deficit. They were baffled by the way that government revenues remained buoyant in 1951 after their own estimates that year had pointed to a slump in trade and soaring unemployment. 'It is difficult to give a precise reason or reasons for this but it is probably due fundamentally to a recovery of confidence in the future of Hong Kong which has brought back a great deal of money into the Colony', declared the Governor in obvious bewilderment, 'and has been evidenced by steep rises in the value of land and of local shares'.[64] It did not occur to him, apparently, that land and share prices might be an indicator of the economy's underlying buoyancy. One serious consequence of the government's ignorance of the true state — both of the labour market and economy as a whole — was its inability to restore business and banking confidence. Panic proved persistent, and employers remained convinced — quite wrongly — in early 1952 that collapse was around the corner. Kadoorie, for example, was still urging that 'when credit was tight, government by its promise of support could encourage banks to give loans more freely' — just as in 1945–46, when the government had encouraged post-war reconstruction.[65] Officials lacked the information needed to convince entrepreneurs and banking executives that their survival was not in question.

The Hong Kong economy was not supposed to grow in this chaotic and haphazard manner. When the UK's Labour Party came to power in 1945, it directed colonial governments to abandon laisser-faire attitudes and accept responsibility for promoting economic and social development. The first goal was to create flourishing economies which would finance the costs of social progress. All colonies, therefore, should draw up development plans to promote business and encourage manufacturing.[66] The Colonial Office promoted a vision of colonial development which Hong Kong did not share, together with a variety of development programmes in which Hong Kong preferred not to participate. Thus, although Hong Kong dutifully set up a committee in 1946 to prepare development plans, work on them soon ground to a halt.[67] Other colonial governments also found this new role of direct responsibility for economic progress difficult to implement in practice, and in 1950, London started to examine further ways to promote industrial expansion in colonial territories.[68] By 1952, a blueprint had been prepared to brief colonial governments on a wide range of initiatives that would speed up industrialisation, including direct government involvement in economic management, investment incentives and protection for infant industries. These measures were what the Hong Kong business community was already seeking and for which it was to lobby in vain over the next 20 years. They were also initiatives which had been endorsed by senior Hong Kong officials before World War II.[69] The colonial administration, nevertheless, chose to ignore this blueprint even though rapid expansion of manufacturing was essential for economic survival as the traditional entrepôt trade disappeared during the Korean War.[70] The decision to cling to laisser faire was made entirely by the colonial administration and in direct defiance of the Colonial Office's advice.

Taxing Issues

The colonial administration also decided to resist tax reforms, and this was to prove crucial to the survival of laisser faire. Before World War II, an official commission had recommended that the colonial administration should accept greater responsibility for both economic and social progress, which should be financed by the introduction of direct taxation. The business representatives on the commission had not disputed the assertion that Hong Kong could afford increased taxation to pay for the new policy.[71] When the colony introduced direct taxation for the first time in 1939, the Financial Secretary mollified business representatives by pointing out that the additional revenue could be used to provide financial help for industrialists.[72] The disruption caused by the impending hostilities against Japan prevented the introduction of development programmes before the outbreak of war, however.

After World War II, London instructed colonial governments to introduce modern systems of income tax to pay for industrial and social development.[73] Hong Kong attitudes had changed since the 1930s, however, and the business community rejected the proposal of a full income tax. Its representatives also expressed implacable opposition to raising the rate of profits tax to the levels which London believed essential to finance a modern government and its development schemes. The colonial administration chose to disobey the Colonial Office's tax directive.[74] There was to be no income tax and no tax on dividends or capital gains for the rest of the century.

Business was now safe from taxation. But, for the business community, this victory had an unintended and unwelcome consequence. Where were the resources to come from to provide subsidised investment schemes, tax concessions and other incentives? Once tax reforms had been rejected, government revenue was barely sufficient to pay for a less than adequate infrastructure, basic public housing and rudimentary health services in the 1950s, and minimal welfare and education in the 1960s. There was nothing left over to subsidise business. With its restricted tax base, the government could not afford to abandon laisser faire. The business community saw the solution in bringing back the reserves held in London. Chapter 10 will explain why the colonial administration steadfastly rejected demands for these overseas resources to be repatriated to Hong Kong to help promote business. To their vexation, entrepreneurs and investors were left without state aid. The private sector would have to fund its own growth.

This outcome was of profound importance for the banking industry. The banks would not have to compete with state-subsidised industrial finance at the expense of their profit margins. There would be no official development plans to tempt the government to interfere with banks' lending policies in order to achieve the colonial administration's goals at the expense of the private sector.

But there were less desirable consequences of the decision that the financing of Hong Kong's growth should be left to the market and be entirely profit-driven. This policy assumed that banks would act rationally and avoid self-destructive behaviour. Later chapters will show that many proved incapable of realising how profitable but safe industrial lending would prove, while large numbers of bank owners and executives could not be trusted to act prudently, even in the interests of their own survival. Uncritical reliance on market forces was to be a feature of monetary policy in both the 1960s and 1970s, when financial secretaries allowed speculation to reach alarming levels (as Chapter 10 argues in some detail).

Conclusions

Overall, the post-war emergencies highlighted the economic resilience of Hong Kong. The banking industry, in particular, seemed designed to thrive under the most adverse circumstances. It found the formulas to survive the Japanese occupation in sufficiently robust shape to resume normal activities as soon as hostilities ended. It prospered despite the chaos of the civil war on the Mainland. The industry — especially the local Chinese-owned banks — gave every impression of being secure, adaptable and well able to manage political and commercial risks. Over the long run, bankers were to come through similar tests of their nerve and professionalism with credit.

Nevertheless, the optimism and resourcefulness that rebuilt Hong Kong's economy so quickly after the Japanese surrender evaporated with surprising speed once the Cold War began. The data deficit played an obvious part, both in encouraging dismal predictions of future trends after the closure of Mainland markets and in underestimating the prospects created by the switch to manufacturing for export to the world's richest and most politically stable countries. Officials and bankers alike foresaw disaster. The banking industry was able to overcome its initial panic, and credit lines to the crucial textile sector before it collapsed. The impact on the government was more severe. As the economy moved from post-war boom to Korean War bust, officials who had displayed considerable initiative and commercial flair during the period of economic reconstruction showed much less ingenuity and enterprise in responding to foreign embargoes and the loss of the China trade. The government had become alarmed about business sentiment in 1948. Its confidence continued to fall, and it abandoned plans for new measures to protect the public, including controls on the public utilities which the Governor believed were exploiting the public so seriously in 1949 that they might have to be nationalised. [75]

The colonial administration was slow to recover its nerve even when fears of economic catastrophe proved false. This pessimistic outlook was to have considerable influence on banking policy. Alarmed by worsening business sentiment in general, officials adopted a protective attitude towards the local Chinese-owned banks in particular and were reluctant to take action against incompetent or dishonest bankers after the enactment of Hong Kong's first banking legislation in 1948. This was not an environment which fostered effective regulation of the banking industry, and it was not to improve until the 1960s, as will be recounted in Chapter 6, 'The Rise and Fall of Chinese Banking'.

4

Financial Centre under Siege

The speed with which Hong Kong rebuilt its economy after the Japanese occupation was not just a cause for astonished admiration overseas. Ironically, the colony's rapid return to business as normal provoked demands from abroad for restraints on its unregulated bankers and traders, and it was to spend the first three decades after World War II in a state of siege. Economic success created new tensions in relations with first the Mainland, then the UK and finally the US. These three external powers made considerable efforts to get Hong Kong to impose controls on its merchants and bankers and its entrepreneurs and industrialists, in order to serve their national interests. This chapter will examine the creation of this superstructure of financial controls imposed by these external pressures that was so much at odds with the way in which the rest of the Hong Kong economy was administered. It will focus on three issues.

- Hong Kong's astonishing post-war recovery — and of its banking, in particular — was viewed by the ruling Guomindang between 1946 and 1948 as threatening the Mainland economy. The result was a campaign to intimidate Hong Kong into enforcing Mainland controls on foreign trade and currency transactions.

- The UK was to be chronically worried until 1972 about the influence of Hong Kong's financial markets on the stability of sterling, and it sought to prevent holders of sterling assets from using the colony to escape into stronger currencies.

- The US was very conscious of how the British colony had always been a secure gateway for Mainland business, even when China was engulfed by war, civil war and revolution. Thus, Hong Kong was a prime concern for Washington during the Cold War as it attempted to maintain a total trade and financial blockade of the People's Republic of China from 1950 until 1971.

There was some sympathy overseas with the hardships which these restrictions would cause Hong Kong, but the colony received no compensation for the damage that its economy suffered — although the UK itself received sufficient economic and military aid from the US to offset its commercial losses from cooperating with Washington's Cold War embargo.[1] In self-defence, Hong Kong rejected these external demands for controls where it could, as this chapter will show. When resistance to these powerful political forces proved futile, senior officials allowed the controls to be evaded and diluted regardless of the law. The colonial administration felt it had little choice. If Hong Kong surrendered to these external pressures and agreed to curtail its international trade and financial activities, how could this small British colony continue to thrive as a regional business centre?

The external pressure which the Guomindang — and, separately, London and Washington — sought to exert on Hong Kong clashed with the colony's basic economic philosophy. The colonial administration was committed to completely free trade, and this doctrine was invaluable in protecting Hong Kong's access to foreign markets against protectionist pressures overseas. Quite simply, the colony's economy had to be 'politically neutral' because its markets had to be open to all comers, whether or not they were allies or rivals of either the UK or the colony (except in time of war).[2] This 'neutrality' had been in force in Hong Kong before World War II when, as Chapter 2, 'Chinese Revolutionaries, Chinese Reformers', noted, the colony had failed to discriminate against Japan's exports and in favour of the British Empire. Because of Hong Kong's dependence on the Mainland, 'neutrality' could not be abandoned during the Cold War.

At the same time, because the government did not intervene in the management of the economy, market forces rather than political agendas were supposed to be in command. [3] As a result, the commitment to laisser faire gave Hong Kong flexibility in adjusting to political as well as economic challenges from abroad.[4] The colonial administration was able to avoid confrontations over diplomatic policies or political principles. Instead, Hong Kong shifted its conflicts with foreign governments to trade and financial issues, so that everything became negotiable, including sovereignty, as was to be evident in its dealings with the Guomindang.

The Mainland Squeeze

The Mainland was always the most direct challenge to British rule, and the colonial administration knew that its survival depended on whether the colony made itself useful to the Mainland, even under Guomindang rule (as this chapter later discusses). In much the same way, the colonial administration had to find ways to cooperate economically with Beijing during the Cold War in order to justify a separate political status for Hong Kong, no matter how much the colonial administration mistrusted the Chinese Communist Party.

In the 1930s, as Chapter 2 explained, the Guomindang had steadily squeezed British and other foreign businesses out of the privileges they had gained from Unequal Treaties in the previous century. But Hong Kong was not under political threat because the Guomindang was not yet ready to confront the British colony directly. During World War II, however, the Allies surrendered what remained of their rights under the Unequal Treaties, and the Mainland business environment no longer offered foreigners a privileged position.[5] The Guomindang then turned its attention to the issue of Hong Kong. Its initial ambition, encouraged by the US, was to use Chinese troops to liberate the colony from the Japanese and thus replace British rule, without further discussion or delay. London, however, outmanoeuvred the Guomindang in Washington, and Admiral Harcourt and the Royal Navy arrived in Hong Kong before the Chinese forces.[6]

After the war, the Guomindang grew increasingly hostile towards the colony, an attitude that was not inspired by national pride alone. The Mainland authorities became convinced that the country's economic woes were aggravated by Hong Kong's pursuit of laisser-faire policies in defiance of China's well-being. They believed they could not hope to stabilise the national economy unless the colony and its bankers were brought to heel. The Guomindang ignored its inability to enforce its own laws in Shanghai and elsewhere, as well as the complicity of the Mainland's own 'native' banks in the illegal currency trade (recounted in the previous chapter). Its view was that the Chinese economy was being bled white by rampant black market currency dealings and the no less extensive smuggling of commodities and manufactured goods, all made possible by laisser-faire Hong Kong. Guomindang officials were convinced that if the colony's free markets could be eliminated, there would be a chance of bringing the Mainland's mounting inflation under control, reviving the foreign trade sector and restoring the national economy to health.

In this period, the Mainland itself was taking urgent steps to reform deposit-taking businesses through modern legislation.[7] The Guomindang expected Hong Kong to follow suit and demanded that the colonial administration should cooperate in banning all trade and currency transactions in Hong Kong that would be illegal on the Mainland.[8] Hong Kong could not ignore these demands once the Guomindang started to mobilise a wave of anti-British patriotism on the Mainland, and an economic blockade of Hong Kong seemed possible. Anti-British sentiment gathered considerable strength, and the British Consulate in Guangzhou was stormed and burnt in January 1948.

The colonial administration beat off pressures from British diplomats to capitulate outright to Guomindang demands. Hong Kong officials were able to retain control of the secret negotiations, principally it seems, because of the highly technical issues involved which required a thorough knowledge of how the colony's financial markets worked. In the end, nevertheless, the Guomindang won major political concessions which had had three important implications for the future.

• Hong Kong accepted, albeit on a temporary basis, that 'complete freedom of movement of goods and foreign exchange between China and Hong Kong' was no longer possible. [9]

• The colony had thus agreed to retreat from its Mainland hinterland and its traditional role in China's economic relations with the rest of the world. Its integration with the Chinese economy was being reversed through a deliberate decision by the Mainland authorities, which neither London nor Hong Kong could resist.

• The colony would no longer be able to depend on its free port and the China trade for its prosperity, whichever side won the civil war. The Guomindang had decided that Hong Kong had become a liability to the Mainland. The Chinese Communist Party was pledged to eradicate both imperialist and capitalist influences from China.

The colony now entered into formal agreements with the Guomindang and enacted legislation to curb the commercial and financial activities to which the Mainland objected.[10] The Guomindang did not achieve its goals of suppressing Hong Kong's free market in hard currencies or of being allowed to inspect the bank accounts of the colony's Chinese residents. But the commercial agreement allowed Mainland customs officials to operate within Hong Kong's boundaries to tackle smuggling, which amounted, as one legislator observed, to a 'leasing of our sovereign rights'.[11] The colonial administration candidly admitted that British sovereignty had been compromised in order to support the Guomindang's efforts to rescue the Mainland from its deepening economic crisis.

> We have placed at the disposal of China our administrative capacity. We have temporarily surrendered some of our sovereign rights at a time when sovereign rights are being ever more jealously hoarded in other parts of the world. But yet we have undertaken all these measures willingly and it is reasonable to ask what we in Hong Kong receive in return for all of this ... The answer is that materially we gain exactly nothing in return ...'[12]

The Guomindang was not satisfied with facilities to arrest smugglers in their Hong Kong base. The colonial administration must take direct steps to suppress the free flow of currency and bullion into the Mainland and the flight of Chinese capital into Hong Kong by introducing legal controls on banking activities in the colony. It is a tribute to the importance of the 'native' banks in the Mainland system that the Guomindang negotiators made the local Chinese-owned firms the primary target of the regulatory system they urged on Hong Kong. Mainland officials recognised that effective controls on the 'native' banks would be impossible until the British introduced legislation to register all firms carrying on banking business. Nor would the Guomindang be able to stem the flight of banks from Shanghai to Hong Kong if the new arrivals could start up in business without having to apply for a government licence. Although the Mainland's central bankers were handicapped in the negotiations by their ignorance of Hong Kong's financial markets,[13] the colonial administration could not refuse to make some conciliatory gestures, and the 1948 Banking Ordinance came into force requiring deposit-taking institutions of almost every kind to be licensed. The colonial administration was able to conceal from the general public that the new law had been enacted solely in response to political pressures from the Mainland. The official explanation for passing Hong Kong's first Banking Ordinance in 1948 sounded very worthy: to prevent under-capitalised firms from setting up as banks and to prevent banks from engaging in speculation or other activities which were in breach of the trade or currency regulations of either Hong Kong or the Mainland.[14]

The new banking ordinance was deeply flawed, highly unpopular within the colonial administration and reluctantly enforced (as Chapter 6, 'The Rise and Fall of Chinese Banking', will demonstrate). Particularly serious was the government's decision to rush through the licensing of as many banks as quickly as possible in 1948, even if they were in breach of normal commercial legislation.[15] This exemption from the laws applying to businesses in general was to set a dangerous precedent for the decades that followed. The irony was that Hong Kong could have had an excellent banking law if officials had simply copied the statute that the Mainland had adopted in 1947, which was a model of prudent regulation (although enacted too late to rescue the Guomindang from financial chaos).[16]

Wasted Appeasement

In retrospect, there had been no need to capitulate to a dying régime. The colonial administration, however, had been blind to the fatal weaknesses of the Guomindang, partly because of the close working relations between senior Hong Kong officials and their Guomindang counterparts, particularly in Guangdong Province.[17] British misconceptions about Mainland politics was an even more powerful factor. The Guomindang had become poor business partners for British firms soon after the war ended, principally because of the inefficiency and corruption of Mainland officials. Relations between the two sides got steadily worse, and the British Embassy sent a stream of reports from 1947 illustrating growing Guomindang hostility.[18] These included attempts to impose political constraints on British nationals and the seizure of British-owned property.[19] Until early 1948, nevertheless, British diplomats believed that they had little choice but to work for the survival of the Guomindang, and they only started to take seriously the possibility of the Chinese Communist Party's victory in May 1948.[20] Guomindang propaganda claimed that the trade and financial agreements forced on Hong Kong had improved Sino-British relations. The British Embassy reported to the Foreign Office in London that 'the factual evidence of Chinese goodwill seems … on the contrary to be deplorably lacking'.[21]

Hong Kong officials seemed slower still to comprehend political realities. For example, the colonial administration organised public celebrations for the inauguration of Chiang Kai-shek as China's President in mid-1948, as if his Guomindang Party would remain in power indefinitely.[22] He was soon to be in humiliating flight to the island of Taiwan. The colonial administration believed that the deals negotiated with the Guomindang had removed a serious political threat to the crucial economic relationship with the Mainland and established a new era of goodwill and cooperation.

But the British compromises and the Hong Kong concessions proved to be wasted exercises in appeasement. The economic reality was that, even before the end of the negotiations with the Guomindang, civil war, hyper-inflation and the collapse of normal life in China's cities were forcing Hong Kong businesses — whether owned by British or local Chinese interests — to switch from the Mainland to new markets, mainly in Southeast Asia. By 1947, the Mainland had already ceased to be the colony's largest trading partner.[23] Meanwhile, the Chinese Communist Party's authority was expanding from city to city.

After Mao Zedong came to power in 1949, China's new rulers had no place for foreign capitalism and no need of a British colony's cooperation in solving the nation's economic crisis. They put a stop to the black markets, the currency speculation and the smuggling on the Mainland without any help from Hong Kong. The UK lost its entire investment portfolio on the Mainland as a result of Mao's victory. The Chinese Communist Party took a very different view of Hong Kong, however. Its leaders understood quite clearly how this British-run enclave could give the Mainland safe access to the hostile, capitalist world of the West throughout the Cold War,[24] and they were ready to put national interests before ideological appearances.[25]

The Weakness and Worries of Sterling

The next source of attack on Hong Kong's financial freedom came from the UK in the course of that country's protracted struggle to protect its currency. Chapter 2 described the considerable effort that was made in the 1930s to establish the Sterling Area as a unified trading and financial bloc for the British Empire, managed from London and based on the British pound. The outbreak of World War II had been followed by the introduction of rigorous regulation of all trade and currency dealings with non-sterling countries, which reinforced the cohesion of the Sterling Area, and 'it became a method by which Britain could control resources for the war effort and for post-war reconstruction.[26]

Before the Japanese invasion in 1941, Hong Kong had been largely exempt from these controls because London accepted that the colony was not an extension of the British economy and could only survive by serving the commercial and financial needs of China. The case for Hong Kong's free-port status and its free financial markets was well understood by officials in London planning for the colony's post-war rehabilitation.[27] Thus, Hong Kong was set to remain exempt from the more onerous Sterling Area restrictions after the war. This generous treatment did not induce the colonial administration to display a sense of obligation, either moral or political, towards the Sterling Area and its woes. Instead, Hong Kong officials fought doggedly to exploit this financial, commercial and political autonomy, regardless of London's priorities and, very often, in defiance of its instructions.[28]

The Allied victory brought peace but not prosperity, and the UK seemed to have little prospect of an early end to dire austerity, chronic shortages and a currency crisis. London became obsessed with the weakness of sterling, whose first line of defence was strict control of foreign trade and currency movements.[29] Grumbling soon began in London about the claims of Hong Kong and other newly liberated territories for special treatment after enemy occupation.[30] The colony deployed three arguments to convince London to allow its special exemptions to continue.[31]

- Leading bankers were warning that Hong Kong could not survive if the economy were cut off from the Mainland by trade and foreign exchange controls.
- The colony had to be freed from the restrictions accepted by the rest of the Sterling Area if Hong Kong were to win a clear lead over other Chinese ports — notably Shanghai — through as rapid a return to pre-war trading conditions as possible.
- The stringent Sterling Area controls were impossible to enforce in Hong Kong. For example, it would prove politically and physically impossible to apply the regulations to US merchant ships using Hong Kong's port facilities for their transit trade with the Mainland.

Self-interest also encouraged the UK to continue to exempt Hong Kong from the full rigours of the economic and financial restrictions in force throughout the rest of the British colonial empire. Hopes of a revival of British fortunes on the Mainland induced London to risk a potentially large outflow of hard currency through allowing Hong Kong to resume its entrepôt role.[32] In the immediate post-war period, the British view was that Hong Kong was the UK's best hope of doing business with China.[33] Consequently, its free port and uncontrolled financial markets seemed worth preserving in much the same way as London modified the UK's exchange controls to protect its own role as an international financial centre.[34]

For a brief spell, Sino-British trade seemed to be doing 'almost too well' in London's view.[35] After the Chinese Communist Party came to power, however, British firms could no longer operate on the Mainland, which made Hong Kong seem even more important as the gateway to China's markets.[36] Relaxation of the normal Sterling Area rules was approved but on the understanding, declared the Colonial Office, that 'the important thing is to facilitate Sterling Area-China trade'.[37]

Nevertheless, the colony was a member of the Sterling Area and legally obliged to impose some degree of regulation on external trade and financial transactions. In the daily round of business, exchange controls in Hong Kong operated at three levels (although this distinction was not made either formally or in public).

- *Transactions involving bank payments outside the Sterling Area.* These were assumed to be related to legitimate trade and investment flows. They were regarded as subject to an acceptable level of control and supervision because the major banks involved were 'authorised' institutions which undertook to abide by Hong Kong's exchange controls. At the same time, London was prepared to accept the existence of a free market to handle transactions in parallel to the 'authorised' banks.

- *Currency dealing, frequently involving physical transfers of banknotes, drafts and similar instruments.* These were not linked to specific trade transactions. However, they were part and parcel of the settlement system for the Mainland's trade through Hong Kong before the Chinese Communist Party came to power in 1949. They remained an essential element in Hong Kong's relations with overseas Chinese businesses after that date. The import and export of banknotes was subject to strict licensing. Yet, with the tolerated free foreign exchange market, it would have been virtually impossible to suppress currency dealing.

- *Bullion dealing.* This business was not linked to legitimate trade transactions. Gold dealing was subject to increasingly severe controls after World War II. London did not recognise any economic justification for Hong Kong's gold trade. But, eventually, it was to accept a political argument for tolerating this business.

London Backs Down

Allegations about Hong Kong's failure to enforce even its minimal obligations to the Sterling Area were made openly in the media and reported confidentially by British diplomats in the region soon after the war, and London began to express serious concern about the costs to the Sterling Area of Hong Kong's privileged position.[38] The colonial administration rejected allegations that Hong Kong was being used to escape from sterling assets vulnerable to devaluation by moving into the US dollar. More persuasively, it repeated Hong Kong's case for special treatment. Freedom from exchange controls was justified, colonial officials told London, because it arose out of Hong Kong's role as an entrepôt for the Mainland's trade with the US and, therefore, had nothing to do with the Sterling Area. This principle, they insisted, had already been accepted by the Colonial Office. London seemed unable to refute these arguments and withdrew its complaints.[39] The Colonial Office's climb-down reflected the political realities. Negotiations were under way with the Guomindang authorities for Hong Kong's cooperation in controlling Mainland black markets, as explained earlier in this chapter. London depended on the colonial administration to manage these complex financial discussions which, if mishandled, could have led to the collapse of the Hong Kong economy. When the colonial administration declared that the Sterling Area was not being damaged by the slack way in which Hong Kong administered exchange controls, London was in no position to contradict the Governor in the middle of the sensitive and very difficult bargaining with the Guomindang.[40]

Although London's pressures had been potentially very perilous to the colony's survival as a regional business and financial centre, the significance of Hong Kong's victory was not widely understood at the time.[41] A lengthy feature in the influential *Economist*, for example, depicted Hong Kong as a staunch defender of sterling. It claimed that exchange controls were now reinforced by the agreements made with the Guomindang to suppress smuggling and that the law was enforced so vigorously that the colony's normal trade was in danger. It was 'the last policeman on the perimeter of the Sterling Area', declared the article, and Hong Kong had 'already closed most of the leaks in the past year'. This was powerful — though misleading — reassurance for London officials.[42]

During the decade that followed, the Sterling Area— its rules and management — evolved considerably, and there were to be fresh alarms over Hong Kong's role as an escape route from the Sterling Area.[43] But the key precedent had been set, and Hong Kong officials reacted to later developments with considerable self-confidence. They displayed little deference towards their London counterparts and carefully calculated what moves would most benefit the colony, regardless of what would be in the UK's interests.[44] Significantly, in 1952, a draft exchange control law was circulated to all colonies for use as a model for local legislation.[45] All sixteen copies of the model ordinance received from London went into a government file in Hong Kong, never to be perused by anyone other than a registry clerk until the end of British rule.[46] A decade later, senior officials were displaying an equally offhand attitude towards London's circulars and instructions on the application of exchange controls.[47] Occasionally, an official within the colonial administration might develop a misplaced sense of economic patriotism and attempt to promote British interests. For example, one Director of Civil Aviation argued that since British aircraft were 'equally as suitable as the American counterparts', the Hong Kong flag-carrier, Cathay Pacific, should not be granted exchange control permission to place orders with US manufacturers. This plea to buy British failed.[48] After all, the Governor had personally instructed that exchange controls should be applied in Hong Kong as mildly as possible.[49]

Why did the Colonial Office and the Bank of England tolerate such a degree of unauthorised autonomy for Hong Kong? Part of the answer was that London could not oversee the colony effectively because of a lack of comprehensive statistical information about Hong Kong's international financial transactions. The Colonial Office tried to collect reliable balance of payments statistics to improve its management of the Sterling Area as the pound came under pressure in the early 1950s.[50] Demands for data were rejected outright by Hong Kong which viewed this statistical exercise as a ploy to increase London's monitoring of how exchange controls were enforced. When, in 1955, the Colonial Office repeated earlier requests for data about the balance of payments, a Hong Kong official replied that the colony would not cooperate because 'the [British] Treasury's main, if not sole, purpose for wanting the figures is … the detection of illegal movements between sterling and dollars through Hong Kong'.[51] Hong Kong's insubordination was made more tolerable by the fact that the limited statistics compiled by Hong Kong's exchange control officials during the period from 1954 to 1959 gave the impression that the local market was both orderly and stable and made no unreasonable demands on the Sterling Area's resources.[52] The data deficit was important in depriving London of the information it needed to monitor accurately the financial relationship between the colony and the UK.[53]

The Rise of Black Markets

The colonial administration had less luck in keeping the gold market in operation. 'Ill-considered articles' published in the *Far Eastern Economic Review* during 1948 'were much read in Whitehall'. According to the colonial administration, these reports led to orders from London to close the local gold market.[54] The colony did its best to argue that gold was an essential element in its financial markets and important to its banking business. London rejected these claims and demanded the total prohibition of gold transactions. The directive from the British minister responsible for the colony hinted that the colony should consider itself fortunate that the free market in hard currencies was not being closed down as well.[55] The ban meant that no lawful consignments of gold could be imported, and the trade withered almost immediately. So draconian were the new controls that jewellers could no longer display the agreed retail price for gold set by their association, and the media could no longer report gold prices, even on an historical basis. Ironically, the *Far Eastern Economic Review* fell foul of this regulation but was not prosecuted, possibly because the editor suggested that he might challenge its legality.[56]

In 1953, London authorised the import of gold once more but solely for transhipment. The Governor publicly described this concession as 'a small present' for gold merchants without revealing how they would benefit from gold that was strictly in transit.[57] The explanation soon emerged. The gold was flown to the nearby Portuguese enclave of Macao and then smuggled back again to Hong Kong. This illegal trade enabled the colony's gold market to revive quickly, as Chapter 7, 'A Dangerous Business Model', will explain. Hong Kong now became the centre for gold smuggling in Asia.

Official tolerance of this illegal activity highlighted the conflicting attitudes towards financial regulation. In the 1940s, exchange controls and the restrictions on gold dealing were still enforced. Customs officials showed some zeal in pursuing illegal movements of currency and gold, despite the bribes on offer for cooperating with the smugglers. The courts, however, proved 'uncooperative', officials complained, and prosecutors found it difficult to obtain convictions.[58] The police believed the new gold regulations would make it easier to tackle crime generally, and officers tried to enforce them. The problem, according to a senior policeman, was that, in the case of gold particularly, 'the ordinances … are incomprehensible to myself and fellow officers'. 'Native' banks, currency dealers and the smaller financial firms were ready to accept compulsory licensing and other controls.[59] They commanded a degree of respect, presumably because economic regulations in general were part of the war effort against Japan and had then played an obviously useful part in the period of post-war reconstruction. In contrast to the public's expectation in this period that laws should be obeyed, the colonial administration had no incentive to improve the legislation, partly because, confessed one senior official, controls 'are not of any particular benefit to Hong Kong' but imposed on the instructions of the UK.[60] The government showed no great enthusiasm for enforcing these measures, and the staff to administer them were recruited sparingly and deliberately employed on temporary terms.[61] Chapter 6 will show that as the credibility of financial regulation evaporated during the 1950s, an environment of cynicism, evasion and contempt for the letter of the law emerged that was to encourage the spread of misconduct among bank owners and executives and the rise of corruption in the decades that followed.

The Cold War Starts

As victory by the Chinese Communist Party loomed larger, Hong Kong did not foresee the radical change that was about to overtake its economic relationship with the Mainland. The previous chapter explained how officials became anxious about a potential collapse of investor confidence, yet business remained buoyant in 1948, the government reported.[62]

> Despite the rapidly deteriorating situation in China, the volume of trade passing through the Colony was greater than it had been in the year before, and there was no apparent lessening in the prosperity of the Colony… Towards the end of the year, a beginning was made in trading with Communist North China, and there are hopes that the trade will prosper …

Runaway inflation, the collapse of the Chinese economy in November that year and the worsening civil war did not lead to a sharp influx of immigrants, apart from wealthy businessmen from Shanghai and Nanjing.[63] Turmoil to the north of Hong Kong had come to seem a natural state of affairs. This complacency was shaken in 1949 when the Chinese Communist Party's victory became inevitable. In mid-1949, rumours were circulating that Hong Kong might be subject to a state of war, which some firms tried to use as an excuse to cancel their import contracts. Otherwise, the colonial administration did not have to deal with widespread panic.[64] The Financial Secretary summed up the colony's reaction:[65]

> … the crossing of the Yangtse by the People's Liberation Army [in 1949] accentuated the feeling of apprehension which was evident among large sections of the population, and a serious exchange crisis developed in May, when the Hong Kong dollar slumped momentarily to eight to the U.S. dollar on the free market. It was not long, however, before confidence was restored.

Emergency legislation was introduced in case Mao Zedong's victory was followed by hostile action against the colony, but a contemporary report observed: 'That there is a state of emergency in Hong Kong is hardly noticed by its citizens'.[66] Gloom only set in, as the previous chapter explained, when trade with the Mainland was brought to a halt in 1950. London, too, regarded Mainland developments with guarded optimism. British businesses in China might enjoy at least a honeymoon period in which the new rulers would want foreign firms to continue normal trading and production to keep the economy going.[67] Hong Kong, it was expected, would play an important part in maintaining British access to the Mainland.

The US viewed the impending military triumph of the Chinese Communist Party very differently.[68] Washington was worried about Hong Kong's role in supplying both the military and the economic needs of the Soviet Union and North Korea, as well as of China itself. Hong Kong was singled out as a special danger by American officials because of its efficiency as a port and its outstanding record in serving the Mainland. Washington wanted Hong Kong to separate itself economically from the Mainland once it became obvious in 1948 that the Guomindang would be defeated in the civil war. This would have been suicidal both for business and for the colonial administration. Washington then focused on blocking the Mainland's access through Hong Kong to overseas export and financial markets. London's response to Washington was sympathetic but unenthusiastic about measures that would endanger the colony's traditional role as a Chinese entrepôt. Only after North Korean troops attacked the south in 1950 did Hong Kong start to apply export controls to strategic goods.

The US' goal was not simply to prevent China from importing strategic supplies and to exclude it from the US domestic market. The embargo was intended to achieve the total isolation of China and its citizens by halting all their commercial and financial transactions with the outside world.[69] The Hong Kong factor made it impossible for London to cooperate with this policy. Apart from the damage to what remained of the entrepôt trade and the colony's dependence on Mainland food supplies, how could the British authorities divide ethnic Chinese residents into those who belonged to Hong Kong and those who belonged to the Mainland?[70] In practice, the US also found it impossible to make clear distinctions and simply mistrusted Hong Kong residents, whatever their race. Thus, the British nationality of a company's ownership and management did not deter American officials when they suspected that a Hong Kong firm was helping the Mainland to get around the US embargo. They conducted investigations in Hong Kong, intimidated the firms under suspicion and their clients, and froze any assets they held in American banks.[71] There was a certain even-handedness about this draconian approach since Washington froze the property of its own citizens if they resided in China. The Colonial Office preferred not to make a fuss about these incidents. It was better not to focus Washington's attention on how the embargo operated, London concluded, 'since the [US] State Department appeared to believe that Hong Kong's trade controls were very firm when in fact they were quite ineffective'.[72] Throughout the life of the embargo, American officials sought to close every possible Hong Kong loophole.[73] As a result, there was considerable tension between the colonial administration and the US Consulate General over its anti-communist activities.[74]

The Embargo Bites

China's military intervention in the Korean conflict led the US to ignore Hong Kong's political status as a British colony and to treat it as part of China's economy. Transhipments of Mainland products to the US were brought to a halt overnight. All American exports to Hong Kong were banned until licensed on a case-by-case basis. Theses US decisions displayed an awareness of Hong Kong's historical success in enabling the Mainland to maintain its access to the outside world, even in periods of armed conflict.

The US economic blockade, reinforced by the United Nations Korean War embargo, had a dramatic effect. China was driven out of world markets, and its principal trading partners were now members of the Soviet Bloc. Before 1949, these countries had accounted for less than one per cent of China's total trade. By 1953, they accounted for three-quarters of all Mainland foreign trade.[75] The pattern of trade also altered dramatically for Hong Kong. While imports from the Mainland hardly changed between 1951 and 1955, the colony's exports to this market fell by almost 90 per cent. The re-export trade was destroyed and with it the colony's traditional source of prosperity. Even more serious for the future, the ban on American shipments to Hong Kong cut off a major source of raw materials, particularly for the textile industry, just as the manufacturing sector was taking off. Worse still, Japan was able to continue to import cheap raw materials from the US, increasing its competitiveness against Hong Kong which was forced to rely on more expensive sources of supply.[76] (The crisis that now confronted Hong Kong, and the way the banks contributed to its solution, was explored in detail in the previous chapter.)

To restore normal commercial relations with the US, the colonial administration set about persuading Washington to treat Hong Kong as a trading partner totally distinct from the rest of China. Negotiations were long and arduous, as the US had to be convinced that the colony had transformed itself into a business centre whose economy was no longer integrated into the Mainland. There were two key issues on which the US had to be reassured:

- that the colonial administration could police the re-export trade to prevent the delivery to the People's Republic of China, North Korea and the Soviet Bloc of American products and strategic goods from other Western sources; and
- that a credible certification mechanism was in place to prevent local factories from using raw materials and other inputs from the Mainland in manufacturing exports for sale to the US.

Not until 1952 did American officials feel that these requirements were being met, allowing a return to a more normal trading relationship. Washington relaxed still further in 1953 after an armistice halted hostilities in Korea.

Nevertheless, the Cold War had forced the colonial administration to adopt a range of stringent controls demanded by the US, simply to survive.

A Regional Financial Centre

Paradoxically, the Cold War restrictions on China business helped Hong Kong to emerge as a regional financial centre. Washington froze the US dollar accounts of Mainland organisations and Chinese citizens in foreign banks, including HSBC, which aggravated these banks' difficulties in dealing with the new government in China.[77] Washington's policies also hit US banks which were now at a disadvantage in Hong Kong because they were unable to provide services for clients who had any connections with the Mainland, however tenuous. In addition, the fact that HSBC and other banks operating in Hong Kong were targets for punitive US measures made it easier for them to foster relationships with Chinese state-owned banks in the next two decades by aiding them to overcome Washington's restrictions on China's access to international financial facilities.

Hong Kong's status as a Sterling Area member was vital to the creation of these relationships. The Sterling Area and its banks, together with London's financial institutions, were beyond the reach of US law, and China's state-owned banks in the colony could carry on business within the Sterling Area free from the threat of Washington's sanctions. Thanks to the Hong Kong dollar, sterling became the currency of transaction for China's commercial and financial relations with countries outside the Soviet Bloc. Thus, the initial disruption which the US caused to Hong Kong's banking activities during the Cold War created the conditions for the emergence of a flourishing regional financial centre in the 1950s.

This development was also encouraged by London's decision in 1957 to ignore the fact that, because exchange controls were not enforced, the free currency market and much of Hong Kong's import and export trade were illegal. The colonial administration wanted the situation to be regularised because the contracts involved could not be enforced by the courts if there were a commercial dispute. The Colonial Office decided that any action to solve the problem might provoke fresh US paranoia about Hong Kong's relationship with the Mainland.[78] (This legal loophole, and the threat of unenforceable contracts, remained unresolved until legislation was introduced in 1967.[79]) Tolerance of one form of illegality made it difficult to take action against other, related activities which were unlawful. Thus, an unintended consequence of London's decision not to regularise the situation through legal means was a reduction of its own ability to prevent the expansion of Hong Kong's freedom from the Sterling Area's rules as it developed its international banking business.

A US investment project offered an important example of the colony's ability to turn the restrictions imposed by foreign governments to its own advantage. In the 1950s, there was sporadic discussion of whether Washington's guarantees for private American investments overseas could be extended to Hong Kong. In 1965, these negotiations were revived only to be held up by the Vietnamese War and US demands that ships bound for North Vietnam should not be allowed to use Hong Kong's port facilities. The colonial administration managed to reassure Washington on this issue, and an investment protection agreement was finalised.[80] Almost immediately, Mobil Oil applied for a US government guarantee to cover what was to be described as 'the world's largest private housing project': the construction of 15,000 middle-class apartments at a projected cost of HKD450 million on a 14-hectare site which Mobil had formerly used as an oil storage depot.[81]

This US corporation did not have to put up any hard cash, however. Its investment took the form of the site itself, which was valued at almost HKD90 million. The balance of the finance was to be obtained from banks in Hong Kong, either in the form of loans to underwrite the sales of apartments ahead of completion (or on mortgages) or through working capital covered by guarantees in New York. These arrangements were in breach of the exchange control regulations. The Financial Secretary personally explained to the developers that, although the government would not apply the regulations to this project, there would be a risk that if legal disputes arose, Hong Kong's courts might refuse to recognise contracts relating to the project because of this illegality. Mobil was undeterred by this prospect.[82] It was this sort of sympathy for business realities and this readiness to find ways around legal constraints in order to facilitate financial engineering that made Hong Kong so attractive to overseas banks. Mobil also demonstrated the importance of the liquidity loophole: the ability to create development finance through the banking system without insisting on physical transfers of foreign capital to Hong Kong, as most other Asian governments would have required. These features of the colony's financial arrangements made Hong Kong the most convenient centre for offshore financial business in the region, and they were the basis of Hong Kong's future role as an international financial centre, as will be explained in Chapter 9, 'From Banking Crisis to Financial Catastrophe'.

Cold War Gains

As long as the Cold War continued and China was the target of a US economic blockade, the colony was the Mainland's most secure centre for international financial transactions and its most reliable source of hard currency. The priority for Hong Kong officials and businessmen was to interpret the Sterling Area exchange controls so as to provide the maximum convenience for China's

Ministry of Finance and its bankers.[83] Circumventing the US blockade was made easier by the colonial administration's refusal to compile balance of payments and similar data.[84] Because of the colonial administration's desire to conceal China's financial activities in Hong Kong, the available banking statistics were made as uninformative as possible in the 1950s.[85] Thus, a sizeable money market grew up in this decade whose operations were largely hidden from contemporary observers, even though it financed a substantial share of China's import bill. These funds were available no matter how strained Beijing's relations were with the rest of the world or how disrupted the Mainland economy was by mass political campaigns. By the mid-1950s, as Table I shows, Hong Kong and Mainland bankers had created a new foreign exchange market in Hong Kong through which the Chinese government was able to buy substantial quantities of sterling which it could use freely and at its own discretion.[86]

For China's leaders, the ability to evade the US' embargo was only part of the agenda. A crucial factor for a centrally planned economy is predictability of inflows of foreign currency. China's receipts from the colony included profits from local assets and remittances from overseas Chinese. But the most important and reliable component was export earnings. The colony's imports of food, raw materials, light industrial products and consumer goods from the Mainland determined the principal costs of production for Hong Kong's exporters (apart from land). For this reason, China's state trading organisations had to keep their prices and thus the colony's production costs low enough to ensure that Hong Kong's domestic exports remained competitive abroad and, at the same time, to undercut any rival sources of these essential imports. The quantity that Hong Kong would import then depended on the performance of its export industries which drove the overall economy, and their growth was sustained and rapid from the early 1950s. The reliability of these Hong Kong dollar earnings allowed Chinese officials to plan the nation's import programme with some assurance in an otherwise highly uncertain world.[87]

The next stage in the process was to convert China's Hong Kong dollar receipts into its 'sterling offtake' (see Table I), which provided the Chinese government with significant amounts of what amounted to convertible currency. The colonial administration allowed China's state-owned banks to make these transactions with almost complete freedom from the constraints of exchange controls.[89] This willingness to bend the law in China's favour continued even during Beijing's worst confrontation with the colonial administration during the Maoist anti-British disturbances in 1967.[90]

A peculiar feature of this tolerance was the widespread ignorance of Hong Kong officials about how these arrangements worked.[91] The Bank of China's operations were an almost impenetrable mystery to the colonial administration. Officials mistrusted Mainland bank executives on political grounds and

Table I: China's Imports and its Sterling Offtake from Hong Kong,
1957–73 (USD million)[88]

Year	China's Total Imports	China's Sterling Offtake from Hong Kong	Offtake/ Imports (%)	Mainland Background
1957	1,510	255	17	Anti-rightist campaign
1958	1,890	266	14	'Great Leap Forward'
1959	2,120	244	12	Sino-Soviet split Natural disasters
1960	1,950	263	13	Natural disasters
1961	1,450	235	16	Natural disasters
1962	1,170	297	25	
1963	1,270	412	32	
1964	1,550	524	34	'Four Cleans' campaign
1965	2,020	636	31	
1966	2,250	714	35	Cultural Revolution
1967	2,020	641	35	Cultural Revolution
1968	1,950	667	34	Cultural Revolution
1969	1,830	679	37	Cultural Revolution
1970	2,330	840	36	Cultural Revolution
1971	2,210	938	42	Cultural Revolution US embargo ends
1972	2,860	1,246	44	Cultural Revolution Nixon visits Beijing
1973	5,160	1,311	25	Cultural Revolution

expected little cooperation from them.[92] They also suspected the Mainland of draining funds out of Hong Kong which should have been used for local business and investment, although senior officials declined to take action on the basis of these suspicions.[93] There was a general assumption that it was best not to interfere with the 'sterling offtake' and the banking arrangements that made it possible.[94]

Both foreign and well-established local Chinese-owned banks were active in this market from the start.[95] HSBC appears to have been the biggest player, nevertheless. In 1967, the political violence on the streets of Hong Kong caused a flight from the banks into cash and from the Hong Kong dollar into foreign currencies. A shortage of sterling developed in Hong Kong, which was an irony because everywhere else sterling was being dumped in anticipation of a devaluation (which occurred in November).[96] The Mainland was still ordering sterling in quantity, however, and HSBC began to fear that it would not be able to buy enough sterling to fulfil its contracts to supply the Bank of China. Fortunately, the political violence ended before the currency situation became desperate. HSBC officials had gone to great lengths to keep the Mainland's foreign exchange market in Hong Kong operating smoothly throughout 1967 — and not just for commercial reasons. The bank's executives understood that these exchange facilities were a major incentive for the Chinese Communist Party to tolerate the British colony in a period when every other concession to foreign imperialism and capitalism was being bitterly attacked throughout the Mainland by the Red Guards.[97]

Table I illustrates how this new financial market grew to be more useful to the Chinese government as the mass campaigns of the Maoist era intensified. The sterling obtained through Hong Kong covered a rising share of China's imports after the failure of the 1958 Great Leap Forward and the famine that followed which killed at least 20 million people between 1959 and 1961.[98] These financial arrangements were essential to maintain the flow of vital imports in this period of natural disasters, especially as the catastrophe was aggravated by the Sino-Soviet dispute and the disruption of economic relations with the Soviet Bloc. The arrangements became even more valuable during the Cultural Revolution (1966–76) which involved an estimated 20 million victims.[99] As this mass campaign got underway in 1966, it caused acute disruption to the domestic economy and led to Beijing's diplomatic isolation. The financial connection with Hong Kong continued to function, however. The volume of sterling obtained through the colony remained considerable for the following six years, as the country struggled first to survive the political turmoil and then to rebuild normal government structures. To maintain the real value of its sterling offtake after the 1967 devaluation of sterling and the continuing weakness of the pound, Beijing adopted a policy of active adjustment of the exchange rate between the RMB and the Hong Kong dollar in combination with sophisticated management of its export prices in the colony. The offtake started to decline in relative importance only in 1973. By this date, the Sterling Area had come to an end. Furthermore, China now had much more freedom in its trade with the rest of the world because the US had lifted its blockade in 1971.

But Hong Kong's usefulness was far from over. Final abolition of the blockade in 1971 ended the risk that the US government might block transactions and freeze assets that could be linked to the Mainland. A new danger now arose. US citizens had claims for debts incurred by the Manchu and Guomindang governments before the Chinese Communist Party came to power and for American-owned assets confiscated on the Mainland since 1949 which were estimated to be worth USD400 million.[100] Firms and individuals could start legal actions for compensation through seizures of Chinese state-owned planes, ships, bank balances and other property within the jurisdiction of US courts. Since China remained a centrally planned economy with its international trade conducted by state-owned agencies, export consignments to the US were also at risk. Sino-American negotiations to remove the complex legal dangers were protracted, and the threat of successful claims against the

Chinese government for bonds issued by the pre-1949 Mainland authorities was only removed in 1984.[101] During this period of legal uncertainty, Hong Kong provided a safe haven for transactions between the Mainland and the US, with China's state-owned banks in the colony creating special US dollar facilities, for example, and Mainland products destined for American markets being transhipped through Hong Kong's port.

Because of the continuing importance of the Hong Kong's contribution to China's foreign exchange earnings, Beijing made a determined effort to maintain the real value of receipts from the colony. When the colonial administration adopted a floating exchange rate in 1974, the RMB was tied to a basket of currencies. Beijing adjusted the rate between the RMB and the Hong Kong dollar almost simultaneously with movements in Hong Kong's exchange rate against major Western currencies. The Mainland's trade surplus with the colony was to become a vital source of funding for China's modernisation. Export earnings from Hong Kong were 'sufficient to cover four-fifths of the total trade deficit with the United States, Western Europe and Japan' during the challenging period of 1978–80 as Deng Xiaoping's 'open door policies' started the transformation of the Mainland's economic relations with the outside world.[102]

Conclusions

The immediate post-war years saw the creation of a framework of legal restraints and official regulation entirely alien to Hong Kong. Controls were mostly imported, usually inconvenient and sometimes damaging to the local economy. Except when under serious external pressure, neither the colonial administration nor the business community had any incentive to cooperate with them. For the economy as a whole, these restrictions had been removed by 1954, and a workable formula had also been agreed with the US to distinguish between exports of locally manufactured products — which were exempt from the American embargo — and Mainland products, which remained banned.[103]

But for the banks and the financial markets, government controls were to become a long-term influence on the business environment and a powerful force in shaping banking behaviour. All free market dealings in foreign currencies and gold were unlawful. This did not stop them from flourishing, but official tolerance of such blatant illegality encouraged a culture of contempt for the law. Bureaucrats and bankers came to disregard not only the controls forced on Hong Kong by foreign governments but also Hong Kong's own banking regulations and the legislation that applied to businesses in general. This tolerance of illegality will be a theme throughout the chapters that follow. At the same time, this chapter has shown how, as Hong Kong rebuilt itself after World War II and then had to adjust to the Cold War, the colonial administration came to believe that Hong Kong had little option but to accept the risks of misconduct and mismanagement within the financial community in order to avoid being stifled by foreign-imposed regulations.

After World War II, both Hong Kong and the UK had to recognise that no post-war Chinese government could tolerate a British colony that allowed its bankers and businessmen to ignore China's policies and priorities. Washington was determined to restrict Hong Kong's links with the Mainland as soon as the Cold War began. The colony's commitment to laisser faire and free trade allowed the government to claim a large measure of 'political neutrality', while membership of the Sterling Area enabled Hong Kong to circumvent US restrictions and establish a new economic relationship with the Mainland. The colony developed, as this chapter has shown, a financial market which provided China with the hard currency it needed, particularly in periods of acute political turmoil or economic disruption. By the end of the 1970s, Hong Kong had created the capacity to act as the principal source of external finance for China's modernisation during the rest of the century.

5

Industrial Take-off: Cut-price and Self-financed

When Guomindang rule collapsed and the Chinese Communist Party came to power in 1949, the state took control of the nation's foreign trade, and foreign investment was to be eliminated. The historical foundations of Hong Kong's prosperity vanished. The colony's economy did not disintegrate, however. Instead, it transformed itself into a manufacturing centre whose exports were soon to be regarded by the UK, the US, Germany and Canada as a major threat to their own domestic producers. This new lease of life came as a surprise to observers because, as a distinguished academic commented in 1956, the colony had few attractions for industrial investors.[1] Even more surprising to contemporaries was the sustained momentum of the manufacturing take-off as the new industries expanded beyond the wildest expectations of business leaders in the 1950s.[2]

Until relatively recently, specialists in development economics were not impressed by Hong Kong's prospects as an industrial city, and they took little interest in how this surprising transformation was engineered.[3] The usual approach is to describe the emergence of Hong Kong as a major textile producer in the 1950s as if it occurred through some form of' spontaneous combustion, with the entrepôt economy able to make a seamless, almost instantaneous, transition from trading to manufacturing. A Foreign Office sinologist-turned-businessman provides a typical example of this view of Hong Kong's industrial take-off.[4]

> The Hong Kong we know today is a creation of the years since the Second World War ... refugees ... provided the catalyst for Hong Kong to transform itself, virtually overnight, from a mere trading post to a manufacturing centre because they included a potent mixture of ordinary people in urgent need of a job, plus wealthy textile entrepreneurs from Shanghai looking for a way of starting up in business again.

The credibility of such 'miraculous' explanations has started to wane. In the absence of an authoritative body of economic analysis to account for Hong Kong's rise to prosperity, recent historians have turned to political and 'ideological' theories for an explanation of its 'economic miracle'. It has now become fashionable to depict Hong Kong's industrial take-off as a triumph of Chinese enterprise over colonial policies hostile to local manufacturers.[5] British banking and commercial interests are described as being afraid they would be overtaken by the Chinese business community if the economy switched from trade to industry.[6] The colonial administration is supposed to have been anxious, therefore, to hold back the advance of modern manufacturing. Furthermore, it has been alleged, the historical record has been manipulated by British attempts to give the credit for the post-war economic 'miracle' to their Shanghainese allies, while suppressing the role of the local Cantonese business community.[7]

In particular, the banks stand accused of cooperating with colonial efforts to stifle the growth of an independent industrial sector. The ideological debate about colonial economic policy has obscured the relationship between banking and economic development and diverted attention from crucial questions about the development process itself and how Hong Kong's industrial take-off after World War II was financed. Ironically, the debate parallels criticism made about the behaviour of Mainland banks before 1949 and the claims that 'they deliberately set up obstacles to China's modern industrial enterprises'.[8] (Chapter 2, 'Chinese Revolutionaries, Colonial Reformers', reviewed allegations that the Mainland banks contributed little to the country's industrial development because the banks were part of the Guomindang system for financing its régime.)

Unaided Growth

The colony's investment environment could hardly have been more discouraging after World War II. The victory of Mao Zedong, a communist pledged to the eradication of colonialism and capitalism from Chinese soil, was followed by the Korean War embargoes against China and the Cold War policies of the US.[9] Not surprisingly then, manufacturing attracted virtually no foreign direct investment during the 1950s, the colonial administration reported confidentially to London. Overseas capital was 'probably of the order of 5% [of total industrial investment] and certainly not more than 10%', it estimated, while total UK investment in the colony averaged less than HKD16 million a year at the end of the decade.[10] Furthermore, Hong Kong was unique among post-war Asian economies because it had no financial institutions, apart from the commercial banks, to provide industry with development or investment capital.[11] The colony had a long-established stock exchange, but this contributed virtually nothing to manufacturing industry in either the 1950s or the 1960s.[12] Foreign aid was almost non-existent, equivalent to a mere 0.28 per cent of total government expenditure between 1947 and 1968, a figure so low as to be a potential political embarrassment to the UK.[13]

Astonishingly, part of the explanation for the lack of external assistance was the colonial administration's refusal to borrow money even on concessionary terms from international agencies. Hong Kong's business leaders urged the colonial administration repeatedly to raise development funds through loans, particularly from overseas. On this issue, officials were particularly sensitive to public criticism, and they did their best to camouflage their reluctance to issue development bonds or to accept loans from such reputable international agencies as the World Bank. Thus, in 1950, the Financial Secretary argued that market conditions were highly unfavourable to floating a local loan and that borrowing in London was hampered by exchange control and other restrictions.[14] In 1960, another Financial Secretary argued that if Hong Kong applied to float a loan in London, the application would probably be rejected on the grounds that 'our rates of taxation are far too low; that there is plenty of money in the Colony; and that there are far more deserving applicants' for access to cheap funds.[15] Indeed, he later stated his belief that 'we do not need to borrow'.[16] By the end of the decade, a third Financial Secretary was fighting off complaints about the failure to borrow development funds to solve the financial bottlenecks impeding Hong Kong's progress. Once again, the government found excuses, this time in market resistance and technical difficulties to do with banking legislation.[17]

The colonial administration could not entirely ignore the business community's complaints about the failure to seek cheap development finance, and it approached the World Bank three times during the 1960s. On each occasion, the Financial Secretary reported, the World Bank had decided that Hong Kong did not need development loans.[18] In their comments on the prospect of World Bank or other loans, officials implied the colony would be willing to accept them if they were available on reasonable terms. But the colonial administration was less than frank with its hand-picked legislators, as well as with the community. Senior officials had no intention of accepting World Bank finance because they were afraid of the consequences for the colonial administration's style of economic management. They feared the World Bank would resume the battle for a modern taxation system from which the Colonial Office had retreated (an issue discussed in chapter 3, 'Post-war Emergencies: from Boom to Bust'). The World Bank would also insist on modern statistics, another fight with Hong Kong which the Colonial Office had abandoned. Similarly, the government refused help from the US during the desperate water shortage of the 1960s because of the reporting and statistical requirements that the donor would expect.[19] The truth was that the colony could have raised funds from overseas, as was made clear in a 1967

World Bank report whose findings were not released to the public. Despite unfavourable conditions on capital markets and the political uncertainties created by the extremism of China's Cultural Revolution (1966–76) then spilling over into Hong Kong, the bank's team concluded that 'the financial strength of the Colony would permit a considerable amount of outside borrowing'. 'There remains little doubt that Hong Kong could assume large amounts of debt on conventional terms', it added.[20]

Self-help and Self-reliance

Hong Kong had locked itself into a policy of self-help because it looked on finance from overseas as a threat to the colony's financial autonomy. This attitude had surfaced first during economic reconstruction after World War II. In that period, officials initially favoured direct help for industry. In mid-1947, a future Financial Secretary, J. J. (later Sir John) Cowperthwaite, expressed concern that 'local industry, which is of increasing importance, is finding it difficult to recover and retain even its pre-war markets owing largely to excessive costs'. He believed that there was a case for 'the provision of interest-free or low-interest loans for the rehabilitation of existing or the installation of new industries'.[21] Nevertheless, he saw no contradiction in persuading senior officials that the colony had nothing to gain either from seeking overseas development assistance or from implementing development projects sponsored by London. He argued that external development assistance would not be economically neutral. It would always be geared to the national interests of the donor, he declared. But, most persuasive of all, he insisted, unlike most colonies, Hong Kong did not need the money.[22]

> Hong Kong ... does not suffer from lack of capital ... and it is largely true that any worthwhile project will find local backers. I am doubtful in any case of the economic wisdom of bringing in outside capital, the return on which leaves the Colony, if it is not strictly necessary ... One of Hong Kong's advantages over less developed colonies is that wealth has tended to remain here rather than return in the shape of dividends to the U. K ... from Hong Kong's point of view we should stand on our own feet and will be all the better for it in the long run. There is still a certain enterprising spirit abroad here; without it Hong Kong might as well pack up.

This self-confident declaration of Hong Kong's capacity for self-financed industrialisation convinced the Governor. He told the Colonial Office in 1950 that the pressing need of local firms was for help with overseas trade promotion; they could manage their financial business unaided.[23] Cowperthwaite's analysis was to dominate the government's response to lobbying from industrialists for subsidised funds over the next quarter of a century.

The business community did not share the colonial administration's belief in self-reliance, and its representatives demanded an industrial development programme similar to the strategies adopted by most other Asian governments, including Malaya (now Malaysia) and Singapore which were still under British rule. The top priority should be cheap finance and other incentives to promote manufacturing. In addition, the government should take steps to 'guide' industrial expansion and restrain 'excessive' or 'cut-throat' competition among local manufacturers.[24] These demands were repeatedly rejected by the colonial administration. It has become fashionable, it was noted earlier, to explain the colonial administration's refusal to finance industrial development as the result of a conspiracy between expatriate officials and the British-dominated financial and commercial sectors to obstruct the rise of a new Chinese manufacturing class which might challenge British political supremacy.[25] In reality, the leading British trading firms joined forces with Cantonese and Shanghainese manufacturers in a protracted campaign for direct measures to aid local industries, including subsidised finance for long-term projects and heavy industry.[26] This business coalition forced the colonial administration to set up a committee in 1959 to review the case for an industrial development corporation or bank.[27] Cowperthwaite, although not yet Financial Secretary, dominated the committee, and its report demolished the arguments in favour of state provision of industrial finance.[28]

- Hong Kong could not be shown to lack investment funds, and the evidence available demonstrated that no reasonable loan request from industry was being denied bank facilities.[29]
- An industrial bank in Hong Kong would divert resources away from booming, export-driven light industry into longer-term projects. These would not be viable unless they were provided with capital at below market cost, which seemed an unnecessary waste of economic resources.

These conclusions were so crushing that not for another decade did the business community mobilise enough support to resume the campaign. It was only after Cowperthwaite's retirement that a scheme was adopted to aid smaller enterprises in 1972.[30] It was wound up in 1976, after failing to produce satisfactory results, and not revived until after 1997.[31]

The Making of a Myth

The conflict over industrial financing reflects the confusion that surrounds the origins of Hong Kong's economic take-off. Did Hong Kong undergo an 'industrial revolution' after World War II, a 'big bang' that was propelled largely by wealthy, well-educated, Westernised entrepreneurs from Shanghai?[32] Or was growth 'organic', generated principally by Cantonese industrialists whose manufacturing facilities had begun to expand rapidly before the war? From the very start of the colony's transition from Mainland trade to global manufacturing centre, Hong Kong's industrial traditions were widely overlooked. The drama unfolding in post-war China pushed into the background the colony's first industrial boom that had followed the start of Japan's open war against China in 1937 and, subsequently, the outbreak of World War II in 1939. Memories of the pre-war foundations of Hong Kong's manufacturing sector almost disappeared as Hong Kong's 'industrial revolution' became Asia's first economic 'miracle' in the 1950s and the stuff of legend.

In the early post-war years, Hong Kong seemed poised, for the first time, to catch up with Shanghai, the nation's richest and most attractive city. This alluring prospect was fuelled not just by that city's decline as an international financial centre (described in Chapter 3) but also by a flight of Mainland industrialists to Hong Kong between 1947 and 1949, in search of refuge both from the civil war and from their apprehensions about the Chinese Communist Party's intentions towards capitalism.[33] The catalyst for the manufacturing take-off was said to be the arrival of refugee textile tycoons from Shanghai with ample capital and considerable technical expertise soon after British rule was restored in 1945. These newcomers have been depicted as specially endowed with the expertise to exploit cheap refugee labour and to mentor an army of would-be entrepreneurs, while the Chinese community's cultural heritage provided the appropriate apolitical, business ethos.[34] Thus was born the belief that Shanghai talent enabled Hong Kong to become, almost overnight, a major source of the Western world's textile imports. The absence of reliable official statistics about industrial activity and the economy's rate of growth in the 1950s allowed this myth to proliferate.[35]

The Governor, Sir Alexander Grantham, endorsed the legend. 'It was the Shanghai-Chinese businessmen, with their capital and their industrial know-how', his memoirs claimed, 'who were largely the economic salvation of Hong Kong'.[36] Despite such distinguished patronage, this mistaken view of Hong Kong's history should not have survived. The senior official responsible for commercial and industrial affairs in the 1950s described the post-war expansion of manufacturing as 'almost incredible' but argued that Hong Kong's industrialisation could be traced back to the previous century. 'It shows just how short and fallible human memory can be', he declared, 'that people generally assume nowadays that our cotton spinning industry dates back only to 1947 [i.e., and the first Shanghainese cotton mills]'.[37] The best-known Hong Kong economist of the decade declared that 'the present widespread industrial development actually started in the 1930s, and was renewed and accelerated after the break caused by the Japanese occupation'.[38] By 1975, academic research had convincingly debunked the claim that Hong Kong's 'industrial revolution' only got under way after World War II.[39] But the myth continues.[40]

Its persistence complicates the task of explaining how the 'industrial revolution' was financed, as the following sections will show.

Shanghai Billionaires

The influx of 'Shanghai billionaires' began almost immediately after the reestablishment of British rule.[41] The Hong Kong community had mixed views about the role of these tycoons. Over the next three years, the sensation of 'the seemingly unending stream of Shanghai billionaires' brought a new glamour to the formerly staid colony whose business landscape they seemed to dominate.[42] Contemporary observers were struck by the 'hundreds of new and mostly modern and efficiently conceived and run factories [which] were established whose existence … is bound to transform the economic nature of the Colony and to place it on a more sound basis'.[43] At the same time, the newcomers from Shanghai were seen as a 'not altogether desirable lot' because 'the great majority [are] financial and commercial adventurers whose activities can only be watched with misgivings'.[44] The complaint was that the bulk of the Shanghai flight capital was devoted to 'any imaginable form of speculation' — principally real estate.[45] 'Only a relatively small number of these opulent immigrants', it was alleged, 'think of business in terms of ordinary trade [and] manufacturing'.[46]

To be fair, the Shanghai entrepreneurs made a major contribution to industrial development. Their spinning mills formed the colony's first large-scale manufacturing sector equipped with world-class technology.[47] The total cost of these new factories was estimated at HKD150 million in 1947–48 (equivalent to 91 per cent of government spending in that financial year). The Shanghai entrepreneurs were not entirely self-financed. They enjoyed a degree of government subsidy that came not from the colonial administration but from the Guomindang, which was still in power. The immigrants made their purchases of advanced textile machinery from abroad with Mainland funds, including cheap foreign exchange allocated by the Guomindang to support national industries during the war against Japan.[48] Not surprisingly, Guomindang officials and newspapers attacked the Shanghainese for a lack of patriotism, although these transactions were facilitated by administrative chaos on the Mainland. Not surprising, either, was the expectation of this group that the colonial administration ought to show a similar generosity towards industrialists who set up plants in Hong Kong by providing the concessions and incentives that manufacturers demanded.[49]

Contemporary comment suggests that the arrival of these entrepreneurs in Hong Kong was not triggered solely by the corruption and mounting chaos on the Mainland under Guomindang rule. Hong Kong offered them the prospect of a considerable market from among the 750 local weaving and knitting factories which had been set up before World War II. The original plan was that the new cotton mills would meet the demands of the local market and leave a small surplus for export. In fact, their overseas sales boomed, and from the mid-1950s, the UK led Western countries in seeking to restrict Hong Kong textile shipments.[50]

Hong Kong did not remain indefinitely an exporter of cotton yarn and grey cloth produced in Shanghai-owned enterprises. The momentum of industrialisation depended, even in its early stages, on diversifying into higher value products. Local Cantonese knitting and weaving factories, a high proportion of them established well before 1949, soon took over from the Shanghainese cotton mills as the main source of manufactured exports.[51] In 1953, Shanghainese textile firms accounted for perhaps 36 per cent of total domestic exports and Cantonese textile producers for 28 per cent. By 1960, the Shanghai share was down to 22 per cent, while the Cantonese textile producers may have accounted for 39 per cent of total domestic exports.[52] This summary account of high-speed manufacturing growth in the 1950s indicates that the initial Shanghainese investment was relatively large but confined to a single, capital-intensive sector of the textile industry. Shanghai entrepreneurs were not viewed by contemporaries as being much involved in other types of industrial activity. In any case, census data demonstrate that the immigrants from Shanghai were too small a community to have engineered the dramatic changes in Hong Kong's economy during that decade so often attributed to them.[53]

Much of the mystery about the origins of Hong Kong's manufacturing take-off arises from confusion about how it was financed. If the Shanghainese contribution to Hong Kong's industrial take-off had been as large as legend claims, industrial finance ought to have presented no great problem. The 'Shanghai billionaires' should have been able to fund the process relatively comfortably from their own resources. But neither contemporary accounts nor later commentaries have suggested that the Shanghainese paid most of the bill. On the contrary, a variety of other sources of industrial capital have been proposed. An influx of external funds, notably flight capital from the Mainland, is said to have played a major role.[54] In fact, manufacturing seems to have attracted very little of the 'hot money' that arrived in the early post-war years. 'Such funds either remained idle (*sic*) within the banking system', one scholar has observed, 'or else were invested in speculative activities such as real estate, stocks, and bullion hoarding'.[55] This view is in line with the contemporary anecdotal evidence, as well as with the analysis presented earlier in this chapter. The Overseas Chinese are often identified as another source of finance for industrialisation. Reportedly, these funds included not only family remittances but also funds escaping from armed conflict in Indochina, racial discrimination in the Philippines and Thailand, and political tensions in Singapore and the states that were to form Malaysia.[56] It is hard to see how these funds would have made their way directly into start-up factories in the 1950s. Nor is it clear why 'flight capital' should tie itself up in manufacturing, given the political and commercial uncertainties of the colony in that decade.[57]

In practical terms, the bulk of inflows from the Mainland, together with other 'hot money' and 'flight capital', would have found a first home within the banking system. It was pointed out earlier that the colony had no institutional arrangements for funding industry other than the banks.[58] But this was not a handicap in Hong Kong's case. To quote an early investigation of how Hong Kong financed its economic modernisation,[59]

> … the availability of commercial bank loans, and advances virtually from the start of industrialization — often to relatively untried businesses against little security — has contributed to the rapid success of industrial development. The Hong Kong commercial banks have, to some degree, accepted risks which elsewhere are the responsibility of equity investors.

This analysis was in line with the 1967 World Bank review of the colony. Its authors accepted the prevailing wisdom that industrial take-off had got underway with the aid of refugee Chinese capital. But they recognised the special contribution of the banks 'which had channelled considerable amounts of funds to manufacturing'. The report also noted the importance of 'medium-term suppliers' credits and direct investments', together with high rates of domestic savings.[60] Part of these funds would have reached the factories through the banking system although this new manufacturing class was not particularly welcomed by the local Chinese-owned banks.[61] Even HSBC and the foreign-owned banks were initially hesitant about this new source of business, despite their experience of lending to industry on the Mainland before 1949. The lukewarm response of the banking industry as a whole to the early period of post-war industrialisation has added to the confusion about how it was paid for and encouraged the view that the bankers were part of a colonial conspiracy against the 'industrial revolution'.

Reluctant Lenders

Bankers were slow to recognise that lending to the colony's industrialists offered the most traditional and conservative sort of banking and that the headlong expansion of manufacturing would transform their business opportunities.[62]. When a bank provided a Hong Kong factory with trade finance and short-term capital, the loans would be safe and rapidly self-liquidating because they were secured against export orders to be produced and shipped within a short period. The bank could also get additional income from foreign currency transactions when the factory was paid by its overseas customers and also if it imported machinery and raw materials. Thus, credit risk was low and simple to manage, while profits were attractive. Bankers ought to have welcomed the buoyant demand for credit from industrialists, as the transition from trading port to manufacturing gathered pace. In practice, banks in general proved far from enthusiastic about doing business with factory owners. Each of the four different banking groups had its own reasons for keeping the industrialists at a distance.

When the Chinese Communist Party came to power in 1949, the state took control of the Mainland's financial system, including the Hong Kong branches of China's banks. Although several of these had considerable experience on the Mainland of lending to industry, especially to Shanghai's textile producers, Hong Kong was unable to take advantage of this expertise in the 1950s.[63] Now under state control, the first priority of these banks was to serve the national interests of China in its overseas financial and commercial activities, which meant that their involvement in the domestic 'capitalist' economy of the colony was minimal. Their principal contribution to the creation of Hong Kong's modern economy was to come later and from participation in the development of its international financial centre.

Otherwise, their available banking resources in Hong Kong were reserved for Mainland-related activities. So much so that the Commissioner of Banking proposed the introduction of legislation in the 1960s to compel this group of banks to lend a minimum proportion of their local deposits for use in Hong Kong.[64] This proposal, though never implemented, is an indication of how isolated this group of banks was from the new Hong Kong economy based on manufacturing for export.

Local Chinese-owned banks ought to have had little difficulty in competing for the new manufacturing customers, and there was an assumption that these banks were a strong source of support for the smaller Hong Kong manufacturer.[65] Yet, they had little appetite for developing trade-based facilities for the local industrialist.[66] HSBC once accused local bankers of providing any 'fly-by-night manufacturer' with easy loans.[67] The evidence for such a commitment to manufacturing by local bankers is far from abundant. The Hang Seng Bank has claimed that in the early post-war period, it lent to small factories 'without a balance sheet or any data to support their loan requests'.[68] Such a policy, however, would have been quite exceptional.

The reality was that local Chinese banking relied very heavily on personal connections. A well-run institution like the Bank of East Asia was very cautious, not just in making loans but in deciding who was permitted to open an account.[69] The typical manufacturer was a new entrepreneur without the sort of business background that would have created a prior relationship with a local banker. In any case, the new industrialists would not have been so easy for a local Chinese-owned bank to serve. They exported to countries where modern commercial banking prevailed and in which transactions had to comply with increasingly strict import and export procedures. These were orderly markets, very different from the Mainland conditions in which local bankers had grown up and flourished before 1949. The average local Chinese-owned bank, as Chapter 7, 'A Dangerous Business Model', will explain, preferred the patterns of the past: financing gold and currency deals and lending to related parties for property projects in particular. Furthermore, unlike personal or property loans, a local Chinese-owned bank could not charge a premium for manufacturing facilities. Industrialists could obtain alternative finance at least as cheaply from HSBC or the foreign-owned banks. Industrial loans also involved a different kind of credit which was not secured by assets in the form of gold, currency or real estate, which were key elements in the local Chinese-owned banks' business model. Increasingly in the 1950s, these banks came to regard property as their priority, particularly after the introduction of instalment terms for the sale of new multi-storey residential flats. Quite simply, local bankers stuck to their traditional business model in which the finance of manufacturing for export to Western markets had played little part.[70]

The local Chinese-owned banks' loyalty to their traditional business created considerable opportunities for their British rivals. An academic generally critical of the colonial record in promoting industry has praised leading British banks and merchant houses for a willingness to relax the normal lending criteria in financing new industries. He has credited this positive approach to industry with making a major contribution to the growth of manufacturing after the entrepôt trade collapsed.[71] While a trading firm like China Engineers has already been shown to have displayed considerable initiative in solving the financial problems of new industrialists, the role of HSBC, the colony's largest 'British' bank, was more complex.

There were risks in lending to manufacturers with limited track records and little experience of Western markets. HSBC had the resources to manage these risks. Its local deposit base was larger and cheaper than any other financial institution in the colony because the confidence of the Chinese community in its sound management and solvency gave it a powerful pull in mobilising the public's deposits. HSBC also benefited from considerable monopolistic advantages because of its size and its special relationship with the colonial administration in the absence of a central bank.[72] Yet, lending to local industry was an innovation that did not come naturally to this very British banking institution. The obstacle was not commercial considerations but the powerful influence on its executives of the expatriate culture of the China treaty ports. Traditionally, the bank had given priority to British firms and Westernised clients. Only in Shanghai had HSBC's expatriate staff been willing to treat the Chinese entrepreneur as a social equal. In Hong Kong, they preferred to transact business with Chinese customers through compradors and other intermediaries. The provision of banking services to local industrialists thus came cautiously in the 1950s, and so did the appointment of Chinese managers.[73] In the 1960s, the gulf between the bank's British staff and Chinese businesses was still wide.[74] As the head of HSBC's Hong Kong operations admitted, there was a 'fear' among 'local businessmen of approaching the Hongkong Bank for money'.[75]

Profits from industrial lending had started to accelerate from 1955 but, even then, the bank remained slow to commit staff resources to this business until the end of the decade. Nevertheless, industrial financing appears to have been highly profitable,[76] and for all its racial prejudice, HSBC's senior management was profit-driven. Although there is some evidence of bank executives agreeing to finance a factory on the grounds that local industry ought to be promoted, a key criterion in making loans was the firm's 'foreign exchange turnover' — 'one of the most lucrative sources of bank profits in Hong Kong' — and the borrower's agreement to give this business to HSBC.[77] With this sort of hard-headed approach, its business model was modified to match the new market realities. Hong Kong's leading banking economist believes that HSBC was the largest single lender to local manufacturers and may have provided as much as half of industry's bank finance during the 1950s.[78]

Foreign Advantages

Before World War II, foreign banks had considerable experience of financing modern factories in China. But their relations had been mainly with the foreign-owned companies that had accounted for over 60 per cent of the Mainland's total industrial capital in 1936.[79] They thus brought to post-war Hong Kong much the same cultural legacy as HSBC, although they benefited considerably from their connections with Hong Kong's new export markets in Western Europe and North America. At the same time, they enjoyed a major advantage over both HSBC and local Chinese banks in lending to the growing industrial sector, thanks to the liquidity loophole. (This issue is discussed more fully in Chapter 11, 'The Exceptional Colony'.) Until the 1964 Banking Ordinance, there were no legal restrictions on bank lending and no statutory requirements to impose a minimum level of liquidity. HSBC, together with the local Chinese banks, had a powerful incentive to adopt voluntary minimum liquidity ratios because they had to keep a safe margin of deposits over outstanding loans in order to meet demands from their customers for cash. Given Hong Kong's political uncertainties and the fragility of its markets overseas, a liquidity crisis was hard to predict and potentially catastrophic. If a bank lent an excessive proportion of its deposits, the colony had no central bank or lender of last resort to rescue it during a liquidity crisis. Overnight funds could be arranged with a 'clearing bank' but at a hefty premium. HSBC or Chartered Bank might come to a bank's assistance during a run but on strictly commercial terms, and in the 1950s, banks which ran out of funds went into liquidation. Even HSBC could not regard itself as invulnerable. Its headquarters was in the colony, and it had no overseas parent to bail it out. It is not accidental that the available statistical evidence shows HSBC to have clung tenaciously to a self-imposed liquidity ratio well above statutory minimum levels.[80]

Foreign-owned banks were in a very different situation. Chapter 11 will explain how banks with their headquarters overseas could cover the liquidity requirements of their Hong Kong branches comfortably through credit facilities made available to them in London and New York because their branches in the colony formed a very small fraction of their global portfolios. The only constraints on the branches' local lending, therefore, were commercial prudence and their ability to borrow Hong Kong dollars with which to meet the normal demand for cash from their customers. They were able to obtain this local currency through the inter-bank market, which allowed them to build up a Hong Kong customer base with the aid of funds lent to them by local Chinese banks.[81] Even after the 1964 Banking Ordinance set a minimum liquidity ratio, foreign banks were effectively exempt from this requirement, as one official explained in confidence to his colleagues.[82]

> … foreign banks branches in Hong Kong are subject to the Banking Ordinance on their business as a separate entity, but funds at call with their Head Office count as a liquid asset. The deposits with their Head Office abroad can be created without the funds actually being transferred over the exchanges so that what it really enables them to do is to finance their business in Hong Kong on local money rather than bringing in their local capital from Japan or America.

There was one potential obstacle to this practice. Until the end of the Sterling Area in 1972, exchange controls should have compelled foreign banks to bring in capital from overseas, while the profits paid to head office by a Hong Kong branch should have been subject to exchange control approval. In practice, foreign banks were never subject to such restrictions.[83] This freedom from exchange controls enabled the liquidity loophole to function smoothly, and it meant that foreign banks could expand their loans in the colony on the basis of a paper transaction with head office. As a result, they were ready to let their loans exceed their deposit base. This liquidity loophole was particularly convenient for financing the industrial transformation of Hong Kong in the 1950s. As was explained earlier in this chapter, there was very little foreign direct investment and no aid from abroad. The foreign-owned banks' liberal attitude towards credit creation helps to explain why the rapid expansion of manufacturing for export was not handicapped by the shortage of capital typical of most Third World economies at that time.

The Statistical Evidence

Published banking data are limited and subject to considerable reservations about their accuracy and coverage before the end of 1964 when the Banking Commission started monthly statistical surveys.[84] The Commission's data were collected for internal use only. They were comprehensive and consistent but are accessible only for a limited number of years and on a restricted range of issues. There are other scattered statistics of variable quality. Nevertheless, these disparate data provide considerable corroboration of the analysis which has been presented so far in this chapter.

Hong Kong's leading banking economist has estimated that during the 1950s, over 60 per cent of total bank loans to industry were allocated to textile manufacturers. He has also calculated that the overall ratio of loans to deposits rose from 48 per cent in 1954 to 70 per cent a decade later, 'reflecting a shift from a generally conservative to a more aggressive posture on the part of the banks to accommodate the increasing loan demand in a growing economy'.[85] An official survey calculated that industry accounted for 18 per cent of total bank loans at the end of 1958 and 21 per cent a year later.[86] It is a fair conclusion from these statistics, despite their drawbacks and defects, that the banking system had responded to the needs of manufacturers in the 1950s and of textile producers in particular.

Once reliable banking statistics became available from the Banking Commission in 1964, manufacturing was seen to take a lower share of total bank lending than its contribution to GDP (and the share declined in the following two decades). These statistics have been taken as evidence of unfair treatment of manufacturers' needs.[87] But critics did not realise that, in supplying statistics to the government, bankers could not easily distinguish between commercial and industrial loans because the loan to a manufacturer almost always involved financing a production run that had been sold in advance to a foreign importer.[88] Thus, loans classified as intended for import or export purposes would have included advances to industry which were used in support of production.

Criticism of the banks' lending policies based on the Banking Commission's data ignores the special characteristics of Hong Kong industry and the type of loan facilities it required. Manufacturing was concentrated overwhelmingly in the light industrial sector, with the bulk of its output sold overseas. The typical factory only started a production run after a foreign buyer had placed a firm order. Output was for immediate sale and not for stock, which meant that the factory could finance its operations through letters of credit and other short-term bank facilities. Turnover, both physical and financial, was rapid. Over a year, a bank loan facility could thus support a much higher level of production in manufacturing than the same sum lent to other sectors, property and construction in particular.

The Liquidity Loophole

Accurate information on the liquidity policies of individual banks only became available from 1964 after the establishment of the Banking Commission. These statistics, which were not released to the public, showed what a difference the liquidity loophole made to the lending behaviour of the foreign-owned bank sector. These banks felt able to create credit far more generously than HSBC or the other two groups of banks (see Table I). In 1964, out of the 35 foreign-owned banks, 11 had loan books which exceeded the total value of their deposits. Only six out of the 38 local Chinese-owned banks had such high loan/deposit ratios (and they were to come under serious strain during the bank runs which began in early 1965). The 13 China state-owned banks had the lowest ratio, reflecting the conservatism which they shared with HSBC (whose ratio was 58 per cent), as well as their lack of participation in the general business of Hong Kong and their strict focus on Mainland-related activities.

Table I: **Ratio of Bank Loans to Deposits, December 1964 (percentages)**[89]

All banks	67
China state-owned banks	51
Local Chinese-owned banks	73
HSBC	58
Foreign-owned banks	81

The Factories' Foreign Friends

Accurate information as to which banks did most to support local manufacturers was not collated by the Banking Commission until 1969, by which time Hong Kong had become a mature manufacturing economy. Industry had offered banks ample opportunities for prudent but profitable lending from the start of the post-war manufacturing take-off, but the risks of lending to industry had been reduced even further by the restrictive practices that followed in the wake of Western protectionism from the 1950s. The colony had transformed the import restrictions imposed by foreign countries into a smoothly operating system which reduced competition both internally and overseas, and the colonial administration had set up a structure of export controls which favoured existing producers and exporters. New entrants were forced to pay a heavy premium to obtain export quota rights, which deterred ruinous price-cutting among local manufacturers. Hong Kong's access to Western textile markets was protected by formal agreements based on past performance, which potential competitors from lower-cost Third World producers did not enjoy. In addition, it was only the volume of Hong Kong exports that was subject to restraint, which encouraged local manufacturers to move up-market because their best hope of improving their sales overseas was through increasing the value of their products.[90]

The appetite for industrial finance had not diminished in the 1960s, and manufacturers' complaints about an inadequate supply of bank loans were to rise to a new crescendo. At the same time, as Chapter 7 will describe, the lending opportunities of local Chinese-owned banks had been reduced by the collapse of the property sector, which was a major element in their business model. Interest in financing manufacturers should have been considerable. Yet, Table II shows how low the priority of industry was with the local Chinese-owned banks in 1969, the first year for which data are available. They lent almost the same amount to building and construction as to manufacturing, while personal lending accounted for 31 per cent of their total lending, compared with only 13 per cent for industry. The China state-owned banks remained detached from the domestic economy, and 58 percent of this group's lending went to finance import, export and wholesale trade.

It was left to the foreign-owned banks and HSBC to finance the factories. Of their total loans and advances, 22 per cent went to manufacturing, and this accounted for 76 per cent of all bank lending to this sector.

Table II: Loans and Advances by Bank Group and Purpose in 1969 (HKD millions)[91]

Banks	Manufacturing	Import, Export & Wholesale	Retail Trade	Building & Construction	Stock Brokers	Professional & Private Individuals	Total
All banks	1,490	2,666	179	803	63	1,004	7,884
China state-owned	55	329	30	47	–	49	570
Local Chinese-owned	303	552	35	307	33	706	2,263
HSBC & foreign-owned	1,132	1,785	114	449	29	249	5,051

Note: The 'Total' column includes items not otherwise listed in the table.

Cut-price Industrialisation

Another important feature of Hong Kong's industrialisation was its relative cheapness. Rapid economic growth could be financed without either state subsidies or foreign aid because this 'industrial revolution' was affordable. As the Industrial Bank Committee pointed out in 1960, Hong Kong's development model required less capital than other developing economies where central planners generally favoured heavy industry or large-scale infrastructure projects. The colony's concentration on light industry meant low capital/output ratios, full employment, rapid repayment of loans and a high turnover of capital.[92] In consequence, the banks had the capacity to meet manufacturing's capital requirements.

In addition, the cost of maintaining the sustained industrial expansion in the 1950s almost certainly declined in relative terms. This cut-price stage of the 'industrial revolution' was propelled by local Cantonese entrepreneurs. A fair proportion of their garment factories, it was noted earlier, was long established and can be assumed to have built up their production capacity over a number of years, using accumulated profits and other personal resources. From at least 1953, manufacturers were able to improve significantly their efficiency, the range and value of their goods and their labour productivity.[93] Furthermore, in this second stage of the industrial take-off, the new textile factories were much smaller than the typical spinning mill and required little capital, most of which was invested in machinery that was operated intensively.[94] Other new industries, which were to play a less conspicuous part in Hong Kong's industrialisation, followed much the same pattern. The average factory in the plastics industry, for example, used simple technology and cheap machinery, did not have to buy raw materials in bulk and could operate efficiently in small premises.[95]

The limited data available about industry's investment behaviour support this picture of manufacturing being expanded on the cheap. The official estimates of capital formation in the 1950s were described by the government's Statistical Branch as 'in an elementary and incomplete stage' and mostly suffering from a 'lack of precision'.[96] Nevertheless, as Table III shows, they provide clear indications of how little capital was required to fuel the manufacturing boom in that decade. Particularly striking is how 'cheap' the high-growth garment sector was in terms of the machinery it required compared with the rest of the textile industry. As a result, the entry costs for would-be industrialists were low, and money poured into manufacturing regardless of the high risks of failure.[97] Investors typically tried to minimise their capital outlay by operating in domestic tenements, squatter areas and

Table III: Industrial Capital Formation during the 1950s:
Private Sector Annual Average (HKD millions)[99]

	Period	Manufacturing
Factory and godown buildings	1950–59	14.6
Textile machinery	1955–59	19.7
Garment machinery	1955–59	5.4
Electric machinery	1955–59	20.9
Other mining, construction and industrial machinery	1955–59	62.8

other illegal premises, which officials tolerated because of the total contribution to the economy from these enterprises.[98] Thus, industry's demand for buildings was remarkably low, especially when compared with the annual investment in private residential buildings, which averaged HKD106 million a year during the 1950s.

Conclusions

The persistent claim that industrial growth was handicapped by a lack of financial support has helped to conceal how, behind the breakneck growth, there was an incremental process at work. This chapter has argued that the expansion of manufacturing for export during the 1950s did not depend principally on an injection of Shanghai capital and entrepreneurial talent. This 'industrial revolution' built on foundations already established before World War II. It was misinterpreted as a 'big bang' because of the data deficit. Chapter 3, 'Post-war Emergencies: From Boom to Bust', showed that neither the government nor business leaders had the statistics needed to demonstrate the speed and success of the manufacturing take-off by the early 1950s.

Despite the absence of credible evidence of bank discrimination against industrialists, historians have been heavily influenced by the manufacturing lobby and have tended to echo its complaints.[100] In fact, the only bottlenecks limiting the growth of Hong Kong industry by the end of the 1950s were the restrictions on Hong Kong exports imposed by Western governments and the acute labour shortage (unemployment had fallen to only 1.3 per cent according to the 1961 Census). What explains, then, the conflict between the manufacturers' perceptions of their financial constraints and their sustained and highly profitable growth performance? It seems quite possible that the long-standing denunciations of the banks for their neglect of industry can be traced back to the initial phase of industrial growth. This chapter has shown that the banks were slow to recognise the implications of a rapidly growing light industrial base. With the sudden disappearance of Mainland markets, they had to make drastic adjustments to their business models as local manufacturers began to replace Mainland traders as the principal source of future profits. New credit risks had to be assessed, and new patterns of customer relationships had to be developed. Bankers were often reluctant to alter the commercial habits of a lifetime, and as a banking group, local Chinese-owned banks never did adjust, as this chapter has explained. The historical reality remains that Hong Kong was unique among Third World economies because it was never short of the capital required for rapid economic development in the first two decades after World War II.[101] For this remarkable performance, this chapter has argued, Hong Kong's banks deserve more credit than they are usually given.

6

The Rise and Fall of the Chinese Banks

In the 1950s, there seemed to be no limit to what Chinese bankers could achieve. The Hang Seng Bank, incorporated in 1952, overtook its local and foreign rivals, including two British note-issuers, and it had become second in size only to HSBC by 1964. The following year saw the downfall of the Hang Seng Bank, which only survived the bank runs of 1965 because it was taken over by HSBC. Its rapid rise and abrupt demise mirror the fortunes of the local Chinese-owned banks as a group.

This chapter starts with a discussion of the colonial administration's banking policies between the 1948 Banking Ordinance and its replacement by a new law in 1964. The government's concerns focused almost exclusively on local Chinese-owned banks in this period, partly because of the political background to the 1948 legislation explained in Chapter 4 'Financial Centre under Siege', and also because officials were convinced of the soundness of the foreign-owned banks. The analysis will show how sensitive officials were to what they regarded as traditional Chinese business practices. It highlights the government's reluctance to tackle the serious problems of local Chinese-owned banks during this period because of its refusal to accept responsibility for protecting depositors. The chapter explains how officials misunderstood the importance of bank liquidity and saw the banks' capital as the key measure of their health. Finally, it discusses the belated realisation that weak regulation was putting the entire system at risk. A striking feature of this period is the way that a single official, A. G. Clarke, dominated the colonial administration's relations with the banking industry even before he was appointed Financial Secretary.

Foreign Challenges

Foreign-owned banks faced considerable obstacles in competing for local business. Although Hong Kong was a British colony, these banks, as aliens in a Chinese world, faced many of the same handicaps they had experienced on the Mainland: 'a formidable language hurdle; low-cost Chinese banks; complex, multiple currencies without a central bank'.[1] From the middle of the nineteenth century, Chinese banks on the Mainland had withstood serious competition from their foreign rivals. After World War I, the failure of several overseas banks operating in China 'left an impression on many Chinese that foreign banks were no longer a safe place to put their money', and Chinese banks on the Mainland were able to compete for deposits on increasingly equal terms.[2] But they were to be less successful in Hong Kong after World War II.

The failure of the Hang Seng Bank — and many other local deposit-takers — to survive cannot be blamed simply on British rule and unfair colonial advantages conferred on foreign businesses. Sir David Li, a prominent Hong Kong banker and vigorous advocate of Chinese banking interests, has observed that 'Chinese businessmen in Hong Kong have never suffered from political or economic repression'.[3] Furthermore, Chinese businessmen dominated the rest of the economy on an increasing scale after World War II. As industrial expansion accelerated in the 1950s, manufacturers — large as well as small — were almost all Chinese.[4] From the 1960s, a new class of Chinese entrepreneurs started to break 'the stranglehold of foreign capital'.[5] By the 1980s, they had taken over many of the largest conglomerates from their British owners — ironically, with the help of HSBC — and had come to dominate the business landscape.[6] Colonial rule had not prevented the capture of the commanding heights of the economy by Chinese entrepreneurs, so why was banking different?

The liquidity loophole gave banks with headquarters overseas a considerable advantage over local Chinese-owned banks. (A detailed explanation of how the loophole operated is presented in Chapter 11, 'The Exceptional Colony'.) Foreign banks used the loophole to service the new manufacturers, a class of borrower of little interest to local Chinese bankers, as Chapter 5, 'Industrial Take-off: Cut-price and Self-financed', explained. HSBC, of course, enjoyed a considerable measure of colonial favouritism, and the government did not start to dismantle this bank's monopolistic privileges until the late 1980s. But even this, the biggest and best-run British bank, was only able to dominate the Hong Kong market because it adapted its very expatriate business culture to establish a mass banking market and to pick the likely winners from among the rising entrepreneurs of post-war Hong Kong.[7] Local Chinese bankers preferred a different business model.

The colonial administration believed that foreign banks were unlikely to default on their local obligations (at least until the banking crisis of the early 1980s and the contagion imported via regional financial institutions).[8] As a result, the local Chinese-owned banks were the principal target for whatever banking regulation was in force, while foreign banks were expected to have appropriate internal systems to ensure sound management and were left to police themselves. This policy, however, was not intended to repress local banks but to protect them, and they were the most privileged group within the industry. Officials placed great store on the survival of the 'Chinese native bank' as a traditional family enterprise which meant, they thought, that these firms ought to be exempt from the full rigours of banking legislation. They should not even be subject to the laws which applied to the rest of the business world. During the 1950s, the status of this favoured group declined, and its numbers shrank. It had failed to make the most of the new profit opportunities created by the modernisation of Hong Kong as the colony switched from entrepôt to manufacturing for export.

Local bankers were not entirely to blame for their own fate. As the 'Introduction' indicated, banking culture is heavily influenced by the behaviour of the bureaucracy. The distinguished economist, Professor William J. Baumol, has argued that it is 'the rules of the game that determine the relative payoffs to different entrepreneurial activities'. Rules can change rapidly in response to official policies and legislation. In some case, he has suggested, these rules may induce the entrepreneur to 'lead a parasitical existence that is actually damaging the economy'.[9] This analysis throws considerable light on how the colony's bureaucratic culture was to contaminate banking behaviour up to 1985. The administrative officers overseeing the banks preferred to regulate the industry in the 1950s according to their own informal rules instead of sticking to statutory requirements. The result was to foster a business culture in which bankers had little expectation of being called to account for misconduct or mismanagement. Official tolerance of illegal or imprudent practices was to have important consequences for the survival of the traditional business model preferred by Chinese bankers, a topic which the next chapter will explore. It was also to influence the conduct of international banks in the 1970s.

Basic Statistics

When licensing of banks was first introduced in 1948, apart from HSBC there were eight China state-owned banks, 12 foreign-owned banks and 111 local Chinese-owned banks. These numbers changed considerably over the next 15 years. In 1964, according to internal government statistics, apart from HSBC there were 13 China state-owned banks; 35 foreign-owned banks; but only 38 local Chinese-owned banks.[10] HSBC and institutions whose headquarters were located outside the colony had become the dominant banking group in the booming, post-war, industrialised economy.

Statistical analysis of this process is handicapped by the government's refusal to compile economic data in this period. The first comprehensive and reliable banking statistics were collected only in late 1964, when Hong Kong was already a mature manufacturing economy. They show the local Chinese-owned banks firmly in second place and unable to improve their position for the rest of the decade (see Table I).

Table I: Banking Market: Percentage Shares of Total Bank Deposits and Loans and Advances by Bank Ownership, 1964–69[11]

Year-end	Total Bank Deposits (HKD million)	China State-owned Banks	Local Chinese-owned Banks	HSBC	Foreign-owned Banks	Total Bank Loans & advances (HKD million)	China state-owned Banks	Local Chinese-owned Banks	HSBC owned	Foreign-owned Banks
1964	6,743	11	33	32	24	4,562	8	26	28	28
1969	12,297	12	32	34	23	7,884	7	29	25	39

Fortunes of War

After Japan surrendered in 1945, Hong Kong's local Chinese-owned banks were among the first businesses to resume normal operations in an economy ravaged by four years of enemy occupation. Their prospects looked very promising. Before World War II, these banks had flourished, handling mostly Mainland-related business. They had successfully financed Mainland trade in a period when China's commerce was constantly disrupted by political anarchy and natural disasters. They had provided access to gold and foreign currencies first when China had multiple domestic currencies before the Guomindang established its authority and then as Japanese aggression provoked an outflow of capital from the Mainland. They had financed real estate activities on the Mainland as well as locally. These Hong Kong banks had continued to operate 'underground' throughout the Japanese occupation, despite the savage penalties for black market activities. They resumed large-scale operation of their normal business of gold and currency dealing and payments for trade consignments less than a month after the end of hostilities in August 1945.[12] Chapter 3, 'Post-war Emergencies: from Boom to Bust', noted that the local banks were able to resume normal business operations much faster than their foreign rivals whose expatriate staff were not immediately free to leave their wartime occupations and return to banking. In any case, Mainland demand for the services of Hong Kong's Chinese-owned banks was booming. In 1948, they seemed to be the most dynamic and enterprising sector of the colony's banking industry. Most of them made 'unprecedented' profits in 1946 and 1947 which were 'many times' their paid-up capital.[13]

The local Chinese-owned banks were popularly divided into two classes. In 1948, there were 33 Chinese-owned commercial banks and 78 'native' banks.

This classification was misleading from the start, however. A 1948 survey of the Chinese-owned group pointed out that the distinction between 'native' and other Chinese banks was 'largely anachronistic'.[14]

> Many local native banks have, for reasons of respectability, no doubt organised their former shops into limited liability companies and they sport, with pride, an 'Ltd' wherever there is a chance to show it off. Thus quite a few of the local so-called native banks have become proper bank companies and ought to be duly acknowledged as commercial banks ... there are many proper commercial banks who would [count] themselves fortunate to transact as many millions as their successful competitors from the 'Chinese city' district

The distinction between Chinese commercial banks and the 'native' variety was further blurred by the efforts of Mainland 'native' banks to shed this label when they transferred their operations to Hong Kong in 1946–47. They tended to go 'to great trouble and expense in registering themselves as companies, and, on the surface at least, follow Western banking methods', noted a senior official.[15] That trend showed how the 'native' classification was being rejected by the industry itself very early in the post-war period.[16] During the 1950s, the gap between 'native' and 'commercial' banking narrowed sharply. The commercial banks within the local Chinese-owned group retained much of the business model developed by Chinese bankers in the past, while the original 'native' banks borrowed from the practices and procedures of conventional modern banking.[17] Although the 'native' label was to linger on for a decade, it proved very confusing. The distinction it conveyed reflected the structure of Mainland banking in another era. There, until the Chinese Communist Party came to power in 1949, a very clear division separated the 'native' from the 'commercial' bank. The Chinese commercial banks were under tight government control, whereas their 'native' competitors operated beyond the government's authority.

Given the dependence of Hong Kong on the Chinese economy before 1949, it was inevitable that the colony's banking industry had been viewed initially in Mainland terms. This tendency was strengthened by the fact that, in the immediate post-war years, the colonial administration was negotiating the future regulation of its banking industry with the Mainland's central banking authorities. The ruling Guomindang blamed Hong Kong and its unregulated financial markets for the relentless collapse of the national currency and galloping inflation on the Mainland after World War II.[18] The colony's 'native' banks — the unincorporated Chinese-owned firms — were identified as the principal culprits. The Guomindang's priority was to extend Mainland financial controls to Hong Kong's 'native' banks and to bring their Mainland activities under the same legal controls as the rest of China's banks. (This campaign and the secret negotiations between the Guomindang and the colonial administration were discussed in Chapter 4.)

In Hong Kong, there was no banking legislation before 1948, and its bankers were free from virtually all official constraints. Until the Chinese Communist Party came to power in 1949, the colony's 'native' banks were described as earning their profits by 'contravening the various laws of the Colony concerning dealings in foreign exchange and gold' and from other activities which commercial banks dared not undertake. All of which 'promised extraordinary profits while risks were negligible'.[19] The Mainland authorities exerted enormous pressure on the colonial administration to restrict their activities. Thus, although the ruling Guomindang was a dying régime, the British made considerable concessions to appease the Mainland authorities, including enactment of the 1948 Banking Ordinance.

This statute was defective from the start, and even its drafters seem to have approached their task with distaste. They forgot, for example, to insert a requirement into the original legislation to require banks to supply their annual accounts to the government, and the law had to be hurriedly amended to remedy this omission.[20] The ordinance also neglected to define a straightforward procedure to allow a bank to cease banking operations and surrender its licence.[21] The colonial administration was to resent having passed this law which introduced the first, though largely nominal, supervision of Hong Kong's banks, and officials showed no enthusiasm for enforcing its provisions. There was no comprehension of how troublesome would be the legacy being shaped by the traditional 'native' banks, to which the government was so indulgent. Officials had no sense of how the continuous pursuit of profits beyond the law would have a corroding effect on banking practices. On the Mainland, by contrast, there was greater realism. Well before World War II, modernisers there had identified such conduct as an obstacle to creating efficient banking enterprises.[22] Hong Kong's experience during the 1950s was to prove these reformers right.

The colonial administration, by contrast, had considerable sympathy for 'native' banks. Officials felt it would be unfair to compel the 'native' bank to abandon its business traditions, accept the corporate structure of conventional commercial banks and adopt their legal obligations and their modern practices because the 'native' firm was financed, not by shareholders but by a network of family and friends, and obtained its deposits, not from the general public but from relatives and business associates.[23] Despite government pampering, nevertheless, the prestige of the 'native' banks was to shrink throughout the decade, even in the eyes of the colonial administration, although the label was not to disappear completely until the 1964 Banking Ordinance. By the end of the 1950s, their previous esteem had been replaced by what one official called a 'dubious reputation' which extended to local Chinese-owned banks as a group.[24] By 1964, there remained only six small, unincorporated holders of bank licences that might be regarded as the last survivors of the 'native' banks which had seemed such a dominant feature of the industry in the early post-war period.[25]

Official Favourites

The eclipse of the local Chinese-owned banks had not been envisaged by the officials who had negotiated with the Guomindang about the level of regulation that would be imposed by the 1948 Banking Ordinance. When the new law was being drafted, Hong Kong had a two-tier banking industry. In the first group were HSBC, the foreign-owned and the China state-owned banks whose stability the government took for granted. The second group consisted of local Chinese-owned banks whose regulation the Mainland authorities had made the primary target of the 1948 Banking Ordinance. Hong Kong's goal during the negotiations had been to frustrate Mainland ambitions for the suppression of these banks and to maintain as much business freedom for them as possible. Official partiality towards family firms was limited to Chinese banks, however, and Western family enterprises were treated with less indulgence.[26]

The new law was so vague that it seemed to apply to any person or firm who handled money or bullion in the colony, and the government declined to clarify the definition of 'bank'. No effort was made to exclude from the licensing process firms which had no deposits, did not describe themselves as a bank and conducted no banking business in the colony.[27] Others were jewellers or goldsmiths who listed their furnace and refining equipment on their balance sheets.[28] The Financial Secretary complained a decade after the ordinance came into effect there were still jewellers who believed they needed a bank licence.[29] Some were money brokers and currency dealers who were able to continue with these businesses after their banking operations became insolvent or they voluntarily surrendered their bank licences.[30] Some were never able to operate because of the confusion caused by the collapse of the Guomindang.[31] Licences were granted to firms which should have been identified as insolvent or fraudulent when they first applied for a licence.[32] It quickly became obvious that once licences had been issued wholesale to 'all and sundry', professional supervision of banking was scarcely possible. What criteria of prudence and integrity could be applied to an industry which included this motley crew?

This indiscriminate approval for firms to operate as banks regardless of their suitability was deliberate policy. The Financial Secretary directed that any applicant trading as a bank when the ordinance came into effect should be considered qualified for a licence without further inquiry. If the bank were in breach of some other legislation, he continued, the question of withdrawing the licence might be considered subsequently and separately.[33] Chapter 1, 'Mismanaged by Mandarins', recorded how officials rejected professional advice and gave bank licences to partnerships contrary to the provisions of the Banking Ordinance, while other firms which were illegal associations under the Companies Ordinance were also licensed without question. This situation could have been avoided if the government had not deleted a requirement in the draft legislation that licences be issued only to incorporated companies. Officials argued that such a restriction would be meaningless because 'rogue' banks tended to have excellent lawyers and to incorporate their businesses. The typical 'native' bank of good repute was, however, unfamiliar with the statutory obligations that incorporation would bring, the Financial Secretary insisted, so that it would be wrong to impose corporate status on such banks.[34] This decision had particularly damaging consequences. Because unincorporated banks were not obliged to have their accounts audited, they were not required to meet the accounting standards set for an ordinary limited company that did not have the right to solicit deposits from the public.

The decision to license all existing deposit-taking institutions without further scrutiny developed into a policy of issuing licences to all new applicants almost without question. The banking and business representatives on the Banking Advisory Committee established by the 1948 Banking Ordinance recorded their dismay at this policy. Clarke was acting as Financial Secretary, and he rejected their advice to be more cautious on the grounds that 'the real purpose of the legislation was not the protection of the public'. But he could not ignore completely the committee's expert opinions. He accepted that a goal of the 1948 Banking Ordinance was 'to stop the setting up of any more mushroom banks'. He agreed, therefore, that future licences would be subject to the condition recommended by the committee that applicants must have a paid-up capital of at least HKD1 million.[35] Even before the new ordinance had been enacted, however, this sum had been derided as totally inadequate for a new bank, particularly by comparison with the capital being invested in Hong Kong's modern spinning mills.[36] In the years that followed, nevertheless, virtually anyone with the minimum capital could obtain a bank licence, provided that nothing seriously discreditable about the applicant was known to the government. Banking competence was not a criterion. It sometimes seemed that the only official concern was to prevent a firm which had not paid for the annual licence fee from being referred to as a bank.[37]

No Nursemaids or Governesses

When London instructed all colonial territories to accept responsibility for safeguarding bank deposits after World War II, Hong Kong responded with a claim to have met this requirement through enacting the 1948 Banking Ordinance.[38] Within the colonial administration, however, a bitter dispute was under way about whether depositors were entitled to any form of government protection. Clarke, who was to hold the post of Financial Secretary from 1952 to 1961, refused to accept that the 1948 Banking Ordinance required the government to intervene on the public's behalf. Other officials disagreed with

Clarke and believed that the 1948 Banking Ordinance required them to make some effort to protect the public. They did not expect to police the entire industry, they conceded, but they should use their statutory powers selectively to 'pick out the occasional bad cases and attempt to enforce the provisions of the ordinance' as a warning to other poorly run banks.[39] Where management was particularly dismal, they might display 'a salutary exercise of the [government's] powers of control' and put it out of business.[40] Clarke's reaction to such activism was revealing. He singled out one colleague for attack, alleging that he 'knew little of the ramifications of Chinese family businesses [and] made use of the [1948 Banking] Ordinance to close down existing banks which were not in a satisfactory position'.[41] This was, of course, a fair summary of what the ordinance required the Government to do.

In this bureaucratic battle, Clarke defied the explicit views of Sir Charles Follows (whom he was to succeed as Financial Secretary). In 1950, Clarke was arguing in favour of virtually unlimited tolerance for local Chinese banks, regardless of whether they were in breach of the 1948 Banking Ordinance or of civil and criminal laws generally. 'We never intended to set ourselves up as nursemaids and governesses to silly people who put their money into shaky institutions', he insisted.[42] Follows made it clear to Clarke that his view of the law was wrong: 'When we see depositors are in danger of losing their money, it is up to us to do something about it'. In a direct rebuttal of Clarke's claim that the government had no duty towards the public, Follows pointed out: to his subordinate: 'The fact that the Ordinance is now on the Statute Book does place a certain responsibility on Government to protect the public in cases where there is reason to believe that all is not well with a bank'.[43] Clarke prevailed, nevertheless, by persuading Follows to rule out any monitoring of a bank's performance 'unless there is a strong prima facie reason to do so'.[44] This decision blocked routine inspections of a bank's affairs and removed the threat of investigation until the bank's problem had become so large that they could no longer be concealed from outsiders. The result was to obstruct all serious banking supervision until 1964.

An Equity Theory of Banking

While Clarke was not prepared to protect depositors, he was ready to give ailing banks the chance to convalesce. This approach was consistent with his view of the traditional Chinese bank. He rightly thought that the proprietors of most local Chinese-owned banks ran their businesses as venture capitalists rather than conventional bankers. Indeed, it was a characteristic of Hong Kong that even 'commercial banks ... to some degree, accepted risks which elsewhere are the responsibility of equity investors'.[45] Thus, under Clarke, the state of a bank's capital was the main focus of such bank examinations as took place:

once these funds were exhausted, the bank was deemed to be in an unhealthy condition. This approach had nothing to do with the modern concept of capital adequacy ratios, and no attempt was made to relate capital to business risks.

The colonial administration's policy had much in common with the official view before World War II that the Chinese community was prepared to lose its deposits because it regarded these funds as capital placed with a bank in the hope of high rates of interest.[46] There seemed to be little realisation in the 1950s that banks were not like other business firms and that, while shareholders invest their capital in a company without any right of repayment, depositors lend funds to a bank on condition that their money may be withdrawn on demand or at the end of some fixed period. In this decade, little attention was paid to the need to oversee the management of a bank's liquidity and its obligation to meet depositors' demands for payment. Overlooked, too, was the related management challenge of how to resolve the conflict between prudence and profits. It was the quality of management that determined a bank's fortunes, but expatriate officials found it hard to deal with bank owners and proprietors, as Chapter 1 explained. Instead, the official prescription for a bank at risk was to persuade it to find more capital.

A bank in trouble, almost always, would be given ample breathing space no matter how unpromising its circumstances, because the policy was to 'go through the drill of requiring the bank to raise further capital', to quote one official.[47] A formal decision to withdraw the bank's licence was not necessarily final if its lawyers wrote an appropriate letter to the Financial Secretary. Even in a case where credit controls were particularly bad and the identity of the owners was unknown, the bank was given a reprieve once it undertook to restore its capital to its original level.[48] Sometimes, the gesture of raising more funds would be enough to win a reprieve even if the sum did not match the amount of capital actually needed.[49] When a bank suspended business because of liquidity problems that indicated defective management, the promise of fresh capital was sufficient to persuade the government not to cancel the licence and allow the bank to re-open.[50] The short-term boost from these capital injections usually provided only a temporary reprieve before final collapse.[51] This policy lingered on until 1963 and the failure of Chiu Tai Bank, whose dire straits were grossly mismanaged by officials, as Chapter 1 pointed out. In this case, its Managing Director's plan was to obtain refinancing from a Japanese bank. The proposal was too uncertain to convince officials. They were, in any case, reluctant to see a Japanese bank enter Hong Kong through the 'back door'. They were also convinced that Chiu Tai Bank would not be able to keep its licence once the tougher requirements of the forthcoming 1964 Banking Ordinance come into force. Even so, there was some regret among officials that they had been forced to decide against letting this hopeless bank linger on.[52]

These policy decisions, taken piecemeal over a number of years, were given coherence and consistency because most were made by Clarke, who largely dictated banking policy from 1948 until 1961. Enforcement of the 1948 banking legislation was adjusted to accommodate what he believed were the traditional practices of the Chinese family firm. The concessions were extended by Clarke and his subordinates to local Chinese banks as a group, whether they were long-established family businesses or newly licensed and incorporated. These decisions amounted to a code of conduct, that is, a set of informal rules made by individual officials that provided local bankers with extensive immunity from inconvenient legal constraints and statutory requirements.

- An almost total exemption from the 1948 Banking Ordinance was granted to the smaller local Chinese-owned banks, while other banks would not normally be subject to inspection.[53]
- Investigation of the suitability of applicants for banking licences imposed a very low threshold of competence. Scrutiny of the affairs of local Chinese-owned banks was perfunctory. Officials did not bother to enforce statutory reporting requirements with any vigour.[54]
- No pressure was imposed on local Chinese-owned banks to ensure the prudent conduct of business or the protection of their depositors. Officials had little interest in their solvency and were prepared to go to considerable lengths to allow the weakest managers to trade their way out of trouble.[55]
- Only when, in exceptional cases, officials perceived a real risk of bank instability leading to serious political protests, did they make full use of their statutory powers to scrutinise applicants and attach the maximum capital requirements to the licence.[56]

The underlying assumption behind this regulatory approach was that friends and relatives would not complain if their 'investments' via a bank went sour and they lost their 'equity', including their deposits. Clarke himself came to the conclusion that the community was not much interested in prudential supervision, arguing 'that Government itself does not seem to have received complaints, direct or indirect, from depositors who have lost their money'.[57] It was true that some of these firms had no public depositors and that they lent money to the same narrow group from which they raised deposits.[58] But these do not appear to have been the norm. The officials' informal rules were applied with consistency so that they created a pattern of anticipated bureaucratic behaviour which set the boundaries for bankers' conduct. Owners and executives had no difficulty in perceiving the rules of the game from the general style of the officials they encountered. Banks could get access to all the information needed to manipulate these rules — in the case of one small, under-capitalised bank, thanks to its lawyer, the Executive Councillor, Sir Man-kam Lo.[59] The code of conduct for the local bank owner and executive which was fostered by the behaviour of officials did nothing to deter imprudence and impropriety. Bankers had ample indications from which to conclude that the officials with whom they dealt had little interest in prudent credit management and even less in law enforcement, not just in terms of compliance with the 1948 Banking Ordinance but with the commercial and criminal law generally.

Clarke eventually became aware of the vulnerability of the local Chinese-owned banks. When the government's policies and performance came under review in 1959, he admitted that the colonial administration could no longer afford to watch complacently as local banks failed, because the collapse of a licensed bank would lead to public criticism of the government. Nevertheless, Clarke saw little scope for improving current practices. When a bank's accounts were unsatisfactory, his officials would exert pressure on management to rectify this situation, he declared. He claimed that this moral suasion was usually effective, although 'small native banks' were ignored and allowed to fail. He agreed that tougher conditions might be considered for future licences: a minimum capital of HKD3 million to HKD5 million; the employment of adequate experienced staff; and a probationary period to monitor the new bank's operations. He warned, however, that these new obstacles to entry would be attacked as direct discrimination against local entrepreneurs in favour of foreign interests. He put the blame for the banking system's vulnerability on the refusal of the colony's Executive Council to approve requests to cancel the licences of poorly run firms.[60]

It was typical of policy-making in Hong Kong that the Financial Secretary's analysis was endorsed, even though it was based on a misleading description of developments during the 1950s. Moral suasion had been successful only in replacing the capital that a bank had lost and had no effect on improving management standards. Nor was it true that the Executive Council refused to revoke bank licences. The official files cited in this chapter contain several instances where the Council approved the cancellation of licences. It was officials rather than Executive Councillors who were reluctant to close down mismanaged banks.[61]

The awakening to the need for serious regulation had come too late. The indulgent code of conduct fostered by the officials' preference for informal rules had become a political liability by the start of the 1960s. The community was acquiring the banking habit, which created a critical mass of public outrage when a bank failed. Thus, in 1961, when the Liu Chong Hing Bank's mismanagement and misconduct became public knowledge, it had to be rescued to protect confidence in the banking system. Clarke's history of benign neglect was no longer sustainable. The full costs of his mistaken view of Chinese banking business were not to become apparent, however, until the 1965 bank runs.

The Liu Chong Hing Bank affair proved a turning point, nevertheless.

Its flagrant involvement in dubious property activities and corruption in the late 1950s were well-known to the colonial administration. Yet, these scandals had raised no apparent alarm about what might be going wrong elsewhere in the bank.[62] The government escaped censure by attributing the crisis to a liquidity problem.[63] Public scandal was avoided by the Managing Director's death which prevented his prosecution for theft. Leading bankers took fright, however, and HSBC led a campaign for new and tougher legislation. After considerable delay, the 1964 Banking Ordinance was passed, introducing professional regulators, imposing minimum liquidity requirements and restricting the freedom to lend to related parties.[64] The new law was introduced to control the sort of risks created by the property sector and its banking connections in particular. But it was too late for the government to fend off disaster. The real estate market was crumbling, and the following year saw the worst banking crisis in Hong Kong's history so far.

Conclusions

The colonial administration displayed almost unlimited patience and goodwill towards the local Chinese-owned banks because officials clung to outdated and misguided notions about the traditional Chinese family firm.[65] The government's starting point had been a desire to preserve commercial arrangements and social practices designed for doing business with the Mainland during periods of political and financial turmoil and when the Chinese economy was barely touched by modernisation. Officials ignored Hong Kong's transition to a manufacturing economy. They did not grasp that the bulk of the colony's business would be with the world's advanced economies where corporate structures were taken for granted; whose banking was relatively large-scale and not confined to a family-based social group; and which engaged in international trade on the basis of considerable documentation and government supervision. While Hong Kong's factories had to adopt not only modern production methods but also new corporate and accounting practices, local Chinese-owned banks were under no such pressure, thanks to the attachment of colonial officials to China's past.

Even in the early 1960s, when the political costs of bank crashes could no longer be ignored, the government remained extremely reluctant to take the initiative to close banks tottering on the edge of insolvency. If bank executives were suspected of criminal activities, the preference was to let the bank collapse under the weight of its own debts rather than through official intervention. This tolerant attitude had nothing to do with leaving the fate of a bank to competitive market forces. Many of these firms were not legally entitled to licences in the first place, and many of the other failures were attributable to a complete absence of the qualifications that any rational regulatory system ought to impose on businesses allowed to call themselves banks. Benign neglect had to end for political reasons once banks started to seek deposits from the general public, but the government acted too late to prevent a serious crisis.

This chapter has presented considerable evidence in support of the claims made in Chapter 1 that expatriates, even the smartest and the most experienced, were ill-qualified to deal with recalcitrant bank owners and executives. It also shows how defective legislation, whose requirements were generously waived by officials, created the expectation among bankers that the law did not matter. They were encouraged to run their businesses on the basis of a flawed code of conduct which they adopted in response to the permissive attitudes of the officials responsible for overseeing the industry. All this is very much in line with Baumol's theory about the influence of government policies and practices on business behaviour, which was introduced at the start of this chapter. The next chapter will show how illegality and imprudence were further encouraged by the links between the local banker's preferred business model and criminal and corrupt activities.

7
A Dangerous Business Model

The most puzzling feature of Hong Kong's banking history is the eclipse of the local Chinese bankers. The previous chapter described their once proud status, their resilience in the face of political turmoil and economic disasters, and their skilful management of credit risks in troubled times. It also explained how their status deteriorated throughout the 1950s in spite of the extra-legal privileges which colonial officials granted them. Their decline was rapid but inevitable. These bankers had clung to their past glories. Adjustment to the economic transformation of Hong Kong after World War II had proved too uncomfortable a challenge for them.

The local Chinese-owned banks failed to capture their full share of the flood of new banking business from manufacturers as industrial exports flourished during the 1950 and 1960s. In 1969, when data on bank-lending patterns first became available, this sector of the economy was mature and more secure than ever before. But these banks were allocating a mere 13 per cent of their loan portfolios to manufacturing. Industrial growth, it seemed fair to conclude, had been fuelled by HSBC and the foreign-owned institutions. These banks devoted 22 per cent of their total lending to manufacturing and, in the process, provided three-quarters of all bank financing for Hong Kong's factories in 1969.[1] It was not that foreign bankers had a bigger appetite for risk. On the contrary, loans to manufacturers producing for export was banking at its most prudent and routine. But, as the next chapter will explain in some detail, industry did not offer the chance for personal premiums and speculative gains to which local bankers were accustomed.

So, what did local Chinese-owned banks do with their depositors' money? They used it very much as if it were part of the owners' equity, an attitude which the colonial administration assumed to be a natural feature of the Chinese banking model.[2] The result was to provide little incentive for this group to upgrade its management standards or to adopt modern corporate practices. Indeed, officials believed that any regulatory pressures on them to do so would be wrong, as the previous chapter has already demonstrated. Most local bankers stuck to what they found most comfortable: gold trading, currency dealing and property speculation. Here again, government policies favoured preserving the past. Albeit accidentally, these boosted the types of business most favoured by local Chinese-owned banks when Hong Kong had still been part of the Mainland economy. The historical foundations of local banking had disappeared when the Chinese Communist Party came to power in 1949. Nevertheless, the colonial administration took a series of decisions in the 1950s which permitted:

- the revival of the gold market;
- the continuation of currency dealing; and
- the dramatic expansion of the property market.

This chapter links the inability of local Chinese-owned banks to dominate the financial landscape, despite cultural advantages and favourable government policies, to their failure to modernise their business model. That was the economic price to be paid for the government's indulgence towards the local Chinese-owned banks which had reduced their incentives to change with the times. There were also serious social costs to these policy decisions — including corruption, smuggling and narcotics trafficking — which this chapter will identify.

The Lure of Gold

Immediately after the 1948 Banking Ordinance was passed, the gold trade seemed destined for extinction.[3] Chapter 4, 'Financial Centre under Siege', explained how London compelled the colonial administration, despite its vigorous protests, to comply with International Monetary Fund (IMF) restrictions and close the free gold market in 1949. Gold trading at free market prices was to remain illegal until 1970. Hong Kong's free market survived, nevertheless, operating in open defiance of the law. It was buoyed up briefly by booming demand from the Mainland for gold and foreign currencies as inflation soared out of the ruling Guomindang's control and then as the Chinese Communist Party's military advance was proving unstoppable. After the fall of the Guomindang régime in 1949, the Mainland market disappeared as China's new rulers quickly sealed the frontier against smugglers and profiteers.

In 1953, London allowed Hong Kong to import gold again but only for transhipment. The trade revived very rapidly because the nearby Portuguese enclave of Macao provided a backdoor through which the Hong Kong gold trade could operate, and the colony became the main centre for gold smuggling in the region. Its largest and most lucrative market was India, but sales soared wherever political confidence in Southeast Asia was undermined by war, revolution or an economic collapse.[4] London bullion dealers dispatched consignments via Hong Kong to Macao, which was not subject to IMF restrictions but lacked shipping and other facilities to distribute gold efficiently around the region. Thus, the gold was smuggled back into Hong Kong, with minimal interference from the colony's law enforcement agencies, to be smuggled to other Asian destinations or to be openly but unlawfully offered for sale by local Chinese-owned banks.[5] In addition, these offered money-changing and other facilities that were crucial to Hong Kong's success in attracting this illicit trade according to a contemporary and very thorough study by a staff member of the US Federal Reserve System.[6]

Hong Kong has numerous financial organizations, many of which maintain close contact with other financial centers of the world, so that the gold dealers have widespread facilities with which to finance their trade. Hong Kong's free market for foreign exchange is also useful, since it enables gold smugglers to convert local currency receipts from the sale of smuggled gold in the various Asian countries into hard currency (dollars, pound sterling) with a minimum of inconvenience.

Macao Mattered

Hong Kong was important to London's attempt to recover its role as a major international gold market in the 1950s. But British commercial interests were not the explanation for the colony's toleration of the gold smugglers. Hong Kong got small benefit from the London firms which accounted for around a quarter of Macao's gold imports towards the end of the decade. Furthermore, the British traders were quick to switch their business to any country in Southeast Asia where an open gold market emerged, regardless of Hong Kong's interests.[7] The most important feature of the gold trade for the UK and the Hong Kong authorities was its contribution to the survival of Macao. The gold trade was the Portuguese enclave's principal source both of foreign exchange and government revenue in that period. There were no other industries which could take its place. British officials felt that Macao needed sympathy and support because they calculated that any threat to Macao's continued existence under Portuguese rule would undermine confidence in Hong Kong's prospects.

In the early years after World War II, Hong Kong officials were unhappy about granting Macao generous concessions over exchange controls.[8] However, on the eve of Mao Zedong's final victory on the Mainland, the Governor successfully applied for London's permission to make concessions to Macao. London subsequently had second thoughts about doing favours for a Portuguese colony. Representations from Hong Kong and Portugal's own pressures through NATO persuaded the Colonial Office to return to a more sympathetic attitude. In 1953, Hong Kong's gold market was re-opened, thanks to the transhipments to Macao. This was to prove a well-timed British concession because the rest of Macao's economy went into a sharp decline that year and lasted until 1956, and Portuguese efforts to rescue their colony's fortunes through a development programme produced meagre results.[9]

By this stage, there was now a well-established British consensus that if the Macao economy collapsed, questions would be raised about Hong Kong's own status.[10] On this political analysis, gold deserved special treatment because it provided the most substantial and secure source of foreign exchange earnings available to Macao at that time. The colonial administration was fully aware of the part played by local Chinese-owned banks in this trade. Indeed, advice from the Hang Seng Bank about the Macao economy and the gold trade was actively sought in framing official policy.[11]

Table I shows the dramatic revival of the gold market in the mid-1950s. It was a highly profitable business which helped to offset the declining fortunes of the rest of the re-export sector. The value of the gold transhipped was equivalent to 19 per cent of re-exports in 1954, rising to 23 per cent in 1956.[12] The ratio of gold transhipments to re-exports reached a peak of 31 per cent in 1959. However, this last figure is somewhat misleading because it also reflected the declining importance of the overall re-export trade. For local Chinese bankers, the profits from continuing their traditional gold trade in Asia must have seemed reasonable compensation for letting foreign banks serve the manufacturers selling to Western markets, a trend which will be reviewed in the next chapter. Local Chinese-owned banks, however, were locking themselves out of the sector that was to dominate the economy until the 1980s.

Table I: Imports of Gold and Specie for Re-export, 1949–60 (HKD million)[13]

Year	Value	Year	Value
1949	155.4	1955	396.3
1950	15.3	1956	490.4
1951	21.7	1957	403.6
1952	8.2	1958	257.9
1953	26.6	1959	302.2
1954	333.1	1960	292.8

The Narcotic Connection

The commitment to laisser faire and the almost complete absence of financial and economic regulation meant that the government took little interest in business behaviour outside the colony's boundaries. Hong Kong banks and other businesses had no need to conceal their failure to comply with the laws of foreign governments. The Hong Kong authorities enforced UK exchange controls and other regulations, Chapter 4 explained, as unenthusiastically as possible because they contributed nothing to Hong Kong's well-being. The colonial administration went along with the US embargo on business with the Mainland, only to the extent that cooperation was essential to maintain Hong Kong's access to North American markets. Officials felt no obligation to respect the IMF restrictions on the bullion trade at the expense of Hong Kong's political interests in Macao's economic survival.

But this trade was illegal under Hong Kong's own laws, and as Chapter 4 explained, the public, as well as the law enforcement agencies, expected legislation to be enforced. The colonial administration only condoned unlawful activities when it believed Hong Kong's best interests were at stake, and the gold trade created a complex management problem for senior officials. Thus, the government was prepared to use its full legal powers to control the flow of gold transhipped through Hong Kong to other Asian centres if it seemed that Macao's share of the gold trade was under threat from these regional rivals in the 1960s.[14] Yet, Macao's gold trade could only prosper if the Hong Kong authorities facilitated the smuggling, and they took steps to prevent disruption of illegal shipments. Unlawful gold consignments should have been intercepted by the Police Marine Division and the Preventive Service. These two agencies, however, were provided with no more resources than would allow a token fraction of the illicit cargoes to be caught. These long-standing but secret arrangements were reconfirmed in 1962 by Hong Kong's Governor after a personal discussion with a Portuguese counterpart in Macao.[15] In 1966, the official in charge of exchange controls discovered accidentally that banks were selling gold illegally and asked what the government's policy was. He was informed that 'on the question of gold returning from Macao ... the [Hong Kong authorities] had always turned a blind eye to it and intended to continue to do so'.[16] There was some concern in 1967 that the IMF would be alerted to how Hong Kong was deliberately tolerating the gold smuggling after the Chief Preventive Officer discussed the value of this trade in public.[17] By now, however, legalisation of gold dealing was about to begin. In 1968, the IMF ended its ban on free markets, and Hong Kong's gold dealings returned to full legality in 1970.[18]

The gold trade was not simply a matter of technical breaches of exchange controls and similar regulations, or of offshore illegality. It created the danger of widespread criminal contamination within the colony's financial system. It is difficult, for example, to see how the banks involved could have kept full and accurate accounts of the business. Even if the gold transactions themselves were recorded openly, creative book-keeping would be necessary to cover the incidental but illicit payments for the smuggling operations. Once bank owners and executives had embarked on accounting practices to conceal one category of transactions from external scrutiny, there was nothing to prevent these practices from contaminating the entire accounting system and enveloping an entire bank in a web of deceit to conceal fraud, as events were to demonstrate dramatically between 1975 and 1984, for example. (Chapter 9, 'From Banking Crisis to Financial Catastrophe', will review that development in which foreign banks were to play a conspicuously shameful role.)

Unfortunately, the criminal contamination was not confined to the banking sector because gold was not the only contraband shipped by the smugglers. An even more profitable cargo was narcotics. The resources denied to the police and customs in order to restrict the interception of gold shipments reduced the ability of these agencies to capture drug consignments. Furthermore, narcotics were a major source of corruption within the police. Consequently, an unintended but alarming consequence of the gold trade with Macao was that Hong Kong operated as 'one of the most drug-ridden places in the world … [and] the major centre for transhipment of and financing of the narcotics business in the Far East'.[19] The link between gold smuggling and narcotics and the role of the banks were topics of widespread speculation in Hong Kong during the 1950s and 1960s. However, as long as the speculation was confined to the colony's Chinese-language press, they were of little concern to British officials in either Hong Kong or London. Such reports could be treated as part of the widespread allegations of corruption and malpractice within the civil service which the colonial administration sought to dismiss as mischievous gossip until the creation of the Independent Commission Against Corruption (ICAC) in 1974. But when English-language publications began to take an interest and London journalists picked up the story, the UK government faced potential political embarrassment.

Confidential documents from the Colonial Office leave little room for doubt that, although its staff did their best to discourage public discussion of the connection between gold and drugs, senior officials were aware that these were related businesses.[20] In the course of preparing a strategy for handling questions on this topic, one candid bureaucrat confessed that the political case for preserving Macao's gold trade outweighed 'any possible connection with the drug trade'. Another official recognised gold as part of the payments system for narcotics. He argued that 'curbing the use of gold in drug transactions' would be almost impossible, while admitting that corruption problems in the police and customs 'have from time to time given some cause for disquiet'. The Governor later tried to reassure the Colonial Office about the integrity of his law enforcement agencies in tackling these problems and produced a declaration from the Commissioner of Police that 'there is no evidence whatever to indicate that racketeers have gained control over any law agency in Hong Kong'. Less than a decade later, a judicial commission would receive information that venality affected virtually every part of the colonial administration and that 'narcotics has always been a tremendously lucrative source of corruption'.[21] The gold trade had brought the Hong Kong end of the transaction into direct contact with the underworld. The gold smugglers were connected to the drugs network which, in turn, was controlled by triads. These were hardly the associates to be welcomed by a modern banking system.

The outside world had little doubt about the unsavoury legacy left by the banks' links to narcotics, which had started with the gold trade. The tolerance shown by the government for the illegal gold trade which facilitated drug smuggling, was to have a long-term effect on Hong Kong's reputation as an international financial centre. There was a widespread belief that the colony's tolerance of dubious practices in the financial field made it easier to fund narcotics. As late as the 1990s, foreign governments claimed that instead of cooperating to combat money laundering linked to narcotics trafficking, Hong Kong officials tried to protect the banking industry through displays of 'denial, naivete, complacency, and outright disingenuousness'.[22] These obstructive tactics had to end in 1994 after there were threats of international sanctions that would have jeopardised Hong Kong's role as an international financial centre. New legislation and enforcement measures were introduced, including codes of ethics for banks; these moves had largely refurbished Hong Kong's reputation by 1998.[23]

The Money Changers

Currency dealing was the second pillar of the Chinese banks' traditional business model. The loss of the black market on the Mainland when the Chinese Communist Party came to power proved a temporary setback. Chapter 3, 'Post-war Emergencies: from Boom to Bust', discussed how the colonial administration succeeded in preserving Hong Kong's free market in US dollars and other hard currencies. The colony, nevertheless, was a member of the Sterling Area, and until 1972, it was under an obligation to enforce the Area's exchange controls. As far as possible, the colony ignored the duties of its membership. The Governor, Sir Alexander Grantham, had personally instructed those in charge of administering exchange controls be very tolerant in enforcing them.[24] A decade later, a UK official complained that, in Hong Kong, the regulations were being evaded through dishonest and illegal means.[25]

The government's professional staff, however, were not willing accomplices in undermining the effectiveness of financial regulations. The colonial administration realised that the Exchange Controller and his staff took their responsibilities seriously and could not be expected to bring the same relaxed attitude to their statutory duties as the administrative officers involved in overseeing the banks. From time to time, exchange control personnel stumbled across flagrant breaches of the regulations, apparently sanctioned by senior officials. In these cases, an effort was made to avoid scandalising them, and they were given personal briefings on policy and its rationale.[26]

The potential contribution of these personnel to better regulate banking in general was considerable. Early in the 1950s, the exchange controller officials came under pressure to approve an increase in the number of banks granted 'authorised' status, which would allow them to deal in foreign exchange at official rates. Unlike the administrative officers who gave bank licences to any firm with a capital of HKD1 million, these officials wanted to be selective about the banks they endorsed.[27] They also took a more hard-headed view of the bank owners and executives when they were consulted on individual banks. For example, a trading company run by the son of a prominent local businessman applied for a banking licence in 1951, and it seemed destined to receive the routine approval that applicants could expect. The Financial Secretary, A. G. Clarke, was more perceptive than his subordinates and asked for the exchange controllers to be consulted on this application. They promptly identified the firm as connected to criminal black market operations overseas. Without this information, the licence would have been granted.[28] These officials identified another bank as run by an individual convicted in Singapore of substantial currency offences, although their Administrative Service colleagues had described the firm as 'doing extremely well'. (In this case, Clarke preferred to take a lenient view of the bank and ignored its record of illegality.)[29]

In theory, the average local Chinese-owned bank was better placed to take advantage of the free currency market than HSBC and the foreign-owned banks. Many of these were classified as 'authorised' institutions, which meant they were trusted to comply strictly with Sterling Area regulations and, in return, were allowed to buy and sell foreign exchange at official rates — without paying the premium that free market transactions involved. In practice, 'authorised' status was not a great constraint on their operations. US banks in Hong Kong had ample access to American dollars, while continental European banks were able to flout Sterling Area requirements in their currency transactions.[30] Nevertheless, the foreign-owned bank sector found it convenient in the 1950s to maintain relations with individual local Chinese-owned banks because, thanks to the free market, they frequently offered faster and more convenient services to customers outside the Sterling Area.[31] But the dependence of foreign banks on these local intermediaries was declining. By the mid-1960s, the 'authorised' banks were open and active players in the free market, regardless of their status.[32]

In the meantime, post-war recovery in Western Europe and Japan meant that the international scarcity of dollars was easing in the 1950s. Early in the following decade, the commercial importance of the free market for local Chinese-owned banks waned still further, and the attractions of sterling increased, thanks to high rates of interest and the general convenience of holding a bank's reserves in sterling, to which the Hong Kong dollar was then tied by a fixed exchange rate. The Hang Seng Bank, for example, stuck to its 'unauthorised' status after being taken over by HSBC in 1965 and thus was free to keep its offshore holdings in any currency it pleased. Despite this freedom from exchange controls, the bank maintained substantial sterling holdings in London which were left uncovered, despite continuous speculation that the pound would devalue.[33]

Other local Chinese-owned banks had started to take a different view of 'authorised' status in the late 1950s. Some local bankers made a belated effort to provide financing for factories and hoped that, with 'authorised' status, they could compete more effectively against foreign banks in the export sector created by the industrial boom.[34] More attractive still was the enhanced market credibility which this status was expected to confer. Local bankers saw it as a way to present themselves as 'being completely trustworthy … an approved bank in the eyes of the world'.[35] This added prestige was more than enough to offset any inconvenience of being subject to Sterling Area regulations, all the more so because officials made little effort to ensure that applicants would comply with their new obligations.[36] Applications for 'authorised' status continued in the 1960s, by which time the distinction between 'authorised' and other banks in terms of banking practice had almost disappeared in spite of the strict 'letter of the law'. In 1968, exchange control staff were still complaining that 'authorised' status was obtained too easily in the colony by comparison with London, where a bank had to satisfy the authorities about its management, and 'the check is rigorous'.[37] The incentive to change status was now plainly the desire of former 'native' banks for greater market credibility through promotion to the ranks of the modern, Western-style financial institutions.[38]

At this stage of Hong Kong's banking development, it should have been possible to exploit the lure of 'authorised' status to persuade local Chinese-owned banks to raise their standards. A future Financial Secretary, J.J. (later Sir John) Cowperthwaite, used the excuse provided by one application in 1959 to question why the bank had a capital of only HKD2 million but had invested HKD2.8 million in land and buildings. He does not seem to have been overly concerned when told that 'the investment represented a use of shareholders' deposits which were not likely to be withdrawn in such a way as to embarrass the bank'. This was an example of the 'equity theory of banking', the drawbacks of which were discussed in the previous chapter. Cowperthwaite, like his colleagues, had missed an opportunity to insist on management reforms.

Hong Kong's failure to enforce exchange control regulations meant that a large proportion of its commercial and financial contracts with the rest of the world were illegal, a fact largely unknown to the business world . The legal profession, however, could not be so complacent. If there were a dispute over these transactions, the courts would be unable to enforce the contracts involved. The colonial administration and the bankers agreed on informal and extra-legal arrangements so that contracts would not be challenged in the courts.[39] Yet, the colonial administration was uncomfortable with the risks involved in relying on backdoor means to deprive aggrieved parties of their right to go to court, and Cowperthwaite argued that 'the enforceability of contracts is the foundation of commerce'. But London blocked the introduction of legislation to solve the problem in 1957. The US government was trying to close every avenue that gave China access to world markets, and the Colonial Office's judgment was that a new law clarifying Hong Kong's exemption from exchange controls would have alarmed Washington.[40] In this case, Hong Kong had little choice but to accept an unlawful situation which was vital to its economic well-being. Not until 1967 was the legislation introduced to regularise the freedom from exchange controls which the business community had always assumed to be an intrinsic feature of the Hong Kong economy.[41]

The Perils of Property

The third leg of the local Chinese-owned banks' business model was property, where, in the 1950s, prospective rewards seemed remarkable and potential risks seemed almost irrelevant. A desperate shortage of residential accommodation in particular was boosting the property market. As the manufacturing boom gathered pace in the early 1950s, it increased the demand for residential space because new factories usually began as domestic workshops which were most easily accommodated in tenement buildings.[42] By the end of the decade, the government's confidential estimate was that 63 per cent of Hong Kong's factories were located in residential buildings.[43] Purpose-built industrial buildings were simply too expensive for the average new or smaller manufacturer.[44]

But the success of the real estate side of the traditional business model contained the seeds of its own collapse. For too many of the banks involved, the speculative features of the development projects to which they lent were masked by the 'real' assets which were involved. Furthermore, in addition to the usual hazards of the property cycle, government policy was a decisive factor in determining the volume of new construction, a factor whose consequences were largely unforeseen by officials and businessmen alike. The risk of self-destruction that property injected into the business model of local Chinese-owned banks increased dramatically in the early 1960s.

Mass Markets

In the early post-war period, property developers faced considerable constraints on their freedom to redevelop urban sites. Tenants were protected from eviction by wartime legislation until 1953, when the law was amended to permit owners to clear occupants from damaged or dangerous premises in order to rebuild them. The result was **a** sharp rise in the level of activity in the property market. Buildings could not be more than five storeys (or 24.4 metres) tall until 1956, when the pre-war restrictions on height were relaxed.[45] Property developers could now use modern building technology to erect multi-storey residential blocks.

The additional finance needed for these much larger development projects was offset by selling individual dwelling units to the public ahead of completion. At first, the business seemed conservative enough, and an official report described how, in 1958, the market had focused on cheaper units but speculation was not a concern. The scale of real estate ventures was altering dramatically, however. The largest development that year offered 397 flats for sale. By the following year, a mass market was emerging, as the average unit became even cheaper and smaller in size. The largest single project contained almost 1,000 units, with flats now as small as 48 square metres.[46] The trend continued into the following decade. Between 1960 and 1965, residential projects accounted for the largest share of new buildings completed by the private sector, and they grew in size and complexity.[47]

These trends were extremely attractive to local Chinese-owned banks.[48] In this business, they had clear advantages over their foreign rivals. Property developers were more likely than the new manufacturing class to have existing personal connections with this group of banks. The business itself was entirely familiar. Unlike industrial finance, it required only local knowledge and demanded no acquaintance with international trade practices or overseas consumer markets. The local Chinese-owned bank frequently had associated companies which were active in property development and construction. Where the developers were not family or friends, bank proprietors and senior executives could become quasi-shareholders in their personal capacities by extorting the right to purchase units in the completed building on concessionary terms or better. A lack of distinction between personal and corporate interests meant, of course, that loans for property projects were not arm's length, and the public's deposits were treated like equity capital, abuses which the government tolerated for reasons discussed in the previous chapter. These dubious practices tended to aggravate the historical dangers of the property cycle which had first led to calls for banking regulation before World War II.[49]

The inability of individual bankers to resist the heady profits offered by property lending became a major threat to banking stability in the late 1950s.

Inevitably, the developers' dependence on their bankers increased, and the commitments of local Chinese-owned banks to real estate rose to a disturbing level, as the government publicly acknowledged.[50] The growing fashion of selling new, multi-storey developments on instalment terms prior to completion increased the project's cash flow and appeared both to reduce a bank's exposure and to allow an increased turnover of its loans. The result was to lull bankers into believing that they could safely increase the leveraging of their property portfolios. The Bank of East Asia was a rare example of respect for basic banking principles. The collapse of other local Chinese-owned banks during the 1950s had impressed its management with the importance of conservative lending, adequate reserves and ample liquidity.[51] The inability of the average local banker to resist the abnormal profits offered by property lending became a major threat to banking stability in this decade. The near-collapse of the Liu Chong Bank in 1961 offered ample evidence of the dangers caused by the property entanglements of a badly managed bank, and leading bankers lobbied hard for a better regulatory system to which the government responded with no great urgency.[52] Catastrophe became only a matter of time in the 1960s after excessively liberal creation of credit by the banks allowed developers to launch over-ambitious property projects that proved financially unsustainable.[53] The government still did not intervene, despite clear warning signs of dangerous expansion of bank credit, as Chapter 8, 'An Avoidable Crisis: The 1965 Bank Runs', will explain. So, the bankers were left to their own devices until 1964 when a new banking law was introduced — but too late to stop the property market from collapsing.

Hang Seng Bank showed how perilous the traditional business model could be, even in the case of the second largest bank in Hong Kong. Its liquidity ratio looked safe enough before the 1965 bank runs started. But it was very vulnerable to any downturn in the real estate sector because property provided the collateral for 90 per cent of its secured lending. In addition, it had the problem of lending to related parties. The bank was part of a corporate complex which had its own real estate company, while its other non-banking interests included trading, taxi and hotel companies.[54] Its inability to survive the 1965 crisis showed how damaging had been the influence of tradition on its business practices, despite the modernising zeal of its redoubtable manager, Lee Quo-wei, perhaps the colony's most influential banker in the second half of the last century. Even before HSBC took over, he had given the bank a well-designed system to assess borrowers and control credit.[55] These were not sufficient, however, to overcome the fundamental flaws in the lending policies of a family-owned bank, wedded to the traditional business model.

Perilous Policies

Thus were laid the foundations of the 1965 bank crisis. Paradoxically, it was to be government intervention in the market that first intensified the property boom and then led to a crash that was followed by the worst bank runs in Hong Kong's history. In 1962, the colonial administration announced that, from 1966, building densities would be reduced. This caused a rush to beat the deadline that would slash profits. The number of new projects begun during the rest of 1962 more than doubled.[56] Developers' plans were based on completion schedules that proved increasingly difficult to achieve.[57] The situation was aggravated by further government controls in 1964, intended to limit the hazards created by demolition and redevelopment of existing buildings. These regulations slowed down the rate at which construction could proceed and increased the risk of breaching building covenants.[58] A collapse of this property boom became increasingly difficult to avoid. Previously, developers would have been able to overcome inconvenient restrictions through their corrupt relations with the bureaucracy, as bankers knew full well. Indeed, the most striking example of how to defy building regulations was provided by a prominent local Chinese-owned bank. In 1955, the Liu Chong Hing Bank had obtained government permission to construct a building no taller than ten storeys. It ignored this restriction together with the safety and health conditions imposed by the Building Authority. When these irregularities were uncovered, its excuse was that the building inspectors had been fully informed of the illegalities. The expatriate officials involved decided not to return to the colony to face an investigation. The bank's owner, Liu Po-shan, successfully lobbied the Governor not to close the building, and, according to an official report, the Governor appears to have made sure that official enquiries were not pursued. Units in the building were then sold off to the public in open breach of the law governing such sales. A judicial inquiry made clear that similar scandals were probably widespread.[59] The government's files reveal that, after the scandals of the Liu Chong Hing Bank project first became known, senior officials went to considerable lengths to protect the staff responsible for enforcing building regulations from bribery investigations, which meant that there was little to deter either developers or their bankers from corrupt practices.[60]

The new restrictions of the 1960s could not be circumvented so easily. In introducing the new regulations, the government had unleashed a building boom that was well beyond the capacity of the construction industry. The developers faced the grim prospect of owning sites on which construction could not start and of being committed to projects that could not be completed. They had financed themselves with bank loans which they could no longer service out of cash flow. Their bankers faced a costly dilemma. They could try to carry the loans on their books, which would be difficult once statutory liquidity ratios and other constraints on lending came into force under the 1964 Banking Ordinance. Or they could enforce the loan agreements and sell off the sites if necessary, which would drive down land values. These market realities were not to be bought off with bribes, as government departments might be. The crisis about to engulf the banks would threaten the survival of the entire local Chinese-owned banking sector. That challenge will be discussed in the next chapter.

Conclusions

The gold trade probably made a significant contribution to the survival of many local banks. At the same time, however, it reduced the incentive to participate in funding the manufacturing for export on which the community's prosperity was being built. The trade involved activities in which modern banks could not be involved without considerable risk because gold was associated with the most dangerous elements of the criminal world. The links with smugglers and drug dealers turned the banks involved into sleeping partners of the triads. A bank could hardly have insulated itself completely from contamination by this source.

The currency dealing side of the traditional business model was relatively harmless. Hong Kong's economic survival depended on being able to operate outside the Sterling Area. When given a chance, the exchange controllers were effective in reinforcing such banking regulation as existed, and they illustrated the contribution that a professional approach could make. They could have been used to encourage local banks eager to acquire 'authorised' status to raise their standards, but the opportunity was lost. The unlawful nature of most transactions involving foreign exchange appears not to have had such a corrupting effect as gold dealing. The business world assumed that Hong Kong residents had the right to choose whether to go through the official exchange controls or use the free market. The colonial administration was able to conceal the fact that there was no such exemption from the law, not only from suspicious foreign governments but also from the general public, thanks to its understanding with the banks that any attempt to litigate the legality of foreign trade and investment contracts would be severely deterred.

The obsession with property was not at all benign. Real estate involved far higher risks in the 1960s than local Chinese bankers had anticipated and for which they were not adequately prepared, either financially or in terms of management capability. In the end, excessive exposure to property was to prove the downfall of significant local Chinese-owned banks, demonstrating the high price to be paid for profits made without proper regard for the risks they involved. The property crash of 1964 triggered the bank crisis of the following year. Both events were aggravated by official policies that were handicapped by defective information and bureaucratic ignorance. Both could have been avoided if the colonial administration had not mismanaged banking regulation throughout the 1950s, as the previous chapter demonstrated. The collapse of the property market marked the demise of the traditional business model, but it did not end the fascination with real estate which afflicted many bankers. The corruption, corporate scandals and bank crashes which occurred between 1961 and 1965 were to be repeated on an even larger scale in the first half of the 1980s. (The bank crisis of that decade, however, was to involve extensive fraud and corruption by foreign-owned banks.)

The overall conclusion of this chapter is that government polices and bureaucratic behaviour were powerful influences on banks and their business strategies. The colonial administration frequently put political convenience before its statutory responsibilities and tolerated widespread corruption in its ranks. The bureaucracy thus became a source of contamination for those banks which did not have a well-established culture and strong internal systems to maintain their integrity. The danger for Hong Kong was not too much state interference but the weaknesses inherent in the colonial approach to government, which was analysed in Chapter 1, 'Mismanaged by Mandarins'.

8

An Avoidable Crisis: The 1965 Bank Runs

As 1965 opened, banking was enjoying a boom, and prospects looked excellent for the economy as a whole. A newspaper headline captured the bullish outlook: 'Prosperity is around the corner. Banking office openings establish record in 1964'.[1] A month later, two banks had failed, runs had begun on other local Chinese-owned banks and the banking industry was under threat.[2] To the astonishment of bankers, bureaucrats and businessmen, Hong Kong's banking was to be brought to the verge of collapse that year.[3]

This was an avoidable crisis. The vulnerable sectors of the banking industry would have been obvious from even a casual study of the state of their liquidity. At the end of 1964, the ratio of loans to advances for local Chinese-owned banks was 73 per cent (compare with 58 per cent for HSBC and 51 per cent for the China state-owned banks). Out of the 36 local Chinese-owned banks, six had 'negative liquidity': they had lent more than the total value of their deposits.[4] Their fragility was unmistakeable, and they were to bear the brunt of the collapse in depositors' confidence. However, these vital figures were not available to the government before January the following year. The colonial administration's long-stranding hostility to statistics meant that even the simplest tools for monitoring the health of financial institutions were missing. This data deficit had handicapped almost every aspect of the colonial administration's management of events leading up to the 1965 crisis.

Manufacturing Prosperity

The banking problems that emerged in the 1960s created a series of doomsday scenarios that seemed to endanger the colony's survival. Yet, as always with Hong Kong's emergencies, whether economic or political, there was a relentless growth dynamic within the economy that might slow — but did not halt — from the mid-1950s until the Asian financial crisis at the end of the century. Thus, while confidence in the smaller banks crumbled in 1965 and the financial system tottered, the momentum of overall growth continued, driven by the sustained expansion of manufacturing. Hong Kong's factories were producing for world markets. Their revenues did not depend on conditions in the local share and property markets. Manufacturing kept the colony buoyant throughout the bank runs of 1965 and the political disturbances of the following two years, as well as the devaluation crisis of 1967. The true measure of this industrial resilience is the fourfold increase in the value of domestic exports during the 1960s (see Table I). Since virtually all industrial output was manufactured for sale overseas, domestic exports were a good indicator of industrial performance for this period. They grew by 16 per cent in 1964. They still increased by 13 per cent in 1965, despite the bank runs. The annual growth rate for the next two years returned to 16 per cent.

Table I: Hong Kong Export Performance, 1960–69[5]

Year	Domestic Exports (HKD millions)	Index (1960 = 100)
1960	3,937	100.0
1961	3,930	99.8
1962	4,388	111.5
1963	4,991	126.8
1964	5,784	146.9
1965	6,529	165.8
1966	7,563	192.1
1967	8,781	223.0
1968	12,712	322.9
1969	15,876	403.3

The shocks and scandals suffered by the banking system during this decade — and, indeed, in the crises that followed until 1985 — could have wreaked financial and political havoc. This danger was made all the more real by the policy errors and confused responses of the colonial administration. In the background to offset these menacing developments was the inherent ability of the Hong Kong economy to grow its way out of trouble and to achieve continuous improvements in profits and earnings. The economy as a whole avoided recession, and overall growth remained positive throughout the decade.

The fact that recession was never economy-wide offered political salvation to the colonial administration. Despite the slump in real estate and the credit squeeze that was to hit the clients of local Chinese-owned banks in particular, there was enough real GDP growth each year to maintain the performance legitimacy of British rule (see Table II). The pain caused by financial failures was nonetheless real, and the number of potential victims was large, following the growth of the banking habit among the community at large. When the pain threatened to become political, it had to be controlled by using the government's reserves to bail out failing banks and their depositors. Sustained economic growth generated the government revenues to make this strategy affordable.

Table II: Gross Domestic Product, 1963–69 (percentage changes)[6]

Year	Nominal Growth	Real Growth
1963	20.1	15.7
1964	14.0	8.6
1965	17.4	14.5
1966	2.3	1.7
1967	8.4	1.7
1968	6.8	3.3
1969	17.5	11.3

Gathering Storm

The banking crisis had been brewing for a long time, and there had been ample warning signs of impending catastrophe. These had failed to stir the senior officials responsible for banking from their customary complacency. In 1961, mismanagement and misconduct had led to a run on the Liu Chong Hing Bank. A rescue was organised to maintain public confidence in the rest of the banking industry. Although the bank's problems were blamed on 'malicious rumours', the fragility of the banking system could no longer be ignored by the colonial administration.[7] An official was borrowed from the Bank of England, and he drafted legislation that would establish a modern regulatory system.

There was no rush to implement his recommendations. Officials miscalculated the resistance from powerful vested interests.[8] Delays were caused by lengthy negotiations with HSBC which had originally lobbied for reforms but was now determined to water down key provisions before the 1964 Banking Ordinance was passed.[9] The result was legislation that was known to be flawed. The Financial Secretary admitted that the new law was marred by three 'strictly unorthodox banking practices', principally in respect of controls on borrowing by directors.[10] The bankers' lobbying meant that the legislation failed to define the boundaries between personal and public interest, thereby condoning misconduct by directors that led to future scandals.[11]

As the process of drafting the new ordinance proceeded at a leisurely pace, officials had used the prospect of new legislation as an excuse to avoid dealing with banks already in trouble. Although increasingly uncomfortable about the risks created by poor management, they stuck to the strategy they had adopted in the late 1940s when bank regulation had first been enacted (which Chapter 6, 'The Rise and Fall of Chinese Banking', described). The failure to penalise the Liu Chong Hing Bank, despite the copious evidence of its scandalous behaviour, reinforced the dangerous message transmitted by lax regulation throughout the 1950s.[12]

- Officials had replaced statutory obligations with informal 'rules' that deliberately overlooked illegalities and imprudence because of a misplaced desire to safeguard 'traditional' Chinese banking practices.
- The bureaucrats' reluctance to act as regulators and enforce the law fostered a banking culture in which legal sanctions were no longer feared. Bank owners and executives had little anxiety about prosecution or cancellation of their licences.[13]
- As a result, bank owners and executives felt free to engage in fraudulent and corrupt behaviour to conceal mounting losses when the stock market fell or real estate slumped.[14]

In 1963, the Chiu Tai Bank ran out of liquidity. Officials had considerable evidence of how badly managed were its affairs, but they made only half-hearted efforts to have it closed.[15] Officials saw no political risk in allowing its depositors to lose their money, and it was allowed to fail. The disintegration of the locally owned Chinese bank sector gathered momentum. There were three more failures in early 1965: the Ming Tak, Canton Trust and Savings, and Hang Seng Banks. Although Hang Seng was the second largest bank in the colony, it commanded little respect with the newly arrived Banking Commissioner. 'I have never had any confidence in the Hang Seng Bank nor did I consider that they were a beneficial influence on the banking community here', he declared.[16] Nevertheless, its closure would have been calamitous. A rescue was feasible because HSBC recognised its commercial attractions. But the Ming Tak and the Canton Trust and Savings Banks were allowed to go into liquidation.

These five public failures did not reveal the full extent of the propensity to self-destruct. Another four locally owned Chinese banks would have suffered the same fate except for secret injections of government liquidity, as total deposits in this group fell by 30 per cent between January and September 1965.[17] The true total number of banks which forfeited their depositors' confidence between 1961 and 1965 was thus nine. The five which failed outright had suffered from one or more management defects that proved fatal to their survival:

- failure to distinguish between the public's deposits and personal assets;

- over-involvement in non-banking businesses, especially property development;[18] and
- dangerous disregard for real estate risks.[19]

The Blame Game

There was an inevitable rush to find culprits for the 1965 emergency. Hong Kong's colonial status fostered mistrust of British banks, which had already faced allegations in 1961 of exacerbating the Liu Chong Hing Bank's woes.[20] In 1965, a colonial conspiracy against Chinese business interests was an obvious explanation for the collapse of local banks, especially after HSBC took over Hang Seng Bank. 'Is the Hang Seng Bank's takeover part of official economic policy?', asked one anti-colonial newspaper, 'If so, the foreign banks will take over one Chinese bank after another as they get into difficulties'.[21] The *Far Eastern Economic Review* put the blame on attempts to reform the industry and the strains created by the new 1964 Banking Ordinance through the introduction of statutory liquidity requirements.[22] The newly arrived Banking Commissioner showed a much better grasp of reality and blamed the previous lack of banking regulation, stating publicly 'that the policy of laissez-faire and banking do not mix; that supervision and direction are essential'.[23] Assigning blame had serious implications for the colonial administration because the political environment was becoming more difficult to manage. The 1960s were a decade of Maoist upheavals on the Mainland; the collapse of sterling and final retreat from empire by the UK; and war and revolution throughout Asia. It was also a decade in which colonialism in Hong Kong faced its most serious challenges since the seamen's strike and the year-long boycott of 1925–26. The post-war myth of a docile society disappeared in street disturbances in 1966 and a summer of Maoist violence in 1967.

What made the 1965 bank runs a serious challenge to British rule was a transformation of the way in which the community and its families managed their money. Incomes had risen in the 1950s, and the banking habit had spread. As the bank network expanded, so did the volume of deposits they attracted. Table III suggests that the banks were highly successful in persuading small depositors to keep their money in savings accounts with a neighbourhood branch. In 1955, savings accounts had amounted to only 11 per cent of total deposits with licensed banks. By 1960, they had reached 20 per cent. Total bank deposits were more than six times higher in 1965 than they had been a decade earlier. But over the same period, savings deposits had expanded by a factor of 12. Members of the general public, it is reasonable to assume, accounted for a significant share of the banking system's customers by 1960, and the potential losses to these customers, if a bank failed, had also increased. The stability of the banking system had a direct impact on the well-being of an increasing proportion of the population. Bank runs could no longer be shrugged off by officials as they had been in the 1950s. Banking for the masses added a political dimension to the management of Hong Kong's money which the colonial administration could not ignore.

Table III: Banking Expansion, 1955–65[24]

Year	Head Offices & Branches (number)	Total Deposits (HKD million)	Savings Deposits (HKD million)
1955	97	1,137	133
1960	124	2,681	537
1965	301	7,250	1,620

At first in 1965, officials assumed that they retained the freedom to decide which illiquid bank would be rescued (they had their choice in the case of the Liu Chong Hing Bank in 1961) and which would be allowed to close with no recompense for their depositors (this had been the fate of the Chiu Tai Bank in 1963). Thus, when a run on the Canton Trust & Commercial Bank began in February 1965, the government decided that it should be treated no differently than the Ming Tak Bank which had been left to fail the previous month. But the Canton Trust had well over 100,000 customers, which created considerable potential for serious unrest. Public resentment ran so deep that the colonial administration had to display some concern for the unfortunate depositors, and the liquidators were eventually provided with public funds to start a protracted process of repaying deposits.[25]

Almost inadvertently, the relationship between a usually remote colonial administration and the community had been redefined. The government could now be called to account for its economic errors, even in the absence of conventional political parties or an elected legislature. The new political factor was obvious from the fact that the colonial administration only intervened to protect the depositors' interests after the Canton Trust's closure had provoked street protests.[26] There was no commercial justification for using public resources to rescue its depositors because the liabilities of the bank were so much larger than its assets that there seemed little hope of either the government or the depositors getting their money back in full.[27] The government loan and the liquidator's efforts were self-evident political gestures, and they set a precedent. After the angry public response to the colonial administration's initial indifference to the fate of the Canton Bank's depositors, no licensed bank would be allowed to collapse at its depositors' expense until 1991 and the closure of the Bank of Credit and Commerce International (BCCI). For the colonial administration, bank runs had become an unacceptable threat to the governability of Hong Kong.[28]

Called to Account

The Financial Secretary tried to shift as much of the blame for the crisis as possible onto the bankers. He skated over most of the misconduct and mismanagement, implying that such defects were confined to the two banks which had not been rescued in early 1965. Nevertheless, the average banker was at fault, he argued, for having been over-indulgent. 'Credit has been rather too easy in Hong Kong for good banking and commercial discipline', he declared, and businesses had become spoiled.[29]

> … many people assumed that once credit was accorded it would never be recalled; where many people assumed that credit would always be forthcoming to meet any demand; and where some banks themselves assumed that their deposits would continue to grow as rapidly as ever and were accordingly over-generous both with their immediate advances and with their promises of future loans. This led to an unhealthy state in some sectors of the economy where the inefficient and incompetent were never called to account; and those bankers who were responsible for failing to call them to account were themselves not called to account.

It was indeed true that bankers had not been called to account, not even by the officials responsible for enforcing the banking legislation, as Chapter 6 explained. Now in 1965, the colonial administration found itself vulnerable, and with good reason, because its own decisions had contributed to the banking turmoil. The government's real estate policies had created the profit opportunities which had lured bankers to disaster. And officials had stood by as speculation had intensified to a stage when only a miracle could have saved the property market from collapse.

The influence of official policies on the property sector had become very apparent soon after World War II, and not just because the government was the sole supplier of new land in the urban areas. Chapter 7, 'A Dangerous Business Model', described how changes in property law and policy affected the banking industry. In brief, wartime rent controls prevented property owners from evicting tenants to redevelop their sites. In addition, the law set the maximum height for a building much lower than modern construction techniques made viable. During the 1950s, these constraints were gradually modified.

- In 1953, a minor change in the law permitted owners to clear occupants from damaged or dangerous premise and to rebuild them.
- From 1955, it became possible to obtain court orders to evict tenants from rent-controlled property if the property were to be redeveloped and the tenants were paid compensation.
- From 1956, the pre-war restriction on building heights was abolished.

The impact of these changes was considerable. The market was freed from the most serious obstacles to redeveloping a city whose housing stock had deteriorated considerably in the previous decade because of lack of maintenance, gross overcrowding and war damage. The response of property developers was immediate. Table IV presents an index of the volume of redevelopment plans which received court approval and thus represented serious investment commitments. Each relaxation of legal restrictions during the 1950s was followed by an upward surge in the index. The market was being allowed to respond to pent-up demand for space — both for living and for work.

The 1950s showed how sensitive property developers were to changes that the government made to the legal environment. In the following decade, they were to respond no less dramatically to shifts in government policies. In 1962, the colonial administration announced a new policy on building densities. The total floor space that could be built on a site would be reduced, which would cut developers' profits. But there would be a breathing space, with the regulations coming into force between 1964 and 1966 (depending on the type of project). This concession was partially offset by tougher safety regulations that took effect in 1964. These were intended to reduce the dangers to neighbouring buildings which the spate of demolition and redevelopment of existing buildings had increased, and these new regulations slowed construction down significantly.

Developers responded to the new measure by accelerating the volume of planned redevelopment to beat the deadlines. Table IV shows how the index rose from 129 in the year before the more restrictive measures were announced to 286 in financial year 1961–62; they reached a peak of 326 in the following year. The density restrictions and the safety regulations started to come into force in the last quarter of financial year 1963–64, and the index fell to 131. (Some decline was probably unavoidable because the construction industry had no capacity left for expansion.) In 1964–65, the index recovered to 155, but the bank runs and political disturbances that marred the rest of the decade pushed the index down to levels not seen since the early 1950s.

As planned investment fell away, work on current projects was running into trouble. The desperate race against the deadline for the lower densities had led to unrealistic building schedules. Projects faced the risk of not being able to meet the deadlines set by their building covenants. By 1964, locally owned Chinese banks were locked into a volume of investment activity which had soared, not because of improving economic fundamentals but because of changes in government policies. Repayment schedules were in danger because of construction delays. The property projects that the banks were financing were often related enterprises. These were not loans that could be liquidated painlessly or quickly. As Chapter 7 pointed out, this sector of the banking industry was now very vulnerable to a fall in property market confidence.

Table IV: Index of Urban Redevelopment Plans for Financial Years
1953–54 to 1972–73 (1959–60 = 100)[30]

Year	Index	Background	Year	Index	Background
1953–54	3	Rebuilding	1963–64	131	Restrictions on
		restrictions			rebuilding works
1954–55	20	relaxed	1964–65	155	Bank runs
1955–56	38	New legislation	1965–66	16	
1956–57	52	facilitates	1966–67	11	Kowloon riots
1957–58	74	redevelopment	1967–68	5	Anti-British riots
1958–59	55		1968–69	9	
1959–60	100		1969–70	n.a.	
1960–61	129		1970–71	119	
1961–62	286	Rush to beat	1971–72	173	
1962–63	326	constraints on desities	1972–73	123	

n.a.: data not available

Missing the Link

Each of the legal and policy changes discussed in the previous section was well-intentioned and easily justified on either economic or social grounds. Nevertheless, their overall impact in the 1960s was to introduce a dangerous distortion into the property market. Booming demand from the property sector for funds to finance the surge in new development in 1962 and 1963 was an irresistible temptation to reckless lending, all the more so when the officials responsible for overseeing the banks showed such little concern for the proper conduct of banking business. The inability of individual bankers to resist the heady profits offered by property lending became a major threat to banking stability in this decade. The developers' dependence on their bankers increased, and the exposure of local Chinese-owned banks grew to levels that alarmed officials in the early 1960s.[31]

The bureaucrats faced a serious dilemma in managing the risks created by the property sector and its banking links, however. The colonial administration felt very dependent on the private sector's contribution of relieving the overcrowding and squalor in which a high proportion of the population was living. When the volume of planned investment was doubling in 1961–62, according to the index of redevelopment plans, the government declared that 'it would be very shortsighted to do anything to discourage' the developer.[32] Catastrophe then became only a matter of time because the excessively liberal creation of credit by the banks allowed developers to launch over-ambitious property projects that proved financially unsustainable.[33] In the aftermath of the 1965 banking crisis, the colonial administration was anxious to deny any involvement in the creation and collapse of the real estate bubble.[34] Nevertheless, the link between government policy and property speculation was undeniable. The Financial Secretary publicly admitted that he had known that 'the vast volume of private plans [in 1963] stimulated and accelerated by the shadow of the forthcoming new building regulations' was leading to alarming 'public problems'.[35] After the banking crisis was over, he faced accusations that the government should have seen how its policies were driving property speculation to dangerous levels and should have intervened. He frankly conceded that he could have choked off speculation in 1963 and brought this market under control through administrative measures. He had decided to do nothing, however, because 'businessmen would have fiercely resisted' any government intervention, and he would have been overwhelmed by a 'torrent of angry protest'.[36]

Thus, before 1965, the government had chosen to ignore the threat that over-exposure to real estate was posing to local Chinese-owned banks. The Financial Secretary's principal anxiety at that time was the strain on the construction industry created by the property boom which was causing delays in the government's public works programme and inflating its costs.[37] He was acting, in fact, like a managing director whose sole concern was with his own firm's trading conditions, rather than as a finance minister responsible for the stability of the banking industry and of the overall economy. In part, this misjudgment was the result of the colonial administration's refusal to collect adequate statistics. Previous chapters have explained how officials misunderstood the way banks created liquidity and how the government had no reliable figure to correct their personal preconceptions about banking practices until the end of 1964. If the statistics on lending patterns had been available a year earlier, the Financial Secretary could have seen that the stability of the financial system was a real cause for concern and that he had every justification for taking direct action to rein in the property market. This data deficit meant that the link between banking behaviour and property market trends could not be tracked with any accuracy.

Selective Bail-outs

In managing the aftershocks from the banking crisis, the colonial administration faced three powerful lobbies seeking government support in surviving the credit squeeze caused both by the public's panic withdrawal of funds from the banking system and by the banks' efforts to recover loans and bolster their reserves: the banks themselves, property developers and manufacturers.

The government showed little hesitation in bailing out the banking system. The government pumped funds into the local Chinese-owned banks regardless of the quality of their management or their loan portfolios.[38] At their peak, these secret injections totalled HK$163 million — equivalent to 9.7 per cent of the total liquidity of the local Chinese-owned banks.[39] The creation of the Banking Commission in 1964 gave the colonial administration the professional expertise and the financial information required to manage this rescue operation with success. The Commissioner's powers to demand detailed statistics meant that threats to individual banks could be identified on the basis of their solvency, their lending patterns and their compliance with statutory liquidity requirements.[40] As a result, the government was able to monitor the impact of changes in depositor confidence on individual banks and to identify the institutions which required immediate injections of liquidity. For the first time, government decisions did not have to rely on business gossip.[41] This new information-led approach to banking supervision transformed the industry's ability to withstand external shocks. It also proved robust during the anti-colonial disturbances of 1966 and the anti-British campaign of the following year when Mao Zedong's Cultural Revolution exported bombs and riots to Hong Kong.

Yet, 1965 was a traumatic experience for the colonial administration, so much so that it abandoned the policy of earmarking government reserves for use in a recession to maintain government spending programmes and 'get on with the task of providing our people with their needs'.[42] Instead, the reserves would be used to offset unexpected deflationary pressures on the banking industry.[43] To ensure that the government would have the necessary funds to prevent future credit squeezes and to counter pressure on the exchange rate during a sudden political or economic shock to Hong Kong, the Financial Secretary adopted a policy of accumulating 'abnormally high' levels of reserves compared with other governments, which were to be kept, as far as practicable, as highly liquid assets overseas.[44] This goal had far-reaching implications. It could only be achieved by holding down the government's spending on social services and the infrastructure in order to produce the annual budget surpluses that provided insurance against banking instability and other financial threats. These funds would have to be invested abroad, thus withdrawing them from the Hong Kong financial system and the pool of local investment funds.

The colonial administration tried to minimise the importance of property in destabilising the banking system. Officials were worried about the political costs of the bank runs and were anxious to avoid a critical examination of their own past policy errors. They also wanted to allay suspicions that property values were based on the reckless expectations of speculators, fearing a surge in panic selling and a slump in demand for new premises. Developers were much less sensitive about either the public mood or market sentiment. They faced bankruptcy unless the government came to their assistance, they claimed, and their sense of impending ruin gave them the courage to present the colonial administration with a set of demands which the Financial Secretary privately described as 'impertinent … and dangerous'. The Real Estate Developers' Association warned of possible public demonstrations against a credit squeeze which was bringing the property sector to its knees. Lack of bank facilities, it declared, had caused 'approximately one half of all private development schemes [to be delayed] … or entirely brought to a halt'. The government rejected the accuracy of this estimate but acknowledged that sales of newly completed premises had slumped, with the possibility of some projects collapsing. The Commissioner of Banking tried to deprive the developers of statistical ammunition to bolster their case and urged that publication of routine property sector figures should be suspended because they showed a large rise in the number of newly completed flats which had not found purchasers. Nevertheless, his confidential advice was that a rescue operation was of 'the utmost importance' because 'the bulk of loans and advances by all banks is secured by property'.[45]

But the Financial Secretary decided to defy the property sector. Developers had only themselves to blame, he insisted. 'Excessive real estate development' had 'aggravated our banking troubles, by freezing so much of our available resources in the form of not readily realizable and temporarily unproductive assets'. Furthermore, he argued, there were no grounds for talking about a property slump.[46]

> Our real estate 'depression' is characterized more by a temporarily excessive increase in supply than by any substantial reduction in demand for new premises and by a tendency at present for the general public to rent rather than purchase.

The available statistics were much less reassuring. Even gloomier than the data on the mounting stock of new flats standing vacant and unsold were the figures on planned investment in residential redevelopment projects, which were the driving force in the property market at that time.[47] The government chose to ignore these statistics which pointed to a total collapse of new investment in the sector which was to persist until the end of the decade (see Table IV).[48] True, the monthly data now being collected by the Banking Commission revealed no decline in the volume of bank business related to property, either in terms of the volume of funding from the banks or as a percentage of total bank lending.[49]. These figures were misleading, however. They covered only current lending for building and construction and did not include loans for investment in land, property purchases or mortgages, for example. 'Depression' was an accurate description of the state of the property sector, regardless of the Financial Secretary's efforts to reinterpret reality.

The Real Estate Developers' Association deserved little sympathy, of course. Its members wanted to be bailed out at public expense from the consequences of the rampant speculation from which the property sector had profited very handsomely in the past. Industrialists had a better case for government support during the pressure on credit facilities that followed the bank runs. The two principal manufacturers' lobbies complained to the colonial administration that local banks were withdrawing facilities and that small factories were being badly hit by this credit squeeze. The manufacturers' representatives urged the government to ensure that the funds it made available to the banks were used to support the smaller firms. In fact, these emergency funds were not intended to prop up industry. Their aim was to offset the flight of depositors from the local Chinese-owned banks.[50] Within the colonial administration, an influential group of officials sympathised with the appeals from industry for more government support. They argued that manufacturers were significantly harmed by a lack of finance, a claim discredited by subsequent surveys.[51] Nevertheless, these officials won a brief victory in the following decade when a scheme to provide loans to small industry was set up in 1972, only to be wound up in 1976.[52]

Hopelessly Wrong

The colonial administration declined to take direct action to relieve the effects of deflation on the economy following the bank runs. This decision was not inspired by a preference for laisser faire. It was another example of the data deficit and the result of Cowperthwaite's adamant refusal to permit the collection of statistics essential for rational policy-making. It was compounded by his curious conviction that 'guesstimates' were likely to prove as useful to a finance minister as accurate information. At best, he declared, official national income figures might be 'more precise and authoritative', but they were unlikely to be 'very accurate'. In response to appeals by business representatives for national income estimates, he replied — astonishingly — that the business community itself would oppose the collection of such data as onerous and expensive. More surprising still, he argued that 'it is not necessary, nor even of any particular value, to have these figures available for the formulation of policy'. 'We have a rough idea of where we are', he claimed, 'certainly enough for any practical purposes'.[53]

This complacency was ill-founded. Cowperthwaite had a very misleading idea of economic trends, and his misconceptions led to contradictory policies during the economic downturn that followed the 1965 banking crisis. In his 1966 budget speech, he insisted that the 1965 bank crisis had been contained.[54] A 'temporary deflation of credit' had occurred, he said, which the government had resolved through injecting liquidity into the banks at risk. He repeatedly poured scorn on claims that the economy had suffered either 'recession' or 'depression'. He clinched his case with the following statement:[55]

The words 'recession' and 'depression' have been freely used during the course of last year [and its bank runs] and, while it is true that some sectors of the economy have receded, the whole economy has done so only in the relative sense of growing less fast. When you have been running at 12–15% and slow down to a trot at, say 6–8% (which is a very rough guess at last year's rate) you have the impression of going backwards — although rivals continue to envy you your speed.

Cowperthwaite's encouraging estimates of the economy's performance were hopelessly wrong. The economy had actually expanded significantly during 1965. The slowdown came in 1966 and 1967, with real GDP growth falling below 2 per cent in both years, well under the trend for the decade (see Table II). Cowperthwaite lacked the data to estimate how long it would take an economy with Hong Kong's growth momentum to slow down, so there was little to prevent him from misunderstanding the impact of the bank runs on business sentiment and misreading the time lag before the rate of growth declined in response to the slump in investor confidence. If Cowperthwaite had not set his face so resolutely against the compilation of national income statistics, he would have been unable to take such an optimistic view of the state of the economy in the 1966 budget. His budget measures that year raised taxes and exerted the maximum restraint on public sector spending. Both policies might have been justified if his belief had been well-founded that the crisis was over and had left the economy growing at six to eight per cent. Because his budget was framed on a flawed estimate of growth trends, it contained deflationary measures inappropriate to Hong Kong's situation in 1966. GDP statistics were far from irrelevant to budgetary policy that year.[56]

Would Cowperthwaite's 1966 budget have been very different if proper GDP data had been available? Despite his general insistence that Hong Kong's special characteristics made it impossible to reflate the economy, Cowperthwaite accepted that the annual budget could provide a useful stimulus. 'Over-spending in the not so good [years] is a sound practice', he admitted.[57] On this principle, his 1966 budget should not have raised taxes and held down public spending. These measures depressed both consumption and investment. Cowperthwaite also ignored another deflationary factor. Chapter 11, 'Colonial Money and its Management', will show how the money supply was affected by changes in the level of reserves which Hong Kong held overseas. When these reserves increased, bank liquidity fell and the economy deflated. During 1965, Hong Kong's sterling holdings had risen by HKD720 million. Cowperthwaite hailed the increase as a sign of economic strength instead of recognising how it added to the credit squeeze. The government increased its sterling assets in 1966, which was a further constraint on liquidity.[58]

It is plain that Cowperthwaite knew that budgetary stringency was not the right prescription when the economy had lost momentum. He also knew that an increase in the overseas reserves would contract the money supply.[59] But in 1965 and 1966, he had no reliable data about how the economy was actually performing. He assumed that the bank runs had caused only a temporary setback in 1965 and that the underlying growth rate remained robust. This was true of domestic exports but not of the overall economy. Because his own analysis was flawed by the data deficit, he could make the assumption that Hong Kong might well benefit from curbing inflationary pressures through a tougher budget for 1966 and a continued build-up in Hong Kong's sterling assets for a second year.

Table II indicates that inflationary pressures were real, quite understandably when export growth from the dominant manufacturing sector was so rapid (as Table I illustrates). Inflation was not supposed to be a policy concern for the colonial administration in the 1960s, however. The Governor had declared in 1964 that 'cost inflation is a sign of increased prosperity and of maturity', a sentiment that Cowperthwaite repeated in later years.[60] The truth was that the colonial administration's macroeconomic response to the 1965 banking crisis was confused. The data deficit meant that neither budgetary nor monetary policies could be framed on the basis of a factual analysis of Hong Kong's economic dynamics or of an informed assessment of the policy options and their consequences.

Bowing to the Bankers

The bank runs themselves were quickly controlled, thanks mainly to the Banking Commission and other reforms introduced in 1964. But how was the banking system to be defended against future crises? The colonial administration found the answer in the bankers' analysis of the causes of banking instability, which identified excessive competition as the culprit. This theory was politically convenient for both bureaucrats and bankers because it distracted attention from the banks' own greed and fraud and the government's failure to police the industry.

Officials were surrendering to lobbying led by HSBC which had started in the 1950s. HSBC and other banks had argued then that new licences should not be issued to foreign banks because Hong Kong had 'more than enough banks already.'[61] The bankers' demands were rejected forcibly in 1959. The Financial Secretary at that time laid down that applications from sound overseas banks should be accepted in accordance with the 'traditional policy of welcoming all forms of business and trade'. He added that, unlike local banks, foreign banks were unlikely to default on their obligations.[62] In any case, the total number of banks was in decline during that decade. When bank licensing began in 1948, there had been 132 licensed banks (of which 12 were foreign and 111 local Chinese). On the eve of the 1965 banking crisis, there were only 87 licensed banks (of which 35 were foreign and 38 local Chinese).[63]

This open-door policy was reversed when Cowperthwaite became Financial Secretary in 1961. He declared that 'another bank in Hong Kong is unwelcome', although he produced no data to show that Hong Kong was over-banked.[64] The Bank of England official who advised on legislation to create a modern regulatory system in 1962 took the same line as the bankers, without offering any supporting statistics. He subsequently wrote a report on the origins of the 1965 runs which showed clearly that mismanagement and misconduct had been the primary causes of the crisis. Nevertheless, his confidential report also complained: 'Too many banks chasing the available business is one of the basic causes of the reckless employment of customers' money'.[65] This assertion was unsupported by any factual analysis. On this anecdotal basis, a moratorium on new bank licences was introduced which lasted until 1981, and the government endorsed an interest-rate cartel that survived until 2001.[66] The indications are that the decision on the cartel was made with little formal discussion.[67]

A recent, authoritative study of the available data has concluded that Hong Kong was not 'over-banked' or threatened by 'excessive' competition in the 1960s: 'The threat to banking in Hong Kong was not the number of banks or their size, but the interlocking ownership of banks and other businesses that were prone to asset market shocks, combined with poor governance'.[68] The cartel did not prevent future crises. Indeed, the scandals worsened over the next two decades. In addition, the costs to the public were significant.[69] The cartel set the interest rates payable on Hong Kong dollar deposits until 2001, thus restricting price competition in the retail market.[70] This impressive study also identifies the true beneficiaries of the cartel. HSBC was now protected against foreign-owned banks, and its newly acquired subsidiary, Hang Seng Bank, was protected against competition from medium-sized banks. The smaller local banks also profited from the government-backed constraints on competition.

The moratorium on new licenses was to have a pernicious effect on the future development of the financial sector. The barrier it imposed on entry to Hong Kong had absurd consequences. As the Financial Secretary was to admit in 1974: 'The fact is that it does prevent the participation in our banking system of some of the most highly reputable international banks in the world and inhibits the emergence of any new local banks'.[71] New entrants were free, however, to enter the colony's market as unlicensed DTCs which the colonial administration chose not to regulate.

The following chapter will show how dangerous these anti-competition measures were to prove in the 1970s and early 1980s. They created new and powerful incentives for banks to escape from the restrictions imposed by their licensed status, and these policies rewarded financial institutions which set up DTCs to operate outside the regulatory constraints imposed on the banking industry. The results were to be even more damaging than the consequences of lax regulation and the tolerance of imprudent and improper behaviour had been for licensed banks between the 1948 and the 1964 Banking Ordinances.

Conclusions

This chapter has demonstrated that 1965 bank runs were an avoidable crisis. Its origins were not just liquidity problems. The 1960s were a period of considerable change in the political landscape, which made it impossible to continue the traditional colonial attitude of indifference to the fate of depositors when banks were mismanaged into insolvency. Mass banking meant that the quality of banking directly affected a growing section of the community. In the absence of representative political institutions, the colonial administration had good reason to fear that depositors would take to the streets seeking redress for their lost savings. Even conservative property tycoons recognised the power of public protests in the aftermath of the credit squeeze that followed the banks runs. As a result, officials had to accept that the government would have to take responsibility for rescuing banks in distress.

The chapter shows the importance of professional regulators. It is hard to imagine how the colonial administration could have coped with the 1965 banking emergency — and the political challenges of 1966 and 1967 — without the modern regulatory structure set up by the 1964 Banking Ordinance. These put the Financial Secretary in a position to identify the banks that needed to be drip-fed back to solvency. The chapter also highlights the costs of the colonial administration's dysfunctional approach to policy making. This problem was aggravated by absence of adequate information. Hong Kong's political arrangements fostered a reluctance to accept responsibility, not just for banking regulation but also for the proper management of monetary affairs and the overall economy (issues discussed in Chapter 10. Officials knew that they would never be called to account for their personal misjudgments which meant that there was little to prevent the errors of one decade from being repeated in the next.

9
From Banking Crisis to Financial Catastrophe

The closing decades of the last century saw no let-up in the pace of Hong Kong's economic expansion. Between 1970 and 1979, the economy in real terms doubled in size, and by 1985, it was three times larger than it had been in 1970 (see Table I). Behind this remarkable performance lay an economic transformation as rapid and as dramatic as the industrial take-off after World War II and from which Hong Kong emerged as a leading international financial centre and a prosperous post-industrial society. There was also a drastic change in the colony's relations with the Mainland between 1970 and 1985. Hong Kong shifted from its role of offshore centre for China's international foreign trade and investment to onshore investor and entrepreneur. But while the colony's reintegration into the Mainland economy began, political strains developed as Hong Kong's return to Chinese rule created diplomatic confrontations and business uncertainty.

The New Economy

The new Hong Kong economy had two engines of growth. The first was manufacturing which continued to flourish, as domestic exports rose by an annual 19 per cent during the 1970s compared with 17 per cent in the 1960s. The second was the services sector which was enjoying a boom that had much in common with the breakneck growth of manufacturing a quarter of a century earlier. Exports of services grew by almost 17 per cent per annum in the 1970s compared with 12 per cent in the previous decade. By 1980, 'financing, insurance, real estate and business services' had almost caught up with manufacturing in terms of value of output, and the two sectors each accounted for some 23 per cent of GDP.[1]

Deindustrialisation got under way with a smoothness that has been described as 'one of the records in world history': 'Given the very low

Table I: GDP Growth, 1970–85 (HKD million)²

Year	Current Market Prices	Year-on-year Growth (%)	Index (1970 = 100)	Constant (2000) Market Prices	Year-on-year Growth (%)	Index (1970 = 100)
1970	23,100	18.9	100	186,010	9.2	100
1971	26,647	15.4	115	199,321	7.2	107
1972	32,168	20.7	139	220,313	10.5	118
1973	41,284	28.3	179	247,425	12.3	133
1974	47,165	14.2	204	253,059	2.3	136
1975	49,567	5.1	215	254,102	0.4	137
1976	63,141	27.4	273	295,337	16.2	159
1977	73,222	16.0	317	330,181	11.8	178
1978	85,698	17.0	371	357,863	8.4	192
1979	112,533	31.3	487	399,461	11.6	215
1980	143,402	27.4	621	440,766	10.3	237
1981	172,965	20.6	749	482,148	9.4	259
1982	195,408	13.0	846	496,529	3.0	266
1983	216,383	10.7	937	525,923	5.9	282
1984	260,761	20.5	1129	578,016	9.9	310
1985	276,823	6.2	1198	582,150	0.7	313

unemployment and underemployment rates prevailing in [these] years, the ease with which employees switched across sectors is a testimony to the famous flexibility of the Hong Kong economy'.[3] Over half the labour force still worked in factories in 1977 and generated almost 30 per cent of GDP. Two decades later, 85 per cent of GDP came from the services sector, which now employed 79 per cent of the labour force.

There was also a significant shift in the colonial administration's economic policies. The colonial administration identified financial services as a major source of the colony's future prosperity. In 1973, the Financial Secretary promised to make Hong Kong a financial centre which matched world standards with 'guidelines which would ensure its growth in a manner which would command the respect of those who decide to conduct their business in or through the Colony'.[4] Despite this commitment to quality, the colony suffered from severe financial crises and acute banking instability between 1970 and 1985. Share and property markets collapsed twice; inflation soared; and the currency came close to free fall in September 1983. Scandals proliferated as never before. Local banks failed, and overseas banks were involved in fraud and corruption on a grand scale, and their executives faced prosecution, together with prominent local lawyers and other professionals.[5]

These crises were aggravated by events outside Hong Kong. The 1970s saw the collapse of traditional international financial relations. The Sterling

Area came to an end in 1972, and Hong Kong cut its currency links with London. The US dollar could no longer cope with the mounting American trade deficit, and, by 1973, the world was switching to floating exchange rates. Singapore seemed better placed than Hong Kong in this turmoil and was reported to be poised to overtake Tokyo as a financial centre after the Asian Currency Unit emerged. This market grew from USD1 billion in 1971 to almost USD10 billion by the end of 1974.[6]

Financial shocks overseas were followed by political clashes with the Mainland which shook business confidence. In 1979, the UK raised the question of Hong Kong's future with China's leaders for the first time. The subsequent negotiations were conducted in secret between 1982 and 1984, but the disputes between the two sides were open and intense until the last few months before agreement was reached in 1984. The Sino-British Joint Declaration signed that year created certainty about the date for the British departure but did not remove anxiety about what lay ahead in the interim.

The colonial administration found it difficult to adjust to Hong Kong's increasingly complex circumstances, particularly in managing financial affairs. The colony plainly needed an active monetary policy. This was a responsibility which the government had rejected in previous decades and which the current Financial Secretary, Sir Philip Haddon-Cave, tried in vain to avoid. But non-interventionism was no longer an option in a world of floating exchange rates. The laisser-faire vision of Hong Kong as a self-regulating economy nevertheless proved a costly myth to which officials clung , regardless of the evidence. (The colonial administration's record in managing monetary affairs and Haddon-Cave's personal performance are reviewed in the next chapter.) Nor did the colonial administration recognise that banking supervision was no long a matter of policing commercial banks whose main business was financing trade and industry. Official were reluctant to accept that the growing sophistication of banking services, both domestic and international, increased the need for effective regulation.[7]

This chapter will trace the origins of Hong Kong's remarkable economic transformation and its emergence as a financial centre in the 1970s. It will show how policy decisions taken after the 1965 bank runs, particularly the introduction of constraints on banking competition, distorted the development of the banking industry with damaging consequences in the 1970s. The chapter will review the government's refusal to expand its regulatory powers, a revival of the reluctance to regulate which had proved pernicious in the 1950s. It will also discuss why the colonial administration lost control over the money supply, leading to a severe instability of the financial system.

In Search of Growth

The years between 1970 and 1985 were a period in which the credibility of the colonial administration was constantly at risk because of its mismanagement of monetary affairs. As in the past, however, the government's performance legitimacy was rescued by real economic growth, year in and year out, almost regardless of world trading conditions and the colony's own uncertainties. The economy faltered occasionally, but the annual expansion was never halted. The government could rely on the astonishing growth momentum, illustrated in Table I, to produce enough surplus resources to buy solutions for every crisis. Thus, after world recession reduced Hong Kong to virtual stagnation in 1975, real growth rebounded to 16 per cent in the following year, the highest annual rate in the entire 15-year period. Similarly, as the currency depreciated and the secret Sino-British talks on Hong Kong's future deteriorated into open conflict, the real growth rate recovered from three per cent in 1982 to almost ten per cent in 1984. Nothing, it seemed, could derail the colony's progress.

Despite the endless economic growth and buoyant industrial exports, pessimism mounted throughout the 1970s. The business community contemplated a bleak future. Land prices, wages and production costs were soaring, and textile exports were threatened by new protectionist measures overseas. Officials shared this sense of approaching disaster and endorsed the colony's first programme for industrial development which gave pride of place to plans for an oil refinery and the creation of a logistics support base for offshore exploration.[8] These ambitious proposals came to nothing, however, and the offshore oil boom failed to materialise.[9]

The banks, too, were looking in new directions. Confidential Banking Commission data provide a snapshot of the business models of the different banking sectors for 1969–72, when Hong Kong was now a mature manufacturing economy and about to expand into a major financial centre (see Table II). Lending priorities were still similar to the pattern of the previous decade described in Chapter 5, 'Industrial Take-off: Cut-price and Self-financed'.

- The priority of Chinese state-owned banks was still trade activities related to the Mainland. They lent virtually nothing to manufacturing.
- Local Chinese-owned banks had allowed HSBC and the foreign-owned banks to dominate the manufacturing market. But local banks had a larger share of property business ('building and construction') and of the market for personal loans ('professional and private individuals').
- HSBC and the foreign banks were the main sources of finance both for manufacturing and for foreign (and wholesale) trade transactions.

Table II: Loans and Advances by Bank Group and Purpose, 1969–72 (HK$ millions)[10]

Year-end	Banks	Manufacturing	Import, Export & Wholesale Trade	Retail Trade	Building & Construction	Stock Brokers	Professional & Private Individuals	Total
1969	All banks	1,490	2,666	179	803	63	1,004	7,884
	China state-owned	55	329	30	47	-	49	570
	Local Chinese-owned	303	552	35	307	33	706	2,263
	HSBC & foreign-owned	1,132	1,785	114	449	29	249	5,051
1970	All banks	1,860	3,527	217	649	143	1,367	9,670
	China state-owned	56	387	41	38	-	60	645
	Local Chinese-owned	450	735	53	315	105	962	3,003
	HSBC & foreign-owned	1,354	2,135	123	296	38	345	6,022
1971	All banks	1,979	3,961	228	723	249	1,862	11,836
	China state-owned	69	394	33	61	-	82	752
	Local Chinese-owned	538	912	65	392	196	1,347	3,915
	HSBC & foreign-owned	1,372	2,655	130	270	53	432	7,169
1972	All banks	2,233	4,770	340	1,090	736	3,746	17,726
	China state-owned	84	424	60	68	5	105	858
	Local Chinese-owned	630	1,025	106	403	533	2,360	5,686
	HSBC & foreign-owned	1,515	3,321	175	619	199	1,281	11,182

Note: The 'Total' column includes items not otherwise listed in the table.

The foreign sector, however, was very responsive to market trends. It could change its lending patterns rapidly to compete head-on with local banks. Personal loans and lending to property rose sharply in 1972, the first evidence of a move by the international banks to change their business model. Henceforward, they would no longer be content with conservative lending to trade and manufacturing for export. They were now in search of the far more lucrative business that followed the new fashion among Chinese family businesses of establishing corporate structures and going public. These banks were also looking for offshore business.

The restructuring of Hong Kong's economy was to transform the entire banking landscape. Life without the manufacturers seemed to be the inevitable trend until, suddenly, at the end of the decade, Hong Kong industrialists were given access to vast supplies of cheap land and labour in neighbouring Guangdong province. The Chinese Communist Party's endorsement of Deng Xiaoping's 'open door' policies and other measures to liberalise the Mainland economy in 1978 started the transfer of the bulk of the colony's manufacturing capacity to Guangdong Province. Some local industrialists had previously moved elsewhere in Asia, attracted by the generous incentive programmes offered by Asian governments. But these inducements were nothing compared with the lure of the Mainland after Deng Xiaoping's reforms were launched in 1978.[11] Hong Kong businessmen gravitated, almost instinctively, towards Guangdong Province and the coastal regions. Guangdong, linguistically, culturally and geographically, was an extension of Hong Kong as far as its businessmen were concerned.[12] China's leaders assigned a key role to the colony in the drive for modernisation, particularly in expanding the Mainland's access to world export markets, importing modern technology and mobilising investment funds.[13] By the end of the century, an estimated five million Guangdong workers were employed in Hong Kong-owned enterprises, 20 times more than the total number of factory workers in Hong Kong. Hong Kong had mobilised USD170 billion for the Mainland by this date, providing 49 per cent of total external direct investment in China.[14] Hong Kong raised the capital and devised the techniques for direct investment in Mainland projects even before China had developed the formal legal and financial structures that foreign investors normally expect.

Hong Kong's special contribution to financing the Mainland's modernisation added a new dimension to its status as an international financial centre.[15] In many ways, however, the colony was simply returning to its historical role: mobilising capital from around the world to finance China's development and investing its own funds and expertise in Mainland ventures just as it had done for a century before Mao Zedong had come to power in 1949.

International Financial Centres

Although Hong Kong's emergence as an international financial centre is usually regarded as part of the process of global financial development in the 1970s,[16] the colony had been Asia's leading financial centre long before World War II. It had remained the premier centre in Asia for offshore financial business after the war, mainly because of its freedom from exchange controls and the large number of international banks in the colony. Chapter 4, 'Financial Centre under Siege', demonstrated how Hong Kong developed a unique international financial sector which provided China with hard currency throughout the Cold War, enabling it to finance national development despite a US embargo and the political and economic turmoil of the Maoist era.

Tokyo overtook the colony in 1960 after Japan had recovered from the war and become a major force in world markets.[17] This development did not persuade the colonial administration that special incentives were needed to boost Hong Kong's offshore activities. On the contrary, the official view in the 1960s was that Hong Kong was already so successful as an international financial centre that it was 'attracting capital from outside … to what could be an embarrassing degree'.[18] In 1972, a new Financial Secretary did not rate Hong Kong so highly. The colony was merely an 'aspirant financial centre'.[19] Hong Kong's offshore financial activities were seen as a relatively new trend whose future expansion would depend on the positive policies to be adopted by the government. There would be no tax concessions, however, so that the main incentive the government could offer would be a pledge of minimal regulatory constraints on foreign-owned financial institutions.[20]

The fear that foreign financial institutions might find Hong Kong unattractive if subjected to statutory controls was entirely without foundation. They had continued to make extraordinary profits both before and after the 1964 Banking Ordinance introduced regulation by professionals. Even US banks did remarkably well, although Washington had long imposed regulatory constraints on overseas banking activities and had limited American banks' overseas lending from the mid-1960s to defend its balance of payments.[21] The liquidity loophole available to the colony's foreign-owned banks enabled them to overcome such obstacles to expanding their business in Hong Kong. (See Chapter 11, 'The Exceptional Colony'.) In 1968, a Hong Kong official reported that 'the six American banks in the colony are operating on a capital of US$1.6 million — less, in fact, than the minimum required by any [single] one'. Yet, he noted, Citibank (then FNCB) had 'over seven years, remitted profits from the Colony in excess of US$6 million'.[22]

In the early 1970s and the Third World, a 'steady stream of merchant banks' arrived in Hong Kong.[23] The colony's attractions for overseas bankers were overwhelming.[24] The immediate inducement was 'the Hong Kong money market … one of the cheapest sources of short term funds available in the world'. In addition, a foreign bank required such little capital to operate in Hong Kong, officials noted, that assets of HKD30 million could support a loan portfolio of an estimated HKD210 million. The only significant constraint on the expansion of Hong Kong as a financial centre was the moratorium adopted after the 1965 bank runs. As the government admitted, the ban on new bank licences stifled the establishment of new local banks and prevented the entry of major international banks.[25] Both types of bank would have been happy to accept statutory regulation as the price of a Hong Kong licence. The colonial administration chose to ignore the evidence that showed so clearly how the exceptional profits that licensed foreign banks could make in Hong Kong were more than adequate compensation for the constraints of the regulators. Officials continued to fear that the development of an international financial centre would be stifled by government regulation, leading the Governor to offer a sweeping public pledge: 'We must not ever on any account discourage enterprise and the willingness to take risks for the sake of profits'.[26]

In reality, the case for extensive regulation of financial instructions, both foreign and local, was to grow stronger in this decade because of the technical transformation that was overtaking the world's banking industry. Foreign-owned banks were fully integrated into the colony's financial system and free to participate in any form of local business. In consequence, Hong Kong could not be insulated from the changes in banking practices and technology taking place in the world's most advanced financial centres. Hong Kong's best-known banking economist has summarised 'the on-going financial innovations that accompany the growth of a financial center' and which led to a banking 'revolution' in this decade.[27]

> In the 1970s alone, new financial techniques, instruments, and services that appeared in Hong Kong included loan syndication, project finance and term lending, currency swaps, leasing, factoring, corporate advice (especially on mergers and acquisitions), certificates of deposits, credit cards, offshore bond issues, autopay, cash-dispenser, bank-managed central provident funds, etc.

These innovations created new challenges for bank regulators whose benchmarks had evolved in the traditional world of commercial banking. Particularly important was the growth of wholesale banking. The switch to large-scale corporate deals and complex financial products was part of a global trend that gave a powerful advantage to international banks during the 1970s. Their business increasingly involved transactions that took place offshore and were not limited to a single national currency, which meant that they were not subject to the same regulatory and other constraints as local banks.[28] The case for regulation was to be ignored, however, just as it had been from 1948 to 1964.

In Fear of Competition

The previous chapter described how, after the 1965 bank runs, the colonial administration decided that the best defence against another banking crisis was less competition. That policy made no sense once the colonial administration had decided to encourage an influx of foreign banks, even though they would not have licensed bank status. They would be excluded from the existing regulatory system but they would not be prevented from challenging the existing financial institutions for business. In addition, the anti-competition measures gave licensed institutions both the incentive and the opportunity to flee from the regulators' supervision and escape from the legal controls designed to prevent improper and imprudent lending.

- The interest-rate cartel applied only to licensed banks and prevented them from competing for deposits on price. Banks thus faced a serious obstacle in expanding their deposit base rapidly in response to new lending opportunities. They could evade the cartel restrictions, however, by shifting part of their activities into unlicensed DTCs which operated outside the regulated system.
- The moratorium on new licences meant that, in practice, new banks could only enter the industry as DTCs. This unlicensed status meant that they avoided the costs of complying with statutory liquidity requirements and their lending was subject to no restrictions.
- To remain competitive against these new 'non-bank' rivals, licensed banks had an additional incentive to transfer activities outside the regulated system by establishing their own DTCs.
- If the parents of these 'non-bank' DTCs were licensed, either locally or overseas, the public regarded them as having the same status as the parent bank. Thus, a new banking sector was created, unlicensed and, at best, regulated only indirectly.

Unlike earlier decades, the strains on the financial system were to come in the first place from the foreign-owned banks. Throughout the industrial take-off and the manufacturing boom, the foreign banks had been comfortable about lending to Hong Kong's factories, despite significant political and currency risks, thanks to the liquidity loophole which they enjoyed: the freedom to set their own liquidity ratios. The 1964 Banking Ordinance introduced legal liquidity requirements, but these did not close the loophole. Foreign banks were allowed to meet the statutory requirements through window-dressing transactions with their head offices.[29] Thus, the foreign-owned banks were able to lend money far more liberally than either the locally owned Chinese banks or HSBC. The liquidity loophole was to have a curious consequence. As foreign banks became involved in stock market activities — and, later in the decade, in the property market — they needed larger quantities of local currency which they had to borrow through the inter-bank market.[30] Local bankers found these deals more attractive and secure than competing to lend to non-bank customers. 'It does seem rather odd that a foreign bank can in fact increase its own business in Hong Kong basically with funds lent to it by local banks', one official observed, 'thus taking away business from local banks with their own funds'.[31] Free from legal restraints on their liquidity, foreign banks could raise the local funds to boost their lending in line with share and property market booms.

The colonial administration was not prepared to restrict the liquidity loophole. In 1973, the Financial Secretary publicly defended foreign-owned banks on the grounds that they were expanding their business through bringing capital into Hong Kong. His own confidential files showed that this assertion was entirely false: they funded their lending through the liquidity loophole.[32] At the end of the 1970s, he was ready to acknowledge that foreign-owned banks were able to circumvent the constraints of statutory liquidity ratios on their lending far more conveniently than their local rivals.[33] Nevertheless, when faced with mounting complaints of imprudent lending by foreign banks, the government still refused to intervene.[34] Furthermore, the attractions of the liquidity loophole were enhanced by the decision of the tax authorities to treat them as arm's-length loans, although in 1985, the Court of Appeal was to rule that they were obviously paper transactions.[35]

Speculation and Inflation

A stock market boom that began in 1971 provided the first evidence of a radical shift in Hong Kong Kong's financial environment. The banking industry devoted an increasing share of its resources to fuelling the speculators (see Table III). HSBC, together with individual China state-owned and local Chinese-owned banks, maintained relatively conservative ratios of loans to advances. Some foreign-owned banks, however, had loan books which were considerably larger than their deposit bases (see Table IV). The liquidity loophole released them from the constraints that prudence and the 1964 Banking Ordinance imposed on other banking groups.[36]

Speculation gathered momentum until the Hang Seng Index reached a peak of 1,775 early in 1973. It then crashed to 400 at year-end and fell to 150 in December 1974.[39] Turnover reached HKD48 billion in 1973 but slumped to HKD11 billion in the following year. Not until the end of the decade did the market make a full recovery (Table V).

The non-bank sector also contributed to the rise in share prices. An estimated 1,500 'finance houses' came into existence to supply the needs of the smaller speculator who had no chance of getting margin facilities from a bank. Most of these firms were under-capitalised and lacked professional

Table III: Bank Lending against Shares Compared with Total Loans and Advances and with Total Deposits (percentages)[37]

	December 1970	December 1971	March 1972	June 1972	September 1972	December 1972
Percentage of total loans & advances	8.2	10.96	12.03	14.57	17.46	18.06
Percentage of total deposits	5.3	6.91	7.47	9.03	11.54	13.39

Table IV: Ratio of Loans to Deposits for Selected Banks (percentages)[38]

Year-end	1970	1971	1972
HSBC	49	43	54
Bank of China	28	34	17
Bank of Communications	33	35	47
Hang Seng Bank	54	53	54
Bank of East Asia	59	61	49
Bangkok Bank	217	165	114
Belgian Bank	127	103	103
Bank of America	302	299	284
FNCB (Citibank)	138	108	246
Chase Manhattan	270	167	255

Table V: Share Prices and Stock Exchange Turnover, 1970–80[40]

	1970	1971	1972	1973	1974	1979	1980
Hang Seng Index (1964 = 100)	187	282	489	786	305	620	1,121
Total annual stock exchange turnover (HKD billions)	5.99	14.79	43.76	48.22	11.25	25.63	95.68

Note: The Hang Seng Index figures are the 'average of indexes as at end of each month' in each year.

management. As long as speculation surged, they could fund their operations relatively easily. The 'finance houses' could compete against the banks for deposits because they were not constrained by the interest-rate cartel, and their lending was not restricted by statutory liquidity ratios. The licensed banks complained in vain about this 'unfair competition' and then realised they could set up their own DTCs outside the regulatory system.[41]

The stock market boom was marked by malpractices and reckless speculation, which officials publicly lamented.[42] The government refused, nevertheless, to regulate DTCs.

- The colonial administration seemed to have nothing to fear politically from the growth of an unregulated financial system. There had been no serious public discontent over the stock market crash, and the community seemed to accept that neither stockbrokers nor DTCs could be expected to behave as prudently as bankers. As for the licensed banks, there had been no scandals and no loss of depositor confidence during the 1973 stock market collapse.

- Officials believed that non-bank DTCs were making a major contribution to Hong Kong's development as a regional financial centre. The government feared many DTCs would be forced into liquidation if they had to comply with statutory regulations when Hong Kong's share and property markets were so depressed and, later, when the economy was hit by the world oil crisis in the mid-1970s. Officials felt that a collapse of the DTCs would undermine the fledgling financial centre.[43]

Speculation reappeared at the end of the decade, again fuelled by the financial system. After Hong Kong adopted a floating exchange rate in 1974, the traditional constraints on the banking system's ability to create liquidity disappeared, as Chapter 10, 'Colonial Money and Its Management,' will show. Officials were slow to realise the link between the new monetary arrangements and excessive bank lending. The government's monetary policies were chaotic, and it lost control of the money supply.[44] The inflation that followed financed a new surge in speculative share and property activities from 1978, which was to lead to further bank excesses (reviewed in later sections). Not until 1979 did the government begin to realise that unless it brought under control the liquidity generated within the banking system, it could not stabilise the money supply and halt reckless bank behaviour.[45]

The New Rich

Although the stock market was not to recover fully until 1980, the boom in 1972 and 1973 had started the process of modernising Hong Kong's corporate environment. Family firms which had grown wealthy during Hong Kong's post-war 'industrial revolution' now began to transform themselves into modern corporations. As a result, the Hong Kong securities market was to become dominated by a group of publicly quoted but tightly held corporations, such as Sun Hung Kai, New World and Henderson, which were launched during the boom.[46] This process required the services of merchant bankers and introduced this new generation of local entrepreneurs to corporate finance.

The wholesale banking market received a further boost from a real estate boom in the second half of the 1970s. The new Chinese-owned corporations had large ambitions and needed jumbo-scale financing which created a demand for syndicated loans particularly for property acquisitions and development projects. With the help of modern banking techniques, these local entrepreneurs expanded so rapidly throughout the 1970s that Li Ka-shing and Sir Yue-kong Pao were able to take over parts of the business empires previously controlled by British family firms such as Jardine Matheson, Hutchison and Wheelock Marden which had previously flourished with the aid of colonial privileges.[47]

As manufacturers gave way to the corporate conglomerates as a primary source of bank profits, bankers adopted a new business model. Highly aggressive and competitive, it seemed thoroughly modern. In fact, it was not very different from the business practices which officials had tolerated as 'traditional banking' before the reforms of the 1964 Banking Ordinance. In particular, wholesale banking in the 1970s was driven by much the same reliance on personal relationships as local banking in the pre-reform era and was marred by a similar failure to distinguish between the borrowers' interests and the protection of the banks' depositors. Chapter 5, 'The Rise and Fall of Chinese Banking', described how, in the 1950s, the government did as little as possible to ensure that licensed banks were managed prudently and their depositors protected. Officials replaced statutory regulations with their own informal rules, so that bankers could ignore both banking and commercial legislation with little risk. There were to be clear parallels between the informal measures taken by the bureaucrats in the 1950s to avoid supervising the licensed banks and the Financial Secretary's policy decisions in the 1970s.[48]

- The Financial Secretary had refused to protect depositors in the 1950s. In the 1970s, the colonial administration openly rejected any duty to ensure 'the prudent conduct of business' by DTCs or 'complete safety for [their] depositors'.
- DTCs were obliged to register with the authorities in 1975, and some controls over their lending were introduced. But, as in the 1950s, there was no machinery to inspect them or to see that they complied with the new regulations.
- In the 1950s, officials responsible for overseeing the banks had failed to hire professional regulators or to make use of the professional expertise that existed within the government. After speculation in shares and property became rampant once again in 1978, the government finally admitted that DTCs could not be trusted to regulate themselves. From 1979, they were to be regulated on a 'broadly similar' basis to the licensed banks. The regulators were not given the resources, however, to do their job.[49]

The less scrupulous and more desperate proprietors and executives could reach much the same conclusion about official attitudes in the 1970s as they had done before the 1964 Banking Ordinance: the colonial administration would tolerate low standards of integrity and was not much interested in law enforcement. The recent past should have provided officials with ample warning of how disastrous such a perception would prove. Lack of effective regulation allowed financial institutions to lend their depositors' money on the basis of personal connections in the 1970s, just as they had in earlier decades. These loans were not subject to proper credit review. When they could not be repaid, fraud seemed the only way to conceal the disastrous state of a bank's accounts, while the struggle to keep the bank afloat led to further criminal behaviour.[50] The Financial Secretary was untroubled, however. 'The safety of Hong Kong's banking system is now assured', he announced in 1978, 'thanks to the system of prudential supervision which has been in force since 1964'. Little did he realise that the colony was moving towards financial catastrophe.[51]

Clash of Cultures

The reluctance to regulate had disastrous consequences for the banking industry. Corporate clients were very different from the manufacturers, whose numbers had been large but whose individual loans had been relatively small. This industrial lending had the additional advantages that it was secured by firm sales contracts and offered rapid turnover at low risk. Corporate transactions, by contrast, were large in scale, technically complex and intensely competitive. This new class of borrower was more sophisticated financially and demanded more from its financiers. Now that the scale of lending to a project was much larger than would have been acceptable previously, bankers had to identify very closely with a client's project because the bank had so much at risk with a single customer.

This new corporate business was attractive to international banks because it offered expatriate bankers the chance to surmount the cultural and linguistic barriers of doing deals with Hong Kong tycoons by providing specialised financial expertise. In addition, many foreign bank executives naively believed that these loans were low risk because of a misplaced assumption that Asian business families would always pool their ample resources to avoid the 'loss of face' from the insolvency of a relative.[52] Thus, a new banking style emerged which was far more aggressive and less conservative than in the past, as a comparison between HSBC and its merchant bank, Wardley, illustrates.

HSBC stuck quite closely to its traditional, cautious conservatism during the 1970s. For example:

- In 1972, HSBC's Deputy Chairman publicly denounced the speculative excesses of the share market.[53] The bank then stopped lending to individuals for investment in shares until May 1974.[54]

- At the end of the decade, HSBC's General Manager openly campaigned for policy reforms after the government's mismanagement of the currency had allowed double-digit inflation which enabled the banking system to fuel renewed speculation in shares and property.[55]
- HSBC exercised considerable self-restraint in managing its lending, despite the opportunities to create credit regardless of the inflationary consequences which the government's misguided monetary policies had created.[56]
- Nevertheless, this self-discipline was not enough to avoid all involvement in the share and property crashes of the 1980s. HSBC accounted for 15 per cent of the external liabilities of Carrian Holdings, the biggest of the corporate scandals.[57]

Wardley's business culture encouraged a much more competitive approach in promoting the interests of the corporate client. For example:

- In 1976, Wardley handled a rights issue for Wheelock Marden that was heavily criticised for failing to supply a balance sheet, among other shortcomings.[58]
- In 1977, the Takeovers and Mergers Code was amended to remove all doubts about a merchant bank's duty to disclose its connections with a client. This followed criticism of Wardley for its limited disclosure of a relationship with Cheung Kong when managing major transactions.[59]
- In 1980, the Takeovers and Mergers Committee criticised Wardley for its behaviour in helping Sir Yue-kong Pao to defeat Jardine Matheson in a take-over of a property-rich company.[60]
- Wardley appears to have lost at least as much as its much larger parent, HSBC, in the Carrian crash and was involved in other corporate disasters in this period.[61]
- A former Chief Executive of Wardley was prosecuted on charges of accepting bribes in the early 1980s.[62]

These cultural changes were not confined to the financial institutions. The decline in bankers' standards, so reminiscent of the pre-1964 era, was matched by officials who showed much the same indifference to misconduct and mismanagement as their predecessors in the 1950s and early 1960s.[63] Regulators did not initiate serious investigations of individual banks and confined their inspections to the banks' compliance with auditing and other technical requirements. They disclaimed any obligation to see that criminal offences were prosecuted on the excuse that information obtained from banks and DTCs was a statutory secret and could not be disclosed to the police or the ICAC. The official who was entrusted with cleaning up the banking industry in 1984 revealed that, in the past, as long as the accounting and other technicalities prescribed by law seemed in order, the regulators would take no further interest in a bank's behaviour.[64]

On the basis of Hong Kong past experiences, the consequences of this erosion of banking standards and the reluctance to regulate were predictable. After 1978, property values surged, with prices rising by almost 50 per cent for residential and retail units by 1981 (and even faster in office and industrial buildings). Interest rates then rose to record heights, and property prices slumped sharply during 1982, generally undermining the stock market and business confidence. Banks and DTCs alike had recklessly expanded their exposure to property and related activities. In 1982, these loans accounted for 35 per cent of local advances by banks and 42 per cent by DTCs.[65] The weaker DTCs and their associated banks made desperate efforts, first to shore up their balance sheets and then to conceal their losses to disguise their liquidity problems. The mounting financial crisis was aggravated by the collapse of the currency in 1983 against a background of acrimonious Sino-British diplomatic negotiations about Hong Kong's future.[66]

The extension of banking-style regulation to the DTCs from 1978 had come too late. They had already contaminated several licensed banks, not surprisingly since 28 of the 124 licensed banks had set up DTC subsidiaries, while a further 187 DTCs were associated with overseas banks (either locally licensed or with representative offices in the colony).[67] Between 1982 and 1986, seven licensed banks failed, brought down not just by the insolvency of corporate clients but by fraud and corruption in their DTCs.[68] To prevent a general collapse in public and business confidence, the government was forced to spend HKD3.8 billion on rescuing and restructuring them.[69] The contribution to GDP from 'financing, insurance, real estate and business services' fell from 23 percent in 1980 to 17 per cent in 1986.[70]

Malpractices could no longer be regarded as a small price to pay for the survival of traditional business practices, which had been the complacent but costly attitude of the colonial administration in the 1950s (as described in Chapter 7, 'A Dangerous Model'). The scale of the crisis in the 1980s was demonstrated by revelations about Dollar Trust. This minor DTC, which collapsed in 1982, had a loan book of some HKD900 million and was connected to a local Chinese-owned banking group (which also failed). Dollar Trust became notorious for what was probably the biggest cheque-kiting scandal in history. It used its American bank accounts to obtain funds by passing worthless cheques to a total value of USD21.7 billion, which highlighted a striking feature of the Hong Kong financial scene at that time.[71]

In the cheque-kiting exercise, experienced bankers and the internal and external audit procedures of, for instance, Citibank or the Hongkong Bank [i.e., HSBC] had not questioned what was almost a daily procedure through their books.

Overseas associations compounded the contagion in a way that had not been true in the 1961–65 bank failures.[72] The Wing On Bank was brought down by the Chief Manager's own fraudulent loans, but it hardly deserved to survive once it became associated with the notorious Australian Nugan Hand Bank.[73] Connections with Malaysia, Singapore and Thailand were aggravating factors in the downfall of the Hang Lung and Overseas Trust Banks and the near-collapse of Ka Wah Bank.[74] The colonial administration could no longer assume that European banks were in a superior class and would never be tainted by dishonourable behaviour. Executives from Lloyds, Barclays and WestLB banks were convicted on criminal and corruption charges.

An additional complication for the colonial administration was the embarrassment that overtook officials.

- After a senior official responsible for regulatory policy retired in 1986, he was invited to run a nightclub by the Chairman of the Hong Kong Stock Exchange (subsequently gaoled on corruption-related charges). The ex-civil servant was dissuaded from embarking on this new career by a public warning that his government pension might be stopped.[75]
- The life style of a former Commissioner of Securities led to his arrest followed by a six-month investigation by the ICAC in 1982.[76] A former Commissioner of Banking and DTCs also aroused the interest of the ICAC, which investigated his financial affairs after his retirement.[77] (Neither man was charged.)
- The Deputy Public Prosecutor who handled criminal cases relating to three major bank failures in this decade was gaoled for eight years on corruption charges relating to their affairs.[78]

Political Shock

There was now a new Financial Secretary, the Swire Group's former Chief Executive, Sir John Bremridge. Before he became Financial Secretary, he had been regarded by the colonial administration as a stout ally when it was resisting demands for some measure of prudential supervision for DTCs.[79] Bremridge was suspicious of regulation and indulgent towards speculation.[80] He deplored the 'excesses and depredations' associated with the stock market boom of 1972–73 but retained serious reservations about the ability of officials to regulate financial markets.[81] Not surprisingly, he proved slow to act during the bank failures and corporate scandals which engulfed him in his new position. In the end, however, he broke with colonial tradition and became a thorough-going reformer, introducing legislation to restore prudence and integrity to the financial markets that marked a clear break with the cynicism and compromises of the past.[82]

The scandals and crises that had so regularly plagued the banking sector and the financial markets for the previous four decades came to an abrupt end. This sudden improvement in financial behaviour after 1985 had much in common with the dramatic results of the colonial administration's commitment to zero tolerance of corruption in 1974. In that year, the ICAC was established as a specialist professional body after the earlier, half-hearted attempts of the colonial administration to clean up the police and other branches of the government had failed dismally. Corruption, almost at once, ceased to be an everyday feature of Hong Kong life. In the 1980s, the colonial administration faced a challenge of similar proportions. The currency had collapsed in 1983. The corporate world was mired in scandal. Bank runs and DTC failures had shaken confidence in the financial system. The Banking Commission was unable to cope. The solution was a reform package adopted in 1986, at the heart of which was a new definition of the banking commissioner's duties.[83]

> ... the commissioner's role is to promote the general stability and effective working of the banking system. He is responsible, among other duties, for ensuring that authorised institutions are operated in a responsible, honest and business-like manner. He is also to promote and encourage proper standards of conduct and sound business practice among these institutions. It is necessary to spell out in the Bill these functions of the commissioner in order to make it clear that his role is greater than merely one of checking that the institutions comply with the various technical requirements.

The Financial Secretary said this job description reflected 'a different and up-to-date emphasis in the approach to prudential supervision'. It was also a damning indictment of the government policies that had previously prevailed. Why, otherwise, should it have been necessary in 1986 to spell out in law the most obvious duties of the official responsible for banking? Why, 50 years after business leaders and bureaucrats had first agreed on the need to supervise the banks did the regulators need to be instructed to ensure 'proper standards of conduct and sound business practice' and not to confine their attention to 'checking that the institutions comply with the various technical requirements'?

Conclusions

In terms of the behaviour of both bureaucrats and bankers, the Hong Kong landscape seemed to change very little between the 1950s and 1970s. In that earlier period, the bureaucrats' replacement of regulations by rules created a banking environment conducive to misconduct. Mismanagement took time to reach self-destructive proportions, and the crisis was postponed until the runs on five banks between 1961 and 1965. Their woes followed over-expansion of credit as the banks financed rampant property speculation. Similarly, the bureaucrats' policies in the 1970s imposed no penalties on mismanaged DTCs, which allowed them to embark on self-destructive behaviour. Financial ruin overtook the worst of them only in the following decade.[84] Creation of bank credit in the 1970s was virtually unrestricted and fuelled an unsustainable rise in property prices before the crash began in 1982.

But there was an important difference in the colonial administration's response to the excesses that led to this financial catastrophe. Bremridge was shocked by the extensive misconduct among bankers and bureaucrats that the latest financial crisis had revealed, which made him personally determined to reform the system. But reforms could not have been postponed by any financial secretary. The political environment had changed completely with the arrival of a handful of indirectly elected members of the legislature in 1985, and for the first time since World War II, the legislature refused to be silenced in 1986 by officials' claims that too much public discussion would imperil Hong Kong's financial survival. Previously, the colonial administration had been able to use the Exchange Fund's resources to conceal the full costs of rescuing failed banks because the fund operated in total secrecy.[85] Now, the Financial Secretary was forced to explain publicly the case for rescuing the latest bank failures and the role of the Exchange Fund.[86] From now on, the colonial administration would face a direct political challenge if the market failures and corporate collapses that had been recurrent problems for the financial sector since World War II did not cease. The government would be taken to task in public by legislators who owed it nothing and who could compel officials to answer their enquiries. It was no coincidence that, subsequently, the banking industry's stability improved remarkably and that Hong Kong's financial markets came through the political uncertainties of transition to Chinese sovereignty and the post-1997 Asian financial crisis so robustly.

10

Colonial Money and Its Management

A stable banking industry and sound financial markets need more than just a robust regulatory régime. They cannot be achieved without effective monetary policies because a government's management of monetary affairs affects the operations of the entire financial system. In Hong Kong, however, the colonial administration consistently refused to accept responsibility for monetary policy. Officials insisted until late in the 1970s that active management of monetary affairs was unnecessary and potentially dangerous. They were convinced that the economy was self-regulating and that the financial system had an automatic adjustment mechanism. This view was widely held throughout the British Empire and had its origins in the 'currency board', an institution that was at the heart of the colonial financial system. Under a currency board, monetary arrangements were of the simplest. The currency was fully backed by foreign assets held by the government, but there was no central bank or other agency to implement interventionist monetary policies.[1] It was assumed, almost universally, that a currency board removed any need for the government to intervene directly in managing monetary affairs and that this system seemed to abolish the need for monetary policy. But monetary affairs is one area in which laisser faire is self-defeating. Under a currency board, the refusal to intervene leads to monetary policy made by default, as this chapter will explain. Thus, ineffective regulation of the banks was aggravated by mistakes in the management of monetary affairs and misconceptions about monetary policy.

The colonial currency board had a respectable history and had provided stable and robust monetary systems for a large range of economies over a long period. The system fell out of favour for political rather than economic reasons as British Dominions set up central banks and British colonies achieved independence. Currency boards returned to fashion in the late twentieth century with claims that, in the contemporary world, they contribute to better rates of growth than other currency arrangements and that they achieve lower rates of inflation.[2] The currency board system has been given much of the credit for the robustness of Hong Kong's currency and financial markets during the 1997 Asian financial crisis,[3] and many economists now look on this institution 'as a panacea for all monetary disorders'. This current acclaim for the boards is in marked contrast to the condemnation that they attracted for several decades after World War II when they were widely denounced 'as a form of colonial subjugation'.[4]

This chapter will argue that, in Hong Kong, the currency board offered a simple but effective defence against the damage done by misguided and ill-informed monetary decisions executed by officials who lacked professional expertise. The evidence suggests that the colonial administration was often confused in its management of monetary affairs and, during the 1970s in particular, was dangerously ill-advised in its monetary policies. The analysis will show that these errors were not caused by the colonial relationship with the UK. They were to be blamed on poor decision-making by individual financial secretaries. This chapter will examine how these men managed the financial resources of the colony and how their policies affected Hong Kong's banks and financial markets.

Support Home Industries

Before World War II, currency boards were not seen as a device to impose a sort of capital levy on colonial territories. In the 1930s, a colonial expert described how they generated considerable profits at London's expense even though the currency they issued 'has no independent existence of its own, but is simply parasitical upon sterling'.[5]

> [A] board keeps a sufficient amount of its sterling resources liquid to meet probable demands and invests the rest, partly in short-dated securities, and the 'hard core' in longer-dated securities. The business is a very profitable one, most of the currency boards have their liabilities for outstanding coins and notes covered to the extent of 110 per cent and pay over large sums to the Colonial Governments from the interest on their securities.

In Hong Kong, the colonial administration took a similarly optimistic view of its overseas reserves and looked on them as assets which ought to be capable of making a contribution to local development. One Governor, Sir Geoffry Northcote, persuaded the Colonial Office to agree in principle that the government could finance development projects with profits from the London investments that backed the currency.[6] Northcote was astute in foreseeing the potential importance of these profits, which were to rise substantially after World War II.[7]

After the war, official attitudes towards these London investments changed. The first priority was to expand the reserves rather than to use them, and their profits were no longer seen as a source of development finance. Although officials were highly sensitive to accusations that the reserves were being used to benefit the UK instead of the colony's economy,[8] the colonial administration did not take advantage until 1964 of the concession won by Northcote and start to include a portion of the accumulated profits in the annual budget.[9] And no post-war financial secretary could be persuaded to use these funds to aid the private sector through a government development programme. Instead, the colonial administration believed that buoyant reserves were the best comfort factor that nervous investors could be offered to offset the political risks of close proximity to the anti-colonialism and anti-capitalism of Mao Zedong's New China and the protectionist threats from Western countries.

Other colonies, by contrast, reduced the level of the sterling backing for their local currencies 'to 77 per cent', the Financial Secretary admitted, issuing government securities to cover the balance, thus freeing funds which could be used for economic and social development. Singapore, for example, withdrew part of its currency board assets to help fund the creation of an Economic Development Board, which was to play a conspicuous role in creating a modern economy.[10] Hong Kong, however, stuck to total backing for the note issue in overseas assets even though it was 'inconceivable' that the public would ever demand '100% redemption of our currency or anything approaching that'. His excuse for not reducing the currency's backing was the need to preserve 'the international standing of the Hong Kong dollar'.[11]

This policy infuriated the business community, especially as almost every year, the government spent less than it gathered in taxes and other revenues and invested its mounting fiscal reserves in London. Other colonies, too, 'generally followed conservative fiscal policies and aimed to produce budget surpluses' but these were regarded as 'a vital element in funding their ten-year [domestic] development plans'.[12] Even so, these surpluses were politically unpopular in the Third World.[13] They provoked complaints from business representatives in Hong Kong's legislature, who called for the government's overseas reserves to be brought back to the colony and invested in the local economy. A long and bitter clash developed between the colonial administration and the business community over these funds, how they should be deployed and where they should be invested. At first, officials managed to head off business criticism with a pledge that, during a recession, the fiscal reserves would be used to maintain government spending (on capital works projects especially) instead of raising taxation.[14] But in the mid-1950s, the Financial Secretary was maintaining these reserves at the astonishing level of the equivalent of a full year's revenue.[15] The business community could not believe that budgetary prudence on this scale was justified. In 1957, its representatives in the legislature argued that the government's overseas reserves should be devoted to supporting the local economy.[16] These demands were to continue into the 1960s.[17] Financial Secretaries refused to budge, however. While conceding that it was 'absolutely right that our funds should be utilized for the benefit of Hong Kong to the widest possible extent', the government insisted that an even more important priority was 'a thoroughly sound monetary policy' to preserve 'the Hong Kong dollar [as] the most trusted currency in the East'.[18]

The Monetary Key

The controversy aroused by the reserves — the government's own reserves and the assets used to back the note issue — reflected their leverage within Hong Kong's monetary arrangements under the currency board system.[19] The management of the reserves and their impact on money supply had major implications for the government's ability to influence economic development. As in any economy, if the money supply increased, the economy inflated, growth accelerated (though not necessarily in real terms), and bank lending expanded. If the money supply declined, the economy deflated, as investment and consumption contracted and bank lending shrank. Under Hong Kong's monetary arrangements, these simple rules worked their way through the financial system via changes at three levels, each of which involved the colony's external reserves.[20]

- *Fiscal reserves.* The government held considerable reserves overseas accumulated principally through regular budget surpluses. When the government transferred a budget surplus overseas, the effect was deflationary. The reserves overseas increased but there was a fall in the banking system's resources for lending to the public. If the government repatriated funds from its overseas reserves to spend locally, the banking system's resources for lending to the public increased, which was inflationary.

- *External assets to back the currency.* The note-issuing banks could only expand the volume of currency in circulation by surrendering an equivalent value in foreign currency to the Exchange Fund. Thus, the effect of a rise in the volume of banknotes was deflationary. It increased the reserves overseas, but there was a fall in the banking system's Hong Kong dollar resources for lending to the public. Unlike other modern economies, an increase in the volume of currency in circulation was not inflationary.[21]

- *Bank liquidity.* The banking system had to maintain prudent levels of liquidity to meet the public's demands for cash, which limited their freedom to create loans and advances. A government decision to impose statutory liquidity ratios increased the banking system's reserves, which was deflationary (as in the case of the statutory liquidity ratios imposed on banks in 1964 and on DTCs at the end of the 1970s).

Monetary policy seemed straightforward enough and to call for little more than monitoring how a rise or fall in the reserves of either the government or the banking system affected the money supply and the level of economic activity.[22] In practice, however, there were two problems to be overcome: the technical competence of the officials responsible for managing Hong Kong's monetary affairs; and technical complications in administering the colonial monetary system.

The technical competence of the colonial administration fell below what was required to adjust official policies and monetary arrangements to meet the challenges of rapid growth. Chapter 1, 'Mismanaged by Mandarins', showed how the élite Administrative Service reduced banking regulation to a state of complacent chaos which was to cost Hong Kong dearly. This chapter will show that the management of monetary affairs in general was marred by disorder and confusion in policy-making throughout the 1960s and 1970s. The problems began at the top of the official hierarchy.

- The two Financial Secretaries in office during the 1960s and the 1970s insisted that the colonial monetary system was self-regulating. In consequence, they argued, Hong Kong was best left to the mercy of market forces because the economy would adjust automatically to the changing environment, no matter how adverse.[23] As a result, they allowed the banking system to finance share and property bubbles regardless of looming market crashes.[24]

- In these two decades, the financial secretaries misunderstood key aspects of the way in which Hong Kong's monetary arrangements worked. Both men appeared to believe, for example, that government deposits within the local banking system were insulated from the rest of the deposit base and did not have the same impact on the money supply as other deposits.[25] As a result, they underestimated the importance of bank lending in creating liquidity.

- There was a deliberate decision not to collect essential information about the financial situation. In the 1960s, the Financial Secretary was determined to starve potential critics of even the most basic data about social and economic conditions.[26] In the 1970s, the Financial Secretary feared that the process of collecting information might imply some responsibility for protecting depositors, which he was determined to avoid.[27] In consequence, the government lacked data essential for rational policy-making.

- Both officials derided the notion that economic analysis was of much help in foreseeing adverse market trends, and they dismissed suggestions that the government should be capable of taking precautionary measures to bring excessive liquidity and speculative markets under control.[28]

Technical complications were difficult for officials to predict and to understand.

- *Fiscal reserves.* If the government kept a budget surplus in Hong Kong, the banking system's resources for lending to the public remained the same; and, unlike other economies which had central banks, the budget surplus was not deflationary because it was not being sterilised within the banking system. In the 1970s, the government's efforts to combat inflation were handicapped by this inability to remove the colonial administration's Hong Kong dollar reserves from the local money supply.

- *External assets to back the currency.* If the note-issuing banks were allowed to increase the volume of currency in circulation without surrendering an equivalent amount in foreign currency to the Exchange Fund, Hong Kong became like other economies: the additional banknotes were inflationary. The banking system's resources for lending to the public remained unchanged but the amount of cash in the public's hands increased. Unbeknown to the government, this situation arose when the Hong Kong exchange rate floated in the 1970s, with disastrous consequences.

- *Bank liquidity.* Statutory liquidity ratios were rigidly enforced on local banks but easily circumvented by banks with headquarters outside Hong Kong.[29] In the 1950s, liberal lending by foreign banks was invaluable in financing rapid industrial take-off. In the 1970s, their unrestrained lending contributed to share and property speculation that was followed by corporate collapses and bank failures in the following decade.

In addition, the banking industry had little to gain from a stable money supply. Banks had to keep the bulk of their statutory liquidity requirements abroad because of the lack of local public debt and similar investment facilities. As a result, if the Hong Kong exchange rate fell, the book value of overseas assets rose and would support an increasingly large volume of loans in Hong Kong dollar terms. Thus, the entire banking industry — both local and foreign-owned — benefited from inflation which caused the local currency to depreciate.

From Orderly Growth to Chaos

Although clear statements of the colonial administration's monetary policy were rare, the government's policy priorities and the way they shifted from one decade to the next can be identified with reasonable accuracy.

1950s

Orderly growth was the priority — appropriate in a period of rapid economic development. Monetary policy was flexible. The Financial Secretary was ready to intervene to restrict liquidity to control speculative share and property bubbles. He was also willing to use the government's reserves to offset business downturns.[30] Currency stability was not an issue because London took responsibility for defending the Sterling Area's exchange rate.[31] There was no central banking mechanism, and the government had no direct control over the money supply or interest rates. The banking industry was largely ignored. Monetary leverage relied on the currency board system and management of the reserves (i.e., their size and the proportions held overseas).

1960s

Growth remained the priority, but monetary policy ceased to be interventionist. The Financial Secretary rejected any government role in expanding the economy.[32] He also declined to manage the money supply to limit speculation in shares and property, preferring to leave markets free to expand as they pleased. Currency stability became a responsibility of the colonial administration for the first time since World War II because London allowed Hong Kong to fix its own exchange rate after sterling devalued in 1967. Banking problems forced the government to regulate the industry, and it became official policy to inject liquidity into the banking system to prevent bank failures.

There was still no central bank, but the Financial Secretary had some influence over interest rates after a formal banking cartel was established. Nevertheless, monetary leverage relied mainly on the currency board system, and, after the 1965 bank runs, the main role of the reserves was to provide the banking system with liquidity in a financial crisis.[33]

1970s

Exchange rate stability became the priority, but clear policy goals became impossible. The Financial Secretary sought initially to influence bank lending to check a stock market bubble. The subsequent crash and the government's ambition to develop an international financial centre deterred him from further market intervention and regulation of financial institutions. Management of the currency became the biggest challenge after the colony cut the link with sterling in 1972 and then adopted a floating rate in 1974. Automatic backing for the entire note issue with foreign assets was abandoned, thus ending the currency board system.[34]

Officials tried to prevent the currency from depreciating under the floating exchange rate but did not realise that there were now only minimal restrictions on the banks' freedom to create liquidity. When late in the decade, the colonial administration tried to tackle these problems, it was hampered by the absence of a central bank and an inability to isolate the government's reserves from private-sector assets in the banking system.[35] The Financial Secretary argued that the government's influence over interest rates was his only practical monetary leverage.[36]

1980s

In this period, a Financial Secretary was appointed from the private sector. Bremidge brought with him from his life-long career in the Swire Group a commitment to 'primitive' laisser faire. 'Wise governments must concentrate on the promotion of true wealth and in Hong Kong this must come from our export trade', he opined while still in the private sector, 'Moreover I dislike deficit financing, except for self-liquidating projects, believe in balanced budgets, abhor expenditure that exceeds income'.[37] He also believed that without speculation, the Hong Kong financial scene would be 'dull, impoverished, and third-rate'.[38] On the same occasion, he also argued (while Maoist extremism was at its height) 'that our great neighbour China has much to teach the Western democracies about financial self-reliance'.

An effective monetary policy came into being only after the 1983 currency crisis and the adoption of a linked exchange rate. With this move came the rapid revival of the currency board system, which was now supported by an increasingly professional team to manage monetary affairs. There was a clear goal for monetary policy — the defence of a fixed exchange rate — which then determined the appropriate level of interest rates, liquidity and management of the reserves.

The rest of this chapter will be devoted to a review of how monetary policy evolved and of the relationship between monetary management and economic development.

No Invisible Hand

In the early years after World War II, the government was relatively flexible in its economic thinking. It did not look on monetary policy as irrelevant nor was it convinced that Hong Kong's fortunes were guided by an invisible hand that steered financial, labour and other markets through an automatic adjustment mechanism. When officials feared that the Korean War embargoes would lead to mass unemployment, they did not disclaim responsibility for preventing a collapse of the economy. But their strategy for countering recession was very much in the style of Victorian England. They refused pleas from the business community to ensure that the banking system had sufficient liquidity to prevent deflation. Instead, the colonial administration made preparations for extensive make-work and relief programmes.[39]

Officials had earlier been forced to abandon laisser faire by the desperate shortage of every kind of commodity and manufactured product after World War II. International markets were not operating normally, and the government had no choice but to organise the procurement and distribution of essential supplies. These were large-scale commercial activities that were surprisingly profitable under bureaucratic management.[40] They led to substantial balances with local banks, where they helped to underwrite the rapid expansion of bank loans and advances to finance post-war reconstruction and rehabilitation.[41] (Chapter 3, 'Post-war Emergencies: from Boom to Bust', discussed the colonial administration's management of post-war rehabilitation.) This ample liquidity made it possible for the colonial administration to reject suggestions that it should espouse 'a policy of Government control of the money market and of the volume of money'.[42]

But the Financial Secretary did not believe that monetary conditions should be left entirely to market forces when speculation, particularly on the local stock market, started to alarm both the government and HSBC in 1955.[43] The bank decided to initiate a credit squeeze, a move which the Financial Secretary, supported. Share prices slumped, and turnover fell on the gold and foreign exchange markets in which the local Chinese-owned banks were heavily involved. The profits of this group of banks shrank, and so did their deposits. Liquidity tightened still further after six local Chinese banks collapsed in late 1955.[44]

Speculation had been squeezed out of the economy, but investment was also drying up. HSBC had not expected its tougher loan policy to lead to such drastic deflation, and it blamed the government for intensifying the initial credit squeeze by continuing to build up its budget surpluses in London. The effect of the government's actions was deflationary because the transfer of official balances from local banks into sterling reduced the money supply.[45] HSBC urged the government to reflate the economy, and the Financial Secretary injected additional liquidity into the banking system by bringing funds back from London.[46]

This incident showed the limitations of HSBC's position. It was not a central bank and, by itself, was unable to set overall monetary goals for the economy, if only because of the decisive role played by the government's management of the reserves in determining overall liquidity. The Financial Secretary, A. G. Clarke, appeared ready to assume this role and referred publicly to the case for the government having 'a much greater say in credit policy' as it assumed responsibility for ensuring an adequate supply of credit.[47] In the end, however, he did not espouse a formal monetary policy. He ceased to transfer budget surpluses to London. There were to be more attempts to manage the money supply directly, and his successor disclaimed any government obligation to do so.[48]

Growth at Any Price

When J. J. (later Sir John) Cowperthwaite became Financial Secretary in 1961, he took a much narrower view of the colonial administration's economic duties than his predecessor. He had a great deal to gain from minimising government responsibility for the state of the economy. During his ten years as Financial Secretary, the colonial administration faced four serious threats to its survival. The first two were political: rioting in 1966 and bombs and Maoist demonstrations during 1967. The other two were financial crises over which he presided and which weakened the colonial administration's credibility: public indignation at the failure to protect depositors during the 1965 bank collapses; and the bungled 1967 devaluation in line with the UK, followed by a humiliating but popular revaluation shortly afterwards. For him, laisser faire was a policy of considerable political convenience.

Cowperthwaite's priority was growth. He was an expansionist who would do nothing to impede the fastest possible increase in the overall economy even when liquidity was growing at an alarming rate.[49] He knew that 'excessive bank lending' led to inflationary pressures. He explained publicly that one of the objectives of statutory liquidity ratios was to prevent banks from creating excessive liquidity.[50] However, he never used the liquidity ratios to counter worrying surges in bank loans. Instead, he insisted that inflationary pressures were the inevitable outcome of rapid economic growth.[51] He also discussed openly how larger budget surpluses and higher taxation would mop up surplus spending power. Again, he failed to use such measures to halt market excesses which the banks were financing. His excuse this time was the possibility of opposition from the legislature (which was then composed entirely of government appointees).[52]

Cowperthwaite produced two reasons for not interfering with excessive growth. The first was his own experience of claims during the 1950s that industry was being allowed to expand at an unsustainable rate. The pessimists had been proved spectacularly wrong by Hong Kong's manufacturing boom.[53] Then, there was the practical problem of identifying 'what rate of expansion of the economy would be "right" ... [and how] to regulate it at that rate'. He saw no way of judging when an industry was suffering from 'over-expansion'. Thus, he was prepared to stand aside even when, as he put it, the growth rate was threatening 'uncomfortable, even injurious, effects on some individuals or some sectors'.[54]

Cowperthwaite did not regard this policy as dangerous or imprudent. He was convinced that the colonial monetary system created a self-regulating mechanism which compelled the economy to adjust automatically to changing business conditions. In a 1955 letter to the Colonial Office, he explained this conviction.[55]

In countries where economic and financial policies may result in internal and external price levels getting out of line and setting up inflationary tendencies (and unfortunately such countries are in the overwhelming majority today) it is very necessary to keep an eye on the balance of payments. *But our economy is almost wholly external … and our balance of payments is self-regulating either through the free exchange market or through our currency mechanism.* (emphasis added)

For the rest of his career, Cowperthwaite insisted that 'the modern school' of economics did not apply to a small open economy like Hong Kong.[56] Keynes, in particular, was anathema, on the grounds that his doctrines would lead to financial irresponsibility and 'create an immediate balance of payments crisis'.[57] Cowperthwaite argued that because the colony's economy was self-regulating, he did not need to worry about the money supply getting out of control. If 'overheating' occurred through 'expansion of domestic credit and domestic demand in excess of current resources', an automatic adjustment mechanism would correct the imbalance.[58] Cowperthwaite stuck to this complacent view even though market behaviour demonstrated dramatically during the 1960s that overheating was a serious threat. Excess liquidity proved a persistent problem during this and the subsequent decade. In 1964, his budget speech reviewed the mounting inflationary trends. He could have restrained them, he said, by transferring budgetary surpluses to London. He had decided, instead, to leave them inside the colony's banking system 'to continue to work for the economy'. A year later, bank runs had brought the financial system close to collapse. In explaining the crisis, Cowperthwaite confessed that 'in recent years, credit has been rather too easy in Hong Kong for good banking and commercial discipline', principally because of 'excessive' expansion of bank lending.[59] By his own admission, the colonial monetary system's 'self-regulation' was neither smooth nor certain, and the colonial administration had knowingly tolerated the market excesses that created the 1965 crisis.

Behind the bluff and bluster of Cowperthwaite's economic pronouncements, the underlying strategy was clear enough. During the upswing of the business cycle — and of share and property booms in particular — the government's policy was to allow the banking industry to fund whatever level of credit it chose, subject only to the statutory liquidity requirements. The colonial administration preferred to make no judgment as to what might constitute an undesirable level of speculation, relying instead on market forces as far as possible. During the downswing, the government continued to rely on market forces and offered no help to markets or industries in trouble because Cowperthwaite insisted that Hong Kong could not spend its way out of an economic downturn.[60]

One sector of the economy, however, qualified for more generous treatment. He introduced special protection for the banks, a policy that was to persist from 1965 until 1991. Cowperthwaite made it a priority to provide sufficient liquidity to prevent the banking industry — and thus the economy at large — from falling victim to the crises created by the banks' misconduct or mismanagement during the heady peak of a boom. This policy gave errant banks a blank cheque because the colonial administration dared not risk the panic about the stability of the banking system as a whole that failure of even a single bank would cause. Thus, during the banking emergency of 1965, two insolvent and another two uncooperative institutions were kept alive through government injections.[61] Chapter 8, 'An Avoidable Crisis: the 1965 Bank Runs', traced the way that Cowperthwaite's economic strategy contributed to the 1965 bank runs, and how his policy errors in responding to that crisis laid the foundations for market excesses and the erosion of banking integrity in the following decade.

Painful Pilgrimage

When C. P. (later Sir Philip) Haddon-Cave took over as Financial Secretary in 1971, he was very ready to become an economic pundit. Although his public pronouncements were remarkable more for prolixity than profundity, his willingness to discuss budgetary and monetary policies was seen as a welcome contrast to his aloof and taciturn predecessor. Haddon-Cave, unfortunately, was to be plagued by gross errors of judgment. His career as Financial Secretary was to prove a painful pilgrimage in search of understanding about the way that Hong Kong's monetary system worked.

At first, his instinct was to tackle rampant speculation on the stock market which was financed by foreign-owned banks in particular. He stuck to 'moral suasion', however, and the bubble soared until early 1973, before sliding into a collapse from which share prices did not recover fully until the end of the decade.[62] This development was a blow to the colonial administration which regarded the booming stock and property markets of the early 1970s as driving Hong Kong's emergence as an international financial centre. As a result, Haddon-Cave decided that, henceforward, he should do nothing that might dampen investor confidence. For this reason, he refused to extend banking regulation to the DTCs, despite their well-publicised excesses. Market sentiment would have sagged and many DTCs would have gone bankrupt, he feared, if they had been required to conduct their affairs in a prudent fashion.[63] This decision damaged the integrity of the secondary banking sector and destabilised the banking industry as a whole, although large-scale corporate collapses were postponed until the following decade. (These developments were reviewed in detail in Chapter 9, 'From Banking Crisis to Financial Catastrophe'.)

At heart, Haddon-Cave shared Cowperthwaite's belief that government policies should do nothing to disturb the markets, an attitude which led

Haddon-Cave into a series of his misjudgments in managing the reserves. The consequences were severe. His flawed monetary policies financed the excesses of the secondary banking market. He lost control of the money supply, and inflation reached an annual rate of close to 15 per cent between 1973 and 1983, twice the level of the previous decade.[64] Hong Kong had to abandon its floating exchange rate in 1983 after the currency had fallen by 28 per cent against its US counterpart that year.

An Absence of Expertise

Chapter 1 noted that a striking feature of the colonial officials directly involved in banking and related matters was their disregard for professional advice. Nowhere were the consequences of this defect to prove more damaging to Hong Kong than in monetary affairs. In 1972, the Hong Kong dollar ceased to be tied to sterling. For the colonial administration, this was a temporary move: the link with sterling would be re-established once the British pound had stabilised. The immediate challenge was what to do about the reserves. If the existing reserves in sterling were run down quickly, there was a chance of heavy losses. Thus, the colonial administration decided that they would not be liquidated for the time being. But what was to be done about new reserves and, in particular, in which currency would Hong Kong keep the assets to back increases in the note issue? Foreign currencies generally seemed so unpredictable in 1972 that it was difficult to select a long-term anchor for the Hong Kong dollar. So, the government decided to end the requirement that the note-issuing banks could only increase the currency in circulation by surrendering an equivalent value in a designated foreign currency (which formerly had been sterling). In future, the Exchange Fund's local bank accounts would be credited with a sum equal to the new notes' value.

Officials did not think that this new practice would materially affect the way that the monetary system operated. Initially, they continued to convert the Hong Kong dollar assets backing the note issue into foreign currencies — but not for long because the government was under no formal obligation to do so. Thus, 'Hong Kong unwittingly entered an era devoid of effective monetary policy'.[65] In any case, as was explained earlier, officials believed that the Hong Kong economy was self-regulating. They seemed to hope that the monetary system would continue to operate automatically, with funds entering and leaving the economy in line with the balances of trade and payments without much need for government intervention.[66]

Within the government, no one realised how drastically this single move would alter the colony's monetary arrangements. The traditional currency system board had controlled increases in the note issue and thus had some influence over the expansion of the money supply. Now, there was no mechanism in place to restrain the banks' creation of liquidity. A perceptive contemporary critic of Hong Kong's mismanagement of its monetary affairs pointed out that 'the period from November 1974 to October 1983 represents a unique experiment in monetary arrangement unparalleled in any other economy, for not only did the Hong Kong authorities allow the price of the currency to be freely determined in the foreign exchange markets, but they also made no provisions to control the quantity of money in Hong Kong'.[67] The government's decision to waive the overseas backing for the currency had been based on ignorance, and the colonial administration itself confessed to its lack of technical expertise. As one of Hong Kong's most experienced central bankers has observed: 'If just one monetary economist had been consulted, the change ... might never have been enacted, even as a temporary measure. It appears, however, that this was regarded as a fund management and operational issue, not an economic one'. He describes the outcome in bleak terms: 'The amount of money created was in practice [now] determined by the banks, free of any obligation to maintain a particular exchange rate or of any technical mechanism inclining them towards one. Monetary policy was largely rudderless and impotent'.[68]

For some time, the colonial administration was able to conceal the decision to back the note issue in Hong Kong dollars, thanks to changes in the presentation of the government's accounts.[69] Bit by bit, however, details of the colonial administration's difficulties in managing the reserves started to emerge. In 1976, the Financial Secretary revealed that the government had ceased to buy overseas assets because of its fear of making book losses on the reserves, given the volatility of foreign exchange markets. But he still managed to conceal his decision to abandon altogether the policy of backing the note issue in foreign currency.[70] The following year, he admitted that, as a temporary measure, Exchange Fund reserves were not being converted into foreign currencies in order to avoid putting pressure on the floating exchange rate.[71] He also claimed that the Exchange Fund assets were 'widely diversified', without explaining that he had 'diversified' them into Hong Kong dollars.[72] Until 1977, the impending crisis was masked by the apparent robustness of the exchange rate, as the effective exchange rate strengthened by almost 11 per cent over its 1971 level. It fell by ten per cent in 1978.[73] The monetary system was under mounting inflationary pressures with no checks on the money supply other than the banks' self-restraint, and Haddon-Cave was finally forced to come clean.[74]

> ... since the middle of 1972, ... and, particularly since the floating of the Hong Kong dollar in November 1974, it has not always been possible to use these Hong Kong dollars [backing the note issue] to acquire foreign currency assets because of the virtual certainty of the foreign exchange market being disturbed. *But with the very ready co-operation of the note-issuing banks this problem can be, and has been from time to time, overcome.* (emphasis added)

The pretence that all was well with the monetary system — thanks to sympathetic banks — could last only a few more months. He then had to reveal the damage his monetary policy had wrought.[75]

> The relative importance of [the Exchange Fund's] Hong Kong dollar balances [in the local banking system] and the rate at which they have increased suggest that the Government has involuntarily contributed to the undesirable growth rates of the money supply and bank advances ever since the growth rate of domestic demand began to play a prominent role in determining the growth rate of the economy.

Stripped of jargon, this was an admission that the colonial administration had enabled the banks to swell the money supply to the point at which inflation had become rampant. But even now, the agony was not over. Haddon-Cave tinkered with the system trying to find a formula that would end the inflationary cycle created by holding the colony's reserves in Hong Kong dollars.[76] Muddle and confusion persisted despite desperate efforts to bring the banking system under control.[77] It was left to Haddon-Cave's successor, Bremridge, to deal with the crisis that the mistaken policies of the 1970s had made inevitable. The collapse of the currency in 1983 forced the colonial administration to realise that, given the peculiarities of Hong Kong's monetary infrastructure and its political circumstances, a return to the currency board was the simplest and safest solution. The linked exchange rate of HKD7.80 = USD1 was introduced, which defined the target for monetary policy and created the opportunity to achieve stability both for the currency and the money supply. The government's relationship with the banking industry was transformed, and officials now took on the direct responsibility for implementing monetary policy that they had so long sought to evade.[78]

Conclusions

Some modern economists argue that it is wrong for the monetary authorities to try to counter excessive liquidity that generates immoderate speculation on share and property markets. They contend that because inadequate banking supervision and defective management are the real causes of 'bubble' conditions — which was certainly true of Hong Kong in the 1960s and 1970s — monetary policy is not the appropriate remedy.[79] But earlier chapters have shown that it was the colonial administration's policies which created the market environment for severe monetary problems and that the government could have averted disaster by accepting responsibility for monetary affairs. The property boom of the 1960s and its collapse can be attributed principally to the abnormal market conditions caused by changes in both building legislation and official policies. Similarly, the chaotic market conditions of the

1970s can be blamed on the colonial administration's mismanagement of the currency and its misunderstanding of the banks' role in the creation of liquidity.

Flawed policies involved significant costs for the community. Once Cowperthwaite had taken the decision to go for growth at all costs, the dangers of speculative markets and financial scandals increased. Haddon-Cave's decision to follow the same policy meant that these risks continued throughout the 1970s and were increased by his loss of control over the money supply. The stability of the financial system now depended not on effective regulation and sound monetary policies but on rescuing insolvent banks. The 1965 bank runs strengthened the obsession with the strength of the Exchange Fund because of its functions in concealing from the public the full costs of the government's policy blunders. This role was made possible by its ample resources and the secrecy of its operations. Bremridge candidly confessed to the legislature: 'I [had] been a Member to this Council for seven years before I became Financial Secretary and I had no idea about the Exchange Fund whatsoever'.[80] These rescue exercises affected the amount of resources available for economic and social programmes because they created an incentive to hold down government spending in order to expand the Exchange Fund's assets. Haddon-Cave's mismanagement of monetary affairs and the financial failures, corporate scandals and currency collapse which followed in the 1980s gave a new importance to the Exchange Fund's role in meeting the government's political liabilities for insolvent banks.

The persistent refusal to introduce reforms except in response to crises produced 'a makeshift banking system', according to a 1982 commentator, which had dangerous characteristics.[81]

> The peculiarities of the Hong Kong system have resulted in a system which ... positively promotes monetary instability because the authorities are virtually powerless to affect the rate of monetary growth, while the banks are not restrained by any external constraint on the rate of credit and money creation and consequently they are free to alternate between phases of exuberant credit expansion and extreme cautiousness and timidity. This results in wide swings in money and credit growth.

All too often, members of the élite Administrative Service made disastrous decisions which could have been avoided with more professionalism. As early as 1962, a prominent development economist had explained the dilemma faced by a government like Hong Kong. If it stuck to the traditional, 'colonial' model of full backing for the currency in overseas assets, a shortage of credit could prove a barrier to higher rates of growth (although, in practice, Hong Kong's modern banking system ensured that the colony never ran short of funds). But once this discipline was abandoned, growth would follow the money supply, with a real risk of 'a balance-of-payments crisis, structural distortions and (very possibly) internal inflation'.[82] After the Hong Kong dollar started to float in the 1970s, the colonial administration ceased to transfer the funds to back the currency overseas. They were held, instead, in Hong Kong bank accounts. The results were exactly as predicted: inflation, distortion of the financial infrastructure and a collapse of the exchange rate in 1983. The only immediate remedy that would restore confidence in the currency was a return to the discipline of a currency board, the colonial administration believed.

Nevertheless, officials still had not fully grasped how weak was the currency board's influence on the money supply in Hong Kong because of the banks' freedom to create liquidity, as discussed earlier in this chapter. Not until 1988 did the government face up to the reality that 'the narrow currency board — based, as it was, only on physical currency — … was insufficient to deliver broader currency stability'. Only then were practical measures introduced to allow the monetary authorities direct influence over the creation of liquidity.[83] In earlier decades, many Third World countries had found it difficult to adopt practical remedies for the limitations of colonial monetary arrangements, even after a currency board had been replaced by a central bank.[84] For all Hong Kong's sophistication as a financial centre, the process of reforming the traditional system had been similarly complex and protracted.

11

The Exceptional Colony

The management of Hong Kong's finances was an issue which provoked constant mistrust of the colonial administration, not just among the public at large but also among the government's hand-picked appointees to the legislature. It proved almost impossible to convince the community that Hong Kong's reserves — the government's budget surpluses and other assets, together with the funds that backed the note issue — remained under the ownership, management and control of Hong Kong even when invested abroad. One popular rumour was that visits by British royalty were a cover for the covert removal of Hong Kong assets.[1] In the early 1980s, the government felt compelled to rebut a widespread belief that Hong Kong remitted large but unpublished subsidies to the UK as a form of colonial tribute.[2] The allegation was given a new lease of life by China's leaders in the final years of British rule in a bid to discredit the colonial administration's motives.[3]

In most colonies, it was difficult enough to understand how the monetary system functioned because of a shortage of reliable data.[4] Observers found Hong Kong particularly baffling. A 1950 survey of the British Empire's currency relations with the UK despaired of making sense of this colony's monetary arrangements, complaining: 'Hong Kong eludes even Imperial authority, and to grapple further would require impossible mental [gymnastics]'.[5] The confusion was intentional because the colonial administration had made a deliberate decision to starve London of economic and financial information. Officials resisted compiling banking statistics throughout the 1950s and did not start to collect comprehensive banking data until 1964. It never acceded to the demands for balance of payments estimates that the Colonial Office first made in 1950 and which London repeated in urgent terms in the decades that followed.[6] These statistical policies were designed to maintain the colony's freedom from London's supervision. The political price to be paid in Hong Kong for this data deficit was the widespread circulation of conspiracy theories about the government's motives and priorities.

Grounds for Suspicion

The UK's monetary arrangements for its imperial possessions seemed specially designed to provoke such suspicions. At the centre of this system was a colonial 'currency board' which issued notes and coins in exchange for sterling assets and controlled the money supply and invested the official reserves in London.[7] Hong Kong seemed little different from the rest of the British Empire. It, too, had a currency board and, before the end of the Sterling Area in 1972, held a substantial proportion of the official reserves in London. Critics have attacked these sterling investments as forced loans to the UK, an export of local capital which, otherwise, would have been available for economic and social development.[8] One historian has argued that 'the placing of Hong Kong's reserves in London represented a direct exploitation of the Hong Kong people … Britain used Hong Kong's colonial status to force a developing territory to extend a loan to a developed country' on disadvantageous terms.[9]

In reality, the British accepted that the colony's financial resources were the property of Hong Kong and not the UK, and Hong Kong's financial secretaries managed the reserves according to their own assessments of Hong Kong's monetary requirements.

- They made up their own minds on how large the reserves should be and turned to the World Bank when they wanted expert advice on this subject.[10]
- Before the demise of the Sterling Area in 1972, the colonial administration did not routinely transfer funds each year to London, contrary to popular belief. No government funds were remitted to London from the end of the 1950s until 1969,[11] and profits from the London portfolio were regularly transferred back to Hong Kong in the 1960s to finance government spending in general.[12]
- Commercial factors played a large part in financial secretaries' decisions about how much to keep in sterling.[13] They were attracted by the interest rates on offer in London, just as the commercial banks were. Thus, when sterling devalued in 1967, it was found that 12 per cent of the total reserves held by Hong Kong's banking industry in London belonged to the Hang Seng Bank. Its management had chosen to ignore the well-known weaknesses of the pound, partly because of the higher interest earnings even though this bank had complete freedom to keep its reserves in US dollars.[14]

This chapter will show that, in spite of popular perceptions to the contrary, Hong Kong was not subject to the economic and monetary constraints that prevailed in other colonies. It had a currency board system, but the currency was issued by commercial banks. The economy was not locked into sterling because a free foreign exchange market operated openly. The banking system was not dominated by London banks but by HSBC, whose headquarters were in Hong Kong and whose business interests were located overwhelmingly in Asia. Economic and financial policies were decided not by the Colonial Office in London but by the colonial administration in Hong Kong. In short, this colony enjoyed a considerable measure of autonomy in the conduct of its monetary affairs, thanks, in part, to precedents established in the 1930s (which were analysed in Chapter 2 'Chinese Revolutionaries, Colonial Reformers').

There was also a China dimension to Hong Kong's monetary arrangements during the colonial era which few critics have recognised. Before World War II and during the planning for post-war reconstruction, the UK had accepted Hong Kong's right to manage its currency independently because of its dependence on the Mainland.[15] The colony joined the Sterling Area only after the collapse of the historical links between the Hong Kong dollar and China's own currency, and it was not forced to accept the rigid exchange controls imposed on the Sterling Area's other members. After the Chinese Communist Party came to power in 1949 and the Cold War embargoes against China began, the colony's vital economic relationship with the Mainland could only be maintained if Hong Kong used sterling as its underlying currency because the US tried to impose a total blockade on China's access to international finance and trade, seizing any assets which appeared to have Mainland connections. The Sterling Area was not subject to American law and thus provided a politically safe currency for the People's Republic of China. The colony's dependence on Mainland imports meant that Hong Kong was stuck with sterling for the same reason as the Chinese government: there was no practical alternative until 1971 when the US embargo ended. For example, when in the 1950s Beijing bought wheat from Canada — which did not belong to the Sterling Area — the currency of the transaction had to be sterling. The deal began in Hong Kong and was completed in London because of the threat of confiscation of the Chinese government's funds if they touched the American financial system.[16] (These issues were analysed in Chapter 4, 'Financial Centre under Siege'.)

A Doubtful Asset

Hong Kong was, in many ways, a disappointing colony. The UK itself was far from convinced that it was a significant asset. The China market, for which Hong Kong had been seized in the nineteenth century, had never lived up to the expectations of British imperialists.[17] By the 1930s, British investment in Hong Kong accounted for perhaps as much as one per cent of total UK overseas investments (compared with the Mainland which was the location for seven per cent of total British foreign investment). Nor was the colony a major market for UK products — an unimpressive situation after almost a century of British rule.[18]

During the 1950s, British ministers began to question the economic worth to the UK of the remaining colonies, and Hong Kong made a dismal showing in a secret exercise to calculate the value of individual territories. Even on the most optimistic calculation, its net contribution to the UK balance of payments was only GBP13 million in 1955. The Colonial Office suggested that, in addition, Hong Kong probably generated more hard currency for the Sterling Area than escaped through its free market.[19] The only substantial benefit to the UK which this secret review could attribute to Hong Kong was as a showcase for British values (rather than for British goods and services).[20]

[Hong Kong] is an outpost of good government, justice and individual freedom ... and a sanctuary for refugees; it is a shop window for the British way of life in that part of the world ... The cost of all this to the United Kingdom Exchequer is slight.

In 1961, ministers began to express fresh doubts about whether it was worthwhile for the UK to remain in Hong Kong. This time, no attempt was made to produce any cash estimates of the benefits derived from the colony. The emphasis was on the costs of quitting. Officials warned that if the British left, the Chinese government would inherit at least GBP100 million from the reserves which the colony had accumulated in London.[21] In 1975, the colonial administration started to worry about the hostile attitude of British politicians towards the continuation of colonial rule, and Hong Kong officials launched an exercise to calculate the benefits to the UK of retaining the colony. The endeavour was abandoned after it failed to produce any credible figures that were likely to convince sceptics in London that Hong Kong was a significant asset for the UK.[22]

These surveys were concealed from the public until their release by public records offices 30 years later, and the colonial administration published no balance of payments or other financial data that would clarify the relationship with the UK. So, conspiracy theories about London's greed for colonial tribute won wide acceptance, reasonably enough since the evidence of colonial exploitation seemed so obvious. Why did the Hong Kong government invest in London instead of in Hong Kong's own economic and social development? Why, too, hold sterling when this currency was in constant danger of devaluation for the first three decades after World War II? The answers seemed obvious: the colonial administration was an active partner in London's attempts to use its rapidly diminishing colonial empire to rescue its own ailing economy. The widespread assumption was that management of Hong Kong's budget, its currency and its reserves was dictated by London and designed to maximise the benefits to the UK from its possession of this vibrant colony.

From the UK's point of view, the reserves held in sterling by the Hong Kong government and the banking system were a mixed blessing. They were a growing and important source of support for sterling in the 1950s and 1960s. But officials in London also saw them as a potential danger for the future, as was noted earlier. If the UK withdrew from the colony, it was pointed out in 1961, 'one heavy cost' would be the surrender of 'the currency backing and a large part of banking and privately held funds' to the Chinese government.[23] The anxiety was that in managing these reserves, Beijing would follow its own agenda even at the expense of sterling's stability — just as India and other former imperial territories had done when the British handed over power.[24]

Hong Kong itself was to demonstrate the validity of London's concerns about the reserves, even before the end of British rule. When the UK devalued sterling in 1967, Hong Kong was allowed to fix its own exchange rate. In the following year, the colony managed to compel the UK to introduce the first guarantees against devaluation ever given to a Sterling Area member. At this stage, Hong Kong accounted for around 15 per cent of the Sterling Area's total balances in London. A significant share in the Hong Kong portfolio belonged to HSBC and was technically classified as 'non-resident' [i.e., offshore] and entitled to be converted into US dollars. The colonial administration and HSBC warned that these funds would be transferred to New York — which would bring down sterling — unless the UK offered guarantees against further devaluations.[25]

London capitulated, and Hong Kong won concessions which independent nations such as Australia and Malaysia had never managed to achieve. This precedent meant that similar protection had be extended to the rest of the Sterling Area at considerable cost to the UK, which now had a powerful incentive to abandon sterling's role as a 'reserve currency'.[26] London had proved vulnerable to an uncooperative government whose reserves were large enough to destabilise the pound.[27] Hong Kong's triumph meant the end of the old 'imperial' Sterling Area. The UK would no longer be free to devalue the pound and force Commonwealth countries and colonial territories to bear the losses involved.[28] Hong Kong had disproved the widespread perceptions of its colonial subordination to sterling and established a claim to be regarded as a financial centre in its own right.[29] Nevertheless, the community continued to harbour considerable misgivings about the reserves and their management, and the government's lack of transparency over their management did nothing to dispel popular misconceptions.

Hong Kong's Special Circumstances

The standard monetary arrangements for colonial territories seemed oppressive by design, hardly surprisingly since they reflected the low level of economic development that prevailed in most parts of the British Empire until at least World War II. Business was conducted mainly on a cash or even a barter basis. There was relatively little banking, and what financial business existed was nearly always handled by branches of banks whose headquarters were in London.[30] As in other parts of the Third World, bank lending played a limited part in the creation of credit because commercial banks tended to maintain high levels of liquidity.[31] Thus, the money supply was dominated by the coins and notes in circulation, and bank loans and advances were only a minor component.[32] The local currency was essentially sterling in another guise, convertible into pounds on demand and fully backed by assets held in London. As a result, the note issue — traditionally, the key component of the money supply — could only increase if an equivalent amount in sterling were available to back it in London, which meant that the money supply expanded and contracted in line with export earnings.[33] The entire economy was very much driven by the foreign trade sector.[34]

With the retreat from empire after World War II, these monetary arrangements came under serious attack because their plain aim was to promote the interests of the UK. In the typical colony, 'local banks were merely branches of London banks, maintaining their basic liquidity in London', and 'the local economy could be regarded substantially as part of the British economy, in much the same way as a state of the USA is part of the Union'.[35] Complaints about these monetary arrangements gained added credibility as the reserves held by colonies in London became increasingly important in defending the Sterling Area and maintaining the value of the pound in the 1950s and 1960s.[36] There seemed to be no escape from subordination to UK interests. 'Whatever political and strategic reasons there may be for their being under the British flag', a well-known colonial economist declared, 'From the standpoint of trade the colonial territories are essentially specialized producing parts of a widespread economy which has its financial, industrial, and managerial center in the UK'.[37] All of which offended the economic as much as the political fashions of the age. The prevailing wisdom was that foreign trade exploited the Third World and that independent monetary policies were an essential tool for rapid economic growth. In addition, colonial monetary arrangements were depicted as unreasonable constraints on a colonial territory's freedom to accelerate growth through 'Keynesian' strategies, including deficit financing and foreign loans.[38]

But the colonial monetary system worked very differently in more sophisticated economies. As the contribution to national income from the domestic economy rose, the money supply would cease to fluctuate mechanically with the level of exchange earnings.[39] In addition, once a territory had developed a modern financial infrastructure, the standard colonial monetary arrangements ceased to be an economic straitjacket. Banks were able to finance business growth through loans and advances, which now became significant components of the money supply.[40] Capital could be created by the banks through their normal lending activities or could be imported through loans raised overseas by business firms.[41] At this stage, the local financial system would acquire a 'discretionary' element instead of adjusting automatically to the amount of foreign exchange available to support the currency. The more developed an economy became, the fewer the constraints imposed by the traditional monetary arrangements. Hong Kong already enjoyed these advantages in the 1930s. Its banking system was then well-developed and not under the control of London banks. The money supply was not confined to cash in circulation. Not surprisingly, Hong Kong was recognised very early during the debates over the traditional colonial monetary arrangements as an exception to the handicaps which they imposed on the typical British colony.[42]

In Hong Kong, banking was a feature of almost every aspect of business. Unlike most colonies before independence, Hong Kong did not depend on highly volatile commodity markets and exports of primary products within the British Empire. Historically, it acted as a commercial and investment centre for China, whose main trading partner was the US. When Hong Kong was still an entrepôt, it was almost impossible for a business to avoid contact with the banking industry. At the very lowest level, each import and export transaction involved a foreign currency and required a financial intermediary. (As late as the 1950s, the boundary between money changers and banks was very thin.) Hong Kong's switch to manufacturing after World War II reinforced this feature of the business landscape. Its emergence as an industrial economy depended on ample bank finance to underwrite its exports to booming consumer markets in the most prosperous Western countries. Because of the high turnover and short production runs typical of light industry (as was explained in Chapter 5, 'Industrial Take-off: Cut-price and Self-financed'), larger enterprises needed continuous banking support to import equipment and raw materials. The daily operations of the smaller sub-contracting factories were often financed by the import-export firms which had placed the original purchase order. These trading houses, in turn, got their working capital from the banks.

Ignoring the Banks

Hong Kong's special circumstances went unrecognised by the colonial administration, however. Officials acted as if Hong Kong were like any other colony in which there was little, if any, room for an active monetary policy since the currency board operated automatically, 'supplying and withdrawing local currency, but merely by a sort of mechanical process; it [had] no power to fix the quantity to be put into circulation'.[43] Officials seemed blind to the fact that with an extensive banking system, 'a significant proportion of the money supply was not currency but bank credit over which the currency board had absolutely no control'.[44] By ignoring the banking sector's role, the colonial administration was able to convince itself that it could disregard most monetary issues because any problems would be temporary and self-solving. Furthermore, it was widely assumed — outside the government as well as by officials — that, thanks to the currency board, the following conditions existed which made government intervention unnecessary.[45]

- Credit creation by the banking system was not a significant or separate source of liquidity.
- Overall liquidity would rise or fall in line with export performance.
- Changes in the money supply would trigger the adjustments within the economy required to ensure the healthy state of the balance of payments.
- Any inflationary pressures were imported.

Because of these assumptions, officials believed that attempts to interfere with the economy would be fruitless and probably counter-productive. In the 1950s, the Financial Secretary publicly rejected 'a policy of Government control of the money market and of the volume of money' on political grounds.[46] In confidential correspondence with the Colonial Office, however, his deputy justified Hong Kong's opposition to government intervention on the grounds that the economy was self-regulating.[47] In the 1960s and 1970s, financial secretaries became increasingly assertive about the way the economy adjusted automatically to the changing business environment. As a result, they argued, markets were best left to find their own equilibrium regardless of the strains and distortions generated by excessive creation of liquidity by the banks which was followed so frequently by reckless speculation (a recurrent theme of Chapters 6 to 9).[48] In the search for currency stability after the collapse of the exchange rate in 1983, the case for an active monetary policy and considerable government involvement in financial markets became overwhelming. But claims that, under a currency board, the economy was self-regulating had become so central to government policy that officials now made a determined effort to conceal the extent of government intervention.[49]

The 'Liquidity Loophole'

The colonial administration did not realise until the late 1970s that the only constraints on bank lending — and hence on a substantial portion of the money supply — were the self-restraint of individual banks and any restrictions imposed by legislation. As a result, officials paid little attention to the way in which banks create money through making loans and advances. Left to their own devices, the only limit on the freedom of banks to lend money is how much cash their customers are likely to demand at short notice. A bank cannot survive if it does not have enough highly liquid assets — as well as money in hand — to cover the withdrawals of its customers. These liquidity requirements reflect the business environment. The more advanced an economy becomes, the more it will rely on cheques and other transfers through the banking system rather than cash. The bigger a firm — or the more international its business — the less cash it will use as a proportion of its total transactions. In Hong Kong, banks also had to take into account the danger that during the colonial era, political events could cause a loss of public confidence in the banking system.

The 1964 Banking Ordinance imposed minimum liquidity ratios on the entire banking system to prevent imprudent bank lending. The colonial administration made it clear that that the aim of this new statutory requirement was partly monetary. 'The minimum liquidity ratio set for banks is designed not only to ensure the ready availability of funds to repay deposits', the Financial Secretary declared, 'but also to prevent the inflationary effects of credit creation through excessive bank lending'.[50] The new law had little impact, however, on the credit policies of local branches of a foreign-owned bank. Their Hong Kong operations were backed by the entire resources of the foreign parent. Head office could provide them with whatever liquidity Hong Kong law required through paper transactions and book-keeping entries, and no cash or assets had to be transferred to the Hong Kong branch.[51] Foreign-owned banks found this practice commercially attractive because they had two significant advantages over HSBC and local Chinese-owned banks in managing liquidity which lowered their costs of operating in Hong Kong.

- The foreign-owned banking sector faced the lowest demands for cash. Their customers were mainly overseas firms or the larger local company, the bulk of whose financial transactions was conducted on a bank-to-bank basis.
- In a political panic, foreign banks would seem less vulnerable than local banks, and so would actually attract depositors in search of security. In addition, because a foreign bank's customers tended to be international, these would respond to a fall in confidence in Hong Kong by transferring their deposits to the bank's branches in other countries rather than shifting to a different bank. [52]

Freedom from statutory liquidity requirements combined with a lower demand for cash created a 'liquidity loophole' for the foreign-owned banking sector. This feature of the Hong Kong banking system allowed an overseas bank to lend out a much higher proportion of its deposits than HSBC or a local Chinese-owned bank was able to do. The liquidity loophole provided Hong Kong with a source of bank-created funding that played a key part in financing Hong Kong's transition to a manufacturing economy and the emergence subsequently of a dominant financial services sector. (How the loophole operated in practice was analysed in earlier chapters.) Thus, Hong Kong's ability to attract international banks was of special help in freeing Hong Kong from the usual constraints of colonial monetary arrangements.

Profits before Patriotism

What made Hong Kong's monetary arrangements particularly unusual among colonial territories was the role of HSBC. As the biggest note-issuing bank, HSBC's influence on the money supply was considerable. It needed sterling for its normal trading activities, so it built up holdings in London for commercial reasons. But it also needed sterling whenever it wanted to expand the note issue. If HSBC issued more banknotes, it would have to hand over the equivalent value in sterling to the government's Exchange Fund (which paid no interest). A larger note issue thus involved a commercial decision about the best use of its assets. HSBC kept in close contact with the Financial Secretary about changes in the note issue.[53] But HSBC was not a government agency, and it did not expand the note issue as an automatic response to Hong Kong's higher exchange earnings — as currency boards did in other colonies.[54] Furthermore, historically, HSBC had not been able to adjust the note issue solely on the basis of Hong Kong's needs. Demand for these banknotes had been high on the Mainland until 1949 where they circulated in quantity but did not form an active part of Hong Kong's money supply.[55] Hong Kong currency began to circulate on the Mainland once more after 1978 and the introduction of Deng Xiaoping's economic reforms.[56]

HSBC's 'diplomatic' policies also reinforced the colony's financial autonomy. The bank played complex, and sometimes confusing, roles in the UK's 'informal empire' in China and within the power structure of colonial Hong Kong. Up to World War I, HSBC was the only British company to enjoy the formal support of the British Foreign Office, which gave it an especially privileged status in an era during which the UK was still firmly wedded to free trade and open competition, even in its imperial pursuits. When British priorities in China switched during the nineteenth century from export domination of Mainland markets to command of its financial system, HSBC became even more useful to London.[57] It was to remain the premier British corporation in China throughout the twentieth century. HSBC, however, was not a docile tool of the UK government, and the bank displayed no sense of 'business patriotism'. It had little to gain from becoming part of the cosy London club that was overseen by an avuncular, but strict, Bank of England and which dominated the British banking scene for much of the last century.[58] It was not dependent on the Bank of England's goodwill because the UK stuck to laisser faire before 1914, and the government did not attempt to control financial markets, unlike most European governments.

In fact, membership of the London banking establishment would have been a disadvantage. HSBC operated offshore and regarded most London financial institutions as potential rivals for international business. The bank preferred to share transactions with non-British banks rather than provide London competitors with an entry to its Asian markets.[59] This attitude made the British Foreign Office less and less convinced of the commercial merits of its special relationship with HSBC, and it had come to an end by 1914.[60] After World War I, HSBC had even less to gain from cooperating with the UK authorities. They wanted all available investment funds to be devoted to the transition to a post-war economy, and the Bank of England persuaded banks not to support loans for overseas borrowers. This informal embargo collapsed in 1922 when HSBC defied the Bank of England and arranged a loan for Thailand.[61] After World War II, the rise of Asian nationalism and the dissolution of the British Empire made it impossible to survive commercially in Asia while serving UK interests.[62] London showed how deep its own mistrust of HSBC had become in the post-colonial world when the Bank of England refused to endorse a Hong Kong takeover of the Royal Bank of Scotland in 1982 because HSBC was not regarded as 'fully committed to the UK public interest'. The deal was also disallowed on the grounds that the colonial administration could not be expected to act on London's behalf and ensure that UK banking policies took priority over Hong Kong interests.[63]

Legally, HSBC was a local bank, whose headquarters remained in Hong Kong until the last decade of British rule. Thus, it could not benefit from the liquidity loophole as foreign-owned banks did. Furthermore, since it dominated the banking system and issued the bulk of the currency, prudence dictated that it maintain high levels of liquidity. As a result, HSBC executives felt deeply about banking stability and the need for a strong currency. Inevitably, its views on banking policy differed, often radically and publicly, from the non-interventionist attitude adopted by the colonial administration, both before and after World War II. There was considerable tension between the bank's interests and the government's priorities — on monetary policy in the 1950s and 1960s; on commercial issues in the 1970s; and on currency board operations throughout the rest of the century.[64]

The Hong Kong public, nevertheless, regarded the bank as a pillar of the colonial establishment, and HSBC remained thoroughly expatriate in its senior personnel and 'British' in its culture until 1997.[65] But HSBC did not see itself as obligated to British business. The bank's management had learnt that profits depended on picking winners first from among the new manufacturing class created by the industrial boom in the 1950s and then from the ranks of the local tycoons who built up impressive corporate empires in Hong Kong. Thus, HSBC showed no hesitation in helping Chinese entrepreneurs, such as Sir Pao Yue-kong and Li Ka-shing, to triumph over long-established British family firms like Jardine Matheson, Hutchison and Wheelock Marden (as was described in Chapter 9, 'From Banking Crisis to Financial Catastrophe').

Conclusions

As a colony, Hong Kong did not live up to the British expectations that had inspired its seizure in the nineteenth century, and there were serious reservations, by the 1950s, about the economic and financial benefits that it was likely to generate for the UK. As this chapter has demonstrated, Hong Kong proved a serious liability for the Sterling Area and hastened its demise, despite its subordinate status as a colonial territory. It was not only a doubtful asset to Britain, it was also a striking exception to the usual pattern of economic development and monetary management that prevailed in the rest of the colonial empire. Hong Kong was never a semi-subsistence, cash-based economy. Its commercial success depended on an extensive banking industry to support the international activities essential to its original role as an entrepôt and to its emergence as a leading exporter of light industrial products. Thus, its economic autonomy began with a modern banking system.

This independence was strengthened by another exceptional feature of the Hong Kong business scene. Unlike the rest of the colonial empire, its leading bank was a local institution which took a thoroughly commercial view of its responsibilities and saw little profit in patriotism. HSBC's dominant position meant that in Hong Kong, UK banks had no opportunity to exert the control over the financial system that was typical of other colonies. In addition, Hong Kong as a financial centre attracted leading banks from the Mainland and around the world. They were not part of the imperial financial system that developed into the Sterling Area, and they had nothing to gain from promoting British interests. Thus, Hong Kong had an advanced banking system and a sophisticated business community which was dominated by Hong Kong interests rather than UK corporations — in marked contrast to the average British territory. This banking and business autonomy made possible the colony's successful transition from trading to manufacturing and then into a substantial financial centre.

Nevertheless, the public remained suspicious about the colonial administration's management of monetary affairs, despite the government's conspicuous lack of commitment to UK interests and its disloyalty to the Sterling Area. Previous chapters illustrated how the colonial administration was able to decide its own economic and financial policies with little interference from London. They also demonstrated how this freedom from UK control was all too often exercised without the wisdom that the people of Hong Kong were entitled to expect. The colony's resilience enabled the colonial administration to resist monetary reforms because the banks continued to flourish and the financial markets recovered regardless of the crises and the collapses which erroneous government decisions made possible.

Conclusions — A Political Deficit

Hong Kong's economic 'miracle' was not based on abrupt breaks with the past or 'revolutions' in production processes and business techniques. The miracle lay in the surprising quality of its performance by comparison with other Chinese cities, British colonies and the rest of the Third World. Hong Kong's enduring feature between 1935–85 was its success as an 'enterprise' economy. The underlying business model for Hong Kong society was so resourceful and resilient that trade and production prospered even under the most adverse circumstances. Growth was largely incremental, and previous chapters have shown how each period of turbulence facilitated an economic surge in the years that followed. The flood of refugees in the 1930s seemed far beyond the colony's capacity to provide for them — even at a subsistence level — but investment confidence was buoyant and industry boomed. A similar immigrant influx after World War II was followed by another boom which began with heavy investment in modern mills to meet the demands of textile factories set up before the war. Meanwhile, during the Japanese occupation, local Chinese-owned banks had turned to new sources of profit, and banking was probably the first business to resume normal operations when peace returned. Then, the Cold War separated the banks from their Mainland hinterland and seemed to threaten their survival. But Hong Kong was able to develop a new offshore financial market in the 1950s to serve China's development needs, despite a US embargo and Sterling Area exchange controls. After 1978, Deng Xiaoping's 'open door' policies could have made Hong Kong's Mainland role redundant. Instead, Hong Kong became the nation's leading source of capital and expertise to modernise southern China.

This 'enterprise' economy survived through a process of constant adaptation. But institutions and individuals differed in the speed and success of their adjustments because the changes required were rarely comfortable and not always immediately obvious. This book has shown how often the optimal strategy and rational decision were postponed and how much depended on the relationship with clients and constituents. Factories and trading houses were directly linked to overseas markets, which compelled them to adopt whatever production or business practices their customers preferred. For bankers, the relationship was not so close. Until the arrival of the large family conglomerates in the 1970s, the Hong Kong borrower was too small to be able to exert much power over a bank, and bankers could remain isolated from radical changes in Hong Kong's economic conditions. In the end, however, they were subject to market forces: failure to adapt would be penalised by lost profit opportunities.

The government displayed much the same pattern. For the most part, bureaucratic rule by colonial mandarins and the absence of an elected legislature meant that there was little direct link between government policy and the community's preferences. The colonial administration could pick and choose its constituents among the business élite, and, in the case of banking, officials had considerable discretion in applying the law. There were no elections to penalise political failure or bureaucratic blunders — in marked contrast to business where bankruptcy could follow customer dissatisfaction and incompetent management. But a threat of public protests on the colony's streets was a powerful incentive for officials to discard their usual disdain for depositors and to reform financial regulation. This book illustrates, too, that the colony's political arrangements meant that the government was free to make the community pay the costs of mistakes in managing monetary affairs. Thus, the government regularly bailed out insolvent banks after 1965 for fear of public indignation if depositors were left to lose their savings. The colony's Exchange Fund financed these rescue operations with money that could have been spent directly on the community's well-being.

Causes of Complaint

Economists are divided about the contribution which banks make to economic modernisation.[1] The banking industry's role in Hong Kong's growth has been portrayed in mainly negative terms. An influential view is that, because of its colonial status, Hong Kong's financial resources were diverted from investment in the local economy and devoted, instead, to protecting the British currency.[2] However, the claim that reserves were held in London as a form of colonial tribute is not supported by the evidence reviewed in Chapter 10, 'Colonial Money and Its Management'. The real costs of maintaining large overseas reserves were social, not economic. After the 1965 bank runs, the colonial administration was determined to build up its reserves overseas to cope with future banking crises or financial collapses. This goal was achieved by under-spending on social services and the infrastructure in order to boost the surpluses on the annual budget. Thus, the price for ill-regulated banking and mismanaged monetary affairs fell heaviest on the ordinary family. For example, free and compulsory primary education was delayed for as long as possible in the 1960s, and housing was mostly squalid and overcrowded, even in the public sector.[3]

Manufacturers and business in general had little difficulty in borrowing from the banks. Nevertheless, Hong Kong industrialists have been depicted as victims of colonial hostility to the rise of a Chinese manufacturing class that might threaten British financial and commercial dominance. As a result, it has been argued, the banking industry neglected manufacturing, and industrial development was handicapped by a lack of capital.[4] It was true that the colonial administration refused to provide the cheap finance and investment incentives common elsewhere in Asia, and Hong Kong's factory owners had to pay a full market price for credit facilities.[5] Yet, manufacturers managed to flourish without the state subsidies and the specialised development and investment banks common to most Asian economies. Chapter 5, 'Industrial Take-off: Cut-price and Self-financed', explained how the banking industry, HSBC and the foreign-owned banks, in particular, filled the investment gap and financed Hong Kong's industrial take-off.[6]

The colony was frequently urged to follow the example of Singapore and other Asian states and introduce state direction and support of economic development. In practice, the colony was less laisser faire than was realised, and a comparative study of Singapore and Hong Kong found that the colonial administration had established an extensive programme to serve the specific needs of manufacturing in terms of industrial sites and buildings, professional and vocational training, productivity and research programmes that was 'probably as significant as that of Singapore'.[7] Surveys of Asian total factor productivity (TFP) growth suggest that Hong Kong's performance was not inferior to Singapore.[8] South Korea and Taiwan cannot claim that they were more successful than laisser-faire Hong Kong in fostering growth through their industrial development programmes.[9]

The colony's manufacturers had a legitimate grievance, nevertheless. Bankers were slow to expand their industrial lending, especially in the early stages of the manufacturing take-off. For new factory owners, the unenthusiastic response they first encountered from the banks seemed an unnecessary obstacle. For the bankers, however, each stage in the process of economic development demanded radical and often painful changes in their business models.

- China state-owned banks used Hong Kong's advantages to meet the Mainland's development needs, both during the Cold War and after the adoption of the 'open door' policies, which assigned an important role to Hong Kong from 1978. This group first had to adjust to the impact on the Mainland's economic management of ideological campaigns during the Maoist era and then, under Deng Xiaoping, had to learn to compete directly for business against capitalist bankers.

- The local Chinese-owned banks played an indispensable part in the period up to 1949 when Hong Kong was integrated into the Mainland economy. Subsequently, they declined to take the lead in financing the new manufacturers and left that role to the international bankers, for which local banks had to pay a price in terms of growth opportunities.
- The international banks (including HSBC), with their experience of industrial economies and Western markets, financed Hong Kong's manufacturing take-off and its emergence as a major exporter in the 1950s, albeit reluctantly at first. In the 1970s, the international banks adapted with excessive enthusiasm to the development of wholesale and offshore banking, and they were caught up in the corporate collapses of the 1980s.

Informal and Illegal

The success with which the different bank groups made these adjustments was heavily influenced by government policy and legislation and, even more, by the way these were implemented. From 1935 to 1985, Hong Kong was ruled by a colonial administration whose instinct was to avoid intervention in economic matters and social affairs. In this period, the impact of the government's 'informal' decisions on banking culture was at least as powerful as its laws, regulations and official policies, a conclusion which helps to explain the frequent self-destructive behaviour of banks, both individually and as groups.[10]

Before World War II, there was no banking supervision, and senior officials and leading businessmen became alarmed at the potential for financial disaster. Regulation began in Hong Kong with the 1948 Banking Ordinance as part of a 'good neighbour' policy towards the Mainland, where the authorities were complaining that Hong Kong banks were destroying the national currency through activities which contravened both Mainland and Hong Kong law.[11] The 1948 ordinance's intention was to define the boundaries of legitimate business conduct within the colony.[12] This objective was abandoned almost immediately. Instead, the government did its best to free local Chinese-owned banks from the letter of the law. The results were disastrous for the group as a whole, and this 'informal' policy had become a threat to the entire economy by 1965. In addition, the colonial administration allowed gold and currency dealing to flourish, although illegal, and government property policies led to reckless expansion of real estate. These three businesses were key elements in the traditional Chinese banking model. The profits they offered were so attractive to local Chinese-owned banks that they neglected the manufacturing sector in the 1950s and 1960s.

The regulators adopted a new 'informal' policy from 1970 to 1985: enforcement of the Banking Ordinance would be confined to technicalities.[13]

Bank owners and executives could safely conclude that the colonial administration had little interest in either prudence or integrity. This message was reinforced by a formal policy decision not to protect the customers of DTCs even though most of these firms were, to all intents and purposes, banking institutions. In this period, HSBC and foreign-owned banks demonstrated that self-imposed prudence has its limits. 'Conservative' corporate cultures can be abandoned with considerable speed when market conditions change and traditional conventions seem to stand in the way of continued profit growth.

Hong Kong's experience indicates that non-interventionism is not a benign strategy when applied to banking and offers considerable evidence in favour of effective regulation. The primary justification for active supervision of the colony's banking industry was law and order. The market itself proved unable to police banking practices, and the industry could not be trusted to conduct its affairs either honestly or efficiently if left entirely without official supervision. Several chapters have explained why, left to themselves, many banks would not resist the temptations offered by the immediate profits from speculative and even unlawful activities. Bankers, all too frequently, were poor judges either of what would endanger their own survival in the case of the smaller, local institutions or of the severe losses that the crash of speculative markets could inflict on international banks. For the most part, however, the colonial administration chose non-interventionism and introduced reforms grudgingly and only when the survival of British rule would be in direct danger from bank runs or financial instability. Not until 1986, after five decades of crisis and scandal, did the colonial administration accept that only the introduction of professional regulation for the entire financial industry would end the recurrent failures of the financial system.

The colonial administration's poor record in monetary affairs is very relevant to the continuing debate over the contribution of laisser faire to Hong Kong's economic success. The dismal fate of the local Chinese-owned banking sector in the first two post-war decades is a warning of how dangerous the colonial administration's approach to business could be even when officials' motives were to protect local interests. The failure to grasp the consequences of allowing an unlicensed banking sector to proliferate in the 1970s and the inability to understand the mechanics of the money supply are even more significant examples of how costly ill-conceived government policies can be. There is no reason to assume that officials would have been any more successful in managing other sectors of the economy if Hong Kong followed Asian fashion and introduced a state development programme. On this analysis, it can be argued that it would have been disastrous if the colonial administration had acceded to demands from all sectors of the business community in the 1950s and 1960s to abandon laisser faire and take charge of industrial progress.

Ramshackle Rule

Hong Kong became such a splendid example of economic prosperity and community well-being that much of the credit has been attributed to the existence of a relatively small, highly disciplined bureaucracy that provided the management for an increasingly sophisticated community and a high-growth, export-dominated economy.[14] The result is to portray British colonialism as having been ideal for Hong Kong and the unique circumstances which its people faced, whatever its defects elsewhere in the world.[15] Seen close up, however, nothing in the record of administrative officers in managing monetary affairs justified their reputation as 'high-minded mandarins, who sought to achieve the Confucianist ideal of disinterested administration and paternalistic concern for the welfare of the society'.[16] In fact, until the 1980s, the Hong Kong government in general presented much the same 'ramshackle appearance' that has been described as typical of public administration throughout the British colonial empire.[17]

Among senior Hong Kong officials, there was widespread hostility towards modern standards of professionalism for which, in the case of banking, budget stringency was invoked as an excuse. In reality, the annual licence fees paid by the banks were more than sufficient to pay for professional inspections in the 1950s.[18] The government simply saw no obligation to use this revenue to employ adequately trained staff to oversee the banking industry.[19] The acceptance of inferior standards reflected an important preconception of the colonial culture: quality was a Western prerogative. This attitude encouraged antipathy towards using professional expertise and mistrust of Western-trained professionals. 'A professional man who has done his training in a wealthy country when given a job to do, naturally wants to do it to the highest professional standards he knows', the Financial Secretary complained in 1962. 'Because of the comparative economic position here', he went on, professionals ought to recognise that Hong Kong should work to lower standards.[20] During this decade, the colonial administration repeatedly warned the community not to compare the quality of its programmes with the UK or Commonwealth countries.[21] By the 1980s, Hong Kong was a mature industrial economy and about to become a leading international business and financial centre. Now, another Financial Secretary denounced those who demanded improvements in public services as irresponsible do-gooders advocating unaffordable Western innovations.[22]

Economic Darwinism was given ample scope, with bank regulation derided by officials as a policy for protecting 'silly people'.[23] Some government policies discussed earlier in this book seemed wilfully harmful to the community's well-being.

- Officials delayed the introduction of banking supervision to protect depositors on the grounds that Chinese bankers would object and that the Chinese community did not expect its deposits to be safe and made little fuss when banks failed.

- The colonial administration deliberately facilitated gold and currency smuggling which were important business activities for many banks. To oblige the Portuguese rulers of Macao, Hong Kong ignored the connection between this illegal trade and drug trafficking.
- The colonial administration was anxious to attract overseas financial institutions to Hong Kong. As a result, international banks were not made subject to the statutory limits on lending, and regulation of DTCs was introduced only reluctantly in the 1970s, despite evidence that their activities fuelled inflation and financed dangerously speculative projects.

It is easy to find parallels in other policy areas that echoed the attitudes towards monetary affairs just quoted and which similarly appeared to put the interests of the least deserving groups ahead of those of the general public. For example:

- Legislation to reduce the length of the working day for factory workers was postponed on the grounds that the business community objected and that Chinese workers liked long hours.[24]
- The colonial administration allowed violent triad gangs to hold cleaning contracts for public housing, which gave them daily access to every household on a housing estate. Officials regarded this arrangement as acceptable because they received no complaints of extortion or intimidation from the tenants.[25]
- The colonial administration was anxious to retain the services of overseas professionals. For this reason, a confidential policy — concealed from the legislature — guaranteed every expatriate child a place in a primary or secondary school from the mid-1950s. Compulsory education for Chinese children was not introduced until 1971 at the primary level, and not until seven years later at the secondary level.[26]

The explanation for this state of affairs lay partly in the political arrangements that left the colonial administration free from community supervision and public accountability. For example, the truth about the dubious decisions listed earlier in this section was buried in official files to which the public had no access. The Executive and Legislative Councils were no safeguard, for government appointees to the legislature had little incentive to challenge official members. But when the process of slow, modest political reforms began in 1985, and a handful of elected members joined the legislature, the quality of financial regulation and monetary policy was rapidly transformed.

The Political Deficit

The connection between the management of monetary affairs and political reform was a discussion topic within the Colonial Office during the 1950s. One London official claimed that the absence of democracy was a guarantee of sound finances.[27]

> ... a Governor with a nominated Legislative Council and a climate of effective opinion, business opinion, which favours private enterprise rather than government activity, should be the best safeguards of responsible and economical financial policy in the colony — certainly better safeguards than would be a constitution giving the vote and influence to the working classes, as distinct from the business classes, because the working classes might be expected to require more of a welfare state and hence a great increase in government expenditure.

Representatives from the business and professional classes filled the colonial power structure, but their presence did not ensure sound policies even in commercial and financial affairs. Appointees from this élite dominated the network of advisory committees and statutory bodies which, in the absence of elections, provided the colonial administration with a substitute for popular endorsement by the Chinese community. But they were not a substitute for the professional policy-maker even when their own commercial survival was in the balance. Thus, when the battle against Western protectionism intensified in the 1960s and a long-term strategy to defend Hong Kong's manufactured exports was urgently needed, business leaders were, for the most part, dangerously confused about what to do, and they had to be cajoled into sensible decisions by senior officials.[28]

The bankers' record was no better. They were prominent in the councils that governed Hong Kong, as well as at the lower levels of the power structure. Somehow, the bankers made little difference to the colonial administration's policy-making or regulatory programmes for banks and financial markets. They did not convince the government to intervene ahead of financial disasters, and they did not call officials to account for costly collapses. Yet, a recurrent theme of this book is how clear were the market signals that disaster was approaching. It was true that HSBC's size and status gave it some leverage over banking policy. But although it acted as a quasi-central bank during the period covered by this book, its private representations and public criticisms did not persuade the colonial administration to introduce timely measures to forestall the dangers of bank scandals and financial failures either in the early 1960s or two decades later.[29] Only after the colonial administration itself made an unconditional commitment to professional regulation of financial institutions in 1986 did the scandals stop. Stability then reigned unshaken by severe political and economic shocks during the rest of the century. Hong Kong's experience is an interesting demonstration that 'irregular' and 'informal' banking practices are not the outcome of excessive government interference with an otherwise efficient business sector, as is often argued.

In the last resort, it was the political environment that mattered most. Banking reforms were piecemeal between 1935 and 1985 and driven mainly by the colonial administration's assessment of public sentiment. During the recession of the mid-1930s, they were a priority because of the fears of general economic collapse. They lost their urgency when a boom started in 1938. The case for reforms revived after Japan's defeat when Hong Kong's banking practices led to outright confrontation between the Mainland and the colony in the dying days of the Guomindang. There were plenty of bank closures and occasional bank runs in the 1950s which were ignored by the colonial administration because the public did not take to the streets. In the 1960s, the political damage caused by bank failures in an age of increasing mass banking became too serious to ignore. Not only were banking reforms introduced, but the government realised that it was no longer politically possible to force depositors to suffer the costs of a bank failure. Full acceptance by the government of responsibility for the integrity of banks and financial markets became unavoidable in 1985 because the political landscape had been transformed by the previous year's Sino-British Joint Declaration. This fixed the date for the end of British rule and unleashed growing demands from the community for greater control over its own affairs. The first indirect elections to the legislature in 1985 made officials accountable in public for the consequences of their policies.[30]

In the absence of accountable government in Hong Kong, only the UK authorities were in a position to insist on reforms, either in the quality of government performance generally or in banking and monetary affairs. London rarely exercised its constitutional powers to force improvements on the colony. There was an obvious irony, for example, in the Bank of England's campaign to improve banking standards at the international level in the 1970s, a decade in which the quality of the colony's management of banking and monetary affairs was allowed to deteriorate dramatically.[31] Thus, despite the unremitting pace of the colony's development, the government was able to cling to the policies and practices in managing monetary affairs that had been designed for African and Asian territories whose financial systems were rudimentary and whose principal banking and commercial institutions were controlled from London. Hong Kong officials made little effort to adapt the traditional monetary arrangements of the currency board to the very different economic conditions of Hong Kong. Indeed, they did not seem to realise that Hong Kong was an exception to the rules and restrictions that applied to the rest of the British Empire

The unacknowledged heroes of Hong Kong's modernisation were the community at large. It might be argued that, by comparison with Maoist extremism on the Mainland and misrule in many other parts of the region during the period, Hong Kong's people were well-off and, in any case, had little choice but to put up with conditions in the colony. Although prudence and self-interest have not prevented communities elsewhere from self-destructive behaviour, Hong Kong's people did not riot when banks failed. Nor did they withdraw their cooperation from the colonial administration. They did not abandon their trust in the banking system as a whole, even when well-known banks had forfeited the confidence of their depositors. They were prepared to patronise foreign banks regardless of the cultural discomforts they often encountered. All in all, the public understood the advantages which modern banking provided for ordinary families as well as to the affluent. They brought the same personal discipline and social maturity to their banking affairs as they did to the rest of their lives, which was fortunate because they had a great deal to provoke them over the years. As a result of this public patience and tolerant pragmatism, Hong Kong prospered on a far greater scale than any other British colony and emerged in the 1980s as the premier business centre for the Asian region and the financial dynamo for the spectacular rise of China in the world economy.

Notes

The following abbreviations are used in the notes:

CO: United Kingdom Colonial Office files in the Public Records Office London
FEER: *Far Eastern Economic Review*
GIS: *Government Information Services* (Daily press releases of the Hong Kong government)
HH: *Hong Kong Hansard* (Official report of the proceedings of the Hong Kong Legislative Council)
HKRS: Government files in the Public Records Office Hong Kong

INTRODUCTION

1. Y. C. Jao, 'The Rise of Hong Kong as a Financial Centre', *Asian Survey*, Vol. 19, No. 7 (July 1979), p. 687.
2. Howard Curtis Reed, 'The Ascent of Tokyo as an International Financial Center', *Journal of International Business Studies*, Vol. 11, No. 3 (Winter 1980), 'Table 3. Rankings of Asian International Bank Centers', p. 28; E. Stuart Kirby, 'Hong Kong and the British Position in China', *Annals*, Vol. 277 (September 1951), pp. 199–200.
3. Measured by comparative levels of non-performing loans and problem assets. Clifford D. Clark and Jung-Chao Liu, 'The Media, the Judiciary, the Banks and the Resilience of East Asian Economies', in Tsu-Tan Fu *et al* (eds), *Productivity and Economic Performance in the Asia-Pacific Region* (Cheltenham: Edward Elgar, 2002), p. 61 Table 3.3, p. 52.
4. Anson Chan, Chief Secretary, *GIS*, 20 January 1998.
5. Y. C. Jao, *The Asian Financial Crisis and the Ordeal of Hong Kong* (Westport: Quorum Books, 2001), p. 117.
6. Joseph Bisignano, 'Suggestions for Improvements', in Gerard Caprio, Jr *et al* (eds), *Preventing Bank Crises: Lessons from Recent Global Bank Failures* (Washington: World Bank, 1998), p. 295.
7. Ricardo, 'Development of Banking in Hong Kong during 1955', *FEER*, 2 February 1956.
8. Y. C. Jao, 'Monetary System and Banking Structure', in H. C. Y. Ho and L. C. Chau (eds), *The Economic System of Hong Kong* (Hong Kong: Asian Research Service, 1988),

p. 59. In 1978, deposits from customers with the 241 DTCs were equivalent to 17 per cent of the total with licensed banks. By 1982, the figure had risen to 22 per cent, only to fall to 10 per cent by 1987, by which date 94 had closed their doors. *Hong Kong Annual Digest of Statistics, 1988 Edition* (Hong Kong: Census and Statistics Department, 1988), pp. 125–8.

9. Gordon Redding, 'Culture and Business in Hong Kong', in Wang Gangwu and Wong Siu Lun (eds), *Dynamic Hong Kong: Business & Culture* (Hong Kong: Centre of Asian Studies, 1997), p. 102.

10. M. 2. Acting Financial Secretary to Governor, 10 September 1968. Hong Kong HKRS229-1-807 'Financial Aid (Including Loans) Received from the United Kingdom and Other Governments Record of ...'; (10) Governor to Secretary of State for the Colonies, 28 March 1962. HKRS163-1-1007 'Finance Estimated Capital Investment in Hong Kong'.

11. 'Report of the Industrial Bank Committee' (Hong Kong Government, January 1960, mimeo), p. 6; M. 10. TID to SID, 3 November 1967. HKRS1056-1-194 'Industrial Survey — Policy'; Catherine R. Schenk, 'Regulatory Reform in an Emerging Stock Market: the Case of Hong Kong, 1945–86', *Financial History Review*, 11.2 (2004), pp. 5–7.

12. Ronald Findlay and Stanislaw Wellisz, 'Hong Kong', in Ronald Findlay and Stanislaw Wellisz (eds), *The Political Economy of Poverty, Equity, and Growth. Five Small Open Economies* (New York: Oxford University Press, 1993), p. 47; Henry Smith, *John Stuart Mill's Other Island. A Study of the Economic Development of Hong Kong* (London: Institute of Economic Affairs, 1966), pp. 18–21.

13. Christopher Howe, 'Growth, Public Policy and Hong Kong's Economic Relationship with China', *China Quarterly*, No. 95 (September 1983), p. 512.

14. Frederick Ma, Secretary for Financial Services and the Treasury, *HH*, 3 July 2002, p. 8208. The trade data suggest that uninterrupted growth probably began in the mid-1950s.

15. Tsang Shu-ki, 'The Economy', in Donald H. McMillen and Man Si-wei (eds), *The Other Hong Kong Report 1994* (Hong Kong: Chinese University Press, 1994), p. 132.

16. Christopher Patten, Governor, *GIS*, 19 November 96.

17. Henry Y. Wan, Jr and Jason Weisman, 'Hong Kong: The Fragile Economy of Middlemen', *Review of International Economics*, Vol. 7, No. 3 (1999), p. 410.

18. F. C. Benham, 'The Growth of Manufacturing in Hong Kong', *International Affairs*, Vol. 32, No. 4 (October 1956), pp. 460–1.

19. Anne O. Krueger, 'Policy Lessons from Development Experience since the Second World War', in Jere Behrman and T. N. Srinivasan (eds), *Development Economics Volume IIIB* (Amsterdam: Elsevier, 1995), pp. 2501, 2504.

20. Bela Belassa, 'Outward Orientation', in Hollis Chenery and T. N. Srinivasan (eds), *Handbook of Development Economics Volume II* (Amsterdam: Elsevier, 1989), pp. 1653–71.

21. Note the comment on the widespread development initiatives based on protection and other incentives for new industries: 'There has been virtually no systematic examination of the empirical relevance of the infant industry argument. This is remarkable in light of the importance of the question, and the fact that thirty years evidence or more has accumulated in a number of countries'. Anne O. Krueger and Baran Tuncer, 'An Empirical Test of the Infant Industry Argument', *American Economic Review*, Vol. 72, No. 5 (December 1982), p. 1142. Hla Myint provided an

early and persuasive overview of the failure of economists to validate their development theories in 'Economic Theory and the Underdeveloped Countries', *Journal of Political Economy*, Vol. 73, No. 5 (October 1965).

22. For an interesting example of how Hong Kong's development experience is treated as of marginal relevance even to the growth process in the other Asian ' miracle' economies, see John Page, 'The East Asian Miracle: Four Lessons for Development Policy' *NBER Macroeconomics Annual*, Vol. 9 (1994).

23. George Hicks, 'The Four Little Dragons: An Enthusiast's Reading Guide', *Asian-Pacific Economic Literature*, Vol. 3, No. 2 (September 1989), pp. 36–7.

24. Cornelis J. A. Jansen and Mark Cherniavsky, 'Current Economic Situation and Prospects of Hong Kong' (Asia Department IBRD, 9 May 1967, mimeo.), p. ii.

25. This sentiment was noted by Shou-eng Koo, 'The Role of Export Expansion in Hong Kong's Economic Growth', *Asian Survey*, Vol. 8, No. 6 (June 1968), p. 508–9.

26. See Y. M. Yeung, 'Introduction', in Y. M. Yeung and Sung Yun-wing (eds), *Shanghai Transformation and Modernization under China's Open Policy* (Hong Kong: Chinese University Press, 1996), pp. 2, 17–8; Wong Siu-lun, 'The Entrepreneurial Spirit: Shanghai and Hong Kong Compared', *ibid.*, p. 43; Joseph Yam, Hong Kong Monetary Authority Chief Executive, *GIS*, 4 September 2000; *China Daily* Hong Kong edition, 18 May 2002. Even Prime Minister Wen Jiabao's assurances of official commitment to a flourishing Hong Kong failed to convince the sceptics. *Hong Kong Economic Journal*, 6 April 2006.

27. The adjustment of the Bank of China to the new Chinese government was made easier by the fact that it had long functioned on lines that bore 'a striking resemblance to the collective socialist organization known under the People's Republic as the *danwei* — the ubiquitous work unit'. Wen-Hsin Yeh, 'Corporate Space, Communal Time: Everyday Life in China's Bank of China', *American Historical Review*, Vol. 100, No. 1 (February 1995), p. 99.

28. 'More than 60 per cent', according to its chairman in 1988. Kevin Rafferty, *City on the Rocks. Hong Kong's Uncertain Future* (London: Viking, 1989), p. 288.

29. HSBC's privileges and how it was stripped of them are analysed in Leo F. Goodstadt, 'Crisis and Challenge: The Changing Role of the Hongkong & Shanghai Bank, 1950–2000', *HKIMR Working Paper No. 13/2005*, July 2005.

30. This assertion comes from one of Hong Kong's most experienced regulators but reflects research covering a large number of banking failures from a variety of countries. Andrew Sheng, 'Bank Restructuring Revisited', in Caprio *et al* (eds), *Preventing Bank Crises: Lessons from Recent Global Bank Failures*, p. 325.

31. See Katherine H. Y. Huang Hsiao, 'Money and Banking in the People's Republic of China: Recent Developments', *China Quarterly*, No. 91 (September 1982), pp. 464, 468.

32. The ideological barrier to direct participation in 'capitalist' activities did not totally prevent the group from participating in such business before 1979 with approval from Beijing.

33. Tommaso Padao-Schioppa, *Regulating Finance: Balancing Freedom and Risk* (Oxford: Oxford University Press, 2004), p. 7. This distinguished central banker makes a strong case for regulation in the current banking environment. The analysis presented here is indebted to this work.

34. London directed that special legislation be rushed through in a single sitting to

remedy this defect (but at no penalty to the banks involved). A. G. Leach, Attorney General, *HH*, 20 March 1895, pp. 38–9.

35. DFS minute to Financial Secretary, 25 January 1950. HKRS41-3-3044 'The Nam Sang Bank: 1. Application from … for a Banking Licence; 2. Balance Sheet of … 3. Cancellation of the Licence of …'.

36. The BCCI collapse provoked runs on four other banks, including Standard Chartered, a note-issuer. In marked contrast to previous decades, no financial crisis developed because the banking system and its regulators were well able to cope with this challenge. See Michael Taylor, 'Hongkong: Exchange of Views', *FEER*, 17 October 1991.

37. A brave bid has been made to prove that the Hong Kong public had adequate information to protect its own interests without government assistance. Kam Hon Chu, 'Free Banking and Information Asymmetry', *Journal of Money, Credit and Banking*, Vol. 31, No. 4 (November 1999), p. 759. This attempt must be regarded as unconvincing because the author gives insufficient attention to the window dressing permitted in published bank accounts to conceal the true liquidity ratios of individual banks, data which were vital to the author's hypothesis.

38. For a detailed analysis of this data deficit, its causes and consequences, see Leo F. Goodstadt, 'Government without Statistics: Policy-making in Hong Kong 1925–85, with special reference to Economic and Financial Management', *HKIMR Working Paper* No. 6/2006, April 2006.

39. Of 14 Asian economies reviewed in a leading historical overview, only Nepal's GDP series starts later than Hong Kong (1962). South Korea's series begins in 1953 (because of the war) and Singapore's in 1960. Balance of payments estimates show a similar pattern: South Korea's series begins in 1951 and Malaysia's in 1956 (and included Singapore until 1963); while the new state of Bangladesh starts its series in 1973. B. R. Mitchell, *International Historical Statistics Africa, Asia & Oceania 1750–1993* (London: Macmillan Reference Ltd, 1998, 3rd edition), pp. 1028–38, 1091–1107.

40. The initial publication covered only 1966–71. C. P. Haddon-Cave, Financial Secretary, *HH*, 28 February 1973, pp. 457–8.

41. The estimates started with 1997. 'HK's Balance of Payments (BoP) Account for 1997 … ', *GIS*, 23 April 1999. The colonial administration refused to compile these statistics even though London was publishing its own estimates from the 1960s without any input from Hong Kong. M. 1. AS(E3) to DES, 20 June 1970; M. 3. Financial Secretary to DES, 24 June 1970; M. 5. and 7. AS(E3) to Financial Secretary, 26 and 29 June 1970; Governor saving despatch to Secretary of State for the Colonies, No. 781, 29 June 1970. HKRS163-9-217 '(A) Meeting of Senior Commonwealth Finance Officials 1970. Sterling Area Balance Of Payments — Developments and Prospects To Mid-1971; (B) Overseas Sterling Area Countries Statistics'.

42. James Riedel, *The Industrialization of Hong Kong* (Tübingen: J. C. B. Mohr [Paul Siebuck], 1974), p. 7.

43. Acting Commissioner of Labour memo to Colonial Secretary, 1 September 1952, covering a report by S. T. Kidd of 26 June 1952. HKRS22-1-19 'Labour Statistics — Policy'; (1A) Commissioner of Labour memo to Colonial Secretary, 'I.L.O. Fifth Asian Regional Conference', 22 January 1963. HKRS1017-2-2 'Labour Department: General Policy (Gibbs Report 1963)'; (19) Commissioner of Labour to

Commissioner, Census & Statistics, 15 May 1970, 'Collection of Statistics on Employment and Related Subjects'. HKRS532-3-22 'Employment Statistics Bill 1972'.

44. M. 52. Colonial Secretary to Governor, 23 December 1948. HKRS170-2-1 'Census Estimate of Population'; M. 9. DCS to Colonial Secretary, 8 December 1954; M. 4. Colonial Secretary to Governor, 27 February 1954; (10) Statistician minute to Director of Commerce and Industry, 15 December 1958; (11) M. 71. Director of Commerce and Industry to DFS(E), 15 December 1958. HKRS22-1-96 'Population Census 1961'.

45. See the following enclosures for 1953: (127), (129), (132); W. Ramsay-Main (Hong Kong) letter to F. F. Richmond (Colonial Office), 27 December 1954; Governor to Secretary of State for the Colonies, 17 April 1957. HKRS163-1-625 'Banking Statistics:1. Supply of ... to S. of S.; 2. Policy Correspondence Concerning'.

46. David Carse, Deputy Chief Executive, Hong Kong Monetary Authority, *GIS*, 3 July 1996.

47. (294) J. J. Cowperthwaite letter to W. F. Seale (Colonial Office), 11 August 1959. HKRS163-1-625.

48. Although officials soon registered doubts about the quality of bank accounts. See (1) H. J. Tomkins memo to Financial Secretary 5 March 1965, 'Suggested Measures to Deal with the Aftermath of the Failure of the Canton Trust & Commercial Bank, Limited', p. 2. HKRS163-3-249 'Banking Emergency 1965 — Matters Arising from ... Staff etc'.

49. Haddon-Cave, *HH*, 8 January 1975, pp. 342–3; F. W. Li, appointed member, *ibid.*, 15 November 1978, p. 172.

50. Catherine R. Schenk, 'The Origins of Anti-competitive Regulation: Was Hong Kong 'Over-banked' in the 1960s?', *HKIMR Working Paper No. 9/2006*, July 2006, pp. 17–27.

51. Branch staff, principally R. J. Brereton and Uisdean McInnes, who, in addition to regular briefings, allowed me to copy data directly from the files containing the Branch's confidential statistical summaries on the banking sector and exchange controls. I was also provided with detailed information on banking conditions by the late Sir Philip Haddon-Cave while he was Financial Secretary (1971–81). The colonial administration provided this access because officials were anxious to prevent the author from misreporting financial trends in the *Far Eastern Economic Review* and the London *Times* and, later, in such specialist publications as *Euromoney* and *Asiabanking* during a period of considerable banking instability and currency uncertainty.

52. P. Selwyn minute to Sir William Gorell Barnes, 6 July 1961. CO1030/1300 'The Future of Hong Kong'.

53. (138) Selwyn (Colonial Office) letter to Cowperthwaite, Financial Secretary, 21 February 1966; (139) Cowperthwaite letter to Selwyn, 19 March 1966; (141) J. Blades (Ministry of Overseas Development) to Cowperthwaite, 28 April 1966; (142) M. D. A. Clinton (Hong Kong) letter to Blades, 11 June 1966. HKRS163-9-88 'Trade. Balance of Payment Statistics. Policy Regarding Preparation of ...'; *Report on the National Income Survey of Hong Kong* (Hong Kong: Government Printer, 1969).

54. A comparison of the final revised estimates with previous figures and well-regarded academic exercises is instructive. *2003 Gross Domestic Product* (Hong Kong: Census and Statistics Department, 2004) p. 14; Cheng Tong Yung, *The Economy of Hong*

Kong (Hong Kong: Far East Publications, 1977), 'Table 8.1. Estimates of G. D. P.', p. 145.

55. It should be noted, nevertheless, that the quality of the statistical information available throughout the Third World was generally poor. Other Asian governments, however, did not refuse to recognise the contribution that good statistics could make to sound policies. A succinct and amusing comment on this issue can be found in Ashok Mitra, 'Underdeveloped Statistics', *Economic Development and Cultural Change*, Vol. 11, No. 3, Part 1 (April 1963).

56. See Lord Hailey's comments in F. Searle *et al*, 'Colonial Statistics', *Journal of the Royal Statistical Society. Series A (General)*, Vol. 113, No. 3 (1950), p. 291. This review indicated that Hong Kong lagged behind other colonial territories.

57. See Stephen Chiu, *The Politics of Laissez-faire. Hong Kong's Strategy of Industrialization in Historical Perspective* (Hong Kong: Hong Kong Institute of Asia-Pacific Studies, 1994), pp. 75–7.

58. The lack of special facilities for industrial lending has been interpreted as evidence of Hong Kong's immaturity as a financial centre. Jao, 'The Rise of Hong Kong as a Financial Centre', *Asian Survey*, p. 693. An alternative — though not very convincing — argument has been made that Hong Kong manufacturers were averse to increasing their size and thus did not take full advantage of all the sources of finance available to them. Irene Eng, 'Flexible Production in Late Industrialization: The Case of Hong Kong', *Economic Geography*, Vol. 73, No. 1 (January 1997), pp. 36–7.

59. Complaints about the lack of bank support began in the 1950s. Stephen W. K. Chiu *et al*, *City States in the Global Economy: Industrial Restructuring in Hong Kong and Singapore* (Boulder: Westview Press, 1997), p. 34.

60. Chiu, *The Politics of Laissez-faire. Hong Kong's Strategy of Industrialization in Historical Perspective*, p. 66.

61. This case is presented vigorously by Alex H. Choi, 'State-Business Relations and Industrial Restructuring', in Tak-wing Ngo (ed), *Hong Kong's History. State and Society under Colonial Rule* (London: Routledge, 1999), pp. 144, 150, 154, in particular.

62. For example, Douglas T. Stuart, 'Paris and London: Between Washington and Beijing', in Yu-ming Shaw (ed), *Mainland China. Politics, Economics and Reform* (Boulder: Westview Press, 1986), pp. 561–3.

63. Cowperthwaite, *HH*, 1 March 1967, p. 83.

64. The comments of the two governments are recorded in CO1030/1718 'The Drug Problem in Hong Kong'.

65. Steve Tsang, *A Modern History of Hong Kong* (London: I. B. Tauris, 2004).

66. The exceptional subordinates who were highly respected as deputies were Cowperthwaite's predecessor, A. G. Clarke, and Cowperthwaite himself.

67. As a prominent civil servant frankly confessed. K. Y. Yeung, 'The Role of the Hong Kong Government in Industrial Development', in Edward K. Y. Chen *et al* (eds), *Industrial and Trade Development in Hong Kong* (Hong Kong: Centre of Asian Studies, 1991), p. 49.

68. The best-known example is the US savings and loan collapses. They suffered high levels of insolvency after they were deregulated without simultaneously reforming the deposit insurance system, which encouraged high-risk lending. Geoffrey P. Miller, 'Banking Crises in Perspective: Two Causes and One Cure', in Caprio *et al* (eds), *Preventing Bank Crises: Lessons from Recent Global Bank Failures*, p. 280.

69. The importance of effective enforcement of legislation in the development of banking systems has been demonstrated in a study of 49 jurisdictions including Hong Kong. Ross Levine, 'The Legal Environment, Banks, and Long-Run Economic Growth', *Journal of Money Credit and Banking*, Vol. 30, No. 3, Part 2 (August 1998), p. 598.

70. William J. Baumol, 'Entrepreneurship: Productive, Unproductive, and Destructive', *Journal of Political Economy* Vol. 98, No. 5, Part 1 (October 1990), pp. 895, 899, 917.

71. See James Hayes, 'East and West in Hong Kong: Vignettes from History and Personal Experience', in Elizabeth Sinn (ed), *Between East and West. Aspects of Social and Political Development in Hong Kong* (Hong Kong: Centre of Asian Studies, 1990), pp. 8, 11.

72. A. J. Youngson, *Hong Kong's Economic Growth and Policy* (Hong Kong: Oxford University Press, 1982), p. 131.

CHAPTER **1**

1. Ambrose Yeo-chi King, 'Administrative Absorption of Politics in Hong Kong: Emphasis on the Grass Roots Level', in Ambrose Y. C. King and Rance P. L. Lee (eds), *Social Life and Development in Hong Kong* (Hong Kong: Chinese University Press, 1981), p. 129.

2. Ian Scott, *Political Change and the Crisis of Legitimacy in Hong Kong* (London: Hurst & Company, 1989), p. 328.

3. See Ian Scott's analysis of this issue, 'Introduction' in Ian Scott (ed), *Institutional Change and the Political Transition in Hong Kong* (London: Macmillan, 1998), p. 5; 'The Public Service in Transition: Sustaining Administrative Capacity and Political Neutrality', in Robert Ash *et al* (eds), *Hong Kong in Transition. The Handover Years* (London: Macmillan Press Ltd, 2000), p. 154.

4. Jermain T. M. Lam, *The Political Dynamics of Hong Kong under Chinese Sovereignty* (Huntington: Nova Science Publishers, Inc., 2000), p. 94; Yun-han Chu, 'State Structure and Economic Adjustment of the East Asian Newly Industrializing Countries', *International Organization*, Vol. 43, No. 4 (Autumn 1989), 662–4.

5. Siu-kai Lau, *Society and Politics in Hong Kong* (Hong Kong: Chinese University Press, 1982), pp. 58–9.

6. Sir Robert Black letter to Sir Hilton Poynton (Colonial Office), 19 July 1958. HKRS270-5-44 'Commercial and Industrial Development — Major Policy'.

7. *HH*, 26 February 1964, p. 36.

8. *HH*, 24 February 1960, pp. 63–4.

9. M. 4. Acting Director of Supplies, Commerce and Industry to Labour Officer, 31 July 1947. HKRS163-1-305 'Retail Price & Wages Index. Preparation of ...'.

10. Acting Financial Secretary minute to Colonial Secretary, 25 April 1957. HKRS163-1-634 'Public Utilities Companies Proposed Control of the Charges and Dividends levied by ...'.

11. 'Completely new industries' were his actual words. *HH*, 30 March 1962, pp. 131–4 and 26 February 1964, p. 45.

12. Philip Haddon-Cave, 'Introduction. The Making of Some Aspects of Public Policy in Hong Kong', in David Lethbridge (ed), *The Business Environment in Hong Kong* (Hong Kong: Oxford University Press, 1980), p. xi.

13. The absence of any economic justification for these loans is revealed by a

comparison between two confidential documents. Industry Development Branch, 'The Case for Improved Access to Loans for Re-equipment Purposes by Small Scale Industry' (Department of Commerce and Industry, IND 2/903, 27 October 1969, mimeo) and 'Memorandum to the Loans for Small Industry Committee' (Commerce and Industry Department, IND 2/903, 4 November 1969, mimeo). The scheme failed and was wound up in 1976. H. C. Y. Ho, *The Fiscal System of Hong Kong* (London: Croom Helm, 1979), p. 62.

14. *HH*, 13 April 1978, p. 812.

15. *Report of the Advisory Committee on Diversification 1979* (Hong Kong: Government Printer, 1979), p. 167.

16. Haddon-Cave was the exception and had an ideological rather than a pragmatic attachment to laisser faire. Only after leaving the post of financial secretary did he declare publicly: 'When faced with an interventionist proposal, the Hong Kong Government does *not* simply respond that such a proposal *must*, by definition, be incorrect'. (*GIS*, 1 February 1982). Previously, he had insisted, even at a junior level, on combating any suggestion 'that bureaucratic judgments are to be preferred to the market process itself'. M. 16. DES to AEO (CG), 4 June 1968. HKRS163-9-511 'Commerce and Industry Dept. Industrial Development Branch'.

17. Ian Scott, 'Generalists and Specialists', in Ian Scott and John P. Burns (eds), *The Hong Kong Civil Service and Its Future* (Hong Kong: Oxford University Press, 1988), pp. 24–5, 39–43; Henry Lethbridge, *Hong Kong: Stability and Change. A Collection of Essays* (Hong Kong: Oxford University Press, 1978), p. 33.

18. Lau, *Society and Politics in Hong Kong*, p. 53.

19. These were linked to calls for a central banking authority, which the International Monetary Fund favoured but the Bank of England, like the colonial administration, did not. Leonidas Cole, Banking Commissioner, letter to Financial Secretary, 9 December 1969. HKRS163-3-249 'Banking Emergency 1965 — Matters Arising from … Staff etc'; Anthony Ockenden, Banking Commissioner, *GIS*, 22 June 1978; Philip Bowring, 'Hongkong Wary of Controls', *FEER*, 2 December 1977; Catherine R. Schenk, *Hong Kong as an International Financial Centre. Emergence and Development 1945–65* (London: Routledge, 2001), pp. 63–5.

20. This unstructured approach to policy, which affected the colonial administration, has been well described by an official who had served in other colonies. Trevor Clark, *Good Second Class* (Stanhope: The Memoir Club, 2004), p. 156.

21. For example, the decision not to enforce the 1948 Banking Ordinance and its policy outcomes were recorded in two files on two minor banks which subsequently went into liquidation, which meant the files ceased to be circulated and consulted. HKRS41-1-3003 'The China Industrial Bank of H. K. Ltd Application from … for a Banking Licence'; HKRS41-3-3044 'The Nam Sang Bank: 1. Application from … for a Banking Licence; 2. Balance Sheet of … ; 3. Cancellation of the Licence of …'.

22. Sir Geoffry Northcote, *HH*, 13 October 1938, p. 117.

23. See, for example, the nervousness about housing surveys. M. 2. AS2 to DCS., 18 May 1957. HKRS41-1-9339(1) 'Pilot Social Survey of Shek Kip Mei Resettlement Area'.

24. M. 4. Colonial Secretary (the future governor, Sir Robert Black) to Governor, 27 February 1954; M. 9. Deputy Colonial Secretary to Colonial Secretary, 8 December 1954. HKRS22-1-96 'Population Census 1961'.

25. DCS minute to Colonial Secretary, 26 May 1950; AS8 minute to DCS, 22 September 1950; (18) Government Statistician letter to Colonial Secretary, 3 May 1950; Acting Government Statistician memo to Colonial Secretary, 4 April 1951. HKRS41-1-4969 'Conferences — The Conference of Colonial Government Statisticians Convened by the Secretary of State for the Colonies at the Colonial Office During March, 1950. Correspondence re …'.

26. Except where otherwise indicated, the discussion of banking statistics that follows is based on the following enclosures for the period 1950–53: (18), (20), (24) and (26) in HKRS163-9-88 'Trade. Balance of Payment Statistics. Policy Regarding Preparation of …'.

27. See the following enclosures for 1953: (127), (129), (132) and Governor to Secretary of State for the Colonies, 17 April 1957. HKRS163-1-625 'Banking Statistics: 1. Supply of to S of S'.

28. (290) Director of Commerce and Industry memo to Colonial Secretary, 6 January 1959. HKRS163-1-625.

29. A good example of unsubstantiated assertions was a reference to a 'potentially dangerous feature' of Hong Kong banking: 'The first obviously unsatisfactory feature … is that there are too many banks'. No comparative figures were offered in support. A striking example of the report's muddle and ignorance of local conditions was the author's assertion: 'There are 87 licensed banks; and it is only a slight exaggeration to say that this means there are 87 different types of bank'. He then proceeds to identify the natural groupings of the banks. H. J. Tomkins, *Report on the Hong Kong Banking System and Recommendations for the Replacement of the Banking Ordinance 1948* (Hong Kong: Government Printer, 1962), pp. 2–3, 7.

30. Officials solved this problem by misleading legislators about the level of confidentiality of the report's contents. On an earlier occasion, documents to the legislature had been drafted to conceal how universal primary education was available to European and other racial minorities but not to Chinese children. Both these incidents and the supporting archival references can be found in Leo F. Goodstadt, 'Business Friendly and Politically Convenient — the Historical Role of Functional Constituencies', in Christine Loh (ed), *Functional Constituencies: A Unique Feature of the Hong Kong Legislative Council* (Hong Kong: Hong Kong University Press, 2006), p. 48.

31. *HH*, 8 January 1975, p. 342–3; 5 November 1975, p. 189; 15 November 1978, p. 173.

32. See F. W. Li's complaints, *HH*, 15 November 1978; Haddon-Cave, *ibid.*, 28 February 1979, p. 554; 17 October 1979, p. 69.

33. Y. C. Jao, 'Monetary System and Banking Structure', in H. C. Y. Ho and L. C. Chau (eds), *The Economic System of Hong Kong* (Hong Kong: Asian Research Service, 1988), p. 59; *Hong Kong Annual Digest of Statistics, 1988 Edition* (Hong Kong: Census and Statistics Department, 1988), pp. 125–8.

34. The Registrar of Companies had stated that he 'was too overworked' to notice the auditors' warnings for seven years about the fragile state of the Bank of Canton whose problems had triggered the banking crisis of 1935. (13) Patterson memo to Financial Secretary, 16 January 1939, p. 2. HKRS170-1-305 'Banking Legislation Miscellaneous Correspondence of the Committee appointed in January 1939 to Consider the Proposed New …'.

35. See (66) and (67) draft banking legislation circulated 15 December 1936; Patterson minute to Colonial Secretary, 31 August 1936. HKRS170-1-307 'Banking Legislation …'.
36. (12)[2] Financial Secretary note to the Committee, 16 February 1939, p. 3. HKRS170-1-305.
37. Acting Financial Secretary minute to Governor, 25 September 1951. HKRS41-1-3095 'Far East Commercial Bank Ltd Application from … for a Banking Licence'.
38. The Accountant General's comments on the ample funds available from the licence fees to cover the costs of investigations were recorded in (38) Circular 34 'Far East Commercial Bank Ltd — Bank Licensing Policy', 18 September 1951. HKRS163-1-679 'Banking Advisory Committee'.
39. Financial Secretary minute to DFS, 30 January 1950. HKRS41-3-3044.
40. Crown Solicitor minute to DFS, 20 May 1949; Financial Secretary minute to Governor, 4 August 1949; Registrar General minute to Colonial Secretary, 12 September 1949. HKRS163-1-440 'Banking: 1. Banking Ordinance; 2. Control over the Opening and Functioning of Native Banks in Hong Kong'. In practice, all pretence of trying to identify beneficial owners on a regular basis was soon dropped. DFS, Floating Sheet, 'Banking Ordinance', 26 January 1950. HKRS163-1-441 'Names and Addresses of Partners of Banks Required for the Banking Ordinance 1948'.
41. At least five firms were granted bank licences even though they were known to be operating illegally because they were not in compliance with the Companies Ordinance. (2) DFS memo to Registrar of Companies, 'Subject: Banking Companies', 11 August 1948. HKRS41-1-3011 'The Provincial Bank of Fukien: 1. Application from … for a Banking Licence; 2. Balance Sheet of …'.
42. See, for example, enclosures (23) to (29), February-March 1954; M. 2. Acting Senior Crown Counsel to DFS, 18 May 1956. HKRS41-1-3024 'Foo Kee: 1. Application from … for a Banking Licence; 2. Balance Sheet of …'.
43. DFS minute to Financial Secretary, 31 October 1950. HKRS41-1-3020 'The On Tai Bank: 1. Application from … for a Banking Licence; 2. Balance Sheet of …'.
44. The details of this episode can be found in Registrar General minute to Financial Secretary, 5 January 1951; DFS minute to Financial Secretary, 9 January 1951; (64) Financial Secretary letter to Registrar of Companies, 5 December 1951; (65) Registrar General letter to Financial Secretary, 21 January 1952. HKRS41-1-3003.
45. See, for example, the efforts made to recover assets from the crash of the relatively large Kar Cheung Chong Bank. *Hong Kong Annual Departmental Report by the Registrar General for the Financial Year 1955–56* (Hong Kong: Government Printer, n.d.), p. 28. He also imposed the same standards on banks as on other companies in enforcing statutes for which his department was responsible, e.g., HKRS41-1-3094 'The Kincheng Banking Corporation H.K. (Trustees) Ltd: 1. Application from … for a Banking Licence; 2. Balance Sheet of …'.
46. (30) Registrar General memo to DCS, 'Chiu Tai Bank, Ltd', 17 October 1961. HKRS163-3-7 'The Chiu Tai Bank Ltd: 1. Application from … for Banking Licence; 2. Balance Sheet of …'.
47. On the importance attached to press reports and legal proceedings in this context, see, for example, DFS minute to Financial, Secretary 8 November 1950. HKRS41-1-3003; Reg. B minute to DFS, 6 September 1950. HKRS41-3-3024.
48. (6) Accountant General (Cashier) memo to DCS, 27 October 1949. HKRS41-1-

3046 'The Ngau Kee Bank: 1. Application from … for a Banking Licence; 2. Balance Sheet of …'.

49. DFS, Floating Sheet, 'Banking Ordinance', 26 January 1950. HKRS163-1-441.

50. Clarke was acting as Financial Secretary during this affair. M. 2. Acting Financial Secretary to DFS, 11 January 1952; M. 4. Acting Financial Secretary note, 12 January 1952. HKRS41-3-3007 'The Fu Shing Bank of H. K. Ltd: 1. Application from … for a Banking Licence; 2. Balance Sheet of …'.

51. A typical example of persistent failure to forward accounts by a poorly managed bank is recorded in HKRS41-1-3057 'The Hang Shun Gold Dealer: 1. Application from … for a Banking Licence; 2. Balance Sheet of …'.

52. DFS minutes to Financial Secretary, 17 May and 29 August 1950; M. 1. DFS to Financial Secretary, 2 April 1952; Financial Secretary minute, 3 April 1952. HKRS41-1-3065 'The Yue Man Banking Co, Ltd: 1. Application from … for a Banking Licence; 2. Balance Sheet of …'.

53. M. 2. Financial Secretary to DFS(E), 3 August 1956. HKRS41-1-3020.

54. (36) DFS letter to bank, 8 August 1955. HKRS41-1-3024.

55. See his response in the case of a bank which had exhausted its capital and had a vault cash ratio of 2.2 per cent. M. 3. DFS(E) note, 15 July 1955. HKRS41-1-3021 'The Wo Cheung Bank: 1. Application from … for a Banking Licence; 2. Balance Sheet of …'. The industry average at the end of 1955 was 12.7 per cent. Y. C. Jao, *Banking and Currency in Hong Kong. A Study of Postwar Financial Development* (London: Macmillan, 1974), 'Table 7.1. Year-end Vault Cash Ratio', p. 173.

56. (302) P. Mardulyn, Manager Banque Belge, letter to DFS, 30 November 1960; (303) DFS's reply to Mardulyn, 3 December 1960; (312) Statistician memo to DES, 'Banking Statistics', 22 April 1961; M. 35. AS(E) to DES, 19 May 1961. HKRS163-1-625.

57. Jao, *Banking and Currency in Hong Kong. A Study of Postwar Financial Development*, 'Table 7.7. Year-end Loan-Deposit Ratio', p. 182. These data are in line with the careful revision of the banking statistics for this period in Catherine R. Schenk, 'The Origins of Anti-competitive Regulation: Was Hong Kong 'Over-banked' in the 1960s?', *HKIMR Working Paper No.9/2006*, July 2006, pp. 4–5.

58. Cowperthwaite does not seem to have clarified his mind on this topic subsequently, judging from Financial Secretary minute to ASE2, 29 January 1966. HKRS163-1-3273 'Banking Statistics Various 1965'.

59. M. 4. DFS note, 6 November 1952; (18)1 accounts for the year ended 31 December 1962. HKRS41-1-3085 'Shun Foo Banking & Investment Co. Ltd: 1. Application from … for a Banking Licence; 2. Balance Sheet of …'.

60. Indeed, the Managing Director put his own construction on Cowperthwaite's advice in explaining subsequent land transactions. DCNT memo to DES, 'Far East Bank Limited', 29 April 1961. HKRS885-3-5 'Far East Bank, Limited'.

61. (9)1 DES note, 10 March 1961; District Officer, Tsuen Wan memo to DCNT, 'Far East Bank Ltd', 26 April 1961; (19) DES note, 3 July 1961. HKRS934-7-104 'Far East Bank — Tsuen Wan'.

62. Commissioner of Banking memo to Financial Secretary, 'Bank Loans — Dao Heng Bank Ltd and Kwong On Bank Ltd', 23 March 1966. HKRS163-3-249.

63. The regulatory problems in manufacturing are illustrated in Eric Peter Ho, *Times of Change. A Memoir of Hong Kong's Governance 1950–1991* (Leiden: Brill, 2005), pp. 48–51.

64. This bank's crash is described in Catherine R. Schenk, 'Banking Groups in Hong Kong, 1945–65', *Asia Pacific Business Review*, Vol. 7, No. 2, (Winter 2000), pp. 145–6. See also, Ng Kwok Leung, 'More Banks in Hongkong', *FEER*, 12 April 1962.

65. See, for example, M. 10. AS(E) to DES, 7 October 1961; M. 38. DES to AS(E), 13 March 1963; M. 44. AS(E) to DES, 12 July 1963. HKRS163-3-7.

66. Tomkins, *Report on the Hong Kong Banking System and Recommendations for the Replacement of the Banking Ordinance 1948.*

67. M. 10. and M. 15. AS(E) to DES, 7 October 1961 and 10 March 1962; M. 13. DES note, 24 October 1961; (45) DES note of a conversation, 21 February 1963. HKRS163-3-7.

68. *South China Morning Post*, 25 March and 12 April 1969.

69. *HH*, 12 April 1967, p. 285.

70. His reluctant retreat towards regulation can be traced in *HH*, 8 January 1975, p. 342; 5 November 1975, p. 189; 3 December 1975, p. 297; 16 November 1978, p. 209; and 28 February 1979, p. 554.

71. See the former regulator Robert Fell, *Crisis and Change. The Maturing of Hong Kong's Financial Markets* (Hong Kong: Longman, 1992), pp. 160, 162, 180–1.

72. *Ibid.*, p. 159. Fell was given responsibility for reforming the regulatory system after the scandals of the early 1980s.

73. Ricardo, 'Development of Banking in Hong Kong during 1955', *FEER*, 2 February 1956.

74. See, for example, *Hong Kong Annual Departmental Report by the Registrar General for the Financial Year 1954–55* (Hong Kong: Government Printer, n.d.), p. 17.

75. Cowperthwaite, *HH*, 16 September 1964, pp. 331–2.

76. These errors are plain from (1) Acting Financial Secretary letter to D. J. Kirkness (Colonial Office), 14 October 1963, pp. 7–8. HKRS160-3-25 'Report on the Financial Situation by the Acting Financial Secretary'.

77. Tai-lok Lui, 'Pressure Group Politics in Hong Kong', in Joseph Y. S. Cheng, (ed), *Political Participation in Hong Kong. Theoretical Issues and Historical Legacy* (Hong Kong: City University of Hong Kong Press, 1999), pp. 150–3.

78. Note the serious concerns the Financial Secretary expressed over the risk of losses and the inadequate size of the Exchange Fund to cope with a floating exchange rate and the impact of the introduction of electronic transfers on the currency markets. C. P Haddon-Cave, *HH*, 25 February 1976, pp. 517–8.

79. The ill-informed, disastrous decisions are summarised lucidly in Y. C. Jao, *Money and Finance in Hong Kong: Retrospect and Prospect* (Singapore: Singapore University Press: 1998), pp. 38–42.

80. T. K. Ghose, *The Banking System of Hong Kong* (Singapore: Buttterworths, 1995, 2nd edition), p. 96.

81. Sir John Bremridge, Financial Secretary, *HH*, 23 February 1983, p. 533.

82. MacLehose's correspondence is recorded in enclosures (168) to (178), December 1959 to January 1960. HKRS163-9-141 'Exchange Control — Individual Problems Arising from Applications of Policy on … in Hong Kong'.

83. *HH*, 17 October 1973, p. 25.

CHAPTER **2**

1. Shanghai's machine-building industry, for example, was Chinese-owned and 'provided a close to complete range of skills for a modern economy of that period'. Mark Elvin, 'Foundations for the Future: the Building of Modern Machinery in Shanghai after the Pacific War', in Ross Garnaut and Yiping Huang (eds), *Growth Without Miracles. Readings on the Chinese Economy in the Era of Reform* (Oxford: Oxford University Press, 2001), p. 56.

2. *Report of the Commission … to Enquire into the Causes and Effects of the Present Trade Recession …* (Hong Kong: Noronha & Co., 1935), p. 71.

3. Tim Wright, 'Coping with the World Depression: The Nationalist Government's Relations with Chinese Industry and Commerce, 1932–1936', *Modern Asian Studies*, Vol. 25, No. 4 (October, 1991), pp. 651–2.

4. Douglas S. Paauw, 'The Kuomintang and Economic Stagnation, 1928–37', *Journal of Asian Studies*, Vol. 16, No. 2 (February 1957), pp. 213–4.

5. T. Wright, 'Entrepreneurs, Politicians and the Chinese Coal Industry, 1895–1937', *Modern Asian Studies*, Vol. 14, No. 4 (1980), p. 596.

6. See Parks M. Coble, Jr, 'The Kuomintang Regime and the Shanghai Capitalists, 1927–29', *China Quarterly*, No. 77 (March 1977).

7. Paauw, 'The Kuomintang and Economic Stagnation, 1928–37', *Journal of Asian Studies*, pp. 218–20.

8. Ch'ao-ting Chi, 'China's Monetary Reform in Perspective', *Far Eastern Survey*, Vol. 6, No. 17 (18 August 1937), pp. 193–4.

9. (1) Commissioner of Inland Revenue memo to Financial Secretary, 8 January 1947, p. 1. HKRS41-1-2769(1) 'Inland Revenue Ordinance 1. General Question of imposing etc …'. No income tax was imposed by the British before the end of their rule.

10. On Guangdong, see John Fitzgerald, 'Increased Disunity: The Politics and Finance of Guangdong Separatism, 1926–1936', *Modern Asian Studies*, Vol. 24, No. 4 (October 1990), pp. 765–8.

11. For a sympathetic analysis of this issue, see Linsun Cheng, *Banking in Modern China: Entrepreneurs Professional Managers and the Development of Chinese Banks, 1897–1937* (Cambridge: Cambridge University Press, 2003), pp. 82–5, 152–3.

12. Leonard T. K. Wu, 'China's Paradox — Prosperous Banks in National Crisis', *Far Eastern Survey*, Vol. 4, No. 6 (27 March 1935), pp. 42–5.

13. A useful analysis of the risks and rewards for banks acting as government brokers can be found in Cheng, *Banking in Modern China: Entrepreneurs Professional Managers and the Development of Chinese Banks, 1897–1937*, pp. 94–5, 99–101 and Chapter 4.

14. *Report of Currency Committee, 1930* (Legislative Council Sessional Paper 7/1930), pp. 105–6 in particular; Steve Tsang, *A Modern History of Hong Kong* (London: I. B. Tauris, 2004), pp. 108–9.

15. (4) Governor's secret letter to Secretary of State for the Colonies, 2 February 1939; (5) Secretary of State letter to Governor, 3 April 1939. HKRS163-1-507 'Excess Population Committee Pre-war Correspondence re …'.

16. A Study Group of the Royal Institute of International Affairs, *Political and Strategic Interests of the United Kingdom. An Outline* (London: Oxford University Press, 1939), p. 218.

17. Except where otherwise indicated, the account that follows of the British position

on the Mainland relies heavily on Jurgen Osterhammel, 'Imperialism in Transition: British Business and the Chinese Authorities, 1931–1957', *China Quarterly*, No. 98 (June 1984), especially pp. 261–3, 285.

18. Evan Luard, *Britain and China* (Baltimore: The John Hopkins Press, 1962), pp. 130, 153; Wong Siu-lun, 'The Entrepreneurial Spirit: Shanghai and Hong Kong Compared', in Y. M. Yeung and Sung Yun-wing (eds), *Shanghai Transformation and Modernization under China's Open Policy* (Hong Kong: Chinese University Press, 1996), p. 26.
19. A good contemporary analysis of the impact of the war on British business can be found in Irving S. Friedman, 'Britain's China Stake on the Eve of European War', *Far Eastern Survey*, Vol. 8, No. 19 (27 September 1939), pp. 219–22.
20. Hong Kong showed no signs of being able to pick up the business that Shanghai was losing in this period. Friedman, 'Britain's China Stake on the Eve of European War', *Far Eastern Survey*, p. 223.
21. Chan Lau Kit-ching, *China, Britain and Hong Kong 1895–1945* (Hong Kong: Chinese University Press, 1990), pp. 171–2, 184, 189–93, 201–4.
22. The Party's role in the industrial disputes of the 1920s, its clandestine operations thereafter and its elimination from Hong Kong before World War II are recounted in Chan Lau Kit-ching, *From Nothing to Nothing. The Chinese Communist Movement and Hong Kong, 1921–1936* (New York: St Martin's Press, 1999).
23. A fuller discussion of reformist trends between the wars can be found in Leo F. Goodstadt 'The Rise and Fall of Social, Economic and Political Reforms in Hong Kong, 1930–1955', *Journal of the Royal Asiatic Society Hong Kong* Branch, Vol. 44, (2004), pp. 58–64.
24. Anthony Howe, *Free Trade and Liberal England, 1846–1946* (Oxford: Clarendon Press, 1997), pp. 275–6.
25. Philip Woodruff, *The Men who Ruled India. The Guardians* (London: Jonathan Cape: 1954), pp. 208–11; S. A. Pakeman, *Ceylon* (London: Ernest Benn Limited, 1964), p. 131.
26. Lennox A. Mills, *British Rule in Eastern Asia. A Study of Contemporary Government and Economic Development in British Malaya and Hong Kong* (London: Oxford University Press, 1942), pp. 395, 410, 414.
27. The employers' arguments against improvements are set out in *Report of the Commission Appointed to Enquire into the Conditions of the Industrial Employment of Children in Hong Kong, and the Desirability and Feasibility of Legislation for the Regulation of such Employment* (Hong Kong: Session Paper 11/1921), Appendices 3A and 4.
28. Nevertheless, its discussions paid disproportionate attention to the tiny European community and its arguments for racially segregated residential areas. *Report of the Housing Commission* (Hong Kong: Session Paper 10/1923), pp. 110, 112, 112, 120, 124–54.
29. *Report of the Housing Commission 1935* (Hong Kong: Noronha & Co., 1938), p. 260.
30. *HH*, 13 October 1938, pp. 119–27.
31. Northcote, and P. S. (later Sir Selwyn) Selwyn-Clarke, Director of Medical Services, *HH*, 16 November 1939, pp. 214–,6 218–20, 228–9.
32. N. J. Miners, 'Plans for Constitutional Reform in Hong Kong, 1946–62'. *China Quarterly*, No. 107 (September 1986), p. 465.
33. For the origins of these resentments, see Lee Pui-Tak, 'Chinese Merchants in the Hong Kong Colonial Context, 1840–1910', in Wong Siu-lun and Toyojiro Maruya

(eds), *Hong Kong Economy and Society: Challenges in the New Era* (Hong Kong: Centre of Asian Studies, 1998), pp. 63–6.

34. Henry Lethbridge, *Hong Kong: Stability and Change. A collection of Essays* (Hong Kong: Oxford University Press, 1978), pp. 20–1, 25; David Faure, 'Reflections on Being Chinese in Hong Kong', in Judith M. Brown and Rosemary Foot (eds), *Hong Kong's Transitions, 1842–1997* (London: Macmillan Press Ltd, 1997), p. 110.

35. R. A. D. Forrest, Acting Colonial Secretary, *HH*, 3 October 1935, p. 201; Sir Arthur Caldecott, Governor, *HH*, 19 March 1936, p. 75. Quotas for expatriates were maintained for the Administrative Service and the police force until the 1984 Sino-British Joint Declaration.

36. *Report of the Commission … to Enquire into the Causes and Effects of the Present Trade Recession*, pp. 71–2, 74, 79, 89–90, 93–4.

37. David Meredith, 'The British Government and Colonial Economic Policy, 1919–39', *Economic History Review*, Vol. 28, No. 3 (August 1975), pp. 485, 498–9.

38. *Report of the Commission … to Enquire into the Causes and Effects of the Present Trade Recession*, pp. 82–3, 86.

39. Derived from *Report on the Social & Economic Progress … for the Year 1938*, pp. 5, 7; *Report on the Social & Economic Progress … for the Year 1939*, p. 1.

40. The average density in 1931 was estimated to have already reached 2,500 persons per hectare, rising to 4,200 in some areas. *Report of the Housing Commission 1935*, p. 267. Density per floor 'in the usual type of three-storey Chinese tenement' rose from 15 to 20 persons to 60 after the refugee influx started in July 1937. *Report on the Social & Economic Progress … for the Year 1938*, p. 7.

41. *Annual Medical Report for the Year 1939*, p. M. 7.

42. Dr. P. S. (later Sir Selwyn) Selwyn-Clarke, Director of Medical Services, *HH*, 14 September, 1939, pp. 127–8 and 16 November 1939, p. 130.

43. 'Appendix M (1) Report of the Chairman, Urban Council', *Annual Medical Report for the Year 1938*, p. M(1) 7.

44. Governor minute to Colonial Secretary, 30 March 1940. HKRS58-1-190-10 'Factory Sites: 1. Suggestion That Government Should Provide … on Favourable Terms to Encourage Industrial Development; 2. Provision of … for Evicted Squatters'.

45. Northcote, *HH*, 13 October 1938, pp. 116–7.

46. The problem was aggravated by the dysfunctional arrangements for the note issue which hindered the smooth expansion of the money supply to match economic growth. *Report of Currency Committee, 1930*, pp. 105–6.

47. (13) J. J. Paterson (Jardine Matheson) letter to Financial Secretary, 17 February 1939. HKRS170-1-305 'Banking Legislation Miscellaneous Correspondence of the Committee appointed in January 1939 to Consider the Proposed new …'.

48. *Report of the Commission … to Enquire into the Causes and Effects of the Present Trade Recession*, p. 104.

49. *Ibid.*, p. 103.

50. *Report on the Social & Economic Progress … for the Year 1939*, p. 45.

51. These included the definition of the minimum Hong Kong content to qualify for preferential tariff treatment and the certification processes to label products as Hong Kong-made. See, for example, *Hong Kong General Chamber of Commerce Report for the Year 1936* (Hong Kong: n.p., 1937), pp. 18–24.

52. Lennox A. Mills, *British Rule in Eastern Asia. A Study of Contemporary Government and Economic Development in British Malaya and Hong Kong*, pp. 456–8.

53. *Report of the Commission … to enquire into the Causes and Effects of the Present Trade Recession*, pp. 83, 85–6.
54. A. C. L. Day, *The Future of Sterling* (Oxford: Clarendon Press, 1954). pp. 38–41; *International Currency Experience: Lessons of the Interwar Period* (Geneva: League of Nations, 1944), pp. 47–9.
55. Useful contemporary analyses of the conflicts involved are provided by Robert B. Stewart, 'Instruments of British Policy in the Sterling Area ', *Political Science Quarterly*, Vol. 52, No. 2 (June 1937) and A. S. J. Baster, 'A Note on the Sterling Area ', *Economic Journal*, Vol. 47, No. 187 (September 1937).
56. Gerold Krozewski, 'Sterling Area, the 'Minor' Territories, and the End of Formal Empire, 1939–1958', *Economic History Review*, Vol. XLVI, No. 2 (1993), pp. 241–2.
57. This account is based on Tony Latter, 'Hong Kong's Exchange Rate Regimes in the Twentieth Century: The Story of Three Regime Changes', *HKIMR Working Paper No. 17/2004*, September 2004, pp. 7–9, 13, 15–6.
58. R. S. Sayers, Financial Policy, 1939–45 (London: HMSO 1956), pp. 226–7.
59. Douglas M. Kendrick, *Price Control and Its Practice in Hong Kong* (Hong Kong: K. Weiss, 1954), p. 188.
60. Caine, Financial Secretary, *HH*, 12 October 1939, pp. 146–7.
61. (9)[1] 'Report of [the 1935 confidential] Committee', p. 6. HKRS41-1-6691 'Banking Operations Legislation for Control of …'.
62. (13) Patterson memorandum, 16 January 1939. HKRS170-1-305.
63. Patterson minute to Colonial Secretary, 31 August 1936. HKRS170-1-307 'Banking Legislation: 1. General Supervision of Banking Concerns in Hong Kong; 2. Appointment of a Committee in 1935 to Consider the Desirability of Specific Legislation for the Regulation of Banking Operations in the Colony; 3. Report of the Committee; 4. Appointment of a Committee in 1939 to Consider Further Action on this Question'.
64. Crown Solicitor minute to Colonial Secretary, 17 July 1936. HKRS170-1-307.
65. Elizabeth Sinn, *Growing with Hong Kong. The Bank of East Asia 1919–1994* (Hong Kong: Hong Kong University Press, 1994), p. 51.
66. (12)2 Financial Secretary note, 16 February 1939, p. 2. HKRS170-1-305.
67. *Report of the Commission … to Enquire into the Causes and Effects of the Present Trade Recession*, p. 104.
68. Sinn, *Growing with Hong Kong. The Bank of East Asia 1919–1994*, pp. 50–1.
69. Legislation was passed allowing this bank to take advantage of changing bullion prices by switching its capital from silver to gold and then back again (Bank of Canton Ltd Capital Conversion Ordinance, 1919 and Bank of Canton Ltd Capital Conversion Ordinance, 1926).
70. (13) Paterson letter to Financial Secretary, 17 February 1939. HKRS170-1-305.
71. (3) Governor letter to Secretary of State for the Colonies, 18 January 1937. HKRS41-1-6691.
72. The full text of the report is preserved in (9)1 'Report of [the 1935 confidential] Committee', p. 7. HKRS41-1-6691.
73. They were summarised in (46) Patterson memorandum to Colonial Secretary, 2 May 1936. HKRS170-1-307.
74. Colonial Treasurer memorandum, 25 August 1936. HKRS170-1-307.
75. Patterson minute to Colonial Secretary, 31 August 1938. HKRS170-1-307.

76. (12)2 Financial Secretary note 'Banking Legislation', circulated 16 February 1939, p. 3. HKRS170-1-305.
77. David Faure (ed), *A Documentary History of Hong Kong. Society* (Hong Kong: Hong Kong University Press, 1997), pp. 10, 181; Ng Sek-hong, 'The Development of Labour Relations in Hong Kong and Some Implications for the Future', in Ian Nish *et al* (eds), *Work and Society. Labour and Human Resources in East Asia* (Hong Kong: Hong Kong University Press, 1996), p. 290.
78. In 1937, the Secretary of State for the Colonies wrote to all colonial governors that, with the end of world depression and the general economic revival, 'it was only right that a fair share of this benefit should be passed on to the workers … in the form of improved social services'. The first step was better supervision of working conditions. The Colonial Office subsequently praised Hong Kong's response to this directive. Colonial Office, *Labour Supervision in the Colonial Empire* (London: HMSO, 1943), pp. 1, 4–5.
79. Ironically, it was again a businessman who was left to demand — in vain — protection for the ordinary depositor. See, for example, Financial Secretary minute to Colonial Secretary, 6 May 1940; Patterson letter to Financial Secretary, 3 June 1940. HKRS41-1-6691.
80. Financial Secretary minute to Colonial Secretary, 12 December 1938. HKRS41-1-6691; Crown Solicitor minute to Financial Secretary 19 March 1940. HKRS170-1-30.
81. Paterson (presumably expressing his views as an HSBC director) memorandum to Financial Secretary, 16 January 1939, p. 4. HKRS170-305.
82. Secretary of State for the Colonies letter to Governor, 7 December 1940. No reply appears to have been sent to London. Instead, the file was marked 'B.[ring] U.[p]' every two months until the last pencilled entry on 11 October 1941. The Japanese Invasion occurred on 7 December 1941, four days before the next review date for the file. HKRS170-1-307.
83. The assumption in 1947 was that the deteriorating security situation in Palestine would prevent the British Mandate authorities from dealing with a request for a copy of their banking law. In fact, by the end of the year, Hong Kong officials had reviewed — and rejected — the Palestine model. Acting Financial Secretary minutes to Attorney General, 14 February and 6 December 1947. HKRS163-1-440 'Banking: 1. Banking Ordinance …'. On the rediscovery of the pre-war file, see M.1. Financial Secretary to the Banking Advisory Committee, 27 March 1952. HKRS41-1-6691.
84. The political factor has been put forward to explain the government's failure to legislate for savings banks. Gillian Chambers, *Hang Seng. The Evergrowing Bank* (Hong Kong: 1991, n.p.), pp. 14–5.
85. The Financial Secretary was singled out for criticism because of his lack of respect for Chinese business views. Li Tse-fong, *HH*, 16 November 1939, p. 212–3.
86. The quality of the economic analysis available to the colonial administration may be gauged from *Report of Currency Committee, 1930*.
87. Northcote warned of the dangers of trying to formulate policy in the absence of reliable data. *HH*, 13 October 1938, p. 117.
88. A remarkable contemporary account of how banking operations were conducted on the Mainland, including in Japanese-occupied areas, is provided by the distinguished Chinese economist, Ta-Chung Liu in 'China's Foreign Exchange

Problems: A Proposed Solution', *American Economic Review*, Vol. 31, No. 2 (June 1941).

89. *Report on the Social & Economic Progress ... for the Year 1939*, p. 45.

90. Among the coincidences were the following business reports. In September 1938, 'six big factories were to be erected in Kowloon by Shanghai Chinese industrialists'. Irving S. Friedman, 'Britain's China Stake on the Eve of European War', *Far Eastern Survey*, p. 223. In early 1948, six large-scale spinning mills were being established by Shanghai industrialists. (The total rose to eight later in the year). *FEER:* 'Industrial Review', 7 April 1948 and 'Cotton Spinning Mills of Hongkong', 27 October 1948.

91. Colonial Treasurer memorandum, 25 August 1936, p. 2. HKRS170-1-307.

CHAPTER 3

1. *Annual Report on Hong Kong for the Year 1946* (Hong Kong: Government of Hong Kong, 1947), pp. 4–5.

2. Anne O. Krueger, 'Policy Lessons from Development Experience since the Second World War', in Jere Behrman and T. N. Srinivasan (eds), *Development Economics Volume IIIB* (Amsterdam: Elsevier, 1995), pp. 2501, 2504.

3. Population estimates for the early post-war years must be used with caution. Apart from the difficulties of keeping track of the flood of immigrants, the colonial administration wanted the published figure to be as high as possible in order to strengthen Hong Kong's case for a greater share of scarce food and other supplies that were allocated through international controls at this period. The figures shown here are from the government's internal discussions. The 1946 figure was based on ration cards. The 1948 figure represented a respectable consensus of various departmental estimates. M. 6., 22 March 1946; M. 13. and M. 21. DSTI to Colonial Secretary, 29 January and 24 February 1947. HKRS170-2-1 'Census Estimate of Population'; 'Report on the Population of the Colony, Mid-Year 1949' (mimeo, Department of Statistics, 12 June 1949), pp. 2, 4, 13. HKRS259-6-1 'Report on the Population of the Colony, Mid-Year 1949'.

4. G. B. Endacott, *Hong Kong Eclipse* (Hong Kong: Oxford University Press, 1978), pp. 262–78, 280; Harold Ingrams, *Hong Kong* (London: HMSO, 1952), p. 243.

5. *Appendix C Hong Kong Departmental Report (1946–1947) Department of Supplies, Trade and Industry* (Hong Kong: n.p., n.d.), p. 11.

6. Most controls were abolished during 1953. (87) Director of Commerce and Industry memo to Financial Secretary, 30 March 1953; (89) UK [Colonial Office] Circular 305/53, 'Price Controls', 2 April 1953. HKRS170-1-418(2) 'Price Control. Machinery and Direction of ...'. See also Alan Birch, 'Control of Prices and Commodities in Hong Kong', *Hong Kong Law Journal*, Vol. 4, Part 2, (1974), pp. 133–50.

7. *Hong Kong Annual Report of the Commissioner of Labour 1st April 1947 to 31st March 1948* (Hong Kong: n.p., n.d.), p. 18.

8. R. R. Todd, Colonial Secretary, *HH*, 29 March, 1950, p. 119; *Hong Kong Annual Departmental Report by the Commissioner of Labour for the Financial Year 1951–2* (Hong Kong: Government Printer, n.d.), p. 54.

9. Much of the machinery removed had been hidden by the factory owners, and there were delays in reinstalling it. The percentages cited are derived from the statistics

obtained from inspections of 75 per cent of the factories recorded by the government and attached to SOII (Industry) minute to DCCCAO (Civil), 16 January 1946. HKRS170-1-710 'Position of Factories in Hong Kong'.

10. The severity of these problems is recorded in detail in HKRS41-1-3378.

11. T. M. Hazelrigg minute to D. M. MacDougall, 8 May 1945. HKRS211-2-20 'Financial Policy'.

12. C. G. S. (later Sir Charles) Follows, Financial Secretary, *HH*, 19 March 1958, pp. 60–1.

13. MacDougall letter to S. (later Sir Sydney) Caine (Colonial Office), 25 January 1946. HKRS170-1-738 'Public Utilities & Other Companies in H. K. Proposed Legislation on the Administration of … after the Restoration of Civil Government'.

14. 'Notes of the Week: Progress of Hongkong', *FEER*, 25 December 1946.

15. *Hong Kong Annual Report of the Commissioner of Labour 1st April, 1948 to 31st March, 1949* (Hong Kong: n.p., n.d.), p. 31.

16. *FEER*: 'Hongkong Business Conditions and Outlook', Mercantile Bank, 28 April 1948; 'The Public Utilities of Hongkong' 11 May 1949; V. A. Grantham, Chartered Bank Chairman, 23 March 1949. But 'Report on Hongkong for 1947 by the Government of Hongkong', *FEER*, 21 April 1948, painted a less glowing picture.

17. *Annual Report on Hong Kong for the Year 1946*, p. 39; *Appendix 1 Labour Office Report (Covering the Period from 1st May, 1946, to 31st March, 1947)* (Hong Kong: n.p., n.d.), p. 1; *Hong Kong Annual Report of the Commissioner of Labour 1st April, 1947 to 31st March, 1948*, p. 4.

18. Financial Secretary memo to DS&D, 13 December 1949. HKRS170-1-418(2); (12) DST & ID memo to Colonial Secretary, 'Cotton Yarn', 19 January 1948. HKRS41-1-3378 'Cotton Textiles: 1. Agreement with Chinese Govt. re Supply of … to Hong Kong; 2. Alternative Supply of … from Japan, U. S. A. and India'; Gene Gleason, *Hong Kong* (London: Robert Hale Ltd, 1964), p. 96.

19. These proposals all came from J. J. (later Sir John) Cowperthwaite, the future Financial Secretary, widely regarded as an uncompromising advocate of laisser faire. Acting Director of Supplies, Trade and Industry minute to Colonial Secretary, 30 December 1947. HKRS163-1-211 'Japan Confidential Correspondence on Trade with …'; (1) Director of Supplies and Distribution memo to Colonial Secretary, 26 January 1950; M. 4. Acting Director of Supplies, Trade and Industry to Labour Officer, 31 July 1947. HKRS163-1-305 'Retail Price & Wages Index. Preparation of …'.

20. G. E. Strickland, Attorney General, *HH*, 20 October 1948, pp. 298–301.

21. M. 4. Acting Director of Supplies, Commerce and Industry to Labour Officer, 31 July 1947. HKRS163-1-305.

22. For details, see HKRS170-1-418(2) and HKRS163-1-602 'China Light & Power Co. Ltd and Hong Kong Electric Co'.

23. Pre-war banks were allowed to operate freely, but new banking firms were subject to 'such terms, conditions and restrictions as the Financial Controller may prescribe'. The legal details are explained in (21) Colonel (CA) Legal memo to Chief Financial Adviser, 'Salt Industry Bank of Szechwan Limited', 6 April 1946. HKRS170-1-240 'Finance. Chinese Government and Other Banks in Hong Kong'.

24. Andrew Whitfield, *Hong Kong, Empire and the Anglo-American Alliance at War, 1941–1945* (Basingstoke: Palgrave, 2001), p. 218.

25. Elizabeth Sinn, *Growing with Hong Kong. The Bank of East Asia 1919–1994* (Hong Kong: Hong Kong University Press, 1994), pp. 70–2.

26. This account comes from K. M. A. Barnett, a colonial official in close contact with 'traditional' society while he was responsible for early post-war banking policy. DFS note, 11 July 1949. HKRS41-1-4095 'Finance (Defence) Regulation, 1940 Request for Information Regarding Bullion Dealers under …'.

27. Commander in Chief Hong Kong top secret telegram to Admiralty, 15 September 1945. HKRS169-2-26 'Currency and Banking'.

28. Commander in Chief top secret telegram to War Office, 21 September 1945. HKRS169-2-26.

29. (59) 'Extract from Fortnightly Intelligence Report No. 5 Period March 1st–15th, 1945'; (65) Minute to J. H. Taggart, 10 May 1945. HKRS170-1-755-2 'Hongkong Electric Co. Ltd …'.

30. Before the war, the three British note-issuing banks had a total expatriate staff of 52. The Colonial Office approved a quota of only 19 for return to Hong Kong in 1945, even though the pre-war system of commercial banks being responsible for issuing the currency and running the financial system was to be resumed immediately. (4) Cowperthwaite memo, 'Banking', 14 June 1945; (5) secret note of a meeting held at the Colonial Office, 19 June 1945, pp. 1, 3. HKRS211-2-21 'British Banks: Question of the Return of … to Hong Kong'.

31. Commander in Chief Hong Kong letter to British Ambassador Chungking, 6 October 1945. HKRS169-2-26.

32. Commander in Chief Hong Kong top secret telegram to Admiralty, 15 September 1945. HKRS169-2-26.

33. Acting Financial Secretary minute to Attorney General, 28 January 1948. HKRS163-1-440 'Banking: 1. Banking Ordinance'. This minute reveals that the Mainland authorities did not understand that this transformation was occurring.

34. The account of Shanghai banking that follows is drawn from an impressive contemporary analysis. John Ahlers, 'Postwar Banking in Shanghai', *Pacific Affairs*, Vol. 19, No. 4 (December 1946), pp. 384–5, 386–7, 490.

35. *Ibid.*, pp. 392–3.

36. This contrast between Hong Kong and Shanghai is well illustrated in Catherine R. Schenk, *Hong Kong as an International Financial Centre. Emergence and Development 1945–65* (London: Routledge, 2001), pp. 20, 25.

37. 'Conditions of Banking in Hongkong', *FEER*, 19 November 1947.

38. Leonard T. K. Wu, 'The Crucial Role of the Chinese Native Banks', *Far Eastern Survey*, Vol. 4, No. 12 (19 June 1935), p. 89.

39. A good summary of how the Hong Kong 'native' banks operated in this period is provided by Schenk, *Hong Kong as an International Financial Centre. Emergence and Development 1945–65*, pp. 53–5.

40. See Ahlers, 'Postwar Banking in Shanghai', *Pacific Affairs*, pp. 389. Wu presents much the same view of the 'native' banks' business model in the 1930s, but in greater detail in 'The Crucial Role of the Chinese Native Banks', *Far Eastern Survey*.

41. 'Open Market Trading in CN$', *FEER*, 20 November 1946.

42. The best account of the economic crisis faced by the Guomindang and of the Hong Kong relationship is Catherine R. Schenk, 'Another Asian Financial Crisis: Monetary Links between Hong Kong and China 1945–50', *Modern Asian Studies*, Vol. 34, No. 3 (2000), pp. 744–6 and 749–50 in particular.

43. Sir Alexander Grantham, Governor, *HH*, 19 March 1948, p. 44.
44. F. C. Benham, 'The Growth of Manufacturing in Hong Kong', *International Affairs*, Vol. 32, No. 4 (October 1956), pp. 460, 463.
45. The author was a Hong Kong academic economist. Frank H. H. King, *Money in British East Asia* (London: Her Majesty's Stationery Office, 1957), pp. 114–5, 118, 124.
46. Sir Robert Black, Governor, *HH*, 26 February 1964, pp. 36–7.
47. Alex Hang-keung Choi, 'The Political Economy of Hong Kong's Industrial Upgrading: A Lost Opportunity', in Benjamin K. P. Leung, (ed), *Hong Kong: Legacies and Prospects of Development* (Aldershot: Ashgate, 2003), p. 279. This author was misled perhaps by the critical standpoint of the source on which he relied for quotations from the Governor's speech, *viz.*, L. F. Goodstadt, 'Towards a Welfare State?', *FEER*, 5 March 1964.
48. A. G. Clarke, Financial Secretary, *HH*, 2 March 1955, p. 60.
49. The largest trade organisation, the Hong Kong General Chamber of Commerce. declined to get involved in export promotion, partly because it 'could not accept that the entrepot trade with China was a dead duck'. (19), 28 October 1964. HKRS270-5-46, 'Commercial and Industrial Development — Major Policy'.
50. The data for domestic exports for 1950–52 are derived from the unpublished monthly reports in HKRS170-1-554-2/3 'Report. Department of Commerce & Industry'. The data for 1953–58 are from the serial publication, *Hong Kong Annual Departmental Report by the Director of Commerce and Industry for the Financial Year* (Hong Kong: Government Printer). Figures for subsequent years and for all total exports are from Census and Statistics Department, *Hong Kong Statistics 1947–1967* (Hong Kong: Government Printer, 1969), p. 88. Re-export data before 1959 shown here represent the difference between total exports and estimated domestic exports. The Commerce and Industry Department estimated domestic export data up to 1958 on the basis of those items for which it had issued Imperial (later Commonwealth) Preference and Comprehensive Certificates of Origin. The former category covered the Sterling Area but not the growing markets in Western Europe. The latter covered exports to US but not to other dollar countries which did not ban trade with the People's Republic of China. Domestic export figures before 1959 are thus underestimated in Table I, while the residual re-export figures are over-estimated.
51. Y. C. Jao, *Banking and Currency in Hong Kong. A Study of Postwar Financial Development* (London: Macmillan, 1974), p. 17.
52. Follows, *HH*, 8 March 1950, p. 46.
53. Changes in trends and mood are illustrated by *FEER*: 'Hongkong's Prosperity', 7 July 1949; 'Commercial Markets', 4 August 1949; 'Trade of Hongkong', 1 September 1949; 'Favourable Business Conditions in HongKong', 1 December 1949; 'A Year of Uncertainty', 12 January 1950.
54. China Engineers was British managed and controlled but always had a significant number of Chinese shareholders according to the company records preserved in HKRS111-4-34 'China Engineers Ltd'. The firm summarised its history in 'The China Engineers Ltd in China', *FEER*, 10 May 1956.
55. W. C. Gomersall, 'The China Engineers, Ltd. & The Textile Trade', in J. M. Braga (comp.), *Hong Kong Business Symposium* (Hong Kong: n.p., 1957), p. 513.
56. *FEER*: Cotton Spinning in Hongkong', 21 September 1950; 'Commercial Reports', 9 November 1950; 'The Hongkong Cotton Mills Pool', 6 September 1951.

57. Financial Secretary minutes to Governor, 17 August 1949 and 27 December 1950. HKRS163-1-634 'Public Utilities Companies Proposed Control of the Charges and Dividends Levied by ...'
58. The labour market figures were known to be hopelessly inadequate. Commissioner of Labour minute to Colonial Secretary, 24 October 1952; Acting Commissioner of Labour memo to Colonial Secretary, 1 September 1952 covering a report by S. T. Kidd of 26 June 1952. HKRS22-1-19 'Labour Statistics — Policy'.
59. But unemployment was almost 20 per cent for females, understandably in a period when outwork was still limited and women were removed from the labour force by frequent pregnancies and child-rearing. M. 8. AS3 to Financial Secretary, 14 December 1951; M. 15. AS3 to Colonial Secretary, Financial Secretary and Political Adviser, 4 January 1952. HKRS163-1-1376 'Industry and Production. Industrial Situation in Hong Kong'. On conditions in squatter areas, note *Annual Departmental Report by the Commissioner of Labour for the Financial Year Ended March 31, 1951* (Hong Kong: Government Printer, 1951), p. 11.
60. Catherine R. Schenk, 'Hong Kong's Economic Relations With China 1949–1955: Blockade, Embargo and Financial Controls', in Lee Pui-tak (ed), *Colonial Hong Kong and Modern China: Interaction and Reintegration* (Hong Kong: Hong Kong University Press, 2005), p. 212.
61. (35) Lawrence Kadoorie note, 'Labour Conditions in Hong Kong as Affected by the U.S. Ban on Raw Materials', 30 December 1950. HKRS163-1-1376. This view was echoed 20 years later by Sir John Cowperthwaite, Financial Secretary. (26) Cowperthwaite letter to Sir Frank Figgures (United Kingdom Treasury), 19 October 1970 and 'A Preliminary Note on the International Monetary Fund with Reference to Dependent Territories (and with Particular Reference to Hong Kong)', p. 11. HKRS163-9-217 '(A) Meeting of Senior Commonwealth Finance Officials 1970. Sterling Area Balance Of Payments — Developments and Prospects To Mid-1971 (B) Overseas Sterling Area Countries Statistics'.
62. The history of the government's plans to cope with widespread unemployment and the reaction of the business community are recorded in HKRS1017-3-4 'Unemployment Relief' and HKRS1017-2-6 'Committee to Review the Unemployment Situation in the Colony'.
63. Colonial Office, *First Conference of Colonial Government Statisticians, 1950* (London: HMSO, 1951, Colonial No. 267), pp. 10–4, 16.
64. Sir Alexander Grantham, *HH*, 5 March 1952, p. 64.
65. (6) Notes on a meeting, Labour Department, 2 April 1952; (11) Labour Officer memo to Commissioner of Labour, 2 May 1952; J. Keswick letter to Commissioner of Labour, 12 May 1952. HKRS1017-3-4.
66. Despatch from the Secretary of State for the Colonies to Colonial Governments, *Colonial Development and Welfare* ... (Cmd 6713/1945), pp. 3–5.
67. The Colonial Office focus was on the typical colonial economy dependent on agriculture. Some projects in the rural New Territories went forward. The history of the committee and its activities can be found in HKRS41-1-796 'Colonial Development and Welfare Committee: 1. Appointment of ...'.
68. On London's disappointment with the failure of its elaborate planning template to produce worthwhile projects, see Sydney Caine, 'British Experience in Overseas Development', *Annals,* Vol. 270 (July 1950), pp. 122–3.
69. This apparent parallel between pre-war Hong Kong thinking and the Colonial

Office's development policies was not entirely coincidental. Hong Kong's Financial Secretary had been transferred to London after the outbreak of war where he became a highly influential figure in the Colonial Office and subsequently the Treasury. He was Director of the London School of Economics from 1957 to 1967.

70. For details of London's initiatives and Hong Kong's response, see HKRS41-1-6032 'Colonial Industrial Development — Legislation to encourage ...'.

71. *Report of the Commission ... to Enquire into the Causes and Effects of the Present Trade Recession* ... (Hong Kong: Noronha & Co., 1935), pp. 74. 79, 86, 89–90, 93–4.

72. S. (later Sir Sydney) Caine, *HH*, 9 November 1939, pp, 187.

73. *Colonial Development and Welfare*, pp. 4–5.

74. This account is based on HKRS41-1-2769(1) 'Inland Revenue Ordinance: 1. General Question of Imposing etc ...'. Hong Kong had managed to escape from London's first attempt in 1922 to introduce modern income tax legislation throughout the colonial empire. See (1) Commissioner of Inland Revenue (E. W. Pudney) memo to Financial Secretary, 8 January 1947, p. 1. HKRS41-1-2769(1).

75. See, in particular, Financial Secretary minutes to Governor, 17 August 1949 and 27 December 1950. HKRS163-1-634 'Public Utilities Companies Proposed Control of the Charges and Dividends Levied by ...'

CHAPTER **4**

1. Wenguang Shao, *China, Britain and Businessmen: Political and Commercial Relations, 1949–57* (Basingstoke: Macmillan, 1991), p. 106. Colonial territories were at a special disadvantage because the Colonial Office was not consulted on their interests until after the Foreign Office had agreed with the US on the trade restrictions to be imposed on them. Frank M. Cain, 'Exporting the Cold War: British Responses to the USA's Establishment of COCOM, 1947–51', *Journal of Contemporary History*, Vol. 29, No. 3 (July 1994), p. 515.

2. This clash between free trade and economic nationalism had been very powerful in British imperial policy until World War II. Thomas G. August, *The Selling of the Empire: British and French Imperialist Propaganda, 1890–1940* (Westport: Greenwood Press, 1985), pp. 32–5.

3. On the limits which laisser faire imposed on government activities in nineteenth century Britain, note Anthony Howe, *Free Trade and Liberal England, 1846–1946* (Oxford: Clarendon Press, 1997), pp. 20, 50.

4. It is generally only the economic dimension to Hong Kong's flexibility that has been recognised. e.g., Deepak Lal and H. Myint, *The Political Economy of Poverty, Equity, and Growth: A Comparative Study* (New York: Oxford University Press, 1996), p.140.

5. The wartime surrender of the last remaining privileges under the Unequal Treaties is reviewed in K. C. Chan, 'The Abrogation of British Extraterritoriality in China 1942–43: A Study of Anglo-American-Chinese Relations', *Modern Asian Studies*, Vol. 11, No. 2 (1977).

6. For a thorough discussion of Guomindang attitudes and aspirations towards Hong Kong during the war, see Andrew Whitfield, *Hong Kong, Empire and the Anglo-American Alliance at War, 1941–1945* (Basingstoke: Palgrave, 2001), pp. 91–100, 106–209.

7. 'Conditions of Banking in Hongkong', *FEER*, 19 Nov 1947.

8. The account that follows of the negotiations between the colonial administration and the Guomindang authorities is based on: (15) Governor to Secretary of State for the Colonies, 13 February 1947; (28) H. H. Thomas, Financial Controller, Consulate General Shanghai, secret telegram to Foreign Office, London 25 February 1947; (86) Officer Administering the Government to Secretary of State for the Colonies, 31 May 1947. HKRS163-1-402 'China Trade And Commerce Aide Memoire re Closer Cooperation between China and Hong Kong in Connection with Trade and Exchange Control'; (289) Governor to Secretary of State for the Colonies, 10 May 1948; Colonial Secretary minute to Governor, 2 July 1948; Governor minute to Colonial Secretary, 30 August 1948. HKRS163-1-403 'China Trade & Commerce Aide Memoire re Closer Cooperation between China and Hong Kong in Connection with Trade and Exchange Control'.

9. (2) Aide memoire from the Chinese side, 27 October 1946. HKRS163-1-402; (165) Letter from Chinese side, 15 August 1947, transmitting the finalised 'Memorandum of Agreement'. HKRS163-1-403.

10. Treaty Series No. 9 (1949), *Exchange of Notes … for the Prevention of Smuggling between Hong Kong and Chinese Ports* (London: Cmd 7615/1949).

11. Sir Man-kam Lo, *HH*, 20 October 1948, p. 389.

12. D. M. MacDougall, Colonial Secretary, *HH*, 6 October 1948, pp. 272–3.

13. Mainland central bankers failed, for example, to realise that Hong Kong had already banned unauthorised trade and financial transactions with the Mainland under wartime Defence Regulations. (262)AFS memo to Attorney General, 15 December 1947. HKRS163-1-403. (The relevant 1941 official circulars which were still in force restricting transactions in the Chinese national currency are on this file.) Trade controls were strengthened after the war. *Appendix D. Report of the Superintendent of Imports and Exports for the Year 1947–8* (Hong Kong: n.p., n.d.), p. 1.

14. J. B. Griffin, Attorney General, *HH*, 17 December 1947, p. 334.

15. (2) DFS memo to Registrar of Companies, 'Subject: Banking Companies', 11 August 1948. HKRS41-1-3011 'The Provincial Bank of Fukien: 1. Application from … for a Banking Licence; 2. Balance Sheet of …'.

16. The British Embassy sent an English version of the new law to the colonial administration on 20 June 1947 which chose to ignore it. HKRS41-1-2485 'China: The Banking Law, 1947'.

17. Cordial relations began under the British Military Administration with the British Commander in Chief, Admiral Sir Cecil Harcourt. They were maintained with some zeal by Sir Alexander Grantham as Governor. HKRS169-2-306 'Visit by H. E. Governor of Hong Kong to Canton'; Wm. Roger Louis, 'Hong Kong: The Critical Phase, 1945–1949', *American Historical Review*, Vol. 102, No. 4 (October 1997), pp. 1068, 1070–2.

18. In 1945–46, Canada and the US faced similar problems. Zhong-ping Feng, *The British Government's China Policy 1945–1950* (Keele: Ryburn Publishing, 1994), pp. 33–5, 44–5.

19. The embassy reports were circulated to the colonial administration in Hong Kong. HKRS41-1-999-1 'Chinese Affairs: Miscellaneous Correspondence from British Embassy Nanking Concerning …'.

20. David C. Wolf, '"To Secure a Convenience": Britain Recognizes China — 1950', *Journal of Contemporary History*, Vol. 18. No. 2 (April 1983), pp. 301–3.

21. J. P. Coghill (British Embassy Nanjing) letter to P. S. W. Y. Scarlett (Foreign Office), 19 October 1948. HKRS41-1-999-1.
22. HKRS41-1-3888 'Inauguration of the President of China. General Holidays and Other Celebrations'.
23. *Annual Report on Hong Kong for the Year 1947* (Hong Kong: Government of Hong Kong. 1948), p. 33.
24. The leadership's attitudes towards Hong Kong are well illustrated in Xu Jiatun, *Xu Jiatun Xianggang Huiyilu* (Taipei: Lianhebao, 1993); Lawrence C. Reardon, *The Reluctant Dragon. Crisis Cycles in Chinese Foreign Economic Policy* (Hong Kong: Hong Kong University Press, 2002); Wong Man Fong, *China's Resumption of Sovereignty over Hong Kong* (Hong Kong: Hong Kong Baptist University, n.d.); Kam Yiu-yu, 'Decision-Making and Implementation of Policy toward Hong Kong', in Carol Lee Hamrin and Suisheng Zhao (eds), *Decision-Making in Deng's China. Perspectives From Insiders* (Armonk: M. E. Sharpe, 1995).
25. P. B. Harris, 'The International Future of Hong Kong' *International Affairs*, Vol. 48, No. 1, January 1972, p. 62. Mao Zedong declined a request from Stalin to expel the British. Michael Yahuda, *Hong Kong. China's Challenge* (London: Routledge, 1996), p. 46.
26. Judith M. Brown and Wm. Roger Louis, *The Oxford History of the British Empire: The Twentieth Century*, Vol. IV (Oxford: Oxford University Press, 1999), p. 95.
27. (15) 'Hong Kong Civil Affairs Policy Directives. Financial Policy', revised draft, 7 July 1944. HKRS211-2-20.
28. See Leo F. Goodstadt, *Uneasy Partners: The Conflict between Public Interest and Private Profit in Hong Kong* (Hong Kong: Hong Kong University Press, 2005), Chapter III, 'The Struggle for Autonomy'.
29. For a useful contemporary account of the UK's controls and how they applied within the Sterling Area, see H. A. Shannon, 'The British Payments and Exchange Control System', *Quarterly Journal of Economics*, Vol. 63, No. 2 (May 1949).
30. Hong Kong was not the only liberated territory where 'the principles behind export control are not fully appreciated'. War Office telegram to Commander in Chief Hong Kong, 7 February 1946. HKRS169-2-53 'Rehabilitation of Business'.
31. Commander in Chief Hong Kong telegram to War Office, 1 November 1945. HKRS169-2-53.
32. To be fair to London officials, there was a general British grasp of how Hong Kong's survival depended on its special relationship with the Mainland economy in this period, as a revealing example shows in War Office secret telegram to Commander in Chief Hong Kong, no. 522263 F5, 22 March 1946. HKRS169-2-26 'Currency and Banking'.
33. Feng, *The British Government's China Policy 1945–1950*, pp. 38–9, 47.
34. In the era of state controls, international financial centres needed 'offshore' markets. London had its own 'free' market' which was exempt from exchange controls, but access to its facilities was confined to non-residents and well-policed (in marked contrast to Hong Kong). New York banks later developed 'offshore' devices to avoid government restrictions on their lending in the 1960s. See Ronen Palan 'Trying to Have Your Cake and Eating It: How and Why the State System Has Created Offshore', *International Studies Quarterly*, Vol. 42, No. 4 (December 1998), pp. 631–3.
35. Aron Shai, 'Britain, China and the End of Empire, *Journal of Contemporary History*, Vol. 15, No. 2 (April 1980), p. 295.

36. David Clayton, *Imperialism Revisited. Political and Economic Relations between Britain and China, 1950–54* (London: Macmillan Press Ltd, 1997), p. 99.

37. Commander in Chief telegram to War Office, 19 January 1946; War Office/ Colonial Office telegram to Commander in Chief Hong Kong, 16 January 1946. HKRS169-2-53; Feng, *The British Government's China Policy 1945–1950*, pp. 34–6.

38. 'Hong Kong's Control of Trade and Finance: Exerted through Supplies, Trade & Industry Department and Exchange Control', *FEER*, 16 Oct 1946; (26) Governor telegram to Secretary of State for the Colonies, 22 February 1947; (116) H. H. Thomas, Financial Counsellor, Consulate General Shanghai, letter to N. E. Young, UK Treasury, 18 June 1947. HKRS163-1-402.

39. Officer Administering the Government telegram to Secretary of State for the Colonies, no. 958, 6 June 1947; S (later Sir Sidney) Caine (Colonial Office) telegram to D. M. MacDougall (Hong Kong), no. 982, 21 June 1947. HKRS163-1-442 'Import and Exchange Control in Hong Kong Proposed Visit of a H.K. Govt. Officer to the U.K. in Connection with …'. In the exchange of correspondence, the colonial administration claimed that a temporary laxity in administering exchange controls had been accidental and caused by the indisposition of the officials responsible.

40. (15) Governor dispatch to Secretary of State for the Colonies, 13 February 1947, p. 9; (101) Officer Administering the Government telegram to Secretary of State for the Colonies, 6 June 1947. HKRS163-1-402.

41. It should be recorded that, contrary to the analysis in this chapter, other studies of this period have argued that there was relatively little opposition in London to granting Hong Kong much more latitude than other Sterling Area members in administering exchange controls. e.g., Clayton, *Imperialism Revisited. Political and Economic Relations between Britain and China, 1950–54*, pp. 97–9.

42. 'Free Trade in Hong Kong', *Economist*, 21 August 1948, p. 304. This article seems to have been 'inspired' by Hong Kong officials.

43. For an authoritative account of these events and the reaction of UK policy-makers, see Catherine R. Schenk, *Hong Kong as an International Financial Centre. Emergence and Development 1945–65* (London: Routledge, 2001), pp. 85–7.

44. See, for example, how the colonial administration responded to London's liberalisation of exchange controls at the end of the decade. (76) DCI memo to DFS, 'Liberalization of Dollar Imports', 2 July 1957; (142)1 DFS note, 'Visit to London, May 1959, Dollar Liberalisation', 20 May 1959; (142) DES memo to AFS (Exchange), 'Exchange Control', 27 March 1961. HKRS163-9-98 'Exchange Control Import Licensing Policy for Dollar Imports'.

45. The pressures on London to control capital outflows were increasing in this period. Samuel I. Katz, 'Sterling Instability and the Postwar Sterling System', *Review of Economics and Statistics*, Vol. 36, No. 1 (February 1954), pp. 85–6.

46. HKRS163-1-15 'Model Exchange Fund Ordinance'.

47. Note the casual way in which the master file for exchange controls was culled. M.1. Acting Financial Secretary, 1 August 1962. HKRS163-1-1366 'Exchange Control Colonial Office Instructions and Circulars …'.

48. The plea was dealt with quite casually. The Director was left free to see if he could induce the airline to change its purchase plans. It did not, and exchange control authorisation was granted without any fuss. (97) Director of Civil Aviation memo to Colonial Secretary, 'Cathay Pacific Airways — Purchase of American Aircraft',

13 August 1957; (98) DFS memo to Director of Civil Aviation, 17 August 1957. HKRS163-9-141 'Exchange Control — Individual Problems Arising from Applications of Policy on ... in Hong Kong'. Cathay Pacific itself used London demands to buy British as a bargaining counter to obtain access to international air routes under UK control. See Gavin Young, *Beyond Lion Rock. The Story of Cathay Pacific Airways* (London: Hutchison, 1988), pp. 203–5, 208, 216.

49. Frank H. H. King, *The Hong Kong Bank in the Period of Development and Nationalism, 1941–1984. From Regional Bank to Multinational Group* (Cambridge: Cambridge University Press, 1991), pp. 345–6.

50. On the importance of balance of payments data for the effective monitoring of the Sterling Area's position, see A. M. Kamarck, 'Dollar Pooling in the Sterling Area: Comment', *American Economic Review*, Vol. 45, No. 4 (September 1955), pp. 652–3.

51. Economic Secretary minute to Financial Secretary, 17 May 1952; (79) J. J. Cowperthwaite letter to W. F. Searle (Chief Statistician, Colonial Office), 8 June 1955. HKRS163-9-88 'Trade. Balance of Payment Statistics. Policy Regarding Preparation of ...'. London denied that the statistics were part of a 'policing' exercise. (80) Searle letter to Cowperthwaite, 28 June 1955. HKRS163-9-88.

52. These confidential data showed that the net amount of sterling allocated for authorised imports into Hong Kong rose by barely three per cent a year between 1954 and 1959. (These statistics did not cover free market transactions, of course.) 'Exchange Control Returns' and M. 6. Financial Secretary to DES, 3 May 1961. HKRS163-1-2660 'Exchange Control Monthly and Half-Yearly Statistics of Foreign Exchange Transactions from January 1961'. See also Schenk, *Hong Kong as an International Financial Centre. Emergence and Development 1945–65*, pp. 76–7.

53. A detailed analysis of UK policy towards Hong Kong's free market (and the sympathetic attitude adopted by the Colonial Office and the Bank of England) can be found in Catherine R. Schenk 'Closing the Hong Kong Gap: The Hong Kong Free Dollar Market in the 1950s', *Economic History Review*, Vol. 47, No. 2 (May 1994).

54. Financial Secretary minute to DFS, 25 May 1949. HKRS41-1-5097 'Defence (Finance) Regulations, 1940, Variation Order 1949, Warning against the Publication of Statements on the Price of Gold on the Black Market'.

55. 'Free gold market and free U.S. dollar market in Hong Kong are both inconsistent with [the UK government's] obligations to International Monetary Fund and inconsistent with policy fixed for official gold prices and exchange rates. But whereas I am prepared to consider free U.S. dollar market for good reasons, I feel case of gold market is very different'. (1)1 Secretary of State for the Colonies secret telegram to Governor, no. 1140, 6 November 1948. HKRS46-1-183 'Legislation Control of Gold by Legislation Exchange Control Dealing in Gold'.

56. C. Y. Kwan & Co., Solicitors, letter to Financial Secretary, 18 August 1949. HKRS41-1-4899 'Kowloon Jewellery, Jadestone, Gold and Silver Ornaments Merchants Association. Question of Displaying Current Gold Price List in Their Shops'; (2) DFS letter to Editor, *FEER*, 10 May 1949; DFS note, 23 May 1949. HKRS41-1-5097.

57. Sir Alexander Grantham, Governor, *HH*, 3 March 1954, p. 17.

58. SIE minute to Financial Secretary, 21 January 1947. HKRS41-1-2871 'Gold Smuggling of ... out of Hong Kong'; (1) Crown Counsel memo to Attorney General, 'Seizure of Gold', 20 April 1950; Financial Secretary minute to Attorney

General, 27 May 1950. HKRS46-1-185 'Legislation Control of Gold by Legislation Seizure of Gold'.

59. For examples of efforts to comply with the law, see DFS minute to SCA, 27 April 1949. HKRS41-1-4095 'Finance (Defence) Regulation 1940 Request for Information Regarding Bullion Dealers under …'; C. Y. Kwan & Co., letter to Financial Secretary, 18 August 1949. HKRS41-1-4899.

60. DCI minute to Commissioner of Police, 7 July 1949; DFS minute to Commissioner of Police, 22 July 1949. HKRS41-1-4897 'Defence (Finance) Regulations 1940. Authorisation of Police Officers …'. Hong Kong was not the only colonial territory which found it difficult to draft effective legislation in this area. Aden sought Hong Kong's advice on how to control the gold trade in 1951. HKRS41-1-182 'Gold Control of Gold by Legislation'.

61. A. G. Clarke, Financial Secretary, *HH*, 5 March 1952, p. 80. The exchange control office had a staff of only ten in 1948–50, of whom eight were clerks. *Hong Kong Annual Report by the Financial Secretary on Exchange Control for the Year Ended the 31st March 1950* (Hong Kong: n.p., n.d.).

62. *Hong Kong Annual Report of the Director of [sic] Department of Commerce and Industry for the Period 1st April, 1948 to 31st March, 1949* (Hong Kong: n.p., n.d.), p. 3.

63. *Hong Kong Annual Report of the Commissioner of Labour 1st April, 1948 to 31st March, 1949* (Hong Kong: n.p., n.d.), p. 34.

64. HKRS41-1-3410 'Trade. Trade between Hong Kong and China'.

65. C. G. S. (later Sir Charles) Follows, Financial Secretary, *HH*, 8 March 1950, p. 46.

66. 'Hongkong's State of Emergency, *FEER*, 20 October 1949.

67. Feng, *The British Government's China Policy 1945–1950*, pp. 101–6.

68. Except where otherwise indicated, the account of the US embargo that follows is based on Chi-kwan Mark, *Hong Kong and the Cold War: Anglo-American Relations 1949–1957* (Oxford: Clarendon Press, 2004),especially pp. 132–9, 142–50, 161–2, 167–9.

69. For details of the US embargo and how it operated, see Richard I. Devane, 'The United States and China: Claims and Assets', *Asian Survey*, Vol. 18, No. 12 (December 1978) unless otherwise indicated.

70. Catherine R. Schenk, 'Hong Kong's Economic Relations With China 1949–1955: Blockade, Embargo and Financial Controls', in Lee Pui-tak (ed), *Colonial Hong Kong and Modern China: Interaction and Reintegration* (Hong Kong: Hong Kong University Press, 2005), p. 210.

71. For some interesting examples, see 'Hongkong Company Meetings', *FEER*, 20 May 1954; Robin Hutcheon, *Shanghai Customs, A 20th Century Taipan in Troubled Times* (Edgecliff: Galisea Publications, 2000), p. 201.

72. Schenk, in Lee (ed), *Colonial Hong Kong and Modern China: Interaction and Reintegration*, p. 212.

73. For example, Anthony Polsky, 'With Forked Tongue', *FEER*, 22 May–1 June 1968.

74. Chi-kwan Mark, 'American "China Hands" in the 1950s', in Cindy Yik-yi Chu (ed), *Foreign Communities in Hong Kong, 1940s–1950s* (New York: Palgrave Macmillan, 2005), pp. 176–8, 181–4.

75. Shao, *China, Britain and Businessmen: Political and Commercial Relations, 1949–57*, pp. 65, 68.

76. *Hong Kong Annual Report 1951* (Hong Kong: Government of Hong Kong, 1952), pp. 7, 9.

77. *Ibid.*, pp. 140–1.
78. The Colonial Office's apprehensions were probably overdone. The background is set out in M. 37. DES to Financial Secretary, 17 June 1964; M. 38. Financial Secretary to DES, 18 June 1964. HKRS163-9-141.
79. J. J. Cowperthwaite, Financial Secretary, *HH*, 26 April 1967, pp. 294–5.
80. Secretary of State for the Colonies savingram to Officer Administering the Government, 'United States Investment Guarantee', 19 October 1965; (20) Financial Secretary note, 18 June 1966. HKRS163-3-269 'Investment Guarantees by the United States Government'.
81. *FEER:* Leo K. Lum, 'US$ in Hongkong', 9–15 July 1967and 'Business Briefs', 8 May 1971.
82. The full details of this astonishing but highly successful operation to defy exchange controls and create development funds can be found in M. 7. and 17. and enclosures (23), (26–7), (29), (34), (39) covering August 1966 to April 1967 in HKRS163-3-269.
83. It was especially important to keep London at a distance from these activities because the UK sought to monitor currency flows out of Hong Kong that might damage the Sterling Area. See, for example, (34) Statistics Office (London) secret memo, 20 September 1956. HKRS163-1-1230 'Trade — Balance Of Payments Statistics (Hong Kong) —Working Papers and Miscellaneous Correspondence re Preparation of …'.
84. See Leo F. Goodstadt, 'Government without Statistics: Policy-making in Hong Kong 1925–85, with special reference to Economic and Financial Management', *HKIMR Working Paper* No. 6/2006, April 2006, pp. 11–13.
85. (294) Cowperthwaite letter to Searle (Colonial Office), 11 August 1959. HKRS163-1-625 'Banking Statistics: 1. Supply of … to S. of S.; 2. Policy Correspondence Concerning'.
86. M. 106. Deputy Economic Secretary to Financial Secretary, 3 February 1968. HKRS163-1-2660 'Exchange Control Monthly and Half-Yearly Statistics of Foreign Exchange Transactions from January 1961'.
87. The background to the place of Hong Kong in China's state planning and details of the Chinese government's management of its trade and currency relations with Hong Kong reflecting discussions with staff of China state-owned banks was described in*FEER:* Leo Goodstadt, 'Currencies: The HK$ Compromise', 15 July 1972 and 'China: Stability, Conservatism and Ingenuity', 25 April 1975.
88. It should be noted that the Chinese Communist Party placed considerable store on balanced trade in the Maoist era, and imports and exports were roughly equal from one year to another. This table was first published, with a description of its sources, in Leo F. Goodstadt, 'Painful Transitions: The Impact of Economic Growth and Government Policies on Hong Kong's "Chinese" Banks, 1945–70', *HKIMR Working Paper* No. 16/2006, November 2006, Table V, p. 22.
89. In particular, China state-owned banks did not comply with the legal requirements governing their offshore assets. M. 13. AS(EM) to Financial Secretary, 29 August 1968. HKRS163-1-3276 'Banking Statistics Various'.
90. M. 42. Assistant Political Adviser, 3 May 1967. HKRS163-1-3275 'Banking Statistics Various — 1967'.
91. M. 13. AS(EM) to Financial Secretary, 29 August 1968. HKRS163-1-3276. The Bank of England early on recognised the difficulties of identifying what China was up

to. P. L. Hogg (Bank of England) letter to N. H. T. Bennett (Hong Kong Exchange Control), 10 August 1955. HKRS163-1-2055.

92. For example, (133) W. Ramsay-Main (Economic Secretary) letter to Searle (Colonial Office), 4 January 1954. HKRS163-1-625.

93. The Commissioner of Banking criticised the use made by the Mainland of the deposits in Hong Kong branches of China state-owned banks. His suggestion of legislation to compel a specific proportion of deposits to be used locally provoked the response: 'I can see many economic advantages, but the political objections would probably outweigh them substantially'. Commissioner of Banking letter to Financial Secretary, 22 March 1966; M. 14. AS(E)2 to DES and Financial Secretary, 2 May 1966. HKRS163-1-3274 'Banking Statistics Various — 1966'.

94. The policy of tolerance developed both because of political realism and the hope of commercial benefits for Hong Kong. (2) AS(E) memo to Financial Secretary, 'Shipments from China via Hong Kong', 29 March 1955; (5) AS(E) memo to DFS(E), 'Exports from China to Transferable Account Area via Hong Kong', 24 July 1956. HKRS41-1-8569 'Exchange Control. Question of ... over Shipment of Goods from China'.

95. (1C) AS(E) memo to Financial Secretary, 29 August 1955. HKRS163-1-2055. 'Exchange Control Monthly Statistics Showing China's Purchases of Sterling and Chinese Inward Remittances'.

96. The problem for Hong Kong was that surplus sterling was transferred for sale to Hong Kong in order to buy US dollars on the colony's free market. When these were not readily available (as during the troubled summer of 1967), potential sellers of sterling (the Gulf States, in particular) had no incentive to bring sterling to Hong Kong. For the background, see M. 76. AS(E)2 to Deputy Economic Secretary/Financial Secretary, 2 March 1966. HKRS163-1-2660.

97. This account of the 1967 crisis is based on the lucid analysis in Catherine R. Schenk, 'The Empire Strikes Back: Hong Kong and the Decline of Sterling in the 1960s', *Economic History Review*, Vol. 57, No. 3 (2004), pp. 562–3.

98. On this tragedy, see Jasper Becker, *Hungry Ghosts. China's Secret Famine* (London: John Murray, 1996).

99. According to an official estimate. *Gongren Ribao*, 29 June 1981.

100. Charles Ford Redick, 'The Jurisprudence of the Foreign Claims Settlement Commission: Chinese Claims', *American Journal of International Law*, Vol. 67, No. 4 (October 1973), p. 739.

101. Monroe Leigh, 'Jackson v. People's Republic of China, 596 F.Supp. 386', *American Journal of International Law*, Vol. 79, No. 2 (April 1985), p. 456.

102. Y. Y. Kueh and Christopher Howe, 'China's International Trade: Policy and Organizational Change and Their Place in the "Economic Readjustment"', *China Quarterly*, No. 100 (December 1984), p. 823.

103. Important exceptions were Cold War strategic controls on trade with the Mainland and Soviet Bloc economies. Sir Alexander Grantham, Governor, *HH*, 3 March 1954, pp. 16–7; C. Blaker, *ibid.*, 17 March 1954, p. 61.

CHAPTER **5**

1. F. C. Benham, 'The Growth of Manufacturing in Hong Kong', *International Affairs*, Vol. 32, No. 4 (October 1956), pp. 460, 463.

2. On fears in the 1950s about limited prospects for cotton spinning and garments, see J. J. (later Sir John) Cowperthwaite, Financial Secretary, *HH*, 28 March 1968, p. 212.
3. George Hicks, 'The Four Little Dragons: An Enthusiast's Reading Guide', *Asian-Pacific Economic Literature*, Vol. 3, No. 2 (September 1989), pp. 36–7. Interest in Hong Kong emerged only after its style of liberal economic management returned to fashion. Hong Kong remained a marginal case, however. See, for example, its treatment in World Bank, *The East Asian Miracle. Economic Growth and Public Policy* (New York: Oxford University Press, 1993).
4. Richard Margolis, 'A History of Paradoxes', in John Elliot (ed), *Hong Kong: Asia's Business Centre* (Hong Kong: Government Information Services, 1992), p. 18.
5. In a World Bank review of Asia's 'miracle' economies, it is has been noted that explanations for this phenomenon fall into two categories. There are the 'fundamentalists' whose starting point is growth models (for which Hong Kong cannot provide adequate data) and the 'mystics' who invoke government intervention (which the colonial administration rejected). Hence, the attractions of 'ideology' in explaining Hong Kong's growth experience. See John Page, 'The East Asian Miracle: Four Lessons for Development Policy' *NBER Macroeconomics Annual*, Vol. 9 (1994), pp. 223–4.
6. Curiously, Hong Kong historians seem unaware of a similar controversy in British economic history about the conflict between industrialists and financial and commercial interests during the nineteenth century. See, in particular, P. J. Cain and A. G. Hopkins, 'Gentlemanly Capitalism and British Expansion Overseas II: New Imperialism, 1850–1945', *Economic History Review*, Vol. 40, No. 1 (February 1987), pp. 6–8.
7. The best-known advocate of this view is Tak-wing Ngo, 'Industrial History and the Artifice of *Laissez-faire* Colonialism', in Tak-Wing Ngo (ed), *Hong Kong's History. State and Society under Colonial Rule* (London: Routledge, 1999). The most impressive history of the financing of Hong Kong's post-war industrialisation is Catherine R. Schenk, 'Finance of Industry in Hong Kong 1950–70: A Case of Market Failure?', *Business History*, Vol. 46, No .4 (October 2004).
8. Such conspiracy theories about Mainland banking history are rejected by Linsun Cheng, *Banking in Modern China: Entrepreneurs Professional Managers and the Development of Chinese Banks, 1897–1937* (Cambridge: Cambridge University Press, 2003), p. 83.
9. The UK government itself had reservations about what investment was appropriate for a colony which would cease to exist no later than 1997. See the British Cabinet document from 1949 quoted in Ngo in Ngo (ed), *Hong Kong's History. State and Society under Colonial Rule*, p. 129.
10. (10) Governor to Secretary of State for the Colonies, 28 March 1962; (15) Secretary of State for the Colonies to Officer Administering the Government, 11 July 1962. HKRS163-1-1007 'Finance Estimated Capital Investment in Hong Kong'.
11. James Riedel, *The Industrialization of Hong Kong* (Tübingen: J. C. B. Mohr [Paul Siebuck], 1974), p. 110.
12. 'Report of the Industrial Bank Committee' (Hong Kong Government, January 1960, mimeo), p. 6; M. 10. TID to SID, 3 November 1967. HKRS1056-1-194 'Industrial Survey — Policy'; Catherine R. Schenk, 'Regulatory Reform in an Emerging Stock Market: the Case of Hong Kong, 1945–86', *Financial History Review*, Vol. 11, No. 2 (2004), pp. 5–7.

13. M.2. Acting Financial Secretary to Governor, 10 September 1968. HKRS229-1-807 'Financial Aid (Including Loans) Received from the United Kingdom and Other Governments Record of …'.

14. The UK's controls on raising capital had been tightened in response not only to domestic problems but also to the impact of the Korean War in 1950. Marvin E. Rozen, 'Investment Control in Post-War Britain, 1945–1955' *Canadian Journal of Economics and Political Science,* Vol. 29, No. 2 (May 1963), p. 185, fn 1.

15. A. G. Clarke, *HH*, 23 March 1960, p. 123. The London capital markets in London were still subject to controls at that date.

16. Clarke, *HH*, 29 March 1961, p. 123.

17. Cowperthwaite, *HH*, 26 March 1969, p. 204.

18. Cowperthwaite, *HH*, 28 February 1968, p. 67; 28 March 1968, p. 214.

19. J. J. Cowperthwaite letter to H. D. Higham (Colonial Office), 11 March 1963. CO1030/1589 'Proposed I.B.R.D Loan for Land Reclamation at Kwai Chung — Hong Kong'; (1) Acting Financial Secretary letter to D. J. Kirkness (Colonial Office), 14 October 1963, pp. 7–8. HKRS160-3-25 'Report on the Financial Situation by the Acting Financial Secretary'. The household supply was reduced to four hours of water every fourth day.

20. Cornelis J. A. Jansen and Mark Cherniavsky, 'Current Economic Situation and Prospects of Hong Kong' (Asia Department IBRD, 9 May 1967, mimeo.), pp. iii, 31.

21. M. 4. Acting Director of Supplies, Trade and Industry to Labour Officer, 31 July 1947. HKRS163-1-305 'Retail Price & Wages Index. Preparation of …'.

22. Acting Director of Supplies, Trade and Industry minute to Colonial Secretary, 8 September 1947. HKRS163-5-2 'Colonial Production Colonial Development Corporation & International Bank Loans'. Cowperthwaite's views reflected a hostility to foreign aid and investment that was voiced by Western economists as well as by Third World political leaders. See, for example, Bernard Goodman, 'The Political Economy of Private International Investment', *Economic Development and Cultural Change*, Vol. 5, No. 3 (April 1957), pp. 270–1, 275.

23. David W. Clayton, 'Industrialization and institutional change in Hong Kong 1842–1960', in Heita Kawakatsu and A. J. H. Latham (eds), *Asia Pacific Dynamism, 1550–2000* (London: Routledge, 2000) p. 161.

24. On fears of excessive competition, see*HH*: H. D. M. Barton, 16 March 1960, p. 94 and 19 March 1962, pp. 73–4; Cowperthwaite, 28 March 1968, p. 213.

25. The most cogent presentation of the colonialist explanation is by Alex H. Choi, 'State-Business Relations and Industrial Restructuring', in Ngo (ed), *Hong Kong's History. State and Society under Colonial Rule*, pp. 144, 150, 154.

26. British interests in the legislature were vociferous in attacking government policy on this issue.*HH*: H. D. M. Barton (Jardine Matheson), 23 March 1960, p. 93 and 19 March 1962, p. 71; W. C. G. Knowles (Swire), 19 March 1962, p. 102; J. D. (later Sir Douglas) Clague (Hutchison), 2 March 1955, p. 119 and 18 March 1959, p. 84. For Wheelock Marden, see Sen San, 'Traveller's Tales', *FEER*, 24 August 1961 and Robin Hutcheon, *Shanghai Customs. A 20th Century Taipan in Troubled Times* (Edgecliff: Galisea Publications, 2000), p. 204.

27. Sir Robert Black, Governor, *HH*, 25 February 1959, pp. 29–30.

28. 'Report of the Industrial Bank Committee', pp. 13–5.

29. Advocates of financial aid to industry — including senior officials — repeatedly failed to produce concrete instances of factories being handicapped on account

of unreasonable bank-lending policies. See, for example, (33) H. A. Angus, Director of Commerce and Industry, letter, 4 June 1959. HKRS163-1-2299 'The Industrial Bank Committee — Proceedings of …'; Industry Development Branch, 'The Case for Improved Access to Loans for Re-equipment Purposes by Small Scale Industry' (Department of Commerce and Industry, IND 2/903, 27 October 1969, mimeo) and 'Memorandum to the Loans for Small Industry Committee' (Commerce and Industry Department, IND 2/903, 4 November 1969, mimeo).

30. Cowperthwaite's final and impressive refutation of the lobbyists can be found in *HH*, 9 October 1970, p. 116.

31. H. C. Y. Ho, *The Fiscal System of Hong Kong* (London: Croom Helm, 1979), p. 62. The post-British scheme was longer-lived but was no better-founded or effective than its colonial predecessor. See Andrew Sheng, Deputy Chief Executive, Hong Kong Monetary Authority, *GIS*, 28 September 1995; Small and Medium Enterprises Committee, *A Report on Support Measures for Small and Medium Enterprises* (Hong Kong: SAR Government, 2001), Chapter 5; Legislative Council Panel on Commerce and Industry, *Progress Report on the Four Funding Schemes for Small and Medium Enterprises*, (CB(1)1670/01-02(03) 13 May 2002).

32. On the attributes of these newcomers, see Wong Siu-lun, *Emigrant Entrepreneurs. Shanghai Industrialists in Hong Kong* (Hong Kong: Oxford University Press, 1988), pp. 126–31.

33. Mao Zedong left his intentions menacingly vague, as in a 1947 speech: 'The new-democratic revolution aims at wiping out only feudalism and monopoly capitalism, only the landlord class and the bureaucrat-capitalist class (the big bourgeoisie), and not at wiping out capitalism in general, the upper petty bourgeoisie or the middle bourgeoisie. … The upper petty bourgeoisie referred to here are small industrialists and merchants employing workers or assistants'. *Selected Works of Mao Tse-tung* (Beijing: Foreign Languages Press, 1967), Vol. IV, p. 168. No successful businessman could be sure of qualifying for the safety of 'petty bourgeois' status.

34. An insightful review of the merits of this sort of 'cultural' approach is provided by Tai-lok Lui and Thomas W. P. Wong, *Chinese Entrepreneurship in Context* (Hong Kong: Hong Kong Institute of Asian-Pacific Studies, 1994), pp. 25–7.

35. For example, the government had only a vague notion of how many workers were employed in different sectors of the economy. In commenting on demands from the Colonial Office for statistical information, the Labour Department declared it would be impossible to collect worthwhile industrial employment, unemployment and non-industrial labour figures. M. 7. Commissioner of Labour to Colonial Secretary, 11 December 1951. HKRS163-1-1376 'Industry and Production. Industrial Situation in Hong Kong'.

36. Alexander Grantham, *Via Ports. From Hong Kong to Hong Kong* (Hong Kong: Hong Kong University Press, 1965), pp. 104–5.

37. H. A. Angus, Director of Commerce and Industry, 'Industrial Developments', *FEER*, 27 October 1955.

38. Edward Szczepanik, *The Economic Growth of Hong Kong* (London: Oxford University Press, 1960), p. 135.

39. Thanks to the pioneering work of Frank Leeming, 'The Earlier Industrialization of Hong Kong', *Modern Asian Studies*, Vol. 9, No. 5 (1975), p. 338.

40. For example, in discussing Shanghai's contribution to Hong Kong's post-war take-off, a well-known economic geographer has asserted: 'What Hong Kong got was

in essence a wholesale transfer of industrialization from the long established industrial base in China … Hong Kong had thus successfully transformed itself into an export-led economy based largely on labor-intensive industries typical of Shanghai in the 1930'. Victor F. S. Sit, 'Hong Kong's "Transferred" Industrialization and Industrial Geography', *Asian Survey*, Vol. 38, No. 9 (September 1998), p. 882.

41. *FEER:* 'Stock & Share Business' and 'Depreciation of CN$', 16 October 1946; 'Financial Notes', 20 November 1946. The magazine used what was then the unusual term, 'billionaire', in describing Shanghai tycoons until 1948. It dropped the term completely from its own lexicon after 1948 and only resumed its regular use in 1972 (in a reference to Tokyo patrons of the arts).

42. 'In its glamour, [Shanghai] outshone the British Crown Colony. Its economic prowess outshone all other Chinese cities'. Wong Siu-lun, 'The Entrepreneurial Spirit: Shanghai and Hong Kong Compared', in Y. M. Yeung and Sung Yun-wing (eds), *Shanghai Transformation and Modernization under China's Open Policy* (Hong Kong: Chinese University Press, 1996), p. 26.

43. The outlook of the era is captured very skilfully in an anonymous article which appears to incorporate a briefing from colonial officials. 'Hongkong's Industrialisation & its Problems', *FEER*, 1 December 1949.

44. 'Exchange & Financial Markets', *FEER*, 2 April 1948. This magazine had earlier lumped the 'Shanghai billionaire refugees' with such undesirables as 'political malcontents, democrats, leftists, alleged Nanking (Wang Ching-wei) collaborationists [with Japan]' who were contrasted with the 'large numbers of merchants, professional men and workers' who had been attracted to Hong Kong. 'Population of Hongkong', *FEER*, 29 January 1947.

45. 'Progress of Construction and Rehabilitation', *FEER*, 34 March 1948.

46. 'Exchange & Financial Markets', *FEER*, 2 April 1948.

47. The colony's only large-scale industrial activity previously had been the factories and shipyards established by British firms before World War I. After World War II, British interest in local industry was limited and diminishing. Except where otherwise indicated, the account of the Shanghai pioneers is based on *FEER*: 'Industrial Review' and 'Industrialisation of Honkong Cotton Spinning Mills', 7 April 1948; 'Cotton Spinning, Weaving and Knitting Industries of Hongkong', 2 March 1949.

48. The original Shanghai spinning tycoons appear to have obtained no funds from Hong Kong for the purchase of their American equipment. (2) Governor savingram to Secretary of State for the Colonies, no. 260, 13 April 1948. HKRS41-1-4118 'Exchange Control Cotton Spinning Plant'.

49. See Wong, *Emigrant Entrepreneurs. Shanghai Industrialists in Hong Kong*, p. 89.

50. By the mid-1950s, Hong Kong was being blamed for the closure of dozens of British mills. 'Expansion of Hongkong Industry and UK Manufacturers', *FEER*, 24 November 1955.

51. Of 200 weaving plants, only 35 had been set up after 1949. Knitting showed a similar pattern. 'Hongkong Textile Industry', *FEER*, 22 November 1956.

52. These estimates are only crude indicators. They are derived from an analysis of unpublished government trade data presented in Ronald Hsia, 'Effects of Industrial Growth on Hong Kong Trade', *Pakistan Development Review*, Vol. II, No. 2 (Summer 1962), p. 585. At that period, 'textile yarn, fabrics, made-up articles and related products' would have been Shanghainese-dominated, while 'clothing'

would have been produced mainly by Cantonese firms. See David R. Meyer, *Hong Kong as a Global Metropolis* (Cambridge: Cambridge University Press, 2000), pp. 151–3.

53. Leo F. Goodstadt, *Uneasy Partners: The Conflict between Public Interest and Private Profit in Hong Kong* (Hong Kong: Hong Kong University Press, 2005), pp. 200, 234–5.

54. I. M. D. Little, *Collection and Recollections Economic Papers and Their Provenance* (Oxford: Clarendon Press, 1999), p. 229; Leonard K. Cheng, 'Strategies for Rapid Economic Development: The Case of Hong Kong', *Contemporary Economic Policy*, Vol. 13, No. 1, 1995, p. 29.

55. Stephen W. K. Chiu, 'Unravelling Hong Kong's Exceptionalism: The Politics of *Laissez-faire* in the Industrial Takeoff', in Law Kam-yee and Lee Kim-ming (eds), *The Economy of Hong Kong in Non-Economic Perspectives* (Hong Kong: Oxford University Press, 2004), p. 163, fn 22.

56. Shou-eng Koo, 'The Role of Export Expansion in Hong Kong's Economic Growth', *Asian Survey*, Vol. 8, No. 6 (June 1968), p. 506; Cheng Tong Yung, *The Economy of Hong Kong* (Hong Kong: Far East Publications, 1977), p. 39.

57. Note the difficulties encountered by the author of a well-known study of remittances in trying to unravel these financial transfers to and through Hong Kong and to arrive at satisfactory estimates of their volumes. Chun-his Wu, *Dollars, Dependents and Dogma: Overseas Chinese Remittances to Communist China* (Stanford: Hoover Institution, 1967), pp. 86, 89, 157.

58. See also John L. Espy, 'Some Notes on Business and Industry in Hong Kong', *Chung Chi Journal*, Vol. 11, No. 1 (April 1972), p. 178. The role of non-institutional financing in the history of Hong Kong's industrial growth was reported in L. F. Goodstadt, 'Hongkong Affairs: Profits in Pawn', *FEER*, 3–19 April 1969.

59. D. W. Stammer, 'Financial Development and Economic Growth in Underdeveloped Countries: Comment', *Economic Development and Cultural Change*, Vol. 20, No. 2 (January 1972), p. 324. This failure to distinguish between bank loans and equity investments was to prove the downfall of several banks in the 1960s, as the following chapter will illustrate.

60. Jansen and Cherniavsky, 'Current Economic Situation and Prospects of Hong Kong', pp. iii, 4, 27.

61. The banking requirements of Cantonese manufacturers rated a single sentence in Y. C. Jao, *Banking and Currency in Hong Kong. A Study of Postwar Financial Development* (London: Macmillan, 1974), p. 210.

62. Credit policies are discussed in Jao, *Banking and Currency in Hong Kong. A Study of Postwar Financial Development*, pp. 46–9.

63. Interesting data on pre-1949 industrial lending by the Bank of China, National Commercial Bank and Yien Yieh Bank are provided by Cheng, *Banking in Modern China: Entrepreneurs Professional Managers and the Development of Chinese Banks, 1897–1937*, pp. 84–6.

64. Commissioner of Banking letter to Financial Secretary, 22 March 1966; M. 14. AS(E)2 to DES and Financial Secretary, 2 May 1966. HKRS163-1-3274 'Banking Statistics Various — 1966'.

65. For example, Jao, *Banking and Currency in Hong Kong. A Study of Postwar Financial Development*, p. 210.

66. Schenk, 'Finance of Industry in Hong Kong 1950–70: A Case of Market Failure?', *Business History*, p. 603.

67. R. H. Leary, interview with M. G. Carruthers, HSBC Hong Kong Manager, *FEER*, 10 June 1965.

68. Gillian Chambers, *Hang Seng The Evergrowing Bank* ((Hong Kong: n.p., 1991), p. 36.

69. Elizabeth Sinn, *Growing with Hong Kong. The Bank of East Asia 1919–1884* (Hong Kong: Hong Kong University Press, 1994), p. 100.

70. The best account of local Chinese banks and their traditional business model is Catherine R. Schenk, 'Banks and the Emergence of Hong Kong as an International Financial Center', *Journal of International Financial Markets, Institutions and Money*, Vol. 12 (2002), pp. 321–40.

71. Nicholas C. Owen, 'Economic Policy', in Keith Hopkins (ed), *Hong Kong: The Industrial Colony. A Political, Social and Economic Survey* (Hong Kong: Oxford University Press, 1971), p. 154.

72. These advantages are analysed in Leo F. Goodstadt, 'Crisis and Challenge: The Changing Role of the Hongkong & Shanghai Bank, 1950–2000', *HKIMR Working Paper No.13/2005*, July 2005, pp. 17–20.

73. Frank H. H. King, *The Hong Kong Bank in the Period of Development and Nationalism, 1941–1984. From Regional Bank to Multinational Group* (Cambridge: Cambridge University Press, 1991), pp. 306–11, 621–5, 704–5.

74. See T. J. F. Marshall, *Whereon the Wild Thyme Blows. Some Memoirs ofSservice with the Hongkong Bank* (Grayshott: Token Publishing Limited, 1986), pp. 107–8, 111–4.

75. Carruthers, *FEER*, 10 June 1965.

76. Y. C. Jao 'Financing Hong Kong's Early Postwar Industrialization: the Role of the Hongkong & Shanghai Banking Corporation', in Frank H. H. King (ed), *Eastern Banking: Essays in the History of the Hong Kong & Shanghai Banking Corporation* (London: The Athlone Press, 1983), pp. 549–50. HSBC's return on assets increased from 1956 to 1960, when it faced a surge in competition. Catherine R. Schenk, 'The origins of Anti-competitive Regulation: Was Hong Kong 'Over-banked' in the 1960s?', *HKIMR Working Paper No.9/2006*, July 2006, p. 9. The data include overseas branches but Hong Kong would have been the major source of business.

77, Jao, *Eastern Banking: Essays in the History of the Hong Kong & Shanghai Banking Corporation*, pp. 550, 552, 553 (fn 21), 554.

78. Jao, *ibid.*, pp. 554, 558–60.

79. This estimate is from Cheng, *Banking in Modern China: Entrepreneurs Professional Managers and the Development of Chinese Banks, 1897–1937*, p. 84.

80. Jao, *Banking and Currency in Hong Kong. A Study of Postwar Financial Development*, 'Table 7.11. Liquidity Ratio of the Hongkong & Shanghai Banking Corporation', p. 192; Goodstadt, *Uneasy Partners: The Conflict between Public Interest and Private Profit in Hong Kong*, pp. 187–8.

81. The clearest account within the colonial administration of how the liquidity loophole worked can be found in M. 9. AS(E3) to DES, 21 August 1972. HKRS163-3-12 'Banking Statistics: 1. Supply of … to S. of S. Policy Concerning …'.

82. M. 11. Exchange Controller to DES, 23 August 1972. HKRS163-3-12.

83. A new Exchange Controller was struck by this exemption of the foreign banks. His suggestion that he examine whether 'it is possible to demand that the capital of foreign banks is remitted and retained in the Colony as long as they operate here' was discreetly blocked. See the response to (1) Exchange Controller memo to Commissioner of Banking, 'Foreign Banks in the Colony', 29 October 1968. HKRS163-3-369 'Foreign Banks in Hong Kong Capitalization Requirements'.

84. In the two years 1958 and 1959, for example, the official figures recorded that total deposits rose by 45 per cent and loans and advances by 57 per cent. Better statistics would have accounted for part of the increases, the Financial Secretary said, and part had been generated by the expansion of branch banking. All he could state for certain was that 'there appears to be no shortage of money'. Clarke, *HH*, 24 February 1960, p. 50.

85. Jao, *Banking and Currency in Hong Kong. A Study of Postwar Financial Development*, pp. 179–82, 205, 210. The published data used for his estimates were not standardised or comprehensive prior to the creation of the Banking Commission in 1964. Professor Schenk (*HKIMR Working Paper No. 9/2006*, pp. 2–4) has identified the chief defects addressed by her revision of key series in these published statistics. In addition, the deposit statistics were distorted beyond repair by allowing local banks to bury their undisclosed 'inner reserves' under the heading of deposits and by permitting foreign banks to window dress, thanks to the liquidity loophole.

86. 'Report of the Industrial Bank Committee', p. 9. Note the comment in the previous footnote on the data available for these two years.

87. Stephen W. K. Chiu *et al*, *City States in the Global Economy: Industrial Restructuring in Hong Kong and Singapore* (Boulder: Westview Press, 1997), p. 134.

88. Bankers warned of how confusion about the distinction between the two classes of loans would create statistical difficulties well before the Banking Commission was created. (304) A. G. Small, Chartered Bank, 2 December 1960 and R. G. L. Oliphant, HSBC, 3 December 1960. HKRS163-1-625 'Banking Statistics: 1. Supply of … to S. of S.; 2. Policy Correspondence Concerning …'.

89. The data in this table and elsewhere in this section are derived from (6) Commissioner of Banking memo to Financial Secretary, 19 March 1965. HKRS163-1-3273 'Banking Statistics Various 1965'.

90. *Hong Kong Report for the Year 1969* (Hong Kong: Government Press, 1970), p. 50; Henry Wai-chung Yeung, *Transnational Corporations and Business Networks. Hong Kong Firms in the Asian Region* (London: Routledge, 1998), pp. 130, 206–7; James H. Weaver and Ira Winakur, 'Impact of United States Cotton Textile Quotas on Underdeveloped Countries', *South Economic Journal*, Vol. 35, No. 1 (July 1968), pp. 26–33.

91. Derived from (76) HKRS163-3-12.

92. 'Report of the Industrial Bank Committee', pp. 12–3.

93. Evidence for the improved performance was identified from the trade data in Hsia, *Pakistan Development Review*, pp. 565, 572–3.

94. Mick Carney and Howard Davies, 'From Entrepot to Entrepot via Merchant Manufacturing: Adaptive Mechanism, Organizational Capabilities and the Structure of the Hong Kong Economy', *Asia Pacific Business Review*, Vol. 6, No. 1, (October 1999), pp. 22–3.

95. D. J. Dwyer and Lai Chuen-yan, *The Small Industrial unit in Hong Kong: Patterns and Policies* (University of Hull Publications, 1967), pp. 35, 37–8.

96. (36) Statistical Branch, 'Problems of making Capital Formation Estimates in Hong Kong', p. 8. HKRS229-1-45 'Capital Formation Estimates'. The data presented in this paragraph are derived from Tables III and IV in this document, which is remarkable for the space devoted to caveats about its statistical defects.

97. The intense competition created by such unrestricted entry in the 1960s so alarmed one economist that he suggested that a government licence should be required

before a new factory could open. Nicholas Owen, 'Competition and Structural Change in Unconcentrated Industries', *Journal of Economics,* Vol. 19, No. 2 (April 1971), pp. 142–3, 147. A more retrospective view of industrial development argued that the style of entrepreneurial behaviour which grew up in the 1950s was an invaluable feature of the long-term Hong Kong economic success model. Tony Fu-lai Yu, 'Hong Kong's Entrepreneurship: Behaviours and Determinants', *Entrepreneurship & Regional Development,* Vol. 12 (2000), pp. 182, 186.

98. See *Hong Kong Annual Departmental Report by the Commissioner of Labour for the Financial Year 1952–3* (Hong Kong: Government Printer, n.d.), p. 13; enclosures (115), (126), (135) and (144). HKRS270-1-2-I 'Industrial Development Flatted Factories Provision of …'.

99. The government statistician calculated machinery figures from his estimates of retained imports plus a 30 per cent margin to cover costs of installation and related expenses.

100. For a useful review of the industrialists' campaign against the banks during the period of fastest post-war growth in manufacturing, see Stephen Chiu, *The Politics of Laissez-faire. Hong Kong's Strategy of Industrialization in Historical Perspective* (Hong Kong: Hong Kong Institute of Asia-Pacific Studies, 1994), pp. 75–7.

101. Ronald Findlay and Stanislaw Wellisz, 'Hong Kong', in Ronald Findlay and Stanislaw Wellisz (eds), *The Political Economy of Poverty, Equity, and Growth. Five Small Open Economies* (New York: Oxford University Press, 1993), p. 47; Henry Smith, *John Stuart Mill's Other Island. A Study of the Economic Development of Hong Kong* (London: Institute of Economic Affairs, 1966), pp. 18–21.

CHAPTER **6**

1. David R. Meyer, *Hong Kong as a Global Metropolis* (Cambridge: Cambridge University Press, 2000), p. 88. For two impressive examples of their ability to counter foreign pressures, see Motono Eiichi, '"The Traffic Revolution": Remaking the Export Sales System in China, 1866–1875', *Modern China,* Vol. 12, No. 1 (January 1986), pp. 96–7, 99–100; Zhongping Chen, 'The Origins of Chinese Chambers of Commerce in the Lower Yangzi Region', *Modern China,* Vol. 27, No. 2 (April 2001), p. 178.

2. Linsun Cheng, *Banking in Modern China: Entrepreneurs Professional Managers and the Development of Chinese Banks, 1897–1937* (Cambridge: Cambridge University Press, 2003), pp. 76–7.

3. David K. P. Li, 'The Development of Chinese Banking in Southeast Asia', in Nyaw Mee-kau and Chang Chak-yan (eds), *Chinese Banking in Asia's Market Economies* (Hong Kong: Chinese University of Hong Kong, 1989), p. 4.

4. Tony Fu-lai Yu, 'Hong Kong's Entrepreneurship: Behaviours and Determinants', *Entrepreneurship & Regional Development,* Vol. 12 (2000), p. 190. Even in the electronics sector, which foreign firms controlled initially because they possessed both the technology and the capital required, local firms soon entered the industry with considerable success even without the sort of government support which Taiwan, for example, gave to local producers. Chyau Tuan and Linda F. Y. Ng, 'Evolution of Hong Kong's Electronics Industry under a Passive Industrial Policy', *Managerial and Decision Economics,* Vol. 16, No. 5 (September-October 1995), pp. 511, 520.

5. Despite claims that Hong Kong businessmen were 'culturally' uncomfortable about

organising large, complex corporate businesses and preferred to leave these to foreign firms. See Mick Carney and Howard Davies, 'From Entrepot to Entrepot via Merchant Manufacturing: Adaptive Mechanisms, Organizational Capabilities and the Structure of the Hong Kong Economy', *Asia Pacific Business Review*, Vol. 6, No. 1 (October 1999), pp. 22–4.

6. See John Scott, *Corporate Business and Capitalist Classes* (Oxford: Oxford University Press, 1997), p. 198.

7. These issues are reviewed in Leo F. Goodstadt, 'Crisis and Challenge: The Changing Role of the Hongkong & Shanghai Bank, 1950–2000', *HKIMR Working Paper No.13/2005*, July 2005.

8. (86) Financial Secretary, 'Memorandum to Members of the Banking Advisory Committee … Licensing Policy', 23 October 1959, p. 2. HKRS163-1-679 'Banking Advisory Committee'.

9. William J. Baumol, 'Entrepreneurship: Productive, Unproductive, and Destructive', *Journal of Political Economy* Vol. 98, No. 5, Part 1, (October 1990).

10. 'Exchange & Financial Markets: Hongkong Licensed Banks & Native Bank Firms', *FEER*, 17 November 1948. The 1964 data are derived from (6) Commissioner of Banking memo to Financial Secretary, 19 March 1965. HKRS163-1-3273 'Banking Statistics Various 1965'. Even now, there was some official confusion about the precise number of licensed banks. (19) Commissioner of Banking memo to AS (E) 231 December 1965; (22) Commissioner of Banking memo to Financial Secretary, 25 January 1966. HKRS163-1-3273.

11. Derived from Goodstadt, 'Crisis and Challenge: The Changing Role of the Hongkong & Shanghai Bank, 1950–2000', *HKIMR Working Paper No.13/2005*, Tables I and II, pp. 24–5.

12. Commander in Chief Hong Kong top-secret telegram to Admiralty, 15 September 1945. HKRS169-2-26 'Currency and Banking'.

13. 'The Position & Business of Chinese Native Banks', *FEER*, 18 February 1948.

14. *Ibid.*

15. Acting Financial Secretary minute to Attorney General, 28 January 1948. HKRS163-1-440 'Banking: 1. Banking Ordinance'.

16. As contemporary observers realised. See 'Conditions of Banking in Hongkong', *FEER*, 19 November 1947.

17. The best accounts of local Chinese-owned banks and their traditional business model are Catherine R. Schenk, 'Banking Groups in Hong Kong, 1945–65', *Asia Pacific Business Review*, Vol. 7, No. 2, (Winter 2000), pp. 131–54, and 'Banks and the Emergence of Hong Kong as an International Financial Center', *Journal of International Financial Markets, Institutions and Money*, Vol. 12 (2002), pp. 321–40.

18. The economic crisis faced by the Guomindang in its Hong Kong relationship is analysed in Catherine R. Schenk, 'Another Asian Financial Crisis: Monetary Links between Hong Kong and China 1945–50', *Modern Asian Studies*, Vol. 34, No. 3 (2000), pp. 744–6 and 749–50 in particular.

19. 'The Position & Business of Chinese Native Banks', *FEER*, 18 February 1948.

20. Official discussion of these and other defects, and the risks to savings depositors in particular, are set out in HKRS163-1-440 'Banking: 1. Banking Ordinance; 2. Control over the Opening and Functioning of Native Banks in Hong Kong'.

21. HKRS41-1-3008 'The Shanghai Commercial & Savings Bank Ltd: 1. Application from … for a Banking Licence; 2. Balance Sheet of …'.

22. Andrea McElderry, 'Confucian Capitalism?: Corporate Values in Republican Banking' *Modern China*, Vol. 12, No. 3 (July 1986), pp. 409–10, 413–4.
23. The account of the decision to protect 'Chinese Native Banks' is drawn from (33) 'Report of the Select Committee' [of the Legislative Council set up to report on the Banking Bill], 14 January 1948. HKRS163-1-440.
24. M. 10. AS(E) to DES, 7 October 1961. HKRS163-3-7 'The Chiu Tai Bank Ltd: 1. Application from ... for Banking Licence; 2. Balance Sheet of ...'.
25. (6) Commissioner of Banking memo to Financial Secretary, 19 March 1965. HKRS163-1-3273.
26. See the discussion about the status of an entirely private bank which was part of a British family-owned group. M.1. DFS to Financial Secretary, 27 February 1948. HKRS41-1-3067 'The H.K. Trust Corp. Ltd: 1. Application from ... for a Banking Licence; 2. Balance Sheet of ...'.
27. For example., HKRS41-1-3034 'The Yee Sang Bank: 1. Application from ... for a Banking Licence; 2. Balance Sheet of ...'; HKRS41-1-3015 'Tong Ho & Co. Ltd: 1. Application from ... for a Banking Licence; 2. Balance Sheet of ...'; HKRS41-1-3013 'The China Trust Co. Ltd Application from ... for a Banking Licence'; HKRS41-1-3076 'Banco Nacional Ultramarino: 1. Application from ... for a Banking Licence; 2. Balance Sheet of ...'.
28. For example, HKRS41-1-3024 'The On Tai Bank: 1. Application from ... for a Banking Licence; 2. Balance Sheet of ...'.
29. Financial Secretary, Circular No. 77 'Chow Sang Sang Jeweller and Goldsmith Co, Ltd', 7 July 1959. HKRS163-1-679.
30. For example, HKRS41-1-3040 'The Hop Kee Bank: 1. Application from ... for a Banking Licence; 2. Balance Sheet of ... ; HKRS41-1-3014 'The Yue Cheong Hong Bank: 1. Application from ... for a Banking Licence; 2. Balance Sheet of ...'; HKRS41-1-3023 'The Tak Fat Bank: 1. Application from ... for a Banking Licence; 2. Balance Sheet of ...'.
31. HKRS41-1-3005 'Agricultural and Industrial Bank of China, Ltd: 1. Application from ... for a Banking Licence; 2. Balance Sheet of ...'.
32. For example, HKRS41-1-3003 'The China Industrial Bank of H. K. Ltd. Application from ... for a Banking Licence'.
33. (2) DFS memo to Registrar of Companies, 'Subject: Banking Companies', 11 August 1948. HKRS41-1-3011 'The Provincial Bank of Fukien: 1. Application from ... for a Banking Licence; 2. Balance Sheet of ...'.
34. Financial Secretary letter to Governor of the Central Bank of China, 19 February 1948. HKRS163-1-440.
35. M. 1. Acting Financial Secretary to Governor, 14 June 1948. HKRS163-1-679.
36. See 'Conditions of Banking in Hongkong', *FEER*, 19 November 1947.
37. For example, the status of every firm described as a 'bank' in one 1951 press report was investigated. HKRS41-1-6690 'Native Banks. Reports on ...'.
38. DFS minute to Financial Secretary, 25 January 1950. HKRS41-3-3044. 'The Nam Sang Bank: 1. Application from ... for a Banking Licence; 2. Balance Sheet of ... ; 3. Cancellation of the Licence of ...'.
39. DFS minute to Financial Secretary, 25 January 1950. HKRS41-3-3044.
40. DFS minute to Financial Secretary, 5 October 1949. HKRS41-1-3003.
41. Acting Financial Secretary minute to Governor, 25 September 1951. HKRS41-1-3095 'Far East Commercial Bank Ltd Application from ... for a Banking Licence'.

Clarke's slur on his colleague was unwarranted since — as Clarke knew — this official had inherited this strategy from the previous incumbent of his post, K. M. A. Barnett, who was a byword for a knowledge of Chinese society unmatched by almost any other member of the Administrative Service at this time, including Clarke. See DFS minute to Financial Secretary, 25 January 1950. HKRS41-3-3044.

42. See the exchanges in HKRS41-1-3044.

43. Financial Secretary minute to DFS, 19 May 1950. HKRS41-1-3065 'The Yue Man Banking Co. Ltd: 1. Application from ... for a Banking Licence; 2. Balance Sheet of ...'.

44. Financial Secretary minute to DFS, 30 January 1950. HKRS41-3-3044.

45. D. W. Stammer, 'Financial Development and Economic Growth in Underdeveloped Countries: Comment', *Economic Development and Cultural Change*, Vol. 20, No. 2 (January 1972), p. 324. This failure to distinguish between bank loans and equity investments was to prove the downfall of several banks in the 1960s, as Chapter 10 will illustrate.

46. Colonial Treasurer memorandum, 25 August 1936. HKRS170-1-307 "Banking Legislation: 1. General Supervision of Banking Concerns in Hong Kong; 2. Appointment of a Committee in 1935 to Consider the Desirability of Specific Legislation for the Regulation of Banking Operations in the Colony; 3. Report of the Committee; 4. Appointment of a Committee in 1939 to Consider Further Action on this question'.

47. M. 3. DFS to Financial Secretary, 18 October 1954. HKRS41-1-3038 'The Wing Cheung Bank: 1. Application from ... for a Banking Licence; 2. Balance Sheet of ...'. This bank's situation was desperate. For details of its dubious background, see HKRS41-1-3054 'The Kwai Kee Bank: 1. Application from ... for a Banking Licence; 2. Balance Sheet of ...'.

48. A good example is recorded in HKRS41-1-3024 'Foo Kee: 1. Application from ... for a Banking Licence; 2. Balance Sheet of ...'.

49. HKRS41-1-3065 'The Yue Man Banking Co. Ltd: 1. Application from ... for a Banking Licence; 2. Balance Sheet of ...'.

50. As recorded in HKRS41-1-3085 'Shun Foo Banking & Investment Co. Ltd: 1. Application from ... for a Banking Licence; 2. Balance Sheet of ...'.

51. On official complacency, see M. 3. Acting DFS to Financial Secretary, 18 July 1956. HKRS41-1-3012 'Yau Tak Bank: 1. Application from ... for a Banking Licence; 2. Balance Sheet of ...'.

52. This reluctance to close the Chiu Tai Bank was not out of fear of triggering a fall in the public's confidence in the banking system. M. 22. Acting Financial Secretary to AS(E), 3 August 1962; M. 36. AS(E)2 to DES, 12 March 1963; M. 37. DES to Financial Secretary, 12 March 1965; M. 38. DES to AS (E) 2, 13 March 1963; (66)A 'Banking Advisory Committee Circular No. 119 Chiu Tai Bank Ltd', 3 December 1963. HKRS163-3-7.

53. Deputy Financial Secretary, 'Banking Ordinance', 26 January 1950; Financial Secretary minute to DFS, 30 January 1950. HKRS163-1-441 'Names and Addresses of Partners of Banks Required for the Banking Ordinance 1948'; Financial Secretary minute to DFS, 30 January 1950.

54. For example, HKRS41-1-3024 'The Foo Kee Bank: 1. Application from ... for a Banking Licence; 2. Balance Sheet of ...'.

55. This tolerance is well illustrated in HKRS41-1-3095 'Far East Commercial Bank Ltd Application from … for a Banking Licence'.
56. HKRS41-1-3099 'The Bank of New Territories, Ltd Application from … for a Banking Licence'.
57. (86) Financial Secretary, 23 October 1959. HKRS163-1-679.
58. HKRS41-1-3018 'The Wing Tai Bank: 1. Application from … for a Banking Licence; 2. Balance Sheet of …'; HKRS41-1-3062 'Cheuk Kee Bank: 1. Application from … for a Banking Licence; 2. Balance Sheet of …'.
59. See the surprisingly sophisticated document (6)1 Proprietor of Nam Sang Bank letter to Clerk of Councils, 13 January 1950, and note the deliberate bracketing of Clarke with Lo in the second paragraph of DES minute to Financial Secretary, 25 January 1950. HKRS41-1-3044. It should be noted that the bank's letter is an exception to the normal practice that solicitors conducted correspondence on behalf of their banking clients. In this case, a special effort seems to have been made to put some distance between the bank's legal adviser and the bank's representations to the government. Clarke's relationship with Lo on banking policy seems to have been unusually close, even for an Executive Councillor. See, for example, (8) Financial Secretary letter to Sir Man-kam Lo, 25 March 1952; (9) Lo letter to Financial Secretary, 26 March 1952. HKRS41-1-6691. 'Banking Operations Legislation for control of …'
60. (86) Financial Secretary, 23 October 1959, pp. 2–4. HKRS163-1-679.
61. The Banking Advisory Committee and Executive Council itself approved Clarke's analysis, nevertheless, which was an important demonstration of the failure of bankers and businessmen to warn the colonial administration of potential crises caused by erroneous policies. (92) Note of a decision made at a meeting of the Banking Advisory Committee, 23 November 1959; (94) memorandum, 'Licensing Policy', 14 January 1960. HKRS163-1-679.
62. For corruption and general disregard of building and related laws, see *Report of the Committee Appointed to Consider Certain Matters concerning the Closure of the Chong Hing Mansion 1971* (Hong Kong: Government Printer, 1972), p. 9. On involvement in land auction scandals, see M. 30. ACS(L) to Colonial Secretary, 11 April 1961. HKRS165-9-226 'Land Sales Question of Upset and Reserved Prices. Auction Rings and Transfers of Ownership Prior to Fulfilment of Conditions of Sale'.
63. The downfall of this bank is summarised elegantly in Catherine R. Schenk, 'Banking Groups in Hong Kong, 1945–65', *Asia Pacific Business Review*, Vol. 7, No. 2, (Winter 2000), pp. 145–6.
64. *Hong Kong Annual Departmental Report by the Registrar General for the Financial Year 1964–65* (Hong Kong: Government Printer, 1965), pp. 4–5.
65. This almost romantic view of the Chinese family enterprise can still be found in analyses of Hong Kong firms with sophisticated modern corporate structures and impressive records of complex transactions on financial markets. An interesting example is Katharyne Mitchell, 'Flexible Circulation in the Pacific Rim: Capitalisms in Cultural Context', *Economic Geography*, Vol. 71, No. 4 (October 1995), pp. 367, 369–70.

CHAPTER 7

1. Loan data are derived from (76). 163-3-12 'Banking Statistics: 1. Supply of … to S. of S. Policy Concerning …'.
2. A pure laisser-faire system may create a temptation to turn depositors into investors. Such a change in the relationship between a bank and its customers would require a specific mechanism, which did not exist in Hong Kong. See the analysis by George A. Selgin and Lawrence H. White, 'How Would the Invisible Hand Handle Money?'. *Journal of Economic Literature*, Vol. 32, No. 4 (December 1994), pp. 1728–9.
3. For a summary of the background to this trade, see Catherine R. Schenk's two articles: 'The Hong Kong Gold Market and the Southeast Asian Gold Trade in the 1950s', *Modern Asian Studies*, Vol. 29, No. 2 (May 1995) and 'Banks and the Emergence of Hong Kong as an International Financial Center', *Journal of International Financial Markets, Institutions and Money*, 12 (2002), pp. 321–40.
4. Richard H. Kaufman, 'The Asian Gold Trade', *Asian Survey*, Vol. 5, No. 5 (May 1965), pp. 236–7, 244.
5. (31) Exchange Control memo to Deputy Economic Secretary, 'Import of Gold', 12 December 1966. HKRS163-1-308 'Import and Export of Gold'.
6. Kaufman, 'The Asian Gold Trade', *Asian Survey*, p. 233.
7. London was the direct and dominant supplier during the brief gold booms of Laos and Sarawak, for example. *ibid.*, pp. 241, 244.
8. The analysis which follows, except where otherwise indicated, is based on enclosures (2), (4), (9), (23), (26), (28) and (33) covering the period 1949–53. HKRS163-1-995 'Exchange Control Transfer by Government of Macau of Surplus Hong Kong Dollar Funds to Portuguese Sterling Account in London'.
9. George V. H. Mosley, 3rd, 'New China and Old Macao', *Pacific Affairs*, Vol. 32, No. 3 (September 1959), pp. 271, 273–4. London's decision does not appear to have been linked directly to the economic downturn in Macao.
10. The sensitivity of London and Hong Kong to the link between the colony's future and developments in Macao was well illustrated in a 1962 analysis for the Foreign Officer by the Political Adviser in Hong Kong. C. M. (later Lord) MacLehose secret letter to A. J. de la Mere (Foreign Office), 13 February 1962. CO1030/1117 'Hong Kong-Macau-China; Inter-relationship'.
11. These contacts with the bank are recorded in: note to the file, 7 May 1963; Hang Seng Bank letter, 7 May 1963; M. 23. and 25., 12 and 18 June 1963. HKRS163-1-308 'Import and Export of Gold'.
12. The re-export data are from Leo F. Goodstadt, 'Dangerous Business Models: Bankers, Bureaucrats & Hong Kong's Economic Transformation, 1948–86', *HKIMR Working Paper No. 8/2006,* June 2006, 'Table I. Domestic Exports & Total Exports, 1950–1960', p. 23.
13. Table 6.2. Census and Statistics Department, *Hong Kong Statistics 1947–1967*, p. 88.
14. (151) Exchange Control memo to DES, 'Gold', 6 November 1967. HKRS163-1-308.
15. M. 10. Governor secret to Colonial Secretary, 20 February 1962. HKRS163-1-308.
16. (31) and (149) AFS(Ex) memos to DES. 'Import of Gold', 12 December 1966 and 5 August 1967. HKRS163-1-308.

17. (149) AFS(EX) to DES, 5 August 1967; M. 72. R. D. Pogue to DES, 15 August 1967. HKRS163-1-308; *China Mail*, 4 August 1967.

18. P. H. M. Jones, 'Phantom Gold', *FEER*, 30 April 1970.

19. Michael G. Whisson, *Under the Rug: the Drug Problem in Hong Kong (A Study in Applied Sociology)* (Hong Kong: Hong Kong Council of Social Service, 1965), pp. 91.

20. The account that follows is based on J. D. Higham minute to PS/Minister of State, 26 March 1965; W. S. Carter minute to Sir Ivo Stourton and W. I. J. Wallace, 12 May 1965; Governor letter to Wallace (Colonial Office), 27 August 1965. CO1030/1718 'The Drug Problem in Hong Kong'.

21. See Second Report of the Commission of Inquiry under Sir Alistair Blair-Kerr (Hong Kong: Government Printer, 1973), especially pp. 23–5, 52.

22. Mark S. Gaylord, 'The Chinese Laundry: International Drug Trafficking and Hong Kong's Banking Industry', in Harold H. Traver and Mark S. Gaylord (eds), *Drugs, Law and the State* (Hong Kong: Hong Kong University Press, 1992), p. 90.

23. *GIS*, 4 July 1999; David Carse, Deputy Chief Executive, Hong Kong Monetary Authority, *GIS*, 15 September 1999.

24. Frank H. H. King, *The Hong Kong Bank in the Period of Development and Nationalism, 1941–1984. From Regional Bank to Multinational Group* (Cambridge: Cambridge University Press, 1991), p. 345.

25. Catherine R. Schenk, *Hong Kong as an International Financial Centre. Emergence and Development 1945–65* (London: Routledge, 2001), p. 92.

26. See, for example, (31) AFS(Ex) memo to DES. 'Import of Gold', 12 December 1966 and enclosures (134), (137) and (149) which record the reluctance with which this exchange control official was briefed on the colonial administration's actual policy. HKRS163-1-308. Also interesting is the cautious briefing of a new Exchange Controller who discovered that foreign banks had been remitting profits from Hong Kong without complying with the proper procedures and who wished to investigate the related question of what capital they had imported into the colony. (1) Exchange Controller memo to Commissioner of Banking, 'Foreign Banks in the Colony', 29 October 1968. HKRS163-3-369 'Foreign Banks in Hong Kong Capitalization Requirements'.

27. Both the Exchange Controller and his UK counterparts complained that that there were already too many 'authorised' banks in 1950. DFS minutes to Financial Secretary, 24 November 1950, 23 May, 24 July and 13 August 1951. HKRS163-1-1000 'Exchange Control Banks Authorised to Deal in Foreign Exchange'.

28. DFS minute to Financial Secretary, 25 October 1951; Financial Secretary minute to DFS, 25 October 1951; AS(E) minute to DFS, 29 October 1951; Commissioner of Police memo to Financial Secretary, 15 November 1951. HKRS41-1-3096 'Asia Trading Co. Ltd. Application for a Banking Licence'.

29. The Colonial Office responded to a request from Clarke for advice on how to act in this case with the comment that 'we find it very hard to give you a decisive answer', which left him free to make up his own mind. (14) Financial Secretary letter to D. Kelvin-Stark (Colonial Office), 22 September 1958; (20) Kelvin-Stark letter to Financial Secretary, 13 January 1959. HKRS163-9-69 'Exchange Control. Banks Authorised to Deal with Foreign Exchange'.

30. The allegation came from HSBC. Circular No. 68 'Deutsch-Asiatische Bank', 10 December 1957; Circular 69 'Banque Nationale pour le Commerce et l'Industrie', 11 December 1957. HKRS163-1-679.

31. These transactions took place with discreet government endorsement. J. J. Cowperthwaite, Financial Secretary, *HH*, 29 March 1963, p. 135.
32. (123)A AFS(Exchange) memo to Financial Secretary, 'Exchange Control: Appointment of Authorised Dealers in Foreign Exchange', 29 October 1965; M. 34. AS(EM) to DES, 14 February 1968. HKRS163-9-69.
33. (92) Commissioner of Banking memo to Financial Secretary, 'Net Balances with Banks in U.K. as at 31st October 1967', 24 November 1967. HKRS163-1-3275.
34. One applicant for this status was quoted as saying: 'This business is now so much more important than the old "native" business'. M. 15. DFS(E) to Financial Secretary, 23 September 1959. HKRS163-9-34.
35. As the first Banking Commissioner was to lament in the following decade. (130) Commissioner of Banking memo to Financial Secretary, 'Hong Kong Industrial and Commercial Bank Limited', 5 February 1968. HKRS163-9-69.
36. (131) Exchange Controller memo to Financial Secretary, 'Hong Kong Industrial and Commercial Bank Ltd', 9 February 1968, and M. 36. and 37., HKRS163-9-69.
37. M. 15. DFS(E) TO Financial Secretary, 23 September 1959; M. 34. AS(EM) to DES, 14 February 1968. HKRS163-9-69.
38. (130) Commissioner of Banking memo to Financial Secretary. 'Hong Kong Industrial and Commercial Bank Limited', 5 February 1968. HKRS163-9-69.
39. The collusion to conceal this illegal situation was described with considerable frankness by Cowperthwaite, *HH*, 26 April 1967, pp. 294–5.
40. M. 37. DES to Financial Secretary, 17 June 1964; Financial Secretary to DES, 18 June 1964. HKRS163-9-141 'Exchange Control — Individual Problems Arising from Applications of Policy on … in Hong Kong'.
41. L. F. Goodstadt, "London Line," *FEER*, 4 May 1967.
42. *Hong Kong Annual Departmental Report by the Commissioner of Labour for the Financial Year 1952–3* (Hong Kong: Government Printer, n.d.), p. 13.
43. This calculation was probably an under-estimate because of the defective statistics compiled by the Labour Department. It did not take into account factories in squatter areas. (135) Commissioner of Labour memo to Director of Commerce and Industry, 'Resettlement Factories', 1 February 1960; (209) Minute to AD, 12 July 1961. HKRS270-1-2-I 'Industrial Development Flatted Factories Provision of …'.
44. (75) 'Report of the Sub-Committee of the Industrial Sites Co-ordination Committee … to Make Recommendations on the Revision of Resettlement Factory Policy'. HKRS270-1-2-II 'Industrial Development Provision of Flatted Factories'.
45. K. M. A. Barnett, Census Commissioner, 'Introduction', in W. F. Maunder, *Hong Kong Urban Rents and Housing* (Hong Kong: Hong Kong University Press, 1969), p. 1.
46. This account is derived from the *Hong Kong Annual Departmental Report by the Registrar General* for financial years 1957–58 (p. 3), 1958–59 (pp. 2–3) and 1959–60 (p.3).
47. The average number of dwelling units per residential building rose from 7.3 to 27 over this period; and average construction cost per unit from HKD18,954 to HKD20,035. Figures are calculated from Census and Statistics Department, *Hong Kong Statistics 1947–1967*, 'Table 10.2. Building (Private Sector): Number and Cost of Completed Buildings by Type, 1951–67', p. 171; 'Table 10.4. Building (Private Sector): Property Redevelopment, 1958–67', p. 173.

48. A good analysis of the importance of property for local Chinese banks is provided by Ng Kwok Leung, 'The Native Banks: Their Structure and Interest Rates', *FEER*, 11 February 1960.
49. The impact of reckless property lending had been a major argument in favour of legislation to regulate banks in 1938. (9) [Ad Hoc Committee 1938], 'Report of Committee', p. 6. HKRS41-1-6691.
50. The danger from involvement in property was a prominent complaint in a Bank of England review of Hong Kong banking. H. J. Tomkins, *Report on the Hong Kong Banking System and Recommendations for the Replacement of the Banking Ordinance 1948* (Hong Kong: Government Printer, 1962), pp. 8–9.
51. Its liquidity ratio averaged 80 pr cent, well above the industry average. Elizabeth Sinn, *Growing with Hong Kong. The Bank of East Asia 1919–1994* (Hong Kong: Hong Kong University Press, 1994), p. 103.
52. Catherine R. Schenk, 'Banking Crises and the Evolution of the Regulatory Framework in Hong Kong 1945–1970', *Australian Economic History Review*, Vol. 43, No. 2, (July 2003), pp. 143–4.
53. Cowperthwaite, *HH*, 24 February 1966, pp. 54–5.
54. Schenk, 'Banking Crises and the Evolution of the Regulatory Framework in Hong Kong 1945–1970', *Australian Economic History Review*, pp. 148–9.
55. See Catherine R. Schenk, 'Finance of Industry in Hong Kong 1950–70: A Case of Market Failure?', *Business History*, Vol. 46, No. 4 (October 2004), pp. 596–7.
56. Roderick O'Brien, 'Rent and Tenure Controls for Pre-War Buildings', *Hong Kong Law Journal*, Vol. 7, No. 1 (1977), 'Table 3 Exclusion Orders', p. 41.
57. The best-known account of the market consequences of the changing government regulations is Stephen N. S. Cheung, 'Rent Control and Housing Reconstruction: The Postwar Experience of Prewar Premises in Hong Kong' *The Journal of Law and Economics*, Vol. XXII, (April 1979), pp. 46–8.
58. M. 9. PACS (L) to DCS, 15 December 1965. HKRS163-1-3284 'Problems Affecting the Real Estate and Allied Industries'.
59. This account is based on 'Report on the First Term of Reference', *Report of the Committee Appointed to Consider Certain Matters Concerning the Closure of the Chong Hing Mansion 1971* (Hong Kong: Government Printer, 1972) and Leo Goodstadt, 'Hongkong: Apart at the Seams', *FEER*, 27 February 1971.
60. On official indifference to bribery, see HKRS163-1-2648 'Corruption — Examination of … in the Buildings Ordinance Office — P.W.D.'

CHAPTER **8**

1. *Hong Kong Tiger Standard*, 4 January 1965.
2. The first to be affected were the Hang Seng, Kwong On, Dao Heng and Wing Lung Banks. *South China Morning Post*, 9 February 1965.
3. HSBC claimed that the first bank failure had been expected but not the subsequent crisis. R. G. L. Oliphant, Deputy Chief Manager, Hongkong & Shanghai Banking Corporation, 'Banks and Economic Expansion in Hongkong', *FEER*, 22 April 1965.
4. These data are derived from (6) Commissioner of Banking memo to Financial Secretary, 19 March 1965. HKRS163-1-3273.'Banking Statistics Various 1965'. Foreign-owned banks, as Chapter 5 noted, had even lower liquidity levels but they had parents overseas to underwrite their Hong Kong lending.

5. Census and Statistics Department, *Hong Kong Statistics 1947–1967* (Hong Kong: Government Printer, 1969), p. 88.
6. *2003 Gross Domestic Product* (Hong Kong: Census and Statistics Department, 2004), pp. 16, 20.
7. Ng Kwok-leung, 'More banks in Hongkong', *FEER*, 12 April 1962.
8. (1) Acting Financial Secretary letter to D. J. Kirkness (Colonial Office), 14 October 1963, pp. 7–8. HKRS160-3-25 'Report on the Financial Situation by the Acting Financial Secretary'.
9. Catherine R. Schenk, *Hong Kong as an International Financial Centre. Emergence andDdevelopment 1945–65* (London: Routledge, 2001), p. 66.
10. '… i.e. unsecured advances to directors, share dealing and property investment, under one overall limit of 55% of capital and reserves (which is the total of the three previously separate limits) and an individual limit for any one of them of 25%; thus limiting total indulgence in these practices while giving some choice as to the extent of indulgence in each one'. J. J. (later Sir John) Cowperthwaite, Financial Secretary, *HH*, 16 September 1964, pp. 331–2.
11. Robert Fell, *Crisis and Change. The Maturing of Hong Kong's Financial Markets* (Hong Kong: Longman, 1992), p. 180. His views carry added weight as a former Commissioner both for Securities and of Banking.
12. The government's extensive information on this bank's questionable record in property development is outlined in *Report of the Committee Appointed to Consider Certain Matters Concerning the Closure of the Chong Hing Mansion 1971* (Hong Kong: Government Printer, 1972) and M. 30. ACS(L) to Colonial Secretary, 11 April 1961. HKRS165-9-226 'Land Sales Question of Upset and Reserved Prices. Auction Rings and Transfers of Ownership Prior to Fulfilment of Conditions of Sale'.
13. See, for example, Catherine R. Schenk, 'Banking Groups in Hong Kong, 1945–65', *Asia Pacific Business Review*, Vol. 7, No. 2, (Winter 2000), pp. 145–6.
14. T. K. Ghose, *The Banking System of Hong Kong* (Singapore: Buttterworths, 1995, 2nd edition), pp. 72–3.
15. For details of bureaucratic ineptitude in dealing with this wholly unsatisfactory bank, see HKRS163-3-7 'The Chiu Tak Bank Ltd: 1. Application from … for Banking Licence; 2. Balance Sheet of …'.
16. Quoted by Catherine R. Schenk, 'Banking Crises and the Evolution of the Regulatory Framework in Hong Kong 1945–1970', *Australian Economic History Review*, Vol. 43, No. 2, (July 2003), p. 148.
17. (6) and (16) Commissioner of Banking memos to Financial Secretary, 19 March and 25 November 1965. HKRS163-1-3273.
18. Schenk, *Hong Kong as an International Financial Centre. Emergence and Development 1945–65*, pp. 69, 146.
19. Schenk, 'Banking Crises and the Evolution of the Regulatory Framework in Hong Kong 1945–1970', *Australian Economic History Review*, pp. 148–9.
20. This attack was carried by the *Far Eastern Economic Review* which at the time was owned by leading British firms, including HSBC. S. C. Chen, 'Bankers Stifling Hongkong Industries?', *FEER*, 12 October 1961.
21. *Fai Po*, 13 April 1965.
22. 'Editorial: A Stitch in Time', *FEER*, 25 March 1965.
23. Leonidas Cole, Banking Commissioner, quoted in *South China Morning Post*, 12 June

1965. He made this assertion in what purported to be a historical reference to the US.

24. HKIMR Historical Database. URL: https://www.hkimr.org/HK%20Economic%20History%20DB.xls. The coverage and quality of these statistics is limited.

25. The Ming Tak's depositors also benefited from this change of heart. With the help of a government loan and vigorous management of their assets in bankruptcy by the Official Receiver, both banks repaid their depositors in full. The former owner of Ming Tak showed considerable real estate skills in assisting the process, and by 1973, a net surplus had been produced. (14) 'Condensed Version of Minutes', 1 February 1966, p. 3. HKRS55-9-3-10 'Ming Tak Bank Minutes of Committee of Inspection'; Official Receiver and Trustee, letter to committee members, 9 November 1973. HKRS55-9-3-174 'Copies of Committee Meetings of Ming Tak Bank Held on 16th September 1969 and The Following Meetings'. The Canton Trust did not repay all its creditors until 1977 (*Hong Kong Standard*, 18 July 1991).

26. *Hong Kong Tiger Standard*, 11 May 1965.

27. On the most favourable estimate, the Canton Trust's losses were projected to 'be more than twelve times the amount of the bank's paid-up capital'. 'Summary of Statement of Affairs … up to 31st March 1966', Companies Winding Up No. 10 of 1965, p. 2. HKRS70-3-6-1 'Canton Trust and Commercial Bank Ltd'.

28. The pressures faced by the colonial administration to rescue ailing banks were well described by the Financial Secretary who presided over the financial failures of the 1980s. Sir John Bremridge, *HH*, 9 April 1986, p. 984.

29. Cowperthwaite, *HH*, 24 February 1966, pp. 54–5.

30. The index is calculated from applications for court exclusion orders to redevelop existing urban tenement buildings. It is derived from Roderick O'Brien, 'Rent and Tenure Controls for Pre-War Buildings', *Hong Kong Law Journal*, Vol. 7, No. 1 (1977), 'Table 3. Exclusion Orders', p. 41. It measures the initial commitment of a developer to a project. It excludes 'greenfield' projects, which would not have been of great significance in this period. The table does not include data for 1969–70.

31. The danger from involvement in property was highlighted in H. J. Tomkins, *Report on the Hong Kong Banking System and Recommendations for the Replacement of the Banking Ordinance 1948* (Hong Kong: Government Printer, 1962), p.6. The position was no better in 1965. (4) Banking Commissioner secret memo to Financial Secretary, 16 September 1965. HKRS163-1-3284 'Problems Affecting the Real Estate and Allied Industries'.

32. Cowperthwaite, *HH*, 17 January 1962, p. 6.

33. Cowperthwaite, *HH*, 24 February 1966, pp. 54–5.

34. M. 9. PACS (L) to DCS, 15 December 1965. HKRS163-1-3284.

35. Cowperthwaite, *HH*, 25 February 1965, p. 65.

36. Cowperthwaite, *HH*, 26 February 1964, p. 45. The contribution of the colonial administration's property laws and policies to this crisis is analysed in a well-known paper, Stephen N. S. Cheung, 'Rent Control and Housing Reconstruction: The Postwar Experience of Prewar Premises in Hong Kong' *Journal of Law and Economics*, Vol. 22, April 1979.

37. Cowperthwaite, *HH*, 26 February 1964, p. 45.

38. On this broadminded policy, see Commissioner of Banking memo to Financial Secretary, 'Bank Loans — Dao Heng Bank Ltd and Kwong On Bank Ltd', 23 March

1966. HKRS163-3-249 'Banking Emergency 1965 — Matters Arising from … Staff etc'.

39. (13) Commissioner of Banking to Financial Secretary, 2 September 1965. HKRS163-1-3273.

40. Bank inspections by selected auditors to ensure the accuracy of the banks' statistical returns were stepped up during the crisis despite anxiety about provoking further falls in public confidence in the banks' integrity. See Minutes of the Banking Advisory Committee Meeting, 18 March 1965, p. 1. HKRS163-1-3185 'Banking Advisory Committee'.

41. Market gossip could be dangerously misleading. For an example, see the withdrawal of the allegation that China state-owned banks had contributed to the crisis. 'Editorial: Post Mortem', *FEER*, 25 February 1965.

42. A. G. Clarke, Financial Secretary, *HH*, 23 March 1960, pp. 128–9.

43. Cowperthwaite, *HH*, 24 February 1966, p. 57 and 1; March 1967, p. 82.

44. (26) Cowperthwaite letter to Sir Frank Figgures (UK Treasury), 19 October 1970 and 'A Preliminary Note on the International Monetary Fund with Reference to Dependent Territories (and with Particular Reference to Hong Kong)', pp. 11, 12. HKRS163-9-217 '(A) Meeting of Senior Commonwealth Finance Officials 1970. Sterling Area Balance Of Payments — Developments and Prospects To Mid-1971; (B) Overseas Sterling Area Countries Statistics'.

45. This account of the clash between the colonial administration and the property magnates is based on (1) Messrs Deacons & Co letter to Colonial Secretary forwarding a 12-page memorandum from the Real Estate Developers Association of Hong Kong, 9 September 1965; M. 1. Financial Secretary to PACS(L), 10 September 1965); (7) Rating and Valuation Department memo to DCS, 'The Real Estate Developers Association of Hong Kong', Appendix D, 16 September 1965; (4) Commissioner of Banking secret memo to Colonial Secretary, 'Real Estate Developers Association, 16 September 1965; M. 9. PACS(L) to DCS, 15 December 1965, HKRS163-1-3284 'Problems Affecting the Real Estate And Allied Industries'. The Banking Commissioner argued that the data might 'all too easily be quoted out of context'.

46. *HH,* 24 February 1966, pp. 57–8, 59.

47. As Cowperthwaite himself subsequently acknowledged. *HH*, 24 March 1966, p. 215.

48. During the government's elaborate but confidential exercise in 1965 to defend itself against the property developers' claims that it had caused the crisis, officials did not bother to examine the figures on redevelopment plans. See HKRS163-1-3284.

49. (128) Commissioner of Banking letter to Financial Secretary, 4 May 1971. HKRS163-3-12 'Banking Statistics: 1. Supply of … to S. of S. Policy Concerning .'.

50. Minutes of 96th meeting, 21 May 1965, p. 4. HKRS163-1-118 'Federation of Hong Kong Industries Minutes of the Meetings of the …'.

51. Despite an attempt by these officials to make the best case possible for financing industry. 'Report on the Fact-Finding Survey of Small-Scale Industry', (Commerce and Industry Department, 9 January 1969, mimeo.); Industry Development Branch, 'The Case for Improved Access to Loans for Re-equipment Purposes by Small Scale Industry' (Department of Commerce and Industry, IND 2/903, 27 October 1969, mimeo); 'Memorandum to the Loans for Small Industry Committee' (Commerce and Industry Department, IND 2/903, 4 November 1969, mimeo).

52. E. P. Ho, Director of Commerce and Industry, *HH*, 11 April 1973, pp. 705–6; H. C. Y. Ho, *The Fiscal System of Hong Kong* (London: Croom Helm, 1979), p. 62.

53. Cowperthwaite, *HH*, 25 March 1970, pp. 495–6.

54. The text is at *HH*, 24 February 1966, p. 54 *et seq.*

55. *Ibid.*, p. 56.

56. Cowperthwaite's misleading analysis was eventually corrected by his successor, not just with the benefit of hindsight but with the aid of GDP estimates reconstructed for the previous decade. See C. P. (later Sir Philip) Haddon-Cave, Financial Secretary, *HH*, 1 March 1972, p. 422 and 15 November 1972, p.163.

57. *HH*, 25 March 1970, p. 490.

58. *HH*, 22 February 1966, p.57; 1 March 1967, p. 82.

59. In 1970, Cowperthwaite specifically referred to the deflationary impact of an increase in the government's overseas holdings. *HH*, 25 February 1970, p. 363.

60. Sir Robert Black, *HH*, 26 February 1964, p. 37; Cowperthwaite, *HH*, 25 February 1965, pp. 64, 66 and 8 October 1969, p. 86.

61. Other members tended to echo the HSBC's sentiments. Circular No. 49 'Yau Yue Commercial Bank', 18 February 1953; Circular No. 53 'Overseas Bank Ltd', 14 October 1953; Circular No. 69 'Banque Nationale pour le Commerce et l'Industrie', 11 December 1957. HKRS163-1-679 'Banking Advisory Committee'.

62. (86) Financial Secretary, 'Memorandum to Members of the Banking Advisory Committee ... Licensing Policy', 23 October 1959, p. 2. HKRS163-1-679 .

63. Apart from HSBC, the rest were owned by the Chinese state. 'Exchange & Financial Markets: Hongkong Licensed Banks & Native Bank Firms', *FEER*, 17 November 1948; (6) Commissioner of Banking memo to Financial Secretary, 19 March 1965. HKRS163-1-3273.

64. Circular No. 95 'Banking Ordinance — Chapter 155 Bank Negara Indonesia', 16 June 1961. HKRS163-1-679.

65. H. J. Tomkins to Financial Secretary, 5 March 1965, 'Suggested Measures to Deal with the Aftermath of the Failure of the Canton Trust & Commercial Bank, Limited', p. 8. HKRS163-3-249.

66. Lifted temporarily in 1972, again between 1975 and 1978, and then substantially relaxed in 1981 covering applications from Hong Kong for the first time. T. K. Ghose, *The Banking System of Hong Kong* (Singapore: Butterworths, 1987), pp. 76–8; Haddon-Cave, *HH*, 27 May 1981, pp. 893–5. Foreign banks were not freed from all restrictions until 2001.

67. See M. D. Cartland, Secretary for Financial Services, *HH*, 27 April 1994, p. 3477.

68. Catherine R. Schenk, 'The origins of Anti-competitive Regulation: Was Hong Kong 'Over-banked' in the 1960s?', *HKIMR Working Paper No.9/2006*, July 2006, pp. 8–9, 11, 15.

69. Rate-fixing was estimated to have cost the banks' customers the equivalent of 0.3 per cent of GDP in 1987 and 0.8 per cent in 1991. Consumer Council, *Are Hong Kong Depositors Fairly Treated?* (Hong Kong: Consumer Council, 1994), p. 7.

70. Until 1995, it had also set the minimum commissions and charges for such services as foreign exchange and securities. Stephen Ip, Secretary for Financial Services, *GIS*, 7 March 2001.

71. Haddon-Cave, *HH*, 3 July 1974, p. 954.

CHAPTER **9**

1. Census and Statistics Department, *2003 Gross Domestic Product* (Hong Kong: Hong Kong SARG, 2004), pp. 14–5, 78–9. Figures for earlier years and more detailed breakdowns are not available.
2. *2003 Gross Domestic Product* (Hong Kong: Census and Statistics Department, 2004), pp. 16, 20.
3. Tsang Shu-ki, 'The Economy', in Donald H. McMillen and Man Si-wei (eds), *The Other Hong Kong Report 1994* (Hong Kong: Chinese University Press, 1994), p. 132.
4. C. P. (later Sir Philip) Haddon-Cave, Financial Secretary, *HH*, 28 February 1973, p. 495.
5. These developments were well reported in *FEER*. See for example, Andrew Davenport, 'Banking: FNCB: Generous to a Fault?', 9 May 1975; Emily Lau, 'Hongkong: Hunting the Fugitives', 3 March 1988 and 'The law: Hongkong Stumbles Again in its Carrian Prosecution: Carry on Carrian', 18 May 1989.
6. *FEER:* John G. Robert, 'The Phantom Dollar', 11 December 1969; Dick Wilson, Asiadollars: Singapore Widens its Lead', 1 April 1972; 'The Asiadollar Market: Asia's Financial Crossroad', 17 September 1973; Peter Simms, 'Asiadollar: A Sign of Independence', 20 December 1974.
7. This issue had become a topic of concern to financial regulators overseas in the previous decade. For the US Federal Reserve System's views, see Frederick R. Dahl, 'International Operations of U.S. Banks: Growth and Public Policy Implications', *Law and Contemporary Problems,* Vol. 32, No. 1, Part 2 (Winter 1967), pp. 101, 129 in particular.
8. *Report of the Advisory Committee on Diversification 1979* (Hong Kong: Government Printer, 1979), p. 167.
9. Suzanne Berger and Richard K. Lester (eds), *Made By Hong Kong* (Hong Kong: Oxford University Press, 1997), p. 21.
10. Derived from Enclosures 76, 116, 157 and 186. HKRS163-3-12 'Banking Statistics: 1. Supply of … to S. of S. Policy Concerning …'.
11. Henry Wai-chung Yeung, *Transnational Corporations and Business Networks. Hong Kong Firms in the Asian Region* (London: Routledge, 1998), Chapter 4. Note his comment on p. 250, fn 11: 'Up to 80 per cent of HKFDI went to the PRC during the 1980s', which indicates the relatively limited proportion that was invested elsewhere in Asia.
12. This geographical convenience is illustrated by Tony Fu-Lai Yu, *Entrepreneurship and Economic Development in Hong Kong* (London: Routledge, 1997), pp. 103, 127.
13. For example, *Yangcheng Wanbao*, 17 March 1982; *Renmin Ribao*, 8 March 1985; Xu Dixin, 'On Hong Kong's Economic Relations with the Chinese Mainland', *Liaowang* (Overseas Edition), 16 September 1985, pp. 22–3; Peng Naidian, 'Reflections on Deepening Economic and Trade Cooperation between Guangdong, Hong Kong, Macao', *Guoji Maoyi*, No. 6, (27 June 1988), pp. 13–6.
14. Chau Tak Hay, Secretary for Commerce and Industry, *GIS*, 21 May 2001. However, an unknown proportion of the funds labelled as of Hong Kong origin represented 'round tripping'. Mainland organisations bought shell companies in Hong Kong that were then used to re-invest the funds in the Mainland and qualify for the generous tax and customs treatment enjoyed by external investors. Yasheng Huang, *FDI in China. An Asian Perspective* (Hong Kong: Chinese University Press, 1998), pp. 56–7.

15. Josephine M. Chesterton and Tushar K. Ghose, *Merchant Banking in Hong Kong* (Hong Kong: Butterworths Asia, 1998), pp. 29–32.

16. Y. C. Jao, 'The Rise of Hong Kong as a Financial Centre', *Asian Survey*, Vol. 19, No. 7 (July 1979), p. 687. The post-colonial government takes a similar view. See Frederick Ma, Secretary for Financial Services and the Treasury, *GIS*, 10 June 2006.

17. Howard Curtis Reed, 'The Ascent of Tokyo as an International Financial Center', *Journal of International Business Studies*, Vol. 11, No. 3 (Winter 1980), 'Table 3. Rankings of Asian International Bank Centers', p. 28.

18. J. J. (later Sir John) Cowperthwaite, Financial Secretary, *HH*, 30 March 1967, p. 251.

19. Haddon-Cave, *HH*, 5 January 1972, p. 318.

20. Haddon-Cave, *HH*, 28 February 1973, pp. 491, 494–5.

21. On the US background, see Andrew F. Brimmer and Frederick R. Dahl, 'Growth of American International Banking: Implications for Public Policy', *Journal of Finance*, Vol. 30, No. 2 (May 1975), pp. 342–3.

22. (1) Exchange Controller memo to Financial Secretary, 'Foreign Banks in the Colony', 26 October 1968; Commissioner of Banking memo to Financial Secretary, 'Foreign Banks in Hong Kong', 12 March 1969. HKRS163-3-369 'Foreign Banks in Hong Kong Capitalization Requirements'.

23. Sir Murray (later Lord) MacLehose, Governor, *HH*, 17 October 1973, p. 26.

24. M. 9. AS (E3) to DES, 21 August 1972. HKRS163-3-12.

25. Haddon-Cave, *HH*, 3 July 1974, p. 955.

26. MacLehose, *HH*, 6 October 1976, p. 9. While expressing such sentiments, the colonial administration paid some lip service to the protection of depositors. Haddon-Cave, *HH*, 15 March 1978, p. 623.

27. Jao, 'The Rise of Hong Kong as a Financial Centre', *Asian Survey*, p. 688.

28. For a good summary of this trend, see Robert Z. Aliber, 'Financial Innovation and the Boundaries of Banking', *Managerial and Decision Economics*, Vol. 8, No. 1 (March 1987), pp. 67–9.

29. These arrangements are described in Y. C. Jao, 'Monetary System and Banking structure', in H. C. Y. Ho and L. C. Chau (eds), *The Economic System of Hong Kong* (Hong Kong: Asian Research Service, 1988), p. 45.

30. In financing manufacturers, loans had a large offshore dimension. They were raised to finance imports of raw materials and machinery and secured, formally or informally, against an export contract and also involved sales and purchases of foreign currency. Loans to finance share and property transactions in Hong Kong were entirely onshore and involved only the Hong Kong dollar which, unlike foreign currencies, could not be supplied by head office.

31. M. 9. AS(E3) to DES, 21 August 1972; M. 11. Exchange Controller to DES, 23 August 1972. HKRS163-3-12.

32. Haddon-Cave, *HH*, 29 November 1973, pp. 229–30. The inaccuracy of this statement to the legislature is evident from M. 11. Exchange Controller to DES, 23 August 1972. HKRS163-3-12.

33. Haddon-Cave, *HH*, 11 April 1979, p. 709.

34. Haddon-Cave, *HH*, 15 November 1979, p. 217.

35. *Banque National de Paris Hong Kong Branch vs CIR* (1985) 2 HKTC 155; A. J. Halkyard, 'Revenue — Deductibility of Interest ...', *Hong Kong Law Journal*, Vol. 16, No. 3 (1986), pp. 439, 441.

36. Note the official attempt to divert public attention away from this issue by Haddon-Cave. *HH*, 29 November 1973, p. 229.
37. Based on Leo F. Goodstadt, 'Crisis and Challenge: The Changing Role of the Hongkong & Shanghai Bank, 1950–2000', *HKIMR Working Paper No.13/2005*, July 2005, p. 26
38. *Ibid.*
39. Frederick Ma, Secretary for Financial Services and the Treasury, *GIS*, 18 November 2002.
40. Derived from *Hong Kong Annual Digest of Statistics* (Hong Kong: Government Printer), 1978 and 1982 editions.
41. Philip Bowring, 'Hongkong's Banks: Newcomers Squeeze the Establishment', *FEER*, 1 April 1974; Y. C. Jao, *Banking and Currency in Hong Kong. A Study of Postwar Financial Development* (London: Macmillan, 1974), p. 96.
42. For example, two-thirds of all public listings were by way of private placements, to the alarm of the government. Haddon-Cave, *HH*, 25 February 1976, p. 501.
43. Haddon-Cave, *HH*, 8 January 1975, p. 340.
44. The Financial Secretary misunderstood what was driving the money supply until the end of the decade. Haddon-Cave, *HH*, 16 November 1978, pp. 208–9 and 28 February 1979, p. 548.
45. The Financial Secretary remained muddled about Hong Kong's monetary system even after he began to link macroeconomic policies to banking operations. Haddon-Cave, *HH*, 12 April 1979, pp. 762–3 and 9 December 1981, pp. 236–7.
46. Note Yen-P'ing Hao, 'Themes and Issues in Chinese Business History', in Robert Gardella *et al* (eds), *Chinese Business History. Interpretative Trends and Priorities for the Future* (Armonk: M. E. Sharpe Inc., 1998), p. 135.
47. This process is summed up by Lau Chi Kuen, *Hong Kong's Colonial Legacy* (Hong Kong: Chinese University Press, 1997), pp. 88–93.
48. The examples which follow are based on Haddon-Cave's statements in *HH*: 5 November 1975, p. 189; 8 January 1975, p. 342; 3 December 1975, p. 297; 16 November 1978, p. 209; 28 February 1979, p. 554.
49. Anthony Rowley, 'Banking/Hongkong: Not-so-super Vision: The Territory Admits Scrutiny of Financial Institutions is Not All it Should be and Summons Outside Help', *FEER*, 1 March 1984.
50. Philip Bowring, in Philip Bowring *et al*, 'Symposium on Prudential Supervision of Financial Institutions in Hong Kong', *Hong Kong Economic Papers*, Vol. 1985, No. 16 (1985 December), p. 98.
51. Haddon-Cave, *HH*, 15 March 1978, p. 623.
52. See, for example, the evidence given in the Carrian case by an HSBC Senior Manager Credit, *South China Morning Post*, 11 March 1986.
53. *FEER*: 'Sandberg and the Market', 23 September 1972; Stewart Dalby, 'Will the bubble burst?', 2 December 1972.
54. 'Hongkong Bank Spurs a Rally', *FEER*, 13 May 1974.
55. See Leo Goodstadt, 'Controls Come to the Rock of Laissez-faire', *Euromoney*, April 1979, pp. 121–3; 'Whatever the Reasons, Hong Kong keeps Growing', *Euromoney*, July 1982, pp. 134–7; 'Why Hong Kong Still Trusts Interests Rates', *Asian Banking*, January 1982, p. 56.
56. This restraint was a display of 'public-spiritedness' according to Kurt Schuler, 'Episodes from Asian Monetary History: A Brief History of Hong Kong Monetary

Standards', *Asian Monetary Monitor*, Vol. 12, No. 5, (September-October 1989), p. 23.

57. *South China Morning Post*, 23 July 1985, 11 April 1986.

58. Philip Bowring, 'Freebooters Must Abide by Ethical Standards', *FEER*, 17 September 1976.

59. *FEER*: 'Extending Code', 16 September 1977; Philip Bowring, 'There is Still Much Investigation Needed', 23 September 1977.

60. Leo Goodstadt, 'The Weekend Wardley Won Wharf for Pao', *Asian Banking*, August 1980.

61. See Christopher Wood, 'Company Profile: The Hongkong Bank Must Diversify While Avoiding Headlong Retreat. Strategy for Survival', *FEER*, 20 September 1984.

62. *South China Morning Post*, 8 April 2000 and 22 March 2002.

63. Anthony Rowley and Philip Bowring, 'Finance: With Cynical Abandon: Hongkong's Authorities Continue to Look on as the Scale of DTC Failure Grows — and Depositors Lose Their Money', *FEER*, 3 March 1983.

64. Robert Fell, *Crisis and Change. The Maturing of Hong Kong's Financial Markets* (Hong Kong: Longman, 1992), p. 159.

65. Andrew F. Freris, *The Financial Markets of Hong Kong* (London: Routledge, 1991), Tables 2.14, 2.15, p. 48.

66. See Josephine M. Chesterton and Tushar K. Ghose, *Merchant Banking in Hong Kong* (Hong Kong: Butterworths Asia, 1998), pp. 24–6.

67. *FEER*: 'The Banking System: Protect Depositors — or Let Jungle Law Prevail', 17 March 1983; Anthony Rowley, 'Banking: A time For Change: More Professionalism is Being Introduced Into Hongkong's Financial Administration', 9 May 1985.

68. A useful though incomplete summary of the bank failures is provided by Freris, *The Financial Markets of Hong Kong*, Table 2.9, pp. 40–1. On p. 39, he misleadingly argues that criminal activities were not a major factor.

69. T. K. Ghose, *The Banking System of Hong Kong* (Singapore: Butterworths, 1987), p. 96. The actual exposure of the Exchange Fund in supporting these banks was probably significantly higher at the height of the crisis.

70. *2003 Gross Domestic Product*, p. 81.

71. Fell, *Crisis and Change. The Maturing of Hong Kong's Financial Markets*, pp. 158–9.

72. For an excellent overview of the complex relations between the banks that failed, their overseas connections and the efforts to rescue them commercially, see Ghose, *The Banking System of Hong Kong*, pp. 88–96.

73. *FEER*: Brian Robins, 'Companies: No Helping Hand: The affairs of Nugan Hand will continue to be probed despite the lack of cooperation from the CIA and FBI', 21 April 1983; Philip Bowring, 'Companies: Milchcow to Turn Sour?: Wing On minority may block bank cash injection', 12 June 1986.

74. Anthony Rowley, 'Hongkong Regulation: Fresh Powers to Tackle a "Deadly Mixture"', *FEER*, 8 May 1986.

75. *South China Morning Post*, 2 November 1987 and 10 October 1988; *Hong Kong Standard*, 24 March 1988.

76. Philip Bowring, 'Hongkong's Hearts Fall at Ease', *FEER*, 13–9 August 1982.

77. On the official embarrassment after disclosure of this investigation, see John Church, 'Booms, Bursts, and Business as Usual', *South China Morning Post*, 6 November 2003.

78. Jonathan Friedland, 'Jailed Lawyer: Testimony Could Reopen Major Cases. Loose Ends', *FEER*, 31 January 1990.

79. Bremridge argued that it was impracticable to 'legislate for the complete protection of fools', as he put it (*HH*, 30 July 1975, p. 949). Haddon-Cave quoted this remark to justify his refusal 'to ensure that deposit-taking companies conduct their businesses with complete safety for depositors' (*HH*, 5 November 1975, p. 189).

80. His arguments against regulation included the difficulties of enforcement in an open economy like Hong Kong but also a defence of 'virtuous' speculation: 'Let us not also forget those little men who have made fortunes by intelligent speculation'. *HH*, 30 July 1975, pp. 948–9.

81. *Ibid.*, pp. 950–1.

82. Bremridge, *HH*, 19 March 1986, p. 771.

83. Bremridge, *HH*, 19 March 1986, p. 771.

84. On the latter period, see the comments of Richard Farrant, Adviser to the Banking Commissioner, in Philip Bowring *et al*, 'Symposium on Prudential Supervision of Financial Institutions in Hong Kong', *Hong Kong Economic Papers*, pp. 104–5.

85. Before World War II, at Hong Kong's own request, London had agreed that the Exchange Fund's secrecy could be relaxed. R. A. C. North, Colonial Secretary, *HH*, 13 October 1937, p. 111. No convincing reason was put forward to explain why total secrecy was imposed after 1945, especially when other territories under British rule, such as Malaya and Singapore, published their accounts. See Frank H. H. King, *Money in British East Asia* (London: HMSO, 1957), pp. 122, 158 *et seq.*

86. See Bremridge, *HH*, 9 April 1986, pp. 981–7. He made it plain that the criticism of the government on legal and political grounds in the legislature had compelled him to defend his record publicly.

CHAPTER **10**

1. For a somewhat uncritical overview of the history and workings of the currency board system, see Steve H. Hanke, 'Currency Boards', *Annals of the American Academy of Political and Social Science*, Vol. 579 (January 2002).

2. Atish R. Ghosh *et al*, 'Currency Boards: More than a Quick Fix?', *Economic Policy*, Vol. 15, No. 31 (October 2000), p. 272.

3. W. Max Corden, 'Exchange Rate Regimes for Emerging Market Economies: Lessons from Asia', *Annals of the American Academy of Political and Social Science*, Vol. 579, (January 2002), pp. 33–4. This analysis indicates that other factors which were important included appropriate fiscal measures and government support for financial institutions under pressure — deviations from the strict currency board régime.

4. Y. C. Jao, 'The Working of the Currency Board: The Experience of Hong Kong 1935–1997', *Pacific Economic Review*, Vol. 3, No. 3 (1998), pp. 219, 220.

5. Gerard L. M. Clauson, 'Some Uses of Statistics in Colonial Administration', *Journal of the Royal African Society*, Vol. 36, No. 145 (October 1937), p. 14.

6. The specific project was urban renewal. (4) Governor secret letter to Secretary of State for the Colonies, 2 February 1939; (5) Secretary of State letter to Governor, 3 April 1939. HKRS163-1-507 'Excess Population Committee Pre-war Correspondence re …'.

7. Exchange Fund profits had swollen the value of sterling assets held to back the

colony's banknotes to 139 per cent of their face value by 1963 compared with 108 per cent in 1956. See *HH*: A. G. Clarke, Financial Secretary, 27 February 1957, p. 32; Cowperthwaite, Financial Secretary, 27 February 1963, p. 36.

8. This point was made specifically in M. 8., 12 May 1964. HKRS163-1-2522 'Finance Investment of Colonial Government Funds'.
9. Cowperthwaite, *HH*, 18 December 1963, pp. 303–4.
10. Economist Intelligence Unit, *The Commonwealth and Europe* (London: Economist Intelligence Unit, 1960), p. 390.
11. Cowperthwaite, *HH*, 18 December 1963, pp. 303–4.
12. The Colonial Office viewed the reserves' role as the source of finance for development programmes. Michael Havinden and David Meredith, *Colonialism and Development: Britain and Its Tropical Colonies, 1850–1960* (London: Routledge, 1993), pp. 269–70.
13. Albert O. Hirschman, 'Economic Policy in Underdeveloped Countries', *Economic Development and Cultural Change*, Vol. 5, No. 4 (July 1957), p. 366.
14. *HH*: Clarke, 29 February 1956, p. 92; Lo Man Wai, 21 March 1956, p. 118; Ngan Shing-kwan, 21 March 1956, pp., 118, 121.
15. Clarke, *HH*, 2 March 1955, p. 52; 29 February 1956, p. 91; 27 February 1957, p. 31; 6 March 1958, p. 47.
16. C. E. M. Terry, *HH*, 20 March 1957, p. 61. Terry was nominated to the Legislative Council by the Hong Kong General Chamber of Commerce.
17. Clarke, *HH*, 23 March 1960, p. 123. A related criticism in the 1960s was the claim by businessmen that the sterling investment portfolio earned less than the profits to be made from investments in Hong Kong. *HH*: S. S. (later Sir Sydney) Gordon, 18 March 1963 p. 101; K. A. Watson, 12 March 1969, p. 127.
18. Clarke, *HH*, 1 March 1961, p. 46.
19. The size and composition of the government's reserves held by the Exchange Fund were withheld from the public during the period covered by this book. Andrew F. Freris, *The Financial Markets of Hong Kong* (London: Routledge, 1991), p. 188.
20. On the relationship between transfers of official reserves to and from sterling and the local money supply in the 1950s, see Frank H. H. King, *Money in British East Asia* (London: HMSO, 1957), p. 120. A formal discussion of key features of Hong Kong's currency board arrangements in later decades can be found in Freris, *The Financial Markets of Hong Kong*, pp. 215–26.
21. This feature of the Hong Kong system was often misunderstood. See Cowperthwaite, *HH*, 6 September 1967, p. 396.
22. Management of Hong Kong's reserves under a currency board requires a much higher level of technical expertise than this simplified account implies. An illustration of the complexity of this task can be found in an exposition by Hong Kong Monetary Authority's Chief Executive. Joseph Yam, *Review of Currency Board Arrangements in Hong Kong* (Hong Kong: Hong Kong Monetary Authority, 1998), p. 12.
23. For example, *HH*: Cowperthwaite, 27 February 1963, p. 41 and 10 March 1966, p. 57; Haddon-Cave, 28 March 1973, p. 645 and 26 February 1975, p. 484, fn 53 and *GIS*, 1 February 1982.
24. The government ignored the warning of dangerous over-exposure to property among locally owned Chinese banks. H. J. Tomkins, *Report on the Hong Kong Banking System and Recommendations for the Replacement of the Banking Ordinance 1948* (Hong

Kong: Government Printer, 1962), p.6. The failure to curb bank property portfolios was a major factor in the 1965 bank crisis. See (4) Banking Commissioner secret memo to Financial Secretary, 16 September 1965. HKRS163-1-3284 'Problems Affecting the Real Estate and Allied Industries'.

25. Cowperthwaite believed (erroneously) that spending government deposits locally would cause a credit squeeze (*HH*, 1 March 1967, p. 82). He seemed muddled about the role of banks in creating liquidity (*HH*, 24 February 1966, pp. 56–7). Haddon-Cave was even more confused about monetary policy and banking (*HH*, 12 April 1979, pp. 762–3 and 9 December 1981, pp. 236–7).

26. For example, *HH*, 25 March 1970, pp. 495–6 and 'Interview', *The Banker*, Vol.120, No. 533 (July 1970), pp. 741–2. His hostility to the release of socio-economic information was evident before he became Financial Secretary. M. 18. to Colonial Secretary, 21 October 1958. HKRS41-1-9339(1) 'Pilot Social Survey of Shek Kip Mei Resettlement Area'.

27. Haddon-Cave was totally unapologetic about the failure to collect data even after the adverse results of this policy had become evident. *HH*, 8 January 1975, pp. 342–3.

28. Cowperthwaite, *HH*, 28 March 1968, p. 212; Haddon-Cave, *HH*, 16 April 1980, p. 733.

29. This loophole seriously weakened the contribution of statutory ratios to regulating the money supply. Tony Latter, 'Hong Kong's Exchange Rate Regimes in the Twentieth Century: The Story of Three Regime Changes', *HKIMR Working Paper No. 17/2004*, September 2004, p. 24.

30. Clarke, *HH*, 2 March 1955, p. 52; 29 February 1956, p. 91; 6 March 1958, p. 65.

31. In theory, there was a separate exchange rate set by the colony's free currency rate. In 1949, it had fallen to HKD8 = USD1 (compared with the official parity of HKD5.7 = USD1). This depreciation was caused by the advances of People's Liberation Army and was resolved politically. C. G. S. (later Sir Charles) Follows, Financial Secretary, *HH*, 8 March 1950, p. 46.

32. Although he accepted that budget deficits could help to offset a business downturn. *HH*, 24 February 1966, p. 57; 25 February 1970, p. 363.

33. Cowperthwaite, *HH*, 24 February 1966, p. 57.

34. A full analysis of these events was provided in Chapter 9, 'From Banking Crisis to Financial Catastrophe'.

35. *Asian Monetary Monitor* published convincing contemporary analyses of how flawed was the colonial administration's management of monetary affairs. For example: 'Hong Kong: An Attempt to Control the Money Supply', Vol. 3, No. 1 (January-February 1979) and 'Hong Kong: Proposals for a Reform of the Monetary System', Vol. 3, No. 2 (March-April 1979).

36. 'For the time being, it is, I believe, more appropriate to continue to depend primarily on interest rates to influence the growth rate of loans and advances, and hence of the money supply' (Haddon-Cave, *HH*, 28 February 1979, p. 554). He had previously claimed that 'our interest rates are no longer determined internally in isolation, but have to adapt to the trend of interest rates world-wide' (*ibid*, 14 November 1974, p. 218). For a powerful critique of this policy, see 'Hong Kong: The Role of Interest Rates in the Adjustment Mechanism', *Asian Monetary Monitor*, Vol. 3, No. 5 (September-October 1979).

37. *HH*, 23 October 1975, p. 107.

38. Bremridge, *HH*, 30 July 1975, p. 948.
39. Details of these events are recorded in HKRS163-1-1376 'Industry and Production. Industrial Situation in Hong Kong' and HKRS1017-3-4 'Unemployment Relief'.
40. The cumulative net profits by the end of the controls were equivalent to almost a quarter of the government's total revenue for the financial year 1954–55. Clarke, *HH*, 2 March 1955, p. 49.
41. Clarke, *HH*, 27 March 1957, p. 116.
42. Clarke, *HH*, 24 March 1954, p. 136.
43. HSBC's decision to redeem a significant quantity of banknotes repatriated from the Mainland after Mao Zedong's victory in 1949 may have added to the inflationary pressures. Letter to Colonial Office, 25 June 1959. HKRS163-1-1943 'Hong Kong Exchange Fund Operations by the Hong Kong & Shanghai Banking Corporation'.
44. Ricardo, 'Development of Banking in Hongkong during 1955', *FEER*, 2 February 1956.
45. On the relationship between transfers of official reserves to and from sterling and the local money supply in the 1950s, see King, *Money in British East Asia*, p. 120.
46. Frank H. H. King, *The Hong Kong Bank in the Period of Development and Nationalism, 1941–1984. From Regional Bank to Multinational Group* (Cambridge: Cambridge University Press, 1991), p. 338.
47. Clarke, *HH*, 27 March 1957, pp. 116–7.
48. Cowperthwaite, *HH*, 1 March 1967, p. 83 and 25 February 1970, p. 363.
49. His thinking on this issue was expressed most clearly in *HH*, 8 October 1965, p. 85.
50. Cowperthwaite, *HH*, 26 March 1969, p. 205. A decade later, the Attorney General advised that the ratio could not be used for monetary purposes, and the law was amended accordingly. Haddon-Cave, *HH*, 11 April 1979, p. 709.
51. Cowperthwaite also argued that the banks would adjust their ratios without government intervention. *HH*, 24 February 1966, p. 76 and 9 October 1970, pp. 113–4.
52. Cowperthwaite, *HH*, 8 October 1969, p. 85.
53. For his personal reminiscences of the lack of confidence even among industrialists, see *HH*, 28 March 1968, p. 212.
54. *HH*, 8 October 1969, p. 85.
55. (79) Cowperthwaite letter to W. F. Searle, Chief Statistician (Colonial Office), 8 June 1955. HKRS163-9-88. 'Trade. Balance of Payment Statistics. Policy Regarding Preparation of ...'. The rest of the letter shows that the principal reason for objecting to the compilation of balance of payments data was that London's 'main, if not sole, purpose for wanting the figures [was] ... the detection of illegal movements between sterling and dollars through Hong Kong'. The colonial administration was not prepared to gather information that might jeopardise the free currency market.
56. Small size had only limited relevance to Hong Kong's policies. There was the possible argument that it was not feasible 'to have a fully-fledged independent monetary system in some of the small isolated territories of the world — Malta, Mauritius and so on?'. A. R. Prest, *Public Finance in Underdeveloped Countries* (New York: Praeger, 1963), p. 108). In addition, the small size of the domestic market precluded the colonial administration from adopting infant industry and similar

policies. *Report of the Commission … to Enquire into the Causes and Effects of the Present Trade Recession …* (Hong Kong: Noronha & Co., 1935), pp. 89–90; Sir Robert Black letter Governor to Sir Hilton Poynton (Colonial Office), 19 July 1958. HKRS270-5-44 'Commercial and Industrial Development — Major Policy'.

57. Cowperthwaite, *HH*, 26 February 1964, p. 47 and 24 February 1966, p. 57. He ignored the contribution which this eminent economist made to monetary stability in the UK during World War II and to the British government's ability to control inflation, in J. M. Keynes, *How to Pay for the War. A Radical Plan for the Chancellor of the Exchequer* (London: MacMillan, 1940).
58. Cowperthwaite, *HH*, 8 October 1969, p. 85.
59. Cowperthwaite, *HH*, 26 February 1964, p. 47.
60. Cowperthwaite, *HH*, 24 February 1966, p. 57. On a later occasion, he conceded that 'there are good policy grounds for underspending in the good years with a view to overspending in the not so good' *HH*, 25 February 1970, p. 363.
61. For details see Commissioner of Banking memo to Financial Secretary, 'Bank Loans — Dao Heng Bank Ltd and Kwong On Bank Ltd', 23 March 1966. HKRS163-3-249 'Banking Emergency 1965 — Matters arising from … Staff etc'; Catherine R. Schenk, 'Banking Crises and the Evolution of the Regulatory Framework in Hong Kong 1945–1970', *Australian Economic History Review*, Vol. 43, No. 2 (July 2003), pp. 149–50.
62. See Leo F. Goodstadt, 'Dangerous Business Models: Bankers, Bureaucrats & Hong Kong's Economic Transformation, 1948–86', *HKIMR Working Paper No. 8/2006*, June 2006, pp. 16–7, 25–6.
63. Haddon-Cave, *HH*, 8 January 1975, p. 340.
64. *Estimates of Gross Domestic Product 1961 to 1994* (Hong Kong: Census and Statistics Department, 1995), p. 20. The technical background is set out lucidly in Y. C. Jao, 'Monetary System and Banking Structure', in H. C. Y. Ho and L. C. Chau (eds), *The Economic System of Hong Kong* (Hong Kong: Asian Research Service, 1988), pp. 44–6. See also Leo Goodstadt, 'How Hong Kong is Moving towards Banking Controls', *Euromoney*, July 1980, pp. 84–5 and 'Temporary Respite for the Hong Kong Dollar', *Euromoney*, December 1981, p. 163.
65. Anthony Latter, 'The Currency Board Approach to Monetary Policy — from Africa to Argentina and Estonia, via Hong Kong', in *Proceedings of the Seminar on Monetary Management Organized by the Hongkong Monetary Authority on 18–19 October 1993* (Hong Kong: Hong Kong Monetary Authority, n.d.), p. 28.
66. This analysis is based on the detailed account of the colonial administration's actions presented by Haddon-Cave, *HH*, 13 December 1972, pp. 218–29. See also *HH*, 14 November 1974, p. 218.
67. John Greenwood, 'The Monetary Framework Underlying the Hong Kong Dollar Stabilization Scheme', *China Quarterly*, No. 99 (September 1984), p. 633.
68. Tony Latter, 'Hong Kong's Exchange Rate Regimes in the Twentieth Century: The Story of Three Regime Changes', *HKIMR Working Paper No. 17/2004*, pp. 22, 24.
69. The split between overseas and local holdings of the reserves was obfuscated, for example, by not distinguishing between the fiscal reserves and Exchange Fund. See Haddon-Cave, *HH*, 27 February 1974, p. 557.
70. Haddon-Cave obscured the real situation by describing the Exchange Fund as actively intervening in the currency market and acquiring US dollars in significant quantities. *HH*, 25 February 1976, pp. 496, 517—8.

71. Haddon-Cave, *HH*, 2 March 1977, pp. 578–80.
72. It is hard to avoid the conclusion that his intention was to mislead the public. Haddon-Cave, *HH*, 20 April 1977, pp. 834–5.
73. Andrew F. Freris, *The Financial Markets of Hong Kong* (London: Routledge, 1991), 'HK Dollar, Effective Exchange Rate Index (Trade-Weighted), 1975–88)', Table 6.1, p. 185.
74. Haddon-Cave, *HH*, 16 November 1978, p. 208.
75. Haddon-Cave, *HH*, 28 February 1979, p. 550.
76. A fair summary of their uselessness after three years' implementation was: 'Under present arrangements, however, we see no prospect of the authorities … being able to stop the slide for long. Unless some serious steps are taken towards monetary reform, it is entirely conceivable that the Hong Kong dollar will continue to slide inexorably downwards' — which it did for a further twelve months. 'Hong Kong: How to Rescue HK$: Three Practical Proposals', *Asian Monetary Monitor*, Vol. 6, No. 5 (September-October 1982), pp. 11–2.
77. For examples of confusion and indecision, see Haddon-Cave, *HH*, 28 February 1979, p. 554; 12 April 1979, pp. 762–3; 9 December 1981, pp. 236–7.
78. John Gray, 'Monetary Management in Hong Kong: The Role of the Hongkong and Shanghai Banking Corporation Limited', in *Proceedings of the Seminar on Monetary Management Organized by the Hongkong Monetary Authority on 18–19 October 1993* (Hong Kong: Hong Kong Monetary Authority, n.d.), p. 60.
79. See the case presented, for example, in Adam S. Posen, 'Why Central Banks Should Not Burst Bubbles', *International Finance*, Vol. 9, No. 1 (2006).
80. *HH*, 15 January 1986, p. 479.
81. 'Hong Kong's Financial Crisis — History, Analysis, Prescription', *Asian Monetary Monitor*, Vol. 6, No. 6 (November-December 1982), p. 5.
82. Dudley Seers, 'A Model of Comparative Rates of Growth in the World Economy', *Economic Journal*, Vol. 72, No. 285 (March 1962), p. 57.
83. Tony Latter, 'Rules versus Discretion in Managing the Hong Kong Dollar, 1983–2006', *HKIMR Working Paper No.2/2007*, January 2007, pp. 10–2.
84. This adherence to the practices of the past in former colonial territories was noted by Prest, *Public Finance in Underdeveloped Countries*, pp. 102–6.

CHAPTER **11**

1. Dick Wilson, *Hong Kong! Hong Kong!* (London: Unwin Hyman, 1990), p. 6.
2. D. W. A. Blye, Secretary for Monetary Affairs, *GIS*, 24 November 1981.
3. President Jiang Zemin claimed that an annual 'profit' of USD5 billion was remitted to the UK. *Wen Wei Po*, 20 March 1993.
4. Hazelwood, 'Colonial External Finance Since the War', *Review of Economic Studies*, pp. 33, 46 fn 4.
5. H. A. Shannon, 'The Sterling Balances of the Sterling Area, 1939–49', *Economic Journal*, Vol. 60, No. 239 (September 1950), p. 549.
6. The refusal to supply London with information is analysed in Leo F. Goodstadt, 'Government without Statistics: Policy-making in Hong Kong 1925–85, with Special Reference to Economic and Financial Management', *HKIMR Working Paper No. 6/2006*, April 2006.
7. The clearest account of how this system worked before the demise of the colonial

empire is Philip W. Bell, *The Sterling Area in the Postwar World: International Mechanism and Cohesion, 1946–1952* (Oxford: Clarendon Press, 1956), pp. 4–8. It should be noted that while the author wrongly assumed that Hong Kong's system operated in the same way as other colonies, he recognised that its monetary arrangements were not identical.

8. In theory, colonies were not compelled to hold their entire reserves in London. See Frank H. H. King, 'Sterling Balances and the Colonial Monetary Systems', *Economic Journal*, Vol. 65, No, 260 (December 1956), p. 719; Ida Greaves, 'Colonial Trade and Payments', *Economica*, Vol. 24, No. 93 (February 1957), p. 55. But they were undoubtedly capital transfers to the UK. See Arthur Hazelwood, 'Colonial External Finance Since the War', *Review of Economic Studies*, Vol. 21, No. 1 (1953—1954), pp. 48–9.

9. Alex H. Choi, 'State-Business Relations and Industrial Restructuring', in Tak-Wing Ngo (ed), *Hong Kong's History. State and Society under Colonial Rule* (London: Routledge, 1999), pp. 149–50.

10. The World Bank view was that the minimum prudent level should be significant enough to cover more than six months recurrent expenditure. Sir John Cowperthwaite, Financial Secretary, *HH*, 26 March 1969, p. 206. However, the precise ratio recommended by the World Bank was fudged in this speech.

11. Cowperthwaite, *HH,* 1 March 1967, p. 83and 25 February 1970, p. 363.

12. These transfers were announced regularly in annual budgets starting from 1964.

13. The government's investment policy was explained in A. G. Clarke, Financial Secretary, *HH*, 27 March 1957, p. 117.

14. On the eve of London's devaluation in 1967, this bank's net sterling balances were HKD194 million: 92 per cent of the total for all 'unauthorised' banks and 12 per cent of the total for the entire banking industry. (92) Commissioner of Banking memo to Financial Secretary, 'Net Balances with Banks in U.K. as at 31st October 1967', 24 November 1967. HKRS163-1-3275 'Banking Statistics Various — 1967'.

15. (15) 'Hong Kong Civil Affairs Policy Directives. Financial Policy', revised draft, 7 July 1944. HKRS211-2-20 'Financial Policy'.

16. (135) AS(E) memo to Financial Secretary, 'Exchange Control Bank of China Trade between Canada and China', 22 April 1958; (1352) Sub-Manager Bank of China letter to AFS(E), 16 April 1958. HKRS163-9-141 'Exchange Control — Individual Problems Arising from Applications of Policy on … in Hong Kong'.

17. British hopes were disappointed even in the nineteenth century. P. J. Cain and A. G. Hopkins, *British Imperialism: Innovation and Expansion, 1688–1914* (London: Longman, 1993), p. 426.

18. Although an authoritative study asserted that 'politically and commercially, Hong Kong is of the very greatest importance to Great Britain', this claim was belied by these statistics which the authors cited. A Study Group of the Royal Institute of International Affairs, *Political and Strategic Interests of the United Kingdom. An Outline* (London: Oxford University Press, 1939), pp. 208–11, 222.

19. The original documents are reproduced in David Faure, *Colonialism and the Hong Kong Mentality* (Hong Kong: Centre of Asian Studies, 2003), pp. 135–6.

20. Board of Trade memo 'The Value and Cost of the Colony of Hong Kong to the United Kingdom', February 1957, top secret, requested by the Prime Minister. CO 1030/859 'Hong Kong — Value and Cost to the United Kingdom'.

21. Sir William Gorrell Barnes secret minute to Secretary of State for the Colonies, 7 July 1961; P. Selwyn minute to Gorell Barnes, 6 July 1961. CO1030/1300 'The Future of Hong Kong'. This file shows that the Bank of England had advised that it was hopeless to try to compile any statistics on the net commercial and financial gains from Hong Kong to the UK.

22. Details of this exercise are taken from N. A. S. Mills, Hongkong Bank Manager, confidential letter to P. B. Williams, Secretary for Administration, 26 November 1975; FCO Telegram 1201 of 1 December 1975; DCA/BILAT/1351C: (38) Director of Civil Aviation to Political Adviser 10 October 1975; (40) and (43) Director of Civil Aviation to Secretary for Administration, 5 and 19 November 1975.

23. Selwyn minute to Gorrell Barnes, 6 July 1961. CO1030/1300.

24. Gerold Krozewski, 'Sterling, the "Minor" Territories, and the End of Formal Empire, 1939–1958', *Economic History* Review, Vol. 46, No. 2 (1993), pp. 247, 250, 251.

25. Personal information from interviews in 1967–70 with Hong Kong officials involved in the negotiations. See also David Faure and Lee Pui-tak (eds), *A Documentary History of Hong Kong. Economy* (Hong Kong: Hong Kong University Press, 2004), pp. 217–31. There are hints about these pressure tactics in Frank H. H. King, *The Hong Kong Bank in the Period of Development and Nationalism, 1941–1984. From Regional Bank to Multinational Group* (Cambridge: Cambridge University Press, 1991), p. 634.

26. The guarantee arrangements were set out in H. M. Treasury, *The Basle Facility and the Sterling Area* (Cmnd 3787/1968).

27. Editorial Staff, 'Bluff and Blackmail', *FEER*, 24–30 November 1968.

28. Y. C. Jao, *Banking and Currency in Hong Kong. A Study of Postwar Financial Development* (London: Macmillan, 1974), pp. 143–8. These developments surprised contemporaries. Benjamin J Cohen, *The Future of Sterling as an International Currency* (London: Macmillan, 1971), p. 183, fn 2.

29. See, for example, Hong Kong's treatment on an equal footing with other major financial centres, in Susan Strange, 'Sterling and British Policy: A Political View', *International Affairs*, Vol. 47, No. 2 (April 1971), pp. 313, 314.

30. Greaves, 'Colonial Trade and Payments', *Economica*, p. 48.

31. A good overview of the characteristics of banking systems in the Third World in the closing stages of the colonial era can be found in Arthur I. Bloomfield, 'Some Problems of Central Banking in Underdeveloped Countries', *Journal of Finance*, Vol. 12, No. 2 (May 1957), especially pp. 192–4.

32. In only a handful of colonies was bank money a significant element in the money supply before World War II. Hong Kong was cited as an example. G. L. M. Clauson, 'The British Colonial Currency System', *Economic Journal*, Vol. 54, No. 213 (April 1944), pp. 2, 22.

33. Krozewski, 'Sterling, the 'Minor' Territories, and the End of Formal Empire, 1939–1958', *Economic History* Review, p. 246 fn 48, p. 251.

34. At the very least, the volume of credit tended to follow the needs of external trade. J. O. W. Olakanpo, 'Monetary Management in Dependent Economies', *Economica*, Vol. 28, No. 112. (November 1961), p. 399 fn 3, citing the experience of Ceylon (Sri Lanka).

35. Anthony Latter, 'The Currency Board Approach to Monetary Policy — from Africa to Argentina and Estonia, via Hong Kong', in *Proceedings of the Seminar on Monetary*

Management Organized by the Hong Kong Monetary Authority on 18–19 October 1993 (Hong Kong: Hong Kong Monetary Authority, n.d.), p. 27. A striking example of the resentments these arrangements created is provided by James H. Mittelman, 'Underdevelopment and Nationalisation: Banking in Tanzania', *Journal of Modern African Studies*, Vol. 16, No. 4. (December 1978), pp. 389–9 in particular.

36. For an extensive review of the way in which the UK ignored the well-being of colonial territories in the effort to rescue sterling from its frequent crises in the 1950s and 1960s, see Krozewski, 'Sterling, the "Minor" Territories, and the End of Formal Empire, 1939–1958', *Economic History Review*.

37. Ida Greaves, 'The Character of British Colonial Trade', *Journal of Political Economy*, Vol. 62, No. 1 (February 1954), pp. 3, 4–6. As she acknowledged, this analysis was derived from John Stuart Mill's theory of international trade.

38. On these issues, see H. W. Singer, 'The Distribution of Gains between Investing and Borrowing Countries', *American Economic Review*, Vol. 40, No. 2 (May 1950), p. 473; Greaves, 'Colonial Trade and Payments', *Economica*, pp. 48–9; Hla Myint, 'Economic Theory and the Underdeveloped Countries', *Journal of Political Economy*, Vol. 73, No. 5 (October 1965), pp. 477–8.

39. Even if full backing in sterling continued, it was noted in the analysis by Olakanpo, 'Monetary Management in Dependent Economies', *Economica*, pp. 397–8.

40. King, 'Sterling Balances and the Colonial Monetary Systems', *Economic Journal*, pp. 719–20.

41. H. Myint, 'An Interpretation of Economic Backwardness', *Oxford Economic Papers*, New Series, Vol. 6, No. 2 (June 1954), p. 158.

42. Clauson, 'The British Colonial Currency System', *Economic Journal*, pp. 17–21, 22.

43. Gerard L. M. Clauson, 'Some Uses of Statistics in Colonial Administration', *Journal of the Royal African Society*, Vol. 36, No. 145 (October 1937), p. 14.

44. This point was made in the context of similar misunderstandings about how currency boards work in another part of the colonial empire. A. N. R. Robinson, *The Mechanics of Independence: Patterns of Political and Economic Transformation in Trinidad and Tobago* (Barbados: University Press of the West Indies, 2001), p. 60.

45. The same view was held even by John Greenwood, the monetary economist who was the most trenchant critic of the colonial administration's mismanagement in the 1970s and 1980s. The list of assumptions that follows is based on his analysis in 'The Monetary Framework Underlying the Hong Kong Dollar Stabilization Scheme', *China Quarterly*, No. 99 (September 1984) pp. 631, 632.

46. Clarke claimed that an active monetary policy would be 'most unpalatable to a considerable proportion of the business community here'. *HH*, 24 March 1954, p. 136.

47. (79) Cowperthwaite letter to W. F. Searle, Chief Statistician (Colonial Office), 8 June 1955. HKRS163-9-88 'Trade. Balance of Payment Statistics. Policy Regarding Preparation of ...'.

48. For example, *HH*: Cowperthwaite, 27 February 1963, p. 41 and 10 March 1966, p. 57; Haddon-Cave, 28 March 1973, p. 645 and 26 February 1975, p. 484, f.n. 53; *GIS*, 1 February 1982. Haddon-Cave provided the clearest statement of the non-interventionist case: 'The Government does not attempt to regulate the economy either through its expenditure decisions or in other conventional ways, using monetary or fiscal devices. This is because the money supply is largely determined by the balance of trade as influenced from time to time by capital movements;

whilst any major attempt to regulate demand through variations in tax rates or internal borrowing would tend to bring about changes in expenditure on imports rather than influence the volume of domestic output in the required direction'. *HH*, 3 April 1975, p. 691, fn 4.

49. 'The lack of transparency at the time, concerning official operations, was probably accounted for by the fact that the authorities did not wish to admit that the much-vaunted automatic adjustment process of the textbook currency board could not be entirely relied upon in practice'. Tony Latter, 'Rules versus Discretion in Managing the Hong Kong dollar, 1983–2006', *HKIMR Working Paper No. 2/2007*, January 2007, p. 9.

50. Cowperthwaite, *HH*, 26 March 1969, p. 205.

51. The absence of restraints on the creation of liquidity in the Hong Kong context was noted by George A. Selgin, 'Central Banking: Myth and Reality', *Hong Kong Economic Papers*, No. 18 (December 1987), pp. 1–2. He focused on the position of the note-issuing banks when the Hong Kong exchange rate floated during the 1970s and the colonial administration ceased to back increases in the currency with an equivalent value in foreign assets. Foreign banks did not have to support their lending with any assets if they chose not to do so. On foreign banks' credit policies in the Third World generally, see Bloomfield, 'Some Problems of Central Banking in Underdeveloped Countries', *Journal of Finance*, pp. 192–3. Bell, however, suggests that UK banks generally had a liquidity advantage over local banks in British colonies. *The Sterling Area in the Postwar World: International Mechanism and Cohesion, 1946–1952*, p. 7.

52. This was the experience of American banks during the 1967 political violence. M. 76. AS(EM) to Financial Secretary, 27 October 1967. HKRS163-1-3275.

53. Memo (secret), 'Note Issuing Banks in Hong Kong', 14 May 1954, pp. 4–5. HKRS163-1-1943 'Hong Kong Exchange Fund Operations by the Hong Kong & Shanghai Banking Corporation'.

54. See Greaves, 'The Sterling Balances of Colonial Territories', *Economic Journal*, p. 436.

55. For estimates of the Hong Kong banknotes in circulation on the Mainland during the inter-war years, see Tony Latter, 'Hong Kong's Exchange Rate Regimes in the Twentieth Century: The Story of Three Regime Changes', *HKIMR Working Paper No. 17/2004*, September 2004, p. 7.

56. A statistical analysis of this revival in the circulation of local banknotes outside Hong Kong is provided by Kenneth S. Chan, 'Currency Substitution between Hong Kong Dollar and Renminbi in South China', *HKIMR Working Paper No. 02 / 2001*, March 2001.

57. Cain and Hopkins, *British Imperialism: Innovation and Expansion, 1688–1914*, pp. 443–4, 446.

58. On the role of the London 'club', see Charles Goodhart and Dirk Schoenmaker, 'Should the Functions of Monetary Policy and Banking Supervision be Separated?', *Oxford Economic Papers*, Vol. 47, No. 4 (October 1995), pp. 540–2.

59. See Clarence B. Davis, 'Financing Imperialism: British and American Bankers as Vectors of Imperial Expansion in China, 1908–1920', *Business History Review*, Vol. 56, No. 2 (Summer 1982), pp. 253, 258–60.

60. David Mclean, 'Finance and "Informal Empire" before the First World War', *Economic History Review*, Vol. 29, No. 2 (May 1976), pp. 301–4.

61. John Atkin, 'Official Regulation of British Overseas Investment', *Economic History Review*, Vol. 23, No. 2 (August 1970), pp. 329–30.
62. For example, King, *The Hong Kong Bank in the Period of Development and Nationalism, 1941–1984. From Regional Bank to Multinational Group*, pp. 340–4.
63. Monopolies and Mergers Commission, *The Hongkong and Shanghai Banking Corporation. Standard Chartered Bank Limited. The Royal Bank of Scotland Group Limited. A Report on the Proposed Mergers* (Cmnd 8472/1982), pp. 88, 90.
64. The conflicts between HSBC executives and the colonial administration are reviewed in Leo F. Goodstadt, 'Crisis and Challenge: The Changing Role of the Hongkong & Shanghai Bank, 1950–2000', *HKIMR Working Paper No.13/2005*, July 2005. See also Tony Latter, 'Rules versus Discretion in Managing the Hong Kong Dollar, 1983–2006', *HKIMR Working Paper No.2/2007*, January 2007, pp. 8, 14, 16.
65. King, *The Hong Kong Bank in the Period of Development and Nationalism, 1941–1984. From Regional Bank to Multinational Group*, pp. 561, 664–9, 916–9 in particular. For the Bank's attempts to adapt its traditional culture and its presentation for the post-colonial era, see Steven Irvine, 'The Culture That Powers HongkongBank', *Euromoney*, February 1997, pp. 44–50.

CONCLUSIONS

1. For a summary of the key issues, see Sanghoon Ahn and Philip Hemmings, *Policy Influences on Economic Growth in OECD Countries: An Evaluation of the Evidence*, Economics Department Working Papers No. 246 (Paris: OECD, 2000), pp. 41–3.
2. Alex H. Choi, 'State-Business Relations and Industrial Restructuring', in Tak-Wing Ngo (ed), *Hong Kong's History. State and Society under Colonial Rule* (London: Routledge, 1999), pp. 147–50.
3. J. J. (later Sir John) Cowperthwaite, Financial Secretary, *HH*, 28 February 1962, p. 57; 25 February 1970, pp. 368–9; 24 February 1971, p. 419. By 1971, the government had rehoused 1.4 million people (36 per cent of the population). Living space per person in public housing was 2.6 square metres compared with 4.7 square metres per person in the private sector. Census and Statistics Department, 'Overcrowding and Sharing of Housing Accommodation in Hong Kong as Revealed in the 1971 Census', *Hong Kong Monthly Digest of Statistics*, January 1973, p. 65.
4. Stephen W. K. Chiu *et al.*, *City States in the Global Economy: Industrial Restructuring in Hong Kong and Singapore* (Boulder: Westview Press, 1997), pp. 34, 66.
5. James Riedel, *The Industrialization of Hong Kong* (Tübingen: J. C. B. Mohr [Paul Siebuck], 1974), p. 110.
6. It should be noted that Korean industrialists also appear to have relied on the banking system to finance their take-off. Sylvia Maxfield, 'Financial Incentives and Central Bank Authority in Industrializing Nations', *World Politics*, Vol. 46, No. 4 (July 1994), pp. 582–3.
7. Teresa Y. C. Wong, 'A Comparative Study of the Industrial Policy of Hong Kong and Singapore in the 1980s', in Edward K. Y. Chen *et al* (eds), *Industrial and Trade Development in Hong Kong* (Hong Kong: Centre of Asian Studies, 1991), pp. 264–5.
8. Deepak Lal and H. Myint, *The Political Economy of Poverty, Equity, and Growth: A Comparative Study* (New York: Oxford University Press, 1996), p. 98; Leonard K. Cheng, 'Strategies for Rapid Economic Development: The Case of Hong Kong',

Contemporary Economic Policy, Vol. 13. No. 1 (1995), pp. 33–4. For a good overview of the debate on this issue, see Edward K. Y. Chen, 'The Total Factor Productivity debate: Determinants of Economic Growth in East Asia', *Asian-Pacific Economic Literature*, Vol. 11, No. 1 (May 1997).

9. I. M. D. Little, *Collection and Recollections Economic Papers and their Provenance* (Oxford: Clarendon Press, 1999), pp. 197, 202, 228–9. 237–8.

10. See William J. Baumol, 'Entrepreneurship: Productive, Unproductive, and Destructive', *Journal of Political Economy* Vol. 98, No. 5, Part 1, (October 1990).

11. Sir Alexander Grantham, Governor, *HH*, 19 March 1948, p. 57; (262) AFS to Attorney General, 15 December 1947. HKRS163-1-403 'China Trade and Commerce Aide Mmemoire re Closer Cooperation between China and Hong Kong in Connection with Trade and Exchange Control'.

12. J. B. Griffin, Attorney General, *HH*, 17 December 1947, p. 334.

13. See the admission about past policy by Sir John Bremridge, Financial Secretary, *HH*, 19 March 1986, p. 771.

14. This flattering view is also a Mainland verdict, despite 'national oppression … under British colonial rule'. Liu Shuyong, *An Outline History of Hong Kong* (Beijing: Foreign Languages Press, 1997), p. 132.

15. On the case against such flattering analyses especially by British historians, see Esther M. K. Cheung, 'The Histories of Hong Kong', *Cultural Studies,* Vol. 15, Issue 3 & 4 (July 2001), pp. 566–8, 564–90.

16. Theodore Geiger, *Tales of Two City-States: The Development Progress of Hong Kong and Singapore* (Washington: National Planning Association, 1973), p. 146.

17. John Darwin, *Britain and Decolonisation: The Retreat from Empire in the Post-War World* (London: Macmillan, 1988), pp. 30–1.

18. Accountant General, (38) Circular 34 'Far East Commercial Bank Ltd — Bank Licensing Policy', 18 September 1951. HKRS163-1-679 'Banking Advisory Committee'.

19. The government's attitude is illustrated by the Financial Secretary's anxiety to retain an annual licence fee for revenue purposes even if the 1948 Banking Ordinance were abolished, as he hoped. (8) Financial Secretary letter to Sir Mankam Lo, 25 March 1952. HKRS41-1-6691 'Banking Operations Legislation for Control of …'

20. The absurdity of Cowperthwaite's assertions was highlighted by his admission: 'I myself would not find it easy to say with precision what lowering of standards is necessary or justifiable'. *HH*, 28 February 1962, p. 58.

21. Cowperthwaite, *HH*, 28 February 1962, p. 58; 26 February 1964, p. 52; 25 February 1965, p. 75; 24 February 1966, pp. 72–3; 24 February 1971, p. 417.

22. Bremridge, *HH*, 29 February 1984, p. 592.

23. See HKRS41-1-3044 'The Nam Sang Bank:1. Application from … for a Banking Licence; 2. Balance Sheet of … ; 3. Cancellation of the Licence of …'.

24. Alistair Todd (Hong Kong) letter to W. S. Carter (Colonial Office), 1 May 1965; I. M. Lightbody (Hong Kong) letter to A. St. J. Sugg (Colonial Office), 14 October 1965. CO1030/1664 'Labour Legislation — Hong Kong'.

25. Officials knew that the triads involved had records of violence. M.1., 21 July 1963; M. 3., 23 July 1963; Governor's minute, 26 July 1963; Commissioner of Police memo, 10 May 1963; Commissioner for Resettlement memo, 2 July 1963. HKRS163-1-2854, 'Cleansing Services in Resettlement Estates'.

26. Details of this piece of racial discrimination can be found in HKRS163-1-1707 'Education. Educational Provision for English-speaking Children', in particular: M.6. Director of Education to Colonial Secretary, 8 February 1954; (8) Acting Director of Education memo to Colonial Secretary, 14 October 1954; M.83. Financial Secretary to Colonial Secretary, 10 March 1956; M.84. Colonial Secretary to Governor, 14 March 1956; M.85. Governor to Colonial Secretary, 16 March 1956; (33) Agenda Item for Finance Committee Meeting, 11 July 1956; M.210. note by Financial Secretary, 20 July 1962.

27. K. G. Ashton minute to W. G. Hulland, 10 July 1956. CO1030/392 'Financial Devolution Hong Kong'. This argument against democracy was challenged on this file by two other London officials. See the minutes by J. B. Johnston (14 July 1956) and R. J. Vile (27 August 1956).

28. Leading manufacturers even opposed the creation of an organisation to promote Hong Kong products in overseas markets. On the government's views of manufacturers' attitudes, see HKRS163-1-2861 'Cotton Textiles Allocation of Quota to Restricted Markets'. On the government's difficulties in getting cooperation from manufacturers, see HKRS270-5-56 'Cotton Advisory Board. Minutes of Meeting'. For manufacturers' opinions, see Minutes of the fourth Meeting of the General Committee of the Federation, 26 August 1960, p. 3; Minutes of an Emergency Meeting, 18 July 1961, p. 2. HKRS270-5-39 'Federation of Hong Kong Industries Minutes of Meetings of the General Committee'; Minutes of 73rd meeting, 3 January 1964, p. 2; Minutes of 75th meeting, 21 February 1964, p. 3; Minutes of 78th meeting, 24 April 1964, p. 3. HKRS163-1-118 'Federation of Hong Kong Industries Minutes of the Meetings of the …'.

29. HSBC's frustrations run contrary to the optimism expressed about the ability of powerful banks in the private sector to promote conservative banking and monetary policies as long as the government does not have to finance substantial budget deficits. Sylvia Maxfield, 'Financial Incentives and Central Bank Authority in Industrializing Nations', *World Politics*, Vol. 46, No. 4. (July 1994), pp. 564–5.

30. An excellent analysis of the dramatic change in Hong Kong's political environment in the 1980s can be found in B. Karin Chai, 'Export-Oriented Industrialization and Political and Class Development: Hong Kong on the Eve of 1997', in Richard Harvey Brown and William T. Liu (eds), *Modernization in East Asia: Political, Economic, and Social Perspectives* (Westport: Praeger, 1992), pp. 111–2.

31. On London's key role in promoting international cooperation to improve bank regulation, see Ethan B. Kapstein, 'Resolving the Regulator's Dilemma: International Coordination of Banking Regulations', *International Organization*, Vol. 43, No. 2 (Spring 1989), p. 329.

Bibliography

Unpublished Sources

DCA/BILAT/1351C
Industry Development Branch, 'Memorandum to the Loans for Small Industry Committee' (Commerce and Industry Department, IND 2/903, 4 November 1969, mimeo)
Industry Development Branch, 'The Case for Improved Access to Loans for Re-equipment Purposes by Small Scale Industry' (Department of Commerce and Industry, IND 2/903, 27 October 1969, mimeo)
'Report of the Industrial Bank Committee' (Hong Kong Government, January 1960, mimeo)

Public Records Office Hong Kong

HKRS22-1-19 'Labour Statistics – Policy'
HKRS22-1-96 'Population Census 1961'
HKRS41-1-182 'Gold Control of Gold by Legislation'
HKRS41-1-796 'Colonial Development and Welfare Committee. 1. Appointment of ...'
HKRS41-1-2485 'China The Banking Law, 1947'
HKRS41-1-2769(1) 'Inland Revenue Ordinance. 1. General question of imposing etc ...'
HKRS41-1-2871 'Gold Smuggling of ... out of Hong Kong'
HKRS41-1-3003 'The China Industrial Bank of H. K. Ltd. Application from ... for a banking licence'
HKRS41-1-3005 'Agricultural and Industrial Bank of China, Ltd. 1. Application from ... for a banking licence; 2. Balance Sheet of ...'
HKRS41-1-3008 'The Shanghai Commercial & Savings Bank Ltd. 1. Application from ... for a banking licence; 2. Balance Sheet of ...'
HKRS41-1-3011 'The Provincial Bank of Fukien. 1. Application from ... for a banking licence; 2. Balance Sheet of ...'

HKRS41-1-3012 'Yau Tak Bank.1. Application from … for a banking licence; 2. Balance Sheet of …'

HKRS41-1-3013 'The China Trust Co. Ltd. Application from … for a banking licence'

HKRS41-1-3014 'The Yue Cheong Hong Bank. 1. Application from … for a banking licence; 2. Balance Sheet of …'

HKRS41-1-3015 'Tong Ho & Co. Ltd. 1. Application from … for a banking licence; 2. Balance Sheet of …'

HKRS41-1-3018 'The Wing Tai Bank. 1. Application from … for a banking licence; 2. Balance Sheet of …'

HKRS41-1-3020 'The On Tai Bank. 1. Application from … for a banking licence; 2. Balance Sheet of …'

HKRS41-1-3021 'The Wo Cheung Bank. 1. Application from … for a banking licence; 2. Balance Sheet of …'

HKRS41-1-3023 'The Tak Fat Bank. 1. Application from … for a banking licence; 2. Balance Sheet of …'

HKRS41-1-3024 'The Foo Kee Bank. 1. Application from … for a banking licence; 2. Balance Sheet of …'

HKRS41-1-3034 'The Yee Sang Bank. 1. Application from … for a banking licence; 2. Balance Sheet of …'

HKRS41-1-3038 'The Wing Cheung Bank. 1. Application from … for a banking licence; 2. Balance Sheet of …'

HKRS41-1-3040 'The Hop Kee Bank. 1. Application from … for a banking licence; 2. Balance Sheet of …'

HKRS41-1-3044 'The Nam Sang Bank. 1. Application from … for a Banking Licence; 2. Balance Sheet of … ; 3. Cancellation of the Licence of …'

HKRS41-1-3046 'The Ngau Kee Bank. 1. Application from … for a banking licence; 2. Balance Sheet of …'

HKRS41-1-3054 'The Kwai Kee Bank. 1. Application from … for a banking licence; 2. Balance Sheet of …'

HKRS41-1-3057 'The Hang Shun Gold Dealer. 1. Application from … for a banking licence; 2. Balance Sheet of …'

HKRS41-1-3062 'Cheuk Kee Bank. 1. Application from … for a banking licence; 2. Balance Sheet of …'

HKRS41-1-3065 'The Yue Man Banking Co., Ltd. 1. Application from … for a banking licence; 2. Balance Sheet of …'

HKRS41-1-3067 'The H.K. Trust Corp. Ltd. 1. Application from … for a banking licence; 2. Balance Sheet of …'

HKRS41-1-3076 'Banco Nacional Ultramarino. 1. Application from … for a banking licence; 2. Balance Sheet of …'

HKRS41-1-3085 'Shun Foo Banking & Investment Co. Ltd. 1. Application from … for a banking licence; 2. Balance Sheet of …'

HKRS41-1-3094 'The Kincheng Banking Corporation H.K. (Trustees) Ltd. 1. Application from … for a banking licence; 2. Balance Sheet of …'

HKRS41-1-3095 'Far East Commercial Bank Ltd. Application from … for a banking licence'

HKRS41-1-3096 'Asia Trading Co. Ltd. Application for a banking licence'

HKRS41-1-3099 'The Bank of New Territories, Ltd. Application from … for a banking licence'

HKRS41-1-3378 'Cotton textiles. 1. Agreement with Chinese Govt. re Supply of … to Hong Kong; 2. Alternative Supply of … from Japan, USA and India'

HKRS41-1-3410 'Trade. Trade between Hong Kong and China'

HKRS41-1-3888 'Inauguration of the President of China. General Holidays and other celebrations'

HKRS41-1-4095 'Finance (Defence) Regulation 1940 Request for Information regarding bullion dealers under …'

HKRS41-1-4118 'Exchange Control Cotton Spinning Plant'

HKRS41-1-4897 'Defence (Finance) Regulations 1940. Authorisation of Police Officers …'

HKRS41-1-4899 'Kowloon Jewellery, Jadestone, Gold and Silver Ornaments Merchants Association. Question of displaying current gold Price List in their shops'

HKRS41-1-4969 'Conferences – The Conference of Colonial Government Statisticians Convened by the Secretary of State for the Colonies at the Colonial Office during March, 1950. Correspondence re …'

HKRS41-1-5097 'Defence (Finance) Regulations, 1940, Variation Order 1949, Warning against the publication of statements on the price of gold on the black market'

HKRS41-1-6032, 'Colonial Industrial Development – Legislation to encourage …'

HKRS41-1-6690 'Native Banks. Reports on …'

HKRS41-1-6691. 'Banking Operations Legislation for control of …'

HKRS41-1-8569 'Exchange Control. Question of … over Shipment of Goods from China'

HKRS41-1-9339(1) 'Pilot Social Survey of Shek Kip Mei Resettlement Area'

HKRS41-1-999-1 'Chinese Affairs: Miscellaneous correspondence from British Embassy Nanking concerning …'

HKRS41-3-3007 'The Fu Shing Bank of H. K. Ltd. 1. Application from … for a banking licence; 2. Balance Sheet of …'

HKRS41-3-3044 'The Nam Sang Bank. 1. Application from … for a banking licence; 2. Balance Sheet of … ; 3. Cancellation of the licence of …'

HKRS46-1-183 'Legislation Control of Gold by Legislation Exchange Control Dealing in Gold'.

HKRS46-1-185 'Legislation Control of Gold by Legislation Seizure of Gold'

HKRS55-9-3-10 'Ming Tak Bank Minutes of Committee of Inspection'

HKRS55-9-3-174 'Copies of Committee Meetings of Ming Tak Bank held on 16th September 1969 and The Following Meetings'

HKRS58-1-190-10 'Factory Sites. 1. Suggestion that Government should provide … on favourable terms to encourage industrial development; 2. Provision of … for evicted squatters'

HKRS70-3-6-1 'Canton Trust and Commercial Bank Ltd'

HKRS160-3-25 'Report on the Financial Situation by the Acting Financial Secretary'

HKRS163-1-15 'Model Exchange Fund Ordinance'

HKRS163-1-118 'Federation of Hong Kong Industries Minutes of the Meetings of the …'

HKRS163-1-211 'Japan Confidential Correspondence on Trade with …'

HKRS163-1-305 'Retail Price &Wages Index. Preparation of …'

HKRS163-1-308 'Import and Export of Gold'

HKRS163-1-402 'China Trade and Commerce Aide memoire re closer cooperation between China and Hong Kong in connection with trade and exchange control'

HKRS163-1-403 'China Trade & Commerce Aide memoire re closer cooperation between China and Hong Kong in connection with trade and exchange control'

HKRS163-1-440 'Banking. 1. Banking Ordinance; 2. Control over the opening and functioning of Native Banks in Hong Kong'

HKRS163-1-441 'Names and Addresses of Partners of Banks required for the Banking Ordinance 1948'

HKRS163-1-442 'Import and Exchange Control in Hong Kong Proposed visit of a H.K. Govt. officer to the U.K. in connection with ...'

HKRS163-1-507 'Excess Population Committee Pre-war correspondence re ...'

HKRS163-1-602 'China Light & Power Co. Ltd. and Hong Kong Electric Co'

HKRS163-1-625 'Banking Statistics. 1. Supply of ... to S of S; 2. Policy Correspondence concerning'

HKRS163-1-634 'Public Utilities Companies Proposed control of the charges and dividends levied by ...'

HKRS163-1-679 'Banking Advisory Committee'

HKRS163-1-995 'Exchange Control Transfer by Government of Macau of surplus Hong Kong dollar funds to Portuguese sterling account in London'

HKRS163-1-1000 'Exchange Control Banks Authorised to Deal in Foreign Exchange'

HKRS163-1-1007 'Finance Estimated Capital Investment in Hong Kong'

HKRS163-1-1230 'Trade – Balance of Payments Statistics (Hong Kong) – Working papers and miscellaneous correspondence re preparation of ...'

HKRS163-1-1366 'Exchange Control Colonial Office Instructions and Circulars ...'

HKRS163-1-1376 'Industry and Production. Industrial Situation in Hong Kong'

HKRS163-1-1707 'Education. Educational provision for English-speaking children'

HKRS163-1-1943 'Hong Kong Exchange Fund Operations by the Hong Kong & Shanghai Banking Corporation'

HKRS163-1-2055 'Exchange Control Monthly Statistics showing China's purchases of Sterling and Chinese inward remittances'

HKRS163-1-2299 'The Industrial Bank Committee – Proceedings of ...'

HKRS163-1-2522, 'Finance Investment of Colonial Government Funds'

HKRS163-1-2648 'Corruption – Examination of ... in the Buildings Ordinance Office – P.W.D.'

HKRS163-1-2660 'Exchange Control Monthly and Half-Yearly Statistics of Foreign Exchange Transactions from January 1961'

HKRS163-1-2861 'Cotton Textiles Allocation of quota to restricted markets'

HKRS163-1-3185 'Banking Advisory Committee'

HKRS163-1-3273 'Banking Statistics Various 1965'.

HKRS163-1-3274 'Banking Statistics Various – 1966'

HKRS163-1-3275 'Banking Statistics Various – 1967'

HKRS163-1-3276 'Banking Statistics Various'

HKRS163-1-3284 'Problems Affecting the Real Estate and Allied Industries'

HKRS163-3-12 'Banking Statistics. 1. Supply of to S. of S. Policy concerning ...'

HKRS163-3-249 'Banking Emergency 1965 – Matters arising from ... staff etc'

HKRS163-3-269 'Investment Guarantees by the United States Government'

HKRS163-3-369 'Foreign Banks in Hong Kong Capitalization Requirements'

HKRS163-5-2 'Colonial Production Colonial Development Corporation & International Bank Loans'

HKRS163-9-69 'Exchange Control. Banks Authorised to Deal with Foreign Exchange'

HKRS163-9-88 'Trade. Balance of Payment Statistics. Policy regarding preparation of ...'

HKRS163-9-98 'Exchange Control Import Licensing Policy for Dollar Imports'

HKRS163-9-141 'Exchange Control – Individual Problems Arising from Applications of Policy on ... in Hong Kong'

HKRS163-9-217 '(A) Meeting of Senior Commonwealth Finance Officials 1970. Sterling Area Balance of Payments – Developments and Prospects to Mid-1971; (B) Overseas Sterling Area Countries Statistics'

HKRS165-9-226 'Land Sales Question of Upset and Reserved Prices. Auction Rings and Transfers of Ownership prior to fulfilment of Conditions of Sale'

HKRS163-9-511 'Commerce and Industry Dept. Industrial Development Branch'

HKRS169-2-26 'Currency and Banking'

HKRS169-2-53 'Rehabilitation of Business'

HKRS169-2-306 'Visit by H. E. Governor of Hong Kong to Canton'

HKRS170-1-240 'Finance. Chinese Government and other Banks in Hong Kong'

HKRS170-1-305 'Banking Legislation Miscellaneous Correspondence of the Committee appointed in January 1939 to consider the proposed new ...'

HKRS170-1-307 'Banking legislation. 1. General supervision of Banking Concerns in Hong Kong; 2. Appointment of a Committee in 1935 to consider the desirability of specific legislation for the regulation of banking operations in the Colony; 3. Report of the committee; 4. Appointment of a Committee in 1939 to consider further action on this question'

HKRS170-1-418(2) 'Price Control. Machinery and Direction of ...'

HKRS170-1-554-2/3 'Report. Department of Commerce & Industry'

HKRS170-1-710 'Position of Factories in Hong Kong'

HKRS170-1-738 'Public Utilities & other Companies in H. K. Proposed legislation on the administration of ... after the restoration of Civil Government'

HKRS170-1-755-2 'Hongkong Electric Co. Ltd ...'

HKRS170-2-1 'Census Estimate of Population'

HKRS211-2-20 'Financial Policy'

HKRS211-2-21 'British Banks: Question of the return of ... to Hong Kong'

HKRS229-1-45 'Capital Formation Estimates'

HKRS229-1-807 'Financial Aid (Including Loans) Received from the United Kingdom and Other Governments record of ...'

HKRS259-6-1 'Report on the Population of the Colony, Mid-Year 1949'

HKRS270-1-2-I 'Industrial Development Flatted Factories Provision of ...'

HKRS270-1-2-II 'Industrial Development Provision of Flatted Factories'

HKRS270-5-39 'Federation of Hong Kong Industries Minutes of Meetings of the General Committee'

HKRS270-5-44 'Commercial and Industrial Development – Major Policy'

HKRS270-5-56 'Cotton Advisory Board. Minutes of Meeting'

HKRS532-3-22 'Employment Statistics Bill 1972'

HKRS885-3-5 'Far East Bank, Limited'

HKRS934-7-104 'Far East Bank – Tsuen Wan'

HKRS1017-2-2 'Labour Department: General Policy (Gibbs Report 1963)'

HKRS1017-2-6 'Committee to Review the Unemployment Situation in the Colony'

HKRS1017-3-4 'Unemployment Relief'

HKRS1056-1-194 'Industrial Survey – Policy'

Public Records Office London

CO1030/392 'Financial Devolution Hong Kong'
CO 1030/859 'Hong Kong – Value and Cost to the United Kingdom'
CO1030/1117 'Hong Kong-Macau-China; Inter-relationship'
CO1030/1300 'The Future of Hong Kong'
CO1030/1589 'Proposed I.B.R.D Loan for Land Reclamation at Kwai Chun — Hong Kong'
CO1030/1718 'The Drug Problem in Hong Kong'

Official Publications

Census and Statistics Department, 'Overcrowding and sharing of housing accommodation in Hong Kong as revealed in the 1971 census', *Hong Kong Monthly Digest of Statistics*, January 1973

——, *Hong Kong Statistics 1947–1967* (Hong Kong: Government Printer, 1969)

——, *Estimates of Gross Domestic Product 1961 to 1994* (Hong Kong: Census and Statistics Department, 1995)

——, *2003 Gross Domestic Product* (Hong Kong: Census and Statistics Department, 2004)

Colonial Office, *First Conference of Colonial Government Statisticians, 1950* (London: HMSO, 1951, Colonial No. 267)

——, *Labour Supervision in the Colonial Empire* (London: HMSO, 1943)

Despatch from the Secretary of State for the Colonies to Colonial Governments, *Colonial Development and Welfare* ... (Cmd 6713/1945)

H. M. Treasury, *The Basle Facility and the Sterling Area* (Cmnd 3787/1968)

HKIMR Historical Database. URL: https://www.hkimr.org/HK%20Economic%20History%20DB.xls

Ingrams, Harold, *Hong Kong* (London: HMSO, 1952)

King, Frank H. H., *Money in British East Asia* (London: Her Majesty's Stationery Office, 1957)

Legislative Council Panel on Commerce and Industry, *Progress Report on the Four Funding Schemes for Small and Medium Enterprises*, (CB(1)1670/01-02(03) 13 May 2002)

Margolis, Richard, 'A History of Paradoxes', in John Elliot (ed), *Hong Kong: Asia's Business Centre* (Hong Kong: Government Information Services, 1992)

Report of Currency Committee, 1930 (Legislative Council Sessional Paper 7/1930)

Report of the Advisory Committee on Diversification 1979 (Hong Kong: Government Printer, 1979)

Report of the Commission ... to Enquire into the Causes and Effects of the Present Trade Recession ... (Hong Kong: Noronha & Co., 1935)

Report of the Commission Appointed to Enquire into the Conditions of the Industrial Employment of Children in Hong Kong, and the Desirability and Feasibility of Legislation for the Regulation of such Employment (Hong Kong: Session Paper 11/1921)

Report of the Committee appointed to consider certain matters concerning the closure of the Chong Hing Mansion 1971 (Hong Kong: Government Printer, 1972)

Report of the Housing Commission (Hong Kong: Session Paper 10/1923)

Report of the Housing Commission 1935 (Hong Kong: Noronha & Co., 1938)

Report on the National Income Survey of Hong Kong (Hong Kong: Government Printer, 1969)

Sayers, R. S., *Financial Policy, 1939–45* (London: HMSO, 1956)

Second Report of the Commission of Inquiry under Sir Alistair Blair-Kerr (Hong Kong: Government Printer, 1973)

Small and Medium Enterprises Committee, *A Report on Support Measures for Small and Medium Enterprises* (Hong Kong: SAR Government, 2001)

Tomkins, H. J., *Report on the Hong Kong Banking System and Recommendations for the Replacement of the Banking Ordinance 1948* (Hong Kong: Government Printer, 1962)

Treaty Series No. 9 (1949), *Exchange of Notes … for the Prevention of Smuggling between Hong Kong and Chinese Ports* (London: Cmd 7615/1949)

Yam, Joseph, *Review of Currency Board Arrangements in Hong Kong* (Hong Kong: Hong Kong Monetary Authority, 1998)

Books and Monographs

A Study Group of the Royal Institute of International Affairs, *Political and Strategic Interests of the United Kingdom. An Outline* (London: Oxford University Press, 1939)

August, Thomas G., *The Selling of the Empire: British and French Imperialist Propaganda, 1890–1940* (Westport: Greenwood Press, 1985)

Becker, Jasper, *Hungry Ghosts. China's Secret Famine* (London: John Murray, 1996)

Bell, Philip W., *The Sterling Area in the Postwar World: International Mechanism and Cohesion, 1946–1952* (Oxford: Clarendon Press, 1956)

Berger, Suzanne, and Richard K. Lester (eds), *Made By Hong Kong* (Hong Kong: Oxford University Press, 1997)

Brown, Judith M., and Wm. Roger Louis, *The Oxford History of the British Empire: The Twentieth Century, Vol. IV* (Oxford: Oxford University Press, 1999)

Cain, P. J., and A. G. Hopkins, *British Imperialism: Innovation and Expansion, 1688–1914* (London: Longman, 1993)

Chambers, Gillian, *Hang Seng. The Evergrowing Bank* (Hong Kong: n.p., 1991)

Chan Cheuk-wah, *The Myth of Hong Kong's Laissez-faire Economic Governance* (Hong Kong: Hong Kong Institute of Asia-Pacific Studies, 1998)

Chan Lau Kit-ching, *China, Britain and Hong Kong 1895–1945* (Hong Kong: Chinese University Press, 1990)

———, *From Nothing to Nothing. The Chinese Communist Movement and Hong Kong, 1921–1936* (New York: St Martin's Press, 1999)

Cheng Tong Yung, *The Economy of Hong Kong* (Hong Kong: Far East Publications, 1977)

Cheng, Linsun, *Banking in Modern China: Entrepreneurs, Professional Managers and the Development of Chinese Banks, 1897–1937* (Cambridge: Cambridge University Press, 2003)

Chesterton, Josephine M., and Tushar K. Ghose, *Merchant Banking in Hong Kong* (Hong Kong: Butterworths Asia, 1998)

Chiu, Stephen, *The Politics of Laissez-faire. Hong Kong's Strategy of Industrialization in Historical Perspective* (Hong Kong: Hong Kong Institute of Asia-Pacific Studies, 1994)

——— et al, *City States in the Global Economy: Industrial Restructuring in Hong Kong and Singapore* (Boulder: Westview Press, 1997)

Clark, Trevor, *Good Second Class* (Stanhope: The Memoir Club, 2004)

Clayton, David, *Imperialism Revisited. Political and Economic Relations between Britain and China, 1950–54* (London: Macmillan Press Ltd, 1997)

Cohen, Benjamin J, *The Future of Sterling as an International Currency* (London: Macmillan, 1971)

Consumer Council, *Are Hong Kong Depositors Fairly Treated?* (Hong Kong: Consumer Council, 1994),

Darwin, John, *Britain and Decolonisation: The Retreat from Empire in the Post-War World* (London: Macmillan, 1988)

Day, A. C. L., *The Future of Sterling* (Oxford: Clarendon Press, 1954)

Dwyer, D. J., and Lai Chuen-yan, *The Small Industrial Unit in Hong Kong: Patterns and Policies* (University of Hull Publications, 1967)

Economist Intelligence Unit, *The Commonwealth and Europe* (London: Economist Intelligence Unit, 1960)

Endacott, G. B., *Hong Kong Eclipse* (Hong Kong: Oxford University Press, 1978)

Faure, David, *Colonialism and the Hong Kong Mentality* (Hong Kong: Centre of Asian Studies, 2003)

—— (ed), *A Documentary History of Hong Kong. Society* (Hong Kong: Hong Kong University Press, 1997)

—— and Lee Pui-tak (eds), *A Documentary History of Hong Kong. Economy* (Hong Kong: Hong Kong University Press, 2004)

Fell, Robert, *Crisis and Change. The Maturing of Hong Kong's Financial Markets* (Hong Kong: Longman, 1992)

Feng, Zhong-ping, *The British Government's China Policy 1945–1950* (Keele: Ryburn Publishing, 1994)

Freris, Andrew F., *The Financial Markets of Hong Kong* (London: Routledge, 1991)

Geiger, Theodore, *Tales of Two City-States: The Development Progress of Hong Kong and Singapore* (Washington: National Planning Association, 1973)

Ghose, T. K., *The Banking System of Hong Kong* (Singapore: Butterworths, 1987)

——, *The Banking System of Hong Kong* (Singapore: Buttterworths, 1995, 2nd edition)

Gleason, Gene, *Hong Kong* (London: Robert Hale Ltd, 1964)

Gomersall, W. C., 'The China Engineers, Ltd. & The Textile Trade', in J. M. Braga (comp), *Hong Kong Business Symposium* (Hong Kong: n.p., 1957)

Goodstadt, Leo F., *Uneasy Partners: The Conflict between Public Interest and Private Profit in Hong Kong* (Hong Kong: Hong Kong University Press, 2005)

Grantham, Alexander, *Via Ports. From Hong Kong to Hong Kong* (Hong Kong: Hong Kong University Press, 1965)

Havinden, Michael, and David Meredith, *Colonialism and Development: Britain and Its Tropical Colonies, 1850–1960* (London: Routledge, 1993)

Ho, Eric Peter, *Times of Change. A Memoir of Hong Kong's Governance 1950–1991* (Leiden: Brill, 2005)

Ho, H. C. Y., *The Fiscal System of Hong Kong* (London: Croom Helm, 1979)

Hong Kong General Chamber of Commerce, *Report for the Year 1936* (Hong Kong: n.p., 1937)

Howe, Anthony, *Free Trade and Liberal England, 1846–1946* (Oxford: Clarendon Press, 1997)

Huang, Yasheng, *FDI in China. An Asian Perspective* (Hong Kong: Chinese University Press, 1998)

Hutcheon, Robin, *Shanghai Customs, A 20th Century Taipan in Troubled Times* (Edgecliff: Galisea Publications, 2000)

Jao, Y. C., *Banking and Currency in Hong Kong. A Study of Postwar Financial Development* (London: Macmillan, 1974)

——, *Money and Finance in Hong Kong: Retrospect and Prospect* (Singapore: Singapore University Press: 1998)

——, *The Asian Financial Crisis and the Ordeal of Hong Kong* (Westport: Quorum Books, 2001)

Jones, Catherine, *Promoting Prosperity: The Hong Kong Way of Social Policy* (Hong Kong: Chinese University Press, 1990)

Kendrick, Douglas M., *Price Control and Its Practice in Hong Kong* (Hong Kong: K. Weiss, 1954)

Keynes, J. M., *How to Pay for the War. A Radical Plan for the Chancellor of the Exchequer* (London: MacMillan, 1940).

King, Frank H. H., *The Hong Kong Bank in the Period of Development and Nationalism, 1941– 1984. From Regional Bank to Multinational Group* (Cambridge: Cambridge University Press, 1991)

Lal, Deepak, and H. Myint, *The Political Economy of Poverty, Equity, and Growth: A Comparative Study* (New York: Oxford University Press, 1996)

Lam, Jermain T. M., *The Political Dynamics of Hong Kong under Chinese Sovereignty* (Huntington: Nova Science Publishers, Inc., 2000)

Lau Chi Kuen, *Hong Kong's Colonial Legacy* (Hong Kong: Chinese University Press, 1997)

Lau, Siu-kai, *Society and Politics in Hong Kong* (Hong Kong: Chinese University Press, 1982)

—— and Kuan Hsin-chi, *The Ethos of the Hong Kong Chinese* (Hong Kong: Chinese University Press, 1988)

League of Nations, *International Currency Experience: Lessons of the Interwar Period* (Geneva: League of Nations, 1944)

Lethbridge, Henry, *Hong Kong: Stability and Change. A collection of essays* (Hong Kong: Oxford University Press, 1978)

Little, I. M. D., *Collection and Recollections Economic Papers and Their Provenance* (Oxford: Clarendon Press, 1999)

Liu Shuyong, *An Outline History of Hong Kong* (Beijing: Foreign Languages Press, 1997)

Luard, Evan, *Britain and China* (Baltimore: The John Hopkins Press, 1962),

Lui, Tai-lok, and Thomas W. P. Wong, *Chinese Entrepreneurship in Context* (Hong Kong: Hong Kong Institute of Asian-Pacific Studies, 1994)

Mao Zedong, *Selected Works of Mao Tse-tung, Vol. IV* (Beijing: Foreign Languages Press, 1967)

Mark, Chi-kwan, *Hong Kong and the Cold War Anglo-American Relations 1949–1957* (Oxford: Clarendon Press, 2004)

Marshall, T J. F., *Whereon the Wild Thyme Blows. Some Memoirs of Service with the Hongkong Bank* (Grayshott: Token Publishing Limited, 1986)

Meyer, David R., *Hong Kong as a Global Metropolis* (Cambridge: Cambridge University Press, 2000)

Mills, Lennox A., *British Rule in Eastern Asia. A Study of Contemporary Government and Economic Development in British Malaya and Hong Kong* (London: Oxford University Press, 1942)

Miners, N. J., *The Government and Politics of Hong Kong* (Hong Kong: Oxford University Press, 1975)

Mitchell, B. R., *International Historical Statistics Africa, Asia & Oceania 1750–1993* (London: Macmillan Reference Ltd, 1998, 3rd edition)

Padao-Schioppa, Tommaso, *Regulating Finance: Balancing Freedom and Risk* (Oxford: Oxford University Press, 2004)

Pakeman, S. A., *Ceylon* (London: Ernest Benn Limited, 1964)

Prest, A. R., *Public Finance in Underdeveloped Countries* (New York: Praeger, 1963)

Rafferty, Kevin, *City on the Rocks. Hong Kong's Uncertain Future* (London: Viking, 1989)

Reardon, Lawrence C., *The Reluctant Dragon. Crisis Cycles in Chinese Foreign Economic Policy* (Hong Kong: Hong Kong University Press, 2002)

Riedel, James, *The Industrialization of Hong Kong* (Tübingen: J. C. B. Mohr (Paul Siebuck), 1974)

Schenk, Catherine R., *Hong Kong as an International Financial Centre. Emergence and Development 1945–65* (London: Routledge, 2001)

Scott, Ian, *Political Change and the Crisis of Legitimacy in Hong Kong* (London: Hurst & Company, 1989)

Scott, John, *Corporate Business and Capitalist Classes* (Oxford: Oxford University Press, 1997)

Shao, Wenguang, *China, Britain and Businessmen: Political and Commercial Relations, 1949–57* (Basingstoke: Macmillan, 1991)

Sinn, Elizabeth, *Growing with Hong Kong. The Bank of East Asia 1919–1884* (Hong Kong: Hong Kong University Press, 1994)

Smart, Alan, *The Shek Kip Mei Myth: Squatters, Fires and Colonial Rule in Hong Kong, 1950–1963* (Hong Kong: Hong Kong University Press, 2006)

Smith, Henry, *John Stuart Mill's Other Island. A Study of the Economic Development of Hong Kong* (London: Institute of Economic Affairs, 1966)

Szczepanik, Edward, *The Economic Growth of Hong Kong* (London: Oxford University Press, 1960)

Tsang, Steve, *A Modern History of Hong Kong* (London: I. B. Tauris, 2004)

Whisson, Michael G., *Under the Rug: The Drug Problem in Hong Kong (A study in applied sociology)* (Hong Kong: Hong Kong Council of Social Service, 1965)

Whitfield, Andrew, *Hong Kong, Empire and the Anglo-American Alliance at War, 1941–1945* (Basingstoke: Palgrave, 2001)

Wilson, Dick, *Hong Kong! Hong Kong!* (London: Unwin Hyman, 1990)

Wong Man Fong, *China's Resumption of Sovereignty over Hong Kong* (Hong Kong: Hong Kong Baptist University, n.d.)

Wong Siu-lun, *Emigrant Entrepreneurs. Shanghai Industrialists in Hong Kong* (Hong Kong: Oxford University Press, 1988)

Woodruff, Philip, *The Men Who Ruled India. The Guardians* (London: Jonathan Cape: 1954)

World Bank, *The East Asian Miracle. Economic Growth and Public Policy* (New York: Oxford University Press, 1993)

Wu, Chun-hsi, *Dollars, Dependents and Dogma: Overseas Chinese Remittances to Communist China* (Stanford: Hoover Institution, 1967)

Xu Jiatun, *Xu Jiatun Xianggang Huiyilu* (Taipei: Lianhebao, 1993)

Yahuda, Michael, *Hong Kong. China's Challenge* (London: Routledge, 1996)

Yeung. Henry Wai-chung, *Transnational Corporations and Business Networks. Hong Kong Firms in the Asian Region* (London: Routledge, 1998)

Young, Gavin, *Beyond Lion Rock. The Story of Cathay Pacific Airways* (London: Hutchison, 1988)

Youngson, A. J., *Hong Kong's Economic Growth and Policy* (Hong Kong: Oxford University Press, 1982)

Yu, Tony Fu-Lai, *Entrepreneurship and Economic Development in Hong Kong* (London: Routledge, 1997)

Articles, Essays and Working Papers

Ahlers, John, 'Postwar Banking in Shanghai', *Pacific Affairs*, Vol. 19, No. 4 (December 1946), 384–93

Ahn, Sanghoon and Philip Hemmings, *Policy Influences on Economic Growth in OECD Countries: An Evaluation of the Evidence,* Economics Department Working Papers No. 246 (Paris: OECD, 2000)

Aliber, Robert Z., 'Financial Innovation and the Boundaries of Banking', *Managerial and Decision Economics*, Vol. 8, No. 1 (March 1987), 67–73

Anon., 'Hong Kong: An Attempt to Control the Money Supply', *Asian Monetary Monitor,* Vol. 3, No. 1 (January-February 1979), 3–10

——, 'Hong Kong: How to Rescue HK$: Three Practical Proposals', *Asian Monetary Monitor*, Vol. 6, No. 5 (September–October 1982), 13–37

——, 'Hong Kong: Proposals for a Reform of the Monetary System', *Asian Monetary Monitor*, Vol. 3, No. 2 (March–April 1979), 9–23

——, 'Hong Kong: The Role of Interest rates in the Adjustment Mechanism', *Asian Monetary Monitor*, Vol. 3, No. 5 (September–October 1979), 10–17

——, 'Hong Kong's Financial Crisis – History, Analysis, Prescription', *Asian Monetary Monitor*, Vol. 6, No. 6 (November–December 1982)

Atkin, John, 'Official Regulation of British Overseas Investment, 1914–1931' *Economic History Review*, Vol. 23, No. 2 (August 1970), 324–35

Barnett, K. M. A., Census Commissioner, 'Introduction', in W. F. Maunder, *Hong Kong Urban Rents and Housing* (Hong Kong: Hong Kong University Press, 1969)

Baster, A. S. J., 'A Note on the Sterling Area', *Economic Journal*, Vol. 47, No. 187 (September 1937), 568–74

Baumol, William J., 'Entrepreneurship: Productive, Unproductive, and Destructive', *Journal of Political Economy* Vol. 98 No. 5, Part 1 (October 1990), 893–921

Belassa, Bela, 'Outward Orientation', in Hollis Chenery and T. N. Srinivasan (eds) *Handbook of Development Economics Volume II* (Amsterdam: Elsevier, 1989)

Benham, F. C., 'The Growth of Manufacturing in Hong Kong', *International Affairs*, Vol. 32, No. 4 (October 1956), 456–66

Birch, Alan, 'Control of Prices and Commodities in Hong Kong', *Hong Kong Law Journal*, Vol. 4, Part 2 (1974), 133–50

Bisignano, Joseph, 'Suggestions for Improvements', in Gerard Caprio, Jr *et al* (eds), *Preventing Bank Crises: Lessons from Recent Global Bank Failures* (Washington: World Bank, 1998)

Bloomfield, Arthur I., 'Some Problems of Central Banking in Underdeveloped Countries', *Journal of Finance*, Vol. 12, No. 2 (May 1957), 190–204

Bowring, Philip *et al*, 'Symposium on Prudential Supervision of Financial Institutions in Hong Kong', *Hong Kong Economic Papers*, Vol. 1985, No. 16 (1985 December), 97–111

Brimmer, Andrew F., and Frederick R. Dahi, 'Growth of American International Banking: Implications for Public Policy', *Journal of Finance*, Vol. 30, No. 2 (May, 1975), 34–63

Cain, Frank M., 'Exporting the Cold War: British Responses to the USA's Establishment of COCOM, 1947–51', *Journal of Contemporary History*, Vol. 29, No. 3 (July 1994), 501–22

—— and A. G. Hopkins, 'Gentlemanly Capitalism and British Expansion Overseas II: New Imperialism, 1850–1945', *Economic History Review*, Vol. 40, No. 1 (February 1987), 1–26

Caine, Sydney, 'British Experience in Overseas Development', *Annals*, Vol. 270 (July 1950), 118–25

Carney, Mick, and Howard Davies ,'From Entrepot to Entrepot via Merchant Manufacturing: Adaptive Mechanisms, Organizational Capabilities and the Structure of the Hong Kong Economy', *Asia Pacific Business Review*, Vol. 6, No. 1 (October 1999),13–32

Chai, B. Karin, 'Export-Oriented Industrialization and Political and Class Development: Hong Kong on the Eve of 1997', in Richard Harvey Brown and William T. Liu (eds), *Modernization in East Asia: Political, Economic, and Social Perspectives* (Westport: Praeger, 1992)

Chan, K. C., 'The Abrogation of British Extraterritoriality in China 1942–43: A Study of Anglo-American-Chinese Relations', *Modern Asian Studies*, Vol. 11, No. 2 (1977), 257–91

Chan, Kenneth S., 'Currency Substitution between Hong Kong Dollar and Renminbi in South China', *HKIMR Working Paper No. 02 / 2001* March 2001

Chen, Edward K. Y., 'The Total Factor Productivity Debate: Determinants of Economic Growth in East Asia', *Asian-Pacific Economic Literature*, Vol. 11, No. 1, (May 1997), 18–38

Chen, Zhongping, 'The Origins of Chinese Chambers of Commerce in the Lower Yangzi Region', *Modern China*, Vol. 27, No. 2 (April 2001), 155–201

Cheng, Leonard K., 'Strategies for Rapid Economic Development: The Case of Hong Kong', *Contemporary Economic Policy*, Vol. 13. No. 1 (1995), 28–37

Cheung, Esther M. K., 'The Hi/stories of Hong Kong', *Cultural Studies*, Vol. 15, Issue 3&4 (July 2001), 564–90

Cheung, Stephen N. S., 'Rent Control and Housing Reconstruction: The Postwar Experience of Prewar Premises in Hong Kong' *The Journal of Law and Economics*, Vol. 22 (April 1979), 27–53

Chi, Ch'ao-ting, 'China's Monetary Reform in Perspective', *Far Eastern Survey*, Vol. 6, No. 17 (18 August 1937), 189–96

Chiu, Stephen W. K., 'Unravelling Hong Kong's Exceptionalism: The Politics of *Laissez-faire* in the Industrial Takeoff', in Law Kam-yee and Lee Kim-ming (eds), *The Economy of Hong Kong in Non-Economic Perspectives* (Hong Kong: Oxford University Press, 2004)

Choi, Alex Hang-keung, 'The Political Economy of Hong Kong's Industrial Upgrading: A Lost Opportunity', in Benjamin K. P. Leung (ed), *Hong Kong: Legacies and Prospects of Development* (Aldershot: Ashgate, 2003)

——, 'State-Business Relations and Industrial Restructuring', in Tak-wing Ngo (ed), *Hong Kong's History. State and Society under Colonial Rule* (London: Routledge, 1999)

Chu, Kam Hon, 'Free Banking and Information Asymmetry', *Journal of Money, Credit and Banking*, Vol. 31, No. 4 (November 1999), 748–62

Clark, Clifford D., and Jung-Chao Liu, 'The media, the judiciary, the banks and the resilience of East Asian economies', in Tsu-Tan Fu *et al* (eds), *Productivity and Economic Performance in the Asia-Pacific Region* (Cheltenham: Edward Elgar, 2002)

Clauson, Gerard L. M., 'Some Uses of Statistics in Colonial Administration', *Journal of the Royal African Society*, Vol. 36, No. 145 (October 1937), 3–16

——, 'The British Colonial Currency System', *Economic Journal*, Vol. 54, No. 213 (April 1944), 1–25

Clayton, David W., 'Industrialization and institutional change in Hong Kong 1842–1960', in Heita Kawakatsu and A. J.H. Latham (eds), *Asia Pacific Dynamism, 1550–2000* (London: Routledge, 2000)

Coble. Parks M., Jr, 'The Kuomintang Regime and the Shanghai Capitalists, 1927–29', *China Quarterly*, No. 77 (March 1977), 1–24

Corden, W. Max, 'Exchange Rate Regimes for Emerging Market Economies: Lessons from Asia', *Annals*, Vol. 579 (January 2002), 26–37

Dahl, Frederick R., 'International Operations of U.S. Banks: Growth and Public Policy Implications', *Law and Contemporary Problems*, Vol. 32, No. 1, Part 2 (Winter 1967)

Davis, Clarence B., 'Financing Imperialism: British and American Bankers as Vectors of Imperial Expansion in China, 1908–1920', *Business History Review*, Vol. 56, No. 2 (Summer 1982), 236–64

Devane, Richard I., 'The United States and China: Claims and Assets', *Asian Survey*, Vol. 18, No. 12 (December 1978), 1267–79

Eiichi, Motono, '"The Traffic Revolution": Remaking the Export Sales System in China, 1866–1875', *Modern China*, Vol. 12, No. 1 (January 1986), 75–102

Elvin, Mark, 'Foundations for the Future: the building of modern machinery in Shanghai after the Pacific War', in Ross Garnaut and Yiping Huang (eds), *Growth Without Miracles. Readings on the Chinese Economy in the Era of Reform* (Oxford: Oxford University Press, 2001)

Eng, Irene, 'Flexible Production in Late Industrialization: The Case of Hong Kong', *Economic Geography*, Vol. 73, No. 1 (January 1997), 26–43

Espy, John L., 'Some Notes on Business and Industry in Hong Kong', *Chung Chi Journal*, Vol. 11, No. 1 (April 1972), 172–81

Faure, David, 'Reflections on Being Chinese in Hong Kong', in Judith M. Brown and Rosemary Foot (eds), *Hong Kong's Transitions, 1842–1997* (London: Macmillan Press Ltd, 1997)

Findlay, Ronald, and Stanislaw Wellisz, 'Hong Kong', in Ronald Findlay and Stanislaw Wellisz (eds), *The Political Economy of Poverty, Equity, and Growth. Five Small Open Economies* (New York: Oxford University Press, 1993)

Fitzgerald, John, 'Increased Disunity: The Politics and Finance of Guangdong Separatism, 1926–1936', *Modern Asian Studies*, Vol. 24, No. 4 (October 1990), 745–75

Friedman, Irving S., 'Britain's China Stake on the Eve of European War', *Far Eastern Survey*, Vol. 8, No. 19 (27 September 1939), 219–24

Gaylord, Mark S., 'The Chinese Laundry: International Drug Trafficking and Hong Kong's Banking Industry', in Harold H. Traver and Mark S. Gaylord (eds), *Drugs, Law and the State* (Hong Kong: Hong Kong University Press, 1992)

Ghosh, Atish R., *et al*, 'Currency Boards: More than a Quick Fix?', *Economic Policy*, Vol. 15, No. 31 (October 2000), 269–335

Goodman, Bernard, 'The Political Economy of Private International Investment', *Economic Development and Cultural Change*, Vol. 5, No. 3 (April 1957), 263–76

Goodstadt, Leo F. 'The Rise and Fall of Social, Economic and Political Reforms in Hong Kong, 1930–1955', *Journal of the Royal Asiatic Society Hong Kong Branch*, Vol. 44 (2004), 57–81

——, 'Business friendly and politically convenient – the historical role of functional constituencies', in Christine Loh (ed), *Functional Constituencies: A Unique Feature of the Hong Kong Legislative Council* (Hong Kong: Hong Kong University Press, 2006)

——, 'Crisis and Challenge: The Changing Role of the Hongkong & Shanghai Bank, 1950–2000', *HKIMR Working Paper No.13/2005*, July 2005

——, 'Dangerous Business Models: Bankers, Bureaucrats & Hong Kong's Economic Transformation, 1948–86', *HKIMR Working Paper No. 8/2006*, June 2006

——, 'Government without Statistics: Policy-making in Hong Kong 1925–85, with special reference to Economic and Financial Management', *HKIMR Working Paper* No. 6/2006, April 2006

——, 'Painful Transitions: The Impact of Economic Growth and Government Policies on Hong Kong's "Chinese" Banks, 1945–70', *HKIMR Working Paper* No. 16/2006, November 2006

Gray, John, 'Monetary Management in Hong Kong: The Role of the Hongkong and Shanghai Banking Corporation Limited', in *Proceedings of the Seminar on Monetary Management organized by the Hongkong Monetary Authority on 18–19 October 1993* (Hong Kong: Hong Kong Monetary Authority, n.d.)

Greaves, I. C., 'The Sterling Balances of Colonial Territories', *Economic Journal*, Vol. 61, No. 242 (June 1951), 433–9

——, 'Colonial Trade and Payments', *Economica*, Vol. 24, No. 93 (February 1957), 47–58

Greenwood, John, 'The Monetary Framework Underlying the Hong Kong Dollar Stabilization Scheme', *China Quarterly*, No. 99 (September 1984), 631–6

Haddon-Cave, Philip, 'Introduction. The Making of Some Aspects of Public Policy in Hong Kong', in David Lethbridge (ed), *The Business Environment in Hong Kong* (Hong Kong: Oxford University Press, 1980)

Halkyard, A. J., 'Revenue – deductibility of interest ...', *Hong Kong Law Journal*, Vol. 16, No. 3 (1986), 439–42

Hanke, Steve H., 'Currency Boards', *Annals*, Vol. 579 (January 2002), 87–105

Hao, Yen-P'ing, 'Themes and Issues in Chinese Business History', in Robert Gardella *et al* (eds), *Chinese Business History. Interpretative Trends and Priorities for the Future* (Armonk: M. E. Sharpe Inc., 1998)

Harris, P. B., 'The International Future of Hong Kong'. *International Affairs*, Vol. 48, No. 1 (January 1972), 60–71

Hayes, James, 'East and West in Hong Kong: Vignettes from History and Personal Experience', in Elizabeth Sinn (ed), *Between East and West. Aspects of Social and Political Development in Hong Kong* (Hong Kong: Centre of Asian Studies, 1990)

Hazelwood, Arthur, 'Colonial External Finance Since the War', *Review of Economic Studies*, Vol. 21, No. 1 (1953–1954), 31–52

Hicks, George, 'The Four Little Dragons: An Enthusiast's Reading Guide', *Asian-Pacific Economic Literature*, Vol. 3, No. 2 (September 1989), 35–49

Hirschman, Albert O., 'Economic Policy in Underdeveloped Countries', *Economic Development and Cultural Change,* Vol. 5, No. 4 (July 1957), 362–70

Howe, Christopher, 'Growth, Public Policy and Hong Kong's Economic Relationship with China', *China Quarterly,* No. 95 (September 1983), 512–33

Hsia, Ronald, 'Effects of Industrial Growth on Hong Kong Trade', *Pakistan Development Review,* Vol. II, Summer 1962, No. 2, 559–86

Hsiao, Katherine H. Y. Huang, 'Money and Banking in the People's Republic of China: Recent Developments', *China Quarterly,* No. 91 (September 1982), 462–77

Jansen, Cornelis J. A., and Mark Cherniavsky, 'Current Economic Situation and Prospects of Hong Kong' (Asia Department IBRD, 9 May 1967, mimeo)

Jao, Y. C., 'Financing Hong Kong's Early Postwar Industrialization: the role of the Hongkong & Shanghai Banking Corporation', in Frank H. H. King (ed), *Eastern Banking: Essays in the History of the Hong Kong & Shanghai Banking Corporation* (London: The Athlone Press, 1983)

——, 'Monetary system and banking structure', in H. C. Y. Ho and L. C. Chau (eds), *The Economic System of Hong Kong* (Hong Kong: Asian Research Service, 1988)

——, 'The Rise of Hong Kong as a Financial Centre', *Asian Survey,* Vol. 19, No. 7 (July 1979), 674–94

——, 'The Working of the Currency Board: The Experience of Hong Kong 1935–1997', *Pacific Economic Review,* Vol. 3, No. 3 (1998), 219–41

Kam Yiu-yu, 'Decision-Making and Implementation of Policy toward Hong Kong', in Carol Lee Hamrin and Suisheng Zhao (eds), *Decision-Making in Deng's China. Perspectives from Insiders* (Armonk: M. E. Sharpe, 1995)

Kamarck, A. M., 'Dollar Pooling in the Sterling Area: Comment', *American Economic Review,* Vol. 45, No. 4 (September 1955), 652–5

Kapstein, Ethan B., 'Resolving the Regulator's Dilemma: International Coordination of Banking Regulations', *International Organization,* Vol. 43, No. 2 (Spring, 1989), 323–47

Katz, Samuel I., 'Sterling Instability and the Postwar Sterling System', *Review of Economics and Statistics,* Vol. 36, No. 1 (February 1954), 81–7

Kaufman, Richard H., 'The Asian Gold Trade', *Asian Survey,* Vol. 5, No. 5 (May, 1965), 233–44

King, Ambrose Yeo-chi, 'Administrative Absorption of Politics in Hong Kong: Emphasis on the Grass Roots Level', in Ambrose Y. C. King and Rance P. L. Lee (eds), *Social Life and Development in Hong Kong* (Hong Kong: Chinese University Press, 1981)

King, Frank H. H., 'Sterling Balances and the Colonial Monetary Systems', *Economic Journal,* Vol. 65, No. 260 (December 1955), 719–21

Kirby, E. Stuart, 'Hong Kong and the British Position in China', *Annals,* Vol. 277 (September 1951),193–202

Koo, Shou-eng, 'The Role of Export Expansion in Hong Kong's Economic Growth', *Asian Survey,* Vol. 8, No. 6 (June 1968), 490–515

Krozewski, Gerold, 'Sterling, the "minor" territories, and the end of formal empire, 1939–1958', *Economic History* Review, Vol. 46, No. 2(1993), 239–65

Krueger, Anne O., 'Policy Lessons from Development Experience since the Second World War', in Jere Behrman and T. N. Srinivasan (eds), *Development Economics Volume IIIB* (Amsterdam: Elsevier, 1995)

—— and Baran Tuncer, 'An Empirical Test of the Infant Industry Argument', *American Economic Review,* Vol. 72, No. 5 (December, 1982), 1142–52

Kueh, Y. Y., and Christopher Howe, 'China's International Trade: Policy and Organizational Change and Their Place in the "Economic Readjustment"', *China Quarterly*, No. 100 (December 1984), 813–48

Latter, Anthony, 'The Currency Board Approach to Monetary Policy – from Africa to Argentina and Estonia, via Hong Kong', in *Proceedings of the Seminar on Monetary Management organized by the Hong Kong Monetary Authority on 18–19 October 1993* (Hong Kong: Hong Kong Monetary Authority, n.d.)

——, 'Hong Kong's Exchange Rate Regimes in the Twentieth Century: The Story of Three Regime Changes', *HKIMR Working Paper No. 17/2004*, September 2004

——, 'Rules versus Discretion in Managing the Hong Kong Dollar, 1983–2006', *HKIMR Working Paper No. 2/2007*, January 2007

Lee Pui-Tak, 'Chinese Merchants in the Hong Kong Colonial Context, 1840–1910', in Wong Siu-lun and Toyojiro Maruya (eds), *Hong Kong Economy and Society: Challenges in the New Era* (Hong Kong: Centre of Asian Studies, 1998)

Leeming, Frank, 'The Earlier Industrialization of Hong Kong' *Modern Asian Studies*, Vol. 9, No. 5 (1975), 337–42

Leigh, Monroe, 'Jackson v. People's Republic of China, 596 F.Supp. 386', *American Journal of International Law*, Vol. 79, No. 2 (April 1985), 456–8

Levine, Ross, 'The Legal Environment, Banks, and Long-Run Economic Growth', *Journal of Money Credit and Banking*, Vol. 30, No. 3, Part 2 (August 1998), 596–613

Li, David K. P., 'The Development of Chinese Banking in Southeast Asia', in Nyaw Mee-kau and Chang Chak-yan (eds), *Chinese Banking in Asia's Market Economies* (Hong Kong: Chinese University of Hong Kong, 1989)

Liu, Ta-Chung, 'China's Foreign Exchange Problems: A Proposed Solution', *American Economic Review*, Vol. 31, No. 2 (June 1941), 266–79

Lockwood, William W., Jr., 'Hongkong – Empire Bulwark or Hostage to Fortune?', *Far Eastern Survey*, Vol. 7, No. 3 (2 February 1938), 25–9

Louis, Wm. Roger, 'Hong Kong: The Critical Phase, 1945–1949', *American Historical Review*, Vol. 102, No. 4 (October 1997), 1052–84

Lui, Tai-lok, 'Pressure Group Politics in Hong Kong', in Joseph Y. S. Cheng (ed), *Political Participation in Hong Kong. Theoretical Issues and Historical Legacy* (Hong Kong: City University of Hong Kong Press, 1999)

Mark, Chi-kwan, 'American "China Hands" in the 1950s', in Cindy Yik-yi Chu (ed), *Foreign Communities in Hong Kong, 1940s–1950s* (New York: Palgrave Macmillan, 2005)

Maxfield, Sylvia, 'Financial Incentives and Central Bank Authority in Industrializing Nations', *World Politics*, Vol. 46, No. 4 (July 1994), 556–588

McElderry, Andrea, 'Confucian Capitalism?: Corporate Values in Republican Banking' *Modern China*, Vol. 12, No. 3 (July 1986), 401–16

McLean, David, 'Finance and "Informal Empire" before the First World War', *Economic History Review*, Vol. 29, No. 2 (May 1976), 291–305

Meredith, David, 'The British Government and Colonial Economic Policy, 1919–39', *Economic History Review*, Vol. 28, No. 3 (August 1975), 484–99

Miller, Geoffrey P., 'Banking Crises in Perspective: Two Causes and One Cure', in Gerard Caprio, Jr *et al* (eds), *Preventing Bank Crises: Lessons from Recent Global Bank Failures* (Washington: World Bank, 1998)

Miners, N. J., 'Plans for Constitutional Reform in Hong Kong, 1946–62', *China Quarterly*, No. 107 (September 1986), 463–82

Mitchell, Katharyne, 'Flexible Circulation in the Pacific Rim: Capitalisms in Cultural Context', *Economy Geography*, Vol. 71, No. 4 (October 1995), 364–82

Mitra, Ashok, 'Underdeveloped Statistics', *Economic Development and Cultural Change*, Vol. 11, No. 3, Part 1 (April 1963), 315–7

Mittelman, James H., 'Underdevelopment and Nationalisation: Banking in Tanzania', *Journal of Modern African Studies*, Vol. 16, No. 4 (December 1978), 597–617

Mosley, George V. H., 3rd, 'New China and Old Macao', *Pacific Affairs, Pacific Affairs*, Vol. 32, No. 3 (September 1959), 268–76

Myint, Hla, 'Economic Theory and the Underdeveloped Countries', *Journal of Political Economy*, Vol. 73, No. 5 (October 1965), 477–91

——, 'An Interpretation of Economic Backwardness', *Oxford Economic Papers*, New Series, Vol. 6, No. 2 (June 1954), 132–63

Naughton, Barry, 'Between China and the World: Hong Kong's Economy Before and After 1997', in Gary G. Hamilton (ed), *Cosmopolitan Capitalists: Hong Kong and the Chinese Diaspora at the End of the Twentieth Century* (Seattle: University of Washington Press, 1999)

Ng Sek-hong, 'The Development of Labour Relations in Hong Kong and Some Implications for the Future', in Ian Nish *et al* (eds), *Work and Society. Labour and Human Resources in East Asia* (Hong Kong: Hong Kong University Press, 1996)

Ngo, Tak-wing, 'Colonialism in Hong Kong revisited', in Tak-Wing Ngo (ed), *Hong Kong's History. State and Society under Colonial Rule* (London: Routledge, 1999)

——, 'Industrial history and the artifice of *laissez-faire* colonialism', in Tak-Wing Ngo (ed), *Hong Kong's History. State and Society under Colonial Rule* (London: Routledge, 1999)

O'Brien, Roderick , 'Rent and Tenure Controls for Pre-War Buildings', *Hong Kong Law Journal*, Vol. 7, No. 1 (1977), 5–43

Olakanpo, J. O. W., 'Monetary Management in Dependent Economies', *Economica*, Vol. 28, No. 112 (November 1961), 395–408

Osterhammel, Jurgen, 'Imperialism in Transition: British Business and the Chinese Authorities, 1931–1957', *China Quarterly*, No. 98 (June 1984), 260–86

Owen, Nicholas C., 'Economic Policy', in Keith Hopkins (ed), *Hong Kong: The Industrial Colony. A Political, Social and Economic Survey* (Hong Kong: Oxford University Press, 1971)

——, 'Competition and Structural Change in Unconcentrated Industries', *Journal of Economics*, Vol. 19, No. 2 (April 1971), 133–47

Paauw, Douglas S., 'The Kuomintang and Economic Stagnation, 1928–37', *Journal of Asian Studies*, Vol. 16, No. 2 (February 1957), 213–20

Page, John, 'The East Asian Miracle: Four Lessons for Development Policy', *NBER Macroeconomics Annual*, Vol. 9 (1994), 219–69

Palan, Ronen, 'Trying to Have Your Cake and Eating It: How and Why the State System Has Created Offshore', *International Studies Quarterly*, Vol. 42, No. 4 (December 1998), 625–43

Peng Naidian, 'Reflections on Deepening Economic and Trade Cooperation between Guangdong, Hong Kong, Macao', *Guoji Maoyi*, No. 6, 27 June 1988, 13–6

Posen, Adam S., 'Why Central banks Should Not Burst Bubbles', *International Finance*, Vol. 9, No 1 (2006), 109–24

Redding, Gordon, 'Culture and Business in Hong Kong', in Wang Gangwu and Wong

Siu Lun (eds), *Dynamic Hong Kong: Business & Culture* (Hong Kong: Centre of Asian Studies, 1997)

Redick, Charles Ford, 'The Jurisprudence of the Foreign Claims Settlement Commission: Chinese Claims', *American Journal of International Law*, Vol. 67, No. 4 (October 1973), 728–40

Reed, Howard Curtis, 'The Ascent of Tokyo as an International Financial Center', *Journal of International Business Studies*, Vol. 11, No. 3 (Winter 1980), 19–35

Rozen, Marvin E., 'Investment Control in Post-War Britain, 1945–1955' *Canadian Journal of Economics and Political Science*, Vol. 29, No. 2 (May 1963), 185–202

Schenk, Catherine R., 'Closing the Hong Kong Gap: The Hong Kong Free Dollar Market in the 1950s', *Economic History Review*, Vol. 47, No. 2 (May 1994), 335–53

——, 'Another Asian Financial Crisis: Monetary Links between Hong Kong and China 1945–50', *Modern Asian Studies*, Vol. 34, No. 3 (2000), 739–64

——, 'Banking Crises and the Evolution of the Regulatory Framework in Hong Kong 1945–1970', *Australian Economic History Review*, Vol. 43, No. 2, July 2003, 140–54

——, 'Banks and the emergence of Hong Kong as an international financial center', *Journal of International Financial Markets, Institutions and Money*, Vol. 12 (2002), 321–40

——, 'Hong Kong's Economic Relations with China 1949–1955: Blockade, Embargo and Financial Controls', in Lee Pui-tak (ed), *Colonial Hong Kong and Modern China: Interaction and Reintegration* (Hong Kong: Hong Kong University Press, 2005)

——, 'Regulatory reform in an emerging stock market: the case of Hong Kong, 1945–86', *Financial History Review*, Vol. 11, No. 2 (2004), 1–25

——, 'The empire strikes back: Hong Kong and the decline of sterling in the 1960s', *Economic History Review*, Vol. 57, No. 3 (2004), 551–80

——, 'The Hong Kong Gold Market and the Southeast Asian Gold Trade in the 1950s', *Modern Asian Studies*, Vol. 29, No. 2 (May 1995)

——, 'The origins of Anti-competitive Regulation: Was Hong Kong "Over-banked" in the 1960s?', *HKIMR Working Paper No.9/2006*, July 2006

Schuler, Kurt, 'Episodes from Asian Monetary History: A Brief History of Hong Kong Monetary Standards', *Asian Monetary Monitor*, September-October 1989, Vol. 12, No. 5, 11–29

Scott, Ian, 'Generalists and Specialists', in Ian Scott and John P. Burns (eds), *The Hong Kong Civil Service and Its Future* (Hong Kong: Oxford University Press, 1988),

——, 'Introduction' in Ian Scott (ed), *Institutional Change and the Political Transition in Hong Kong* (London: Macmillan, 1998)

——, 'The Public Service in Transition: Sustaining Administrative Capacity and Political Neutrality', in Robert Ash *et al* (eds), *Hong Kong in Transition. The Handover Years* (London: Macmillan Press Ltd, 2000)

Searle, W. F. *et al*, 'Colonial Statistics', *Journal of the Royal Statistical Society. Series A (General)*, Vol. 113, No. 3 (1950), 271–98

Seers, Dudley, 'A Model of Comparative Rates of Growth in the World Economy', *Economic Journal*, Vol. 72, No. 285 (March 1962), 45–78

Selgin, George A., 'Central Banking: Myth and Reality', *Hong Kong Economic Papers*, No. 18 (December 1987), 1–13

——, and Lawrence H. White, 'How would the Invisible Hand Handle Money?', *Journal of Economic Literature*, Vol. 32, No. 4 (December 1994), 1718–49

Sen, Amartya Kumar, 'On the Usefulness of Used Machines', *Review of Economics and Statistics,* Vol. 44, No. 3 (August 1962), 346–48

Shai, Aron, 'Britain, China and the End of Empire', *Journal of Contemporary History,* Vol. 15, No. 2 (April 1980), 287–97

Shannon, H. A., 'The British Payments and Exchange Control System', *Quarterly Journal of Economics,* Vol. 63, No. 2 (May 1949), 212–37

——, 'The Sterling Balances of the Sterling Area, 1939–49', *Economic Journal,* Vol. 60, No. 239 (September 1950), 531–51

Sheng, Andrew, 'Bank Restructuring Revisited', Gerard Caprio, Jr *et al* (eds), *Preventing Bank Crises: Lessons from Recent Global Bank Failures* (Washington: World Bank, 1998)

Singer, H. W., 'The Distribution of Gains between Investing and Borrowing Countries', *American Economic Review,* Vol. 40, No. 2 (May 1950), 473–85

Sit, Victor F. S., 'Hong Kong's "Transferred" Industrialization and Industrial Geography', *Asian Survey,* Vol. 38, No. 9 (September 1998), 880–904

So, Alvin Y., 'The Economic Success of Hong Kong: Insights from a World-System Perspective', *Sociological Perspectives,* Vol. 29, No. 2 (April 1986), 241–58

Stammer, D. W., 'Financial Development and Economic Growth in Underdeveloped Countries: Comment', *Economic Development and Cultural Change,* Vol. 20, No. 2 (January 1972), 318–25

Stewart, Robert B., 'Instruments of British Policy in the Sterling Area', *Political Science Quarterly,* Vol. 52, No. 2 (June 1937), 174–207

Strange, Susan, 'Sterling and British Policy: A Political View', *International Affairs,* Vol. 47, No. 2 (April 1971), 302–15

Stuart, Douglas T., 'Paris and London: Between Washington and Beijing', in Yu-ming Shaw (ed), *Mainland China. Politics, Economics and Reform* (Boulder: Westview Press, 1986)

Tsang Shu-ki, 'The Economy', in Donald H. McMillen and Man Si-wei (eds), *The Other Hong Kong Report 1994* (Hong Kong: Chinese University Press, 1994)

Tsang, Steve, 'Strategy for Survival: The Cold War and Hong Kong's Policy towards Guomindang and Chinese Communist Activities in the 1950s', *Journal of Imperial and Commonwealth History,* Vol. 25, No. 2 (May 1997), 294–317

Tsui-Auch , Lai Si, 'Has the Hong Kong Model Worked? Industrial Policy in Retrospect and Prospect', *Development and Change,* Vol. 29 (1998), 55–79

Tuan, Chyau, and Linda F. Y. Ng, 'Evolution of Hong Kong's Electronics Industry under a Passive Industrial Policy', *Managerial and Decision Economics,* Vol. 16, No. 5 (September–October 1995), 509–23

Wan, Henry Y, Jr, and Jason Weisman, 'Hong Kong: The Fragile Economy of Middlemen', *Review of International Economics,* Vol. 7, No. 3 (1999), 410–30

Weaver, James H., and Ira Winakur, 'Impact of United States Cotton Textile Quotas on Underdeveloped Countries', *South Economic Journal,* Vol. 35, No. 1 (July 1968), 26–33

Wolf, David C. Wolf, ' "To Secure a Convenience": Britain Recognizes China – 1950', *Journal of Contemporary History,* Vol. 18. No. 2 (April 1983), 299–326

Wong Siu-lun, 'Modernization and Chinese Culture', *China Quarterly,* No. 106 (June 1986), 306–25

——, 'The Entrepreneurial Spirit: Shanghai and Hong Kong Compared', in Y. M. Yeung and Sung Yun-wing (eds), *Shanghai Transformation and Modernization under China's Open Policy* (Hong Kong: Chinese University Press, 1996)

Wong, Teresa Y. C., 'A Comparative Study of the Industrial Policy of Hong Kong and Singapore in the 1980s', in Edward K. Y. Chen *et al* (eds), *Industrial and Trade Development in Hong Kong* (Hong Kong: Centre of Asian Studies, 1991)

Wright, Tim, 'Coping with the World Depression: The Nationalist Government's Relations with Chinese Industry and Commerce, 1932–1936', *Modern Asian Studies*, Vol. 25, No. 4 (October, 1991), 649–74

——, 'Entrepreneurs, Politicians and the Chinese Coal Industry, 1895–1937', *Modern Asian Studies*, Vol. 14, No. 4 (1980), 579–602

Wu, Leonard T. K., 'China's Paradox — Prosperous Banks in National Crisis', *Far Eastern Survey*, Vol. 4, No. 6 (27 March 1935), 41–5

——, 'The Crucial Role of the Chinese Native Banks', *Far Eastern Survey*, Vol. 4, No. 12 (19 June 1935), 89–93

Yeh, Wen-Hsin, 'Corporate Space, Communal Time: Everyday Life in China's Bank of China', *American Historical Review*, Vol. 100, No. 1 (February 1995), 97–122

Yeung, K. Y., 'The Role of the Hong Kong Government in Industrial Development', in Edward K. Y. Chen *et al* (eds), *Industrial and Trade Development in Hong Kong* (Hong Kong: Centre of Asian Studies, 1991)

Yeung, Y. M., 'Introduction', in Y. M. Yeung and Sung Yun-wing (eds), *Shanghai Transformation and Modernization under China's Open Policy* (Hong Kong: Chinese University Press, 1996)

Yu, Tony Fu-lai, 'Hong Kong's entrepreneurship: behaviours and determinants', *Entrepreneurship & Regional Development*, Vol. 12 (2000), 179–94

Zhongping Chen, 'The Origins of Chinese Chambers of Commerce in the Lower Yangzi Region', *Modern China*, Vol. 27, No. 2 (April 2001), 155–201

Index